Street by Stre

BRISTOL, BATH
CLEVEDON, PORTISHEAD,
WESTON-SUPER-MARE, YATE

Avonmouth, Bradley Stoke, Chipping Sodbury, Congresbury, Keynsham, Kingswood, Long Ashton, Mangotsfield, Nailsea, Pucklechurch, Thornbury, Yatton

3rd edition November 2008
© Automobile Association Developments Limited 2008

Original edition printed May 2001

 This product includes map data licensed from Ordnance Survey® with the permission of the Controller of Her Majesty's Stationery Office. © Crown copyright 2008. All rights reserved. Licence number 100021153.

The copyright in all PAF is owned by Royal Mail Group plc.

 Information on fixed speed camera locations provided by RoadPilot © 2008 RoadPilot® Driving Technology.

Published by AA Publishing (a trading name of Automobile Association Developments Limited, whose registered office is Fanum House, Basing View, Basingstoke, Hampshire RG21 4EA. Registered number 1878835).

Produced by the Mapping Services Department of The Automobile Association. (A03728)

A CIP Catalogue record for this book is available from the British Library.

Printed by Oriental Press in Dubai

Ref: ML060y

Key to map pages	ii-iii
Key to map symbols	iv-1
Enlarged map pages	2-7
Main map pages	7-127
Index – towns & villages	128
Index – streets	129-151
Index – featured places	151-154
Acknowledgements	154

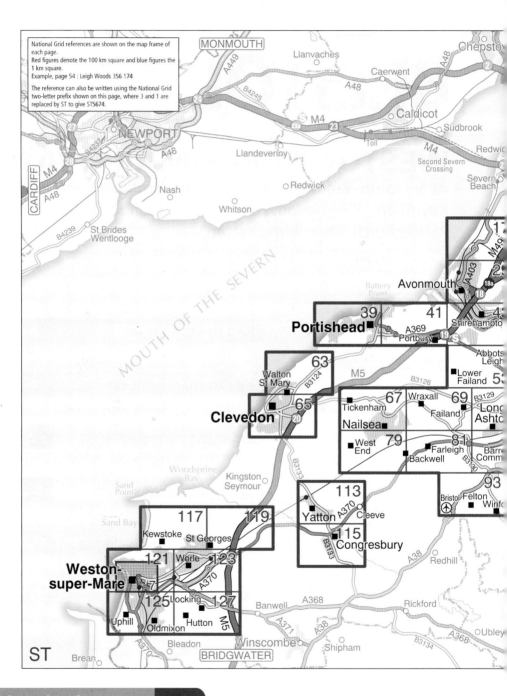

National Grid references are shown on the map frame of each page.
Red figures denote the 100 km square and blue figures the 1 km square.
Example, page 54 : Leigh Woods 356 174

The reference can also be written using the National Grid two-letter prefix shown on this page, where 3 and 1 are replaced by ST to give ST5674.

Enlarged scale pages 1:10,000 6.3 inches to 1 mile

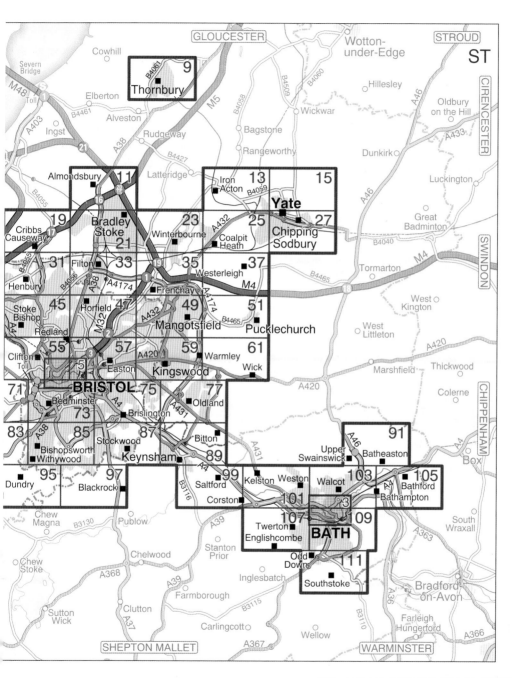

4.2 inches to 1 mile · **Scale of main map pages** 1:15,000

Junction 9	Motorway & junction	Railway & minor railway station
Services	Motorway service area	Underground station
	Primary road single/dual carriageway	Light railway & station
Services	Primary road service area	Preserved private railway
	A road single/dual carriageway	*LC* Level crossing
	B road single/dual carriageway	Tramway
	Other road single/dual carriageway	Ferry route
	Minor/private road, access may be restricted	Airport runway
← ←	One-way street	County, administrative boundary
	Pedestrian area	Mounds
	Track or footpath	**17** Page continuation 1:15,000
	Road under construction	**3** Page continuation to enlarged scale 1:10,000
	Road tunnel	River/canal, lake, pier
30	Speed camera site (fixed location) with speed limit in mph	Aqueduct, lock, weir
V	Speed camera site (fixed location) with variable speed limit	465 ▲ Winter Hill · Peak (with height in metres)
40	Section of road with two or more fixed camera sites; speed limit in mph or variable	Beach
50→ ←50	Average speed (SPECS™) camera system with speed limit in mph	Woodland
P	Parking	Park
P+	Park & Ride	Cemetery
	Bus/coach station	Built-up area
	Railway & main railway station	**IKEA** IKEA store

	Industrial/business building		Abbey, cathedral or priory
	Leisure building		Castle
	Retail building		Historic house or building
	Other building	Wakehurst Place NT	National Trust property
	City wall		Museum or art gallery
A&E	Hospital with 24-hour A&E department		Roman antiquity
PO	Post Office		Ancient site, battlefield or monument
	Public library		Industrial interest
i	Tourist Information Centre		Garden
i	Seasonal Tourist Information Centre		Garden Centre Garden Centre Association Member
	Petrol station, 24 hour Major suppliers only		Garden Centre Wyevale Garden Centre
†	Church/chapel		Arboretum
	Public toilet, with facilities for the less able		Farm or animal centre
PH	Public house AA recommended		Zoological or wildlife collection
	Restaurant AA inspected		Bird collection
Madeira Hotel	Hotel AA inspected		Nature reserve
	Theatre or performing arts centre		Aquarium
	Cinema	V	Visitor or heritage centre
	Golf course		Country park
▲	Camping AA inspected		Cave
	Caravan site AA inspected		Windmill
	Camping & caravan site AA inspected		Distillery, brewery or vineyard
	Theme park	•	Other place of interest

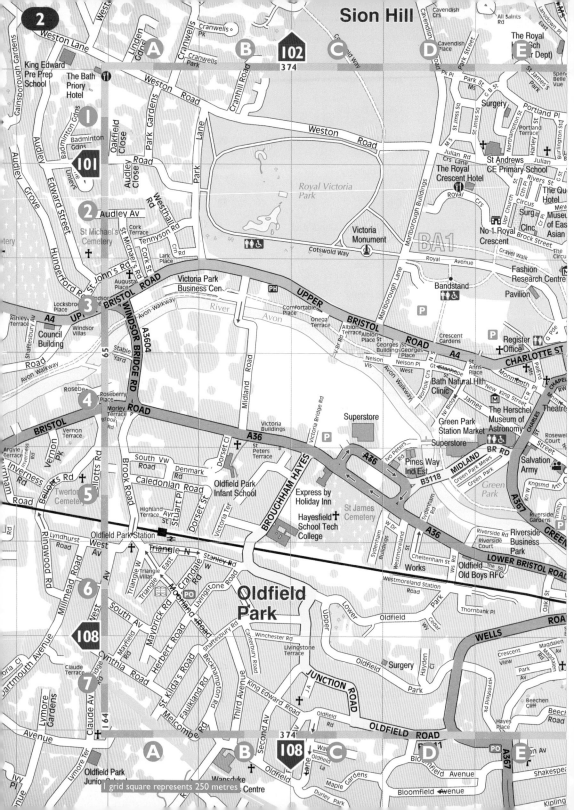

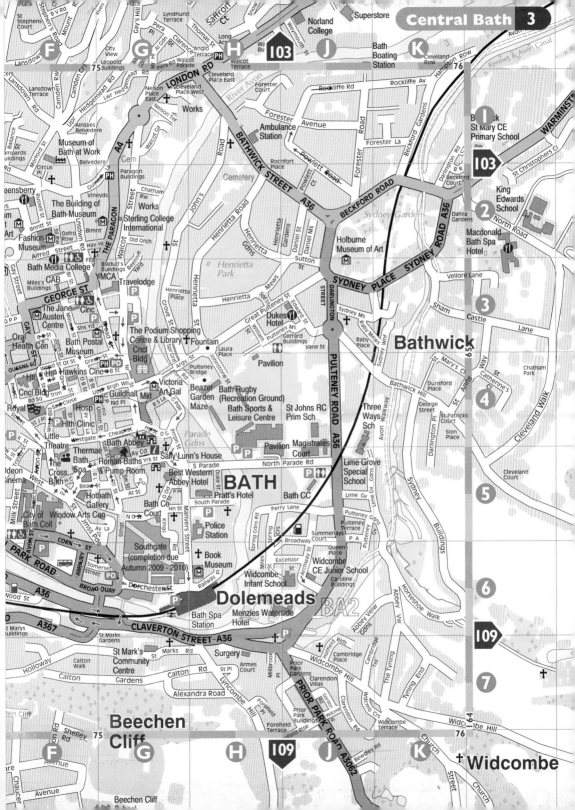

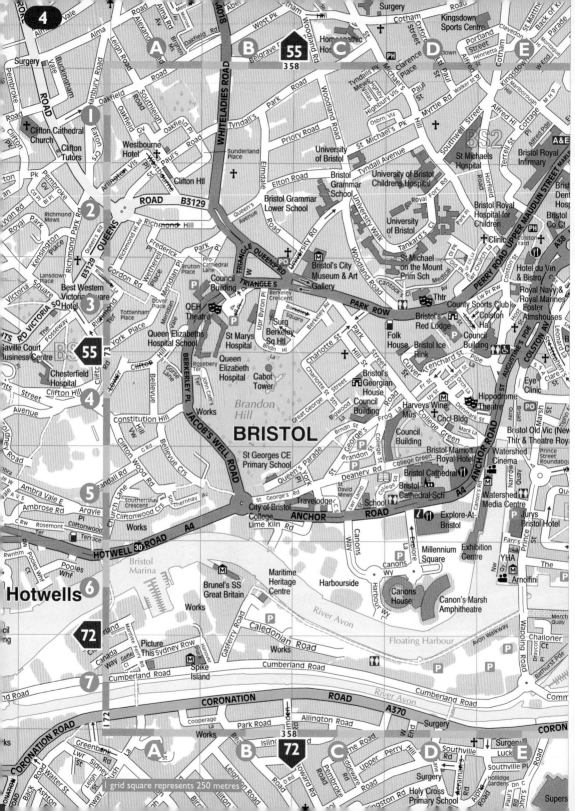

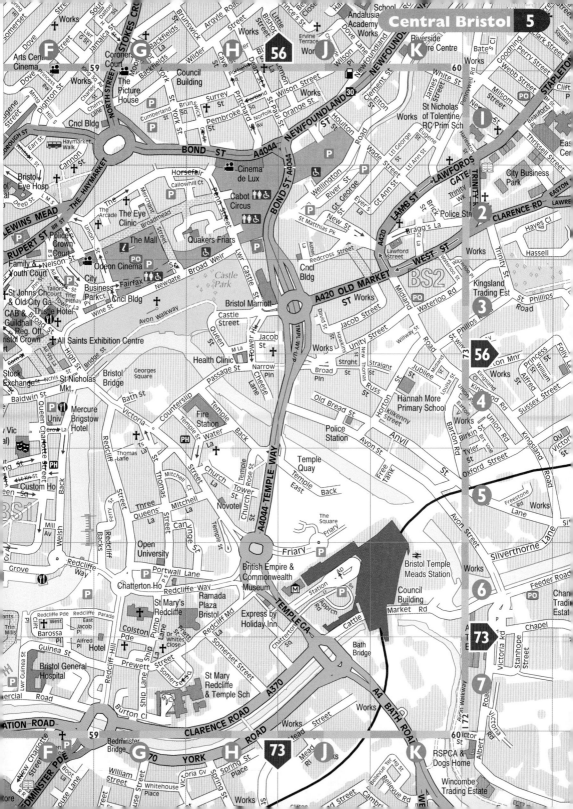

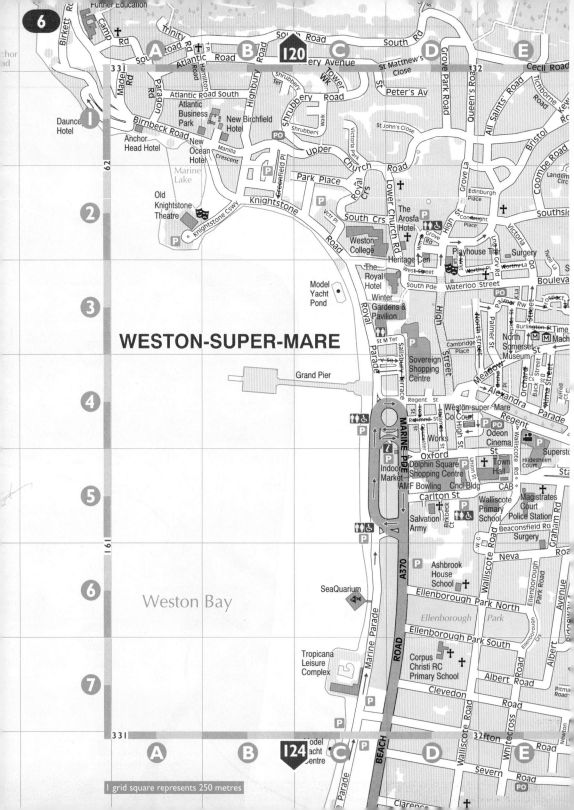

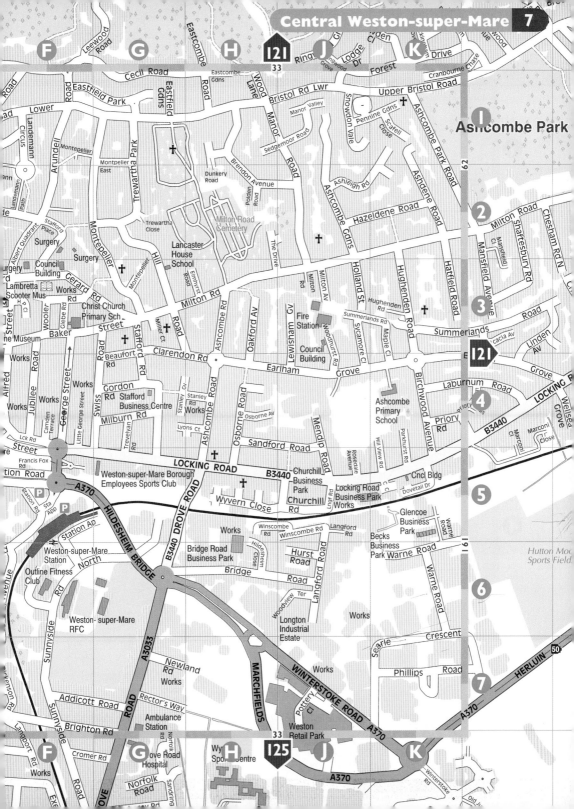

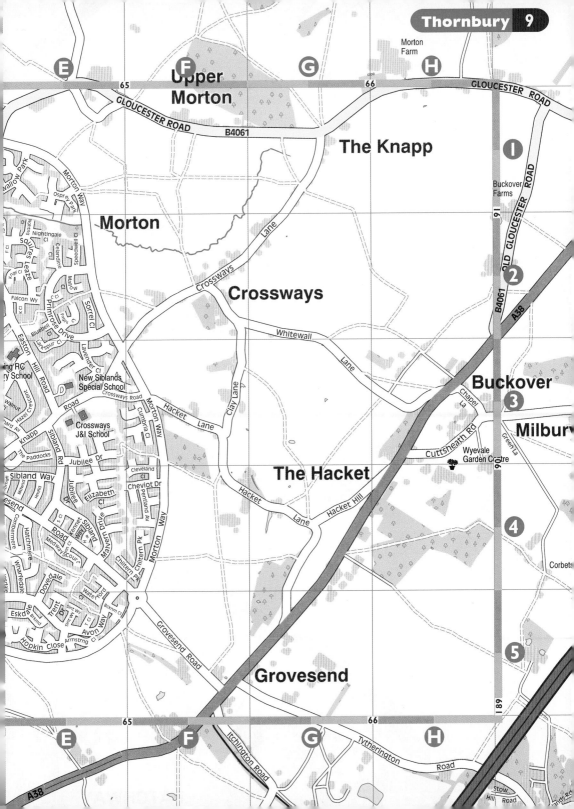

E 65 F G 66 H

Morton Farm

GLOUCESTER ROAD

Upper Morton

GLOUCESTER ROAD

B4061

The Knapp

I

Buckover Farms

Morton

Morton Way

Osprey Park

Swallow Park

Nightingale Cl

Speedwell Cl

Celandine

Mallow

Sorrel Cl

Crossways Lane

Lane

OLD GLOUCESTER ROAD

191

2

B4061

A38

Nepeta Cl

Squires Leaze

Falcon Wy

Primrose Drive

Bluebell Cl

Lavender Cl

Crossways

Whitewall

Lane

Crossways

Easton Hill Road

Walnut

Hazel Crescent

Orchard Av

New Siblands Special School

Crossways Road

Clay Lane

Hacket Lane

ing RC ry School

Knapp

Sibland Rd

Crossways J&I School

Morton Way

Cumbria Cl

Buckover

Chapel La

Green La

3

Milbur

The Paddocks

Jubilee Dr

Cleveland Cl

Cheviot Dr

Cuttsheath Rd

196

Sibland Way

Gresend

Jubilee

Elizabeth Cl

Pentland Av

Chiltern Pk

The Hacket

Wyevale Garden Centre

Condermere

Hatchmere

Road

Kennet Way

Medway Court

Sibland

Maytern Drive

Chiltern Pk

Hacket Lane

Hacket Hill

4

Corbets

Wharfedale

Dovedale

Trent Dri

Sint Wy

Water Road

Bcknm Cl

Sirti Wy

Avon Way

Armstrng

Grovesend Road

5

Eskdale

Brnfd

Hopkin Close

189

Grovesend

E 65 F Itchington Road G 66 Tytherington H

A38

Road

Stow Hill Road

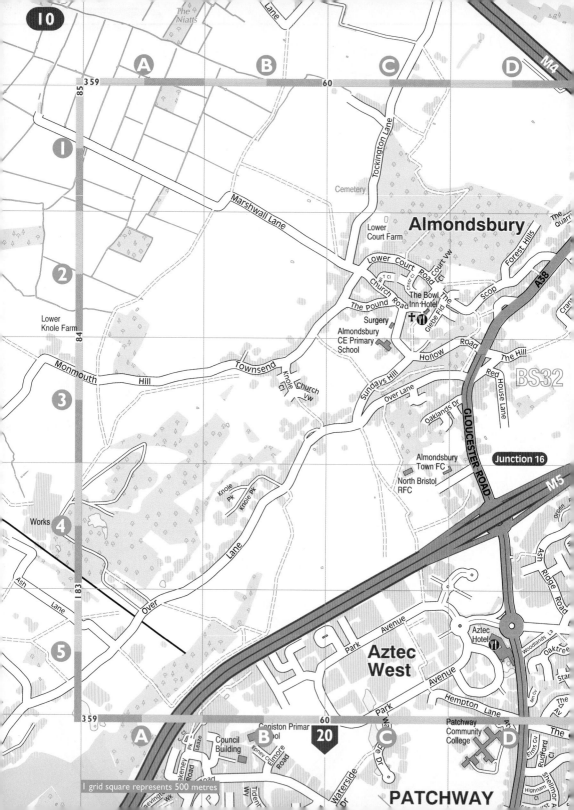

Woodhouse
Down

Fernhill Farm

E F G H

61 62 63

85

Woodhouse Avenue

Ferr Cl

Woodhouse Close

South Road

Hortham
Wood

1

Old Aust Road

Bishop's
Wood

GLOUCESTER ROAD

Hortham Lane

Hickory La

Hortham
Farm

Hortham Lane

M5

Florence Park

Cope Pk

Woodlands Lane

2

Crantock Dr

84

Junction 20/15

3

Golf Course

Brothersw'd

Woodlands

Apex
Ct

St J's Ct

New Leaze

Eagles Wood
Business
Park

Great Pk Rd

Woodlands Pk

Eagles Wd

Hawkley Dr

Almondsbury
Business Cen

4

Park

Ottrells Mead

Cooks Close

Trench
Lane

Crows Grove

Pye Cft

Woodlands
Park

The Park

Pear Tree

Cooks
Road

Foxfield Avenue

Bramling Cl

Westfield Way

M4

Woodlands Golf
& Country Club

Grange

Apseleys Md

Orchard Gd

Rush Cl

Chessel Cl

Paddock Cl

Bowsland
Way

183

Bradley
Stoke Way

PO

Mallard Cl

Ladwing Cl

Bowsland

Tresham

Trench La

St Marys
RFC

West Country
Water Park

5

Crescent

shaws Close

Ferndene

Bradley

Bowsland Green
Primary School

Ormonds Way

Ellicks Close

Trench Lane

The
Close

Common

Brook'nd

The Common
East

Harvest Cl

Stoke
Way

Wheatfield
Primary School

Wheatfield Drive

21

Savage's
Wood

E F 21 G H

61 62 63

Cranham Av

St Chads
Patchway CE
Primary School

Cornfield Cl

Brook

Wheatfield
Way

Dewfalls Dr

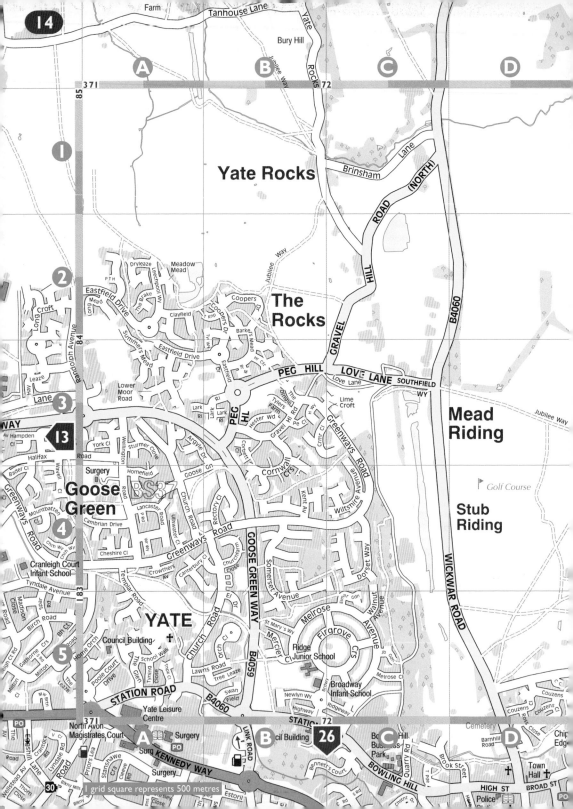

16

351 52

A B C D

1

82

2

3

81

4

5

180

351 52

A B C D

28

Fuel Depot

Fuel Depot

Kings Weston Lane

Stores

St Andrews

Road

Severnside
Trading
Estate

Rockingham
Works

Dean Rd

Ironchurch Road

ST ANDREW'S ROAD

A403

SMOKE LANE

Poplar Way

Burcott Road

Humber Wy

Bank Road

Worthy

1 grid square represents 500 metres

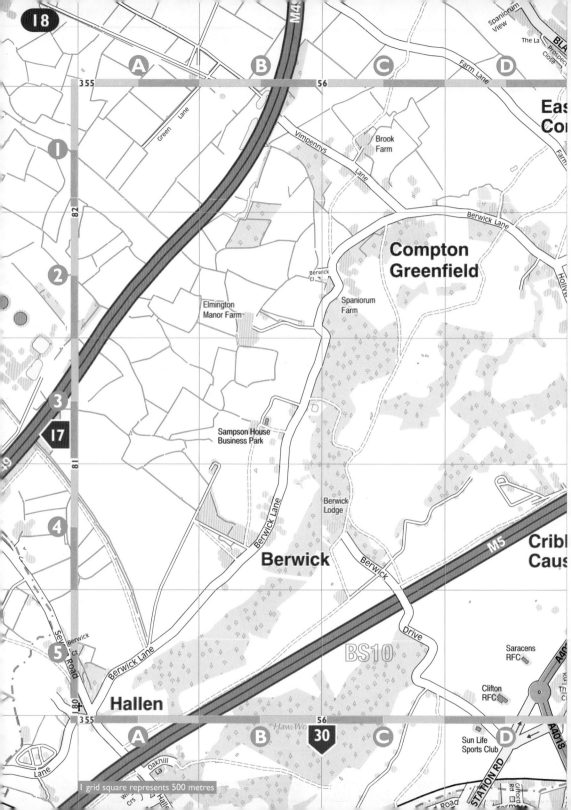

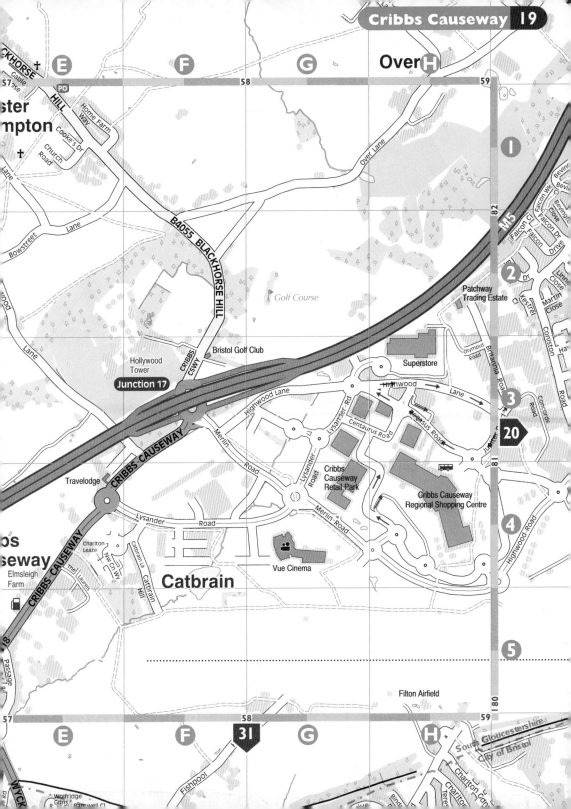

Over

E F G H

I

CKHORSE
Gable
57 5e

HILL

PO

E

ster
mpton

Home Farm Way

Cooke's Dr

Church Road

Bowstreet

Lane

Lane

Lane

B4055 BLACKHORSE HILL

Golf Course

Over Lane

M5
82

Patchway Trading Estate

Falcon Wk
Falcon Cl
Falcon Dri
Falcon Drive

Bevin

Falcon Dr

Kestrel

Linne Close

Martin Close

Conist on

2

Olympus Road

Britannia Road

Superstore

Hollywood Tower

Bristol Golf Club

CRIBBS CSWY

Junction 17

Highwood Lane

Highwood

Lane

Pegasus Road

Concorde Road

Highwood Road

3

20

Highwood Lane

Lysander Rd

Centaurus Road

Juniter

CRIBBS CAUSEWAY

Travelodge

Merlin

Road

Lysander

Road

Cribbs Causeway Retail Park

Cribbs Causeway Regional Shopping Centre

4

Lysander Road

Merlin Road

CRIBBS CAUSEWAY

bs
seway

Elmsleigh Farm

Charlton Leaze

NW Cn W

The Laurels

Catbrain La

Catbrain Hill

Catbrain

Vue Cinema

5

I 80

57 58 59

Filton Airfield

E F 31 G H

South Gloucestershire
City of Bristol

Charlton Gdns

Charlton Terre

WYCK

Wolfridge Cdns
Barnwell Cl

Fishpool

Passage

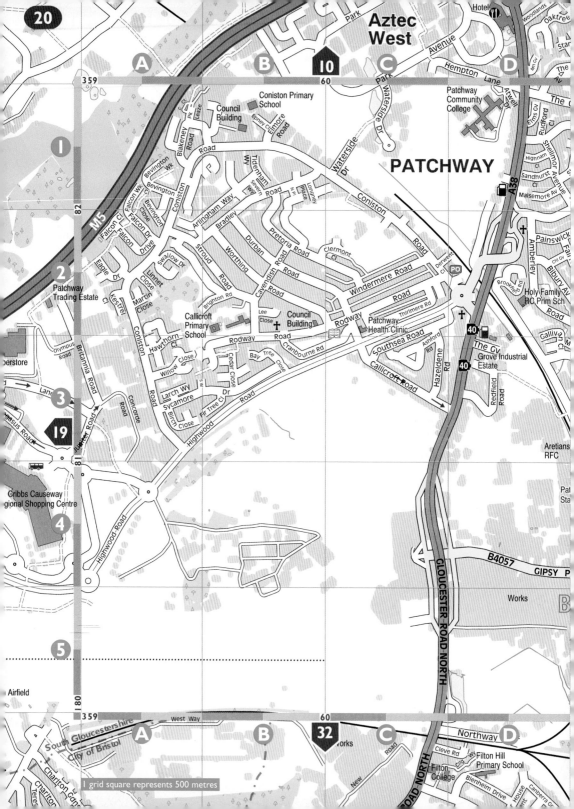

St M___est Country
RFC WaterPark

A B C D

Trench Lane

363

64 B4427

Woods

The Grange
Hotel

1

82

Swan Lane

High Lane

2

Bradley Brook

B4427

Juniper Way

Lavender Wy

Fennel Dr

Juniper
Way

Webbs Wd Rd

St Mary's
Catholic
Primary Sch

OLD GLOUCESTER ROAD

3

Marjoram
Pl

Webbs Wd Rd

Palmers Leaze

21

Coriander
Cl

Baileys Ct

Green Lane

Great Meadow Road

Breaches Ga

Ellan Hay
Road

Bradley Stoke Way

Ellan Hay Rd

Bradley Brook

Baileys Court
___rim Sch

M4

Church Lane

Church Lane

4

The Meadow Md

Berkeleys

___

Robbins

The Vale

Berkeleys Md

The Worthys

Wir

The
Huckley

BEACON

WINTERBOURNE ROAD

Knightwood Rd

The
Orch

Bakers Grnd Rd

LANE B4057

PO

Flax___

Dragon

Green

Dragon Rd

Birdstn

**Great
Stoke**

Bakers
Gnd

WINTERBOURNE HL

Cedar Wy

Rd

Harc___

5

Parsons
Av

Rock La

Trevelyan
Wk

Ct Stoke Wy

Newprick Cl

Simmons
Vw

Hunts Gnd Rd

363

A B C D

34

OLD GL___

Dragon
Road

B4058 ___

Mill

Star Av

Kings ___

Halls Gardens

Vygr

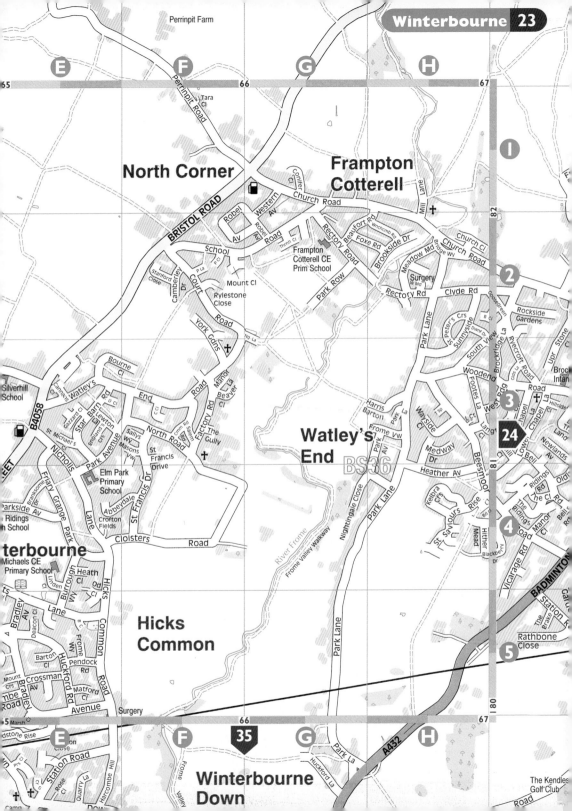

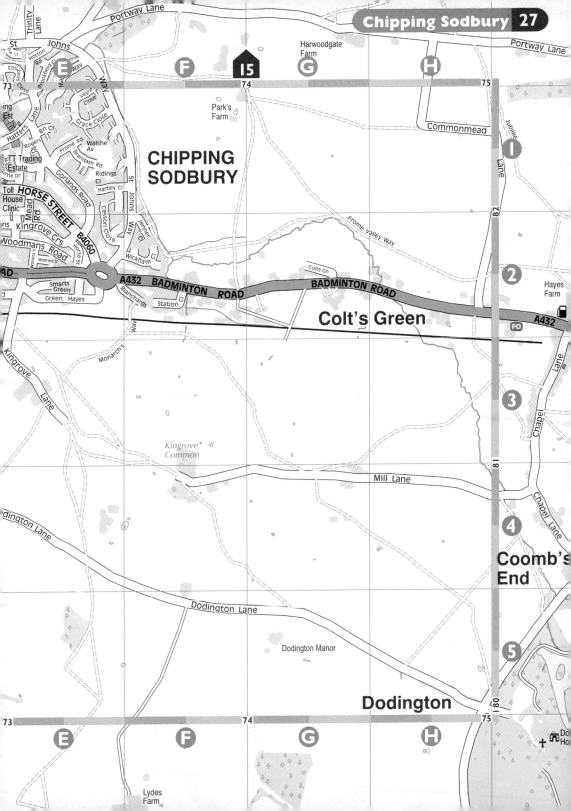

A   B   16   C   D
52

351
80

Fuel Depot

1

St Andrews
Road Station

Kings Weston Lane
Stores
Road

Works
Acid   Workshop   Spar   Boundary
Road   Rd   Road   Road

ANDREW'S ROAD

Severn Road

Cadmium Rd

Zinc   Road

Retort Rd   I.S.F. Rd

St Georges
Industrial Estate

79

Hydro
Estate

2

AVONMOUTH

ST

Haslemere
Industrial
Estate

Jubilee Wy

A403

Docks

3

LC

King Rd Av

Fire Station
Lane

St Brendans
Trading Estate

Avonmouth Wy W

Haslemere
Industrial Estate

Third
Way

Ballast

Willment Way

Avon

CROWLEY WAY

Nova Wy

Avonmouth Way

Severnside
Trading Estate

First Way

Second Way

Lescren Way

178

4

King St

Napier St

Clayton St

Grove St
Meadow St

Gloucester Road

Richmond Ter

Jufland Rd

McLaren Rd

St Andrew's Rd

LC

Avonmouth
Station

Green Lane

Napier Rd

St Brendan's Wy

Police Stn

PO

Avonmouth
Medical Cen

Davis St

Collins St

BRISTOW BROADWAY

M5

Avonbridge
Trading
Estate

Atlantic Road

Avonbridge
Trading
Estate

M5

Avon
Primary School

The Bean Acres

Barrack's La

Shire Gdns

Merrimans Rd

Merrima Rd

5

Council
Building

Portview Road

Cook St

Farr St

Poole St

Marsh St

Pages Rd

Catherine St

Avonmouth
Road

Akeman Wy

Leeming

Robin Cousins
Sports Centre

PORTWAY

Council
Building

Surgery

Portview
Trading
Estate

Victoria

Primary
School

West Town Rd

Watling St

Meadow Grove

Old Park Rd

Kings Weston Rd

Old Oak

HIGH STREET

351

A   B   42   C   D
52

Avon
Riverside
Estate

Avon G
Industrial

Portway
Trading Estate

West Town Rd   Corston   Barrow

Shirehampton

City of

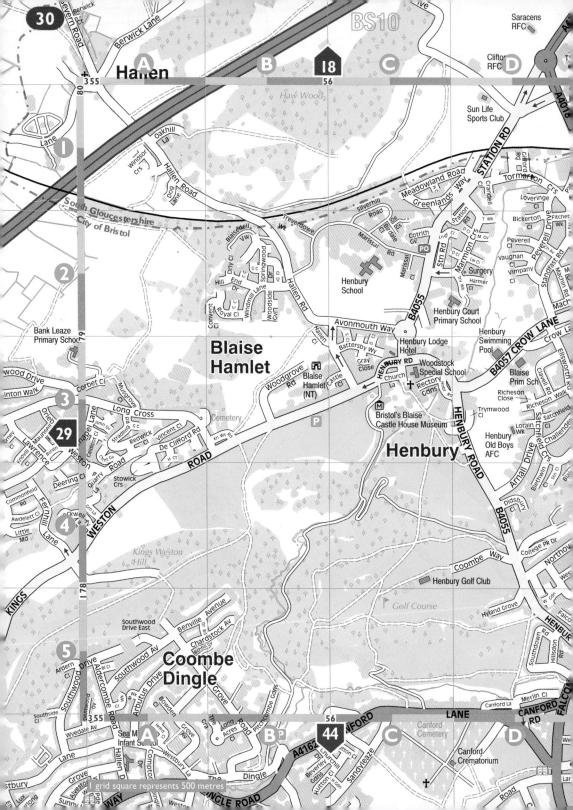

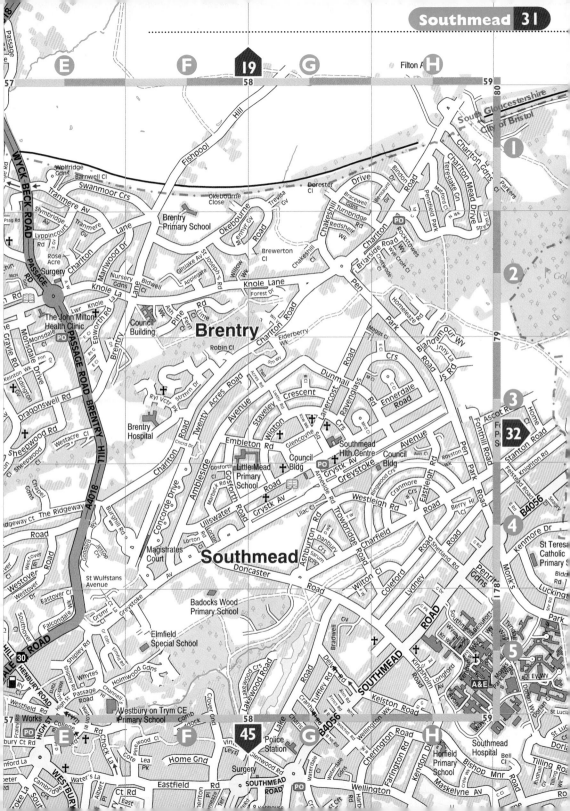

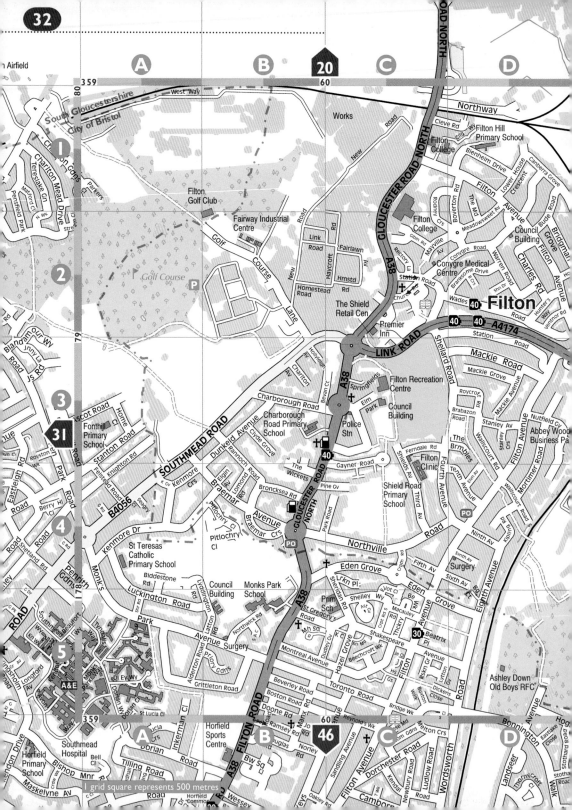

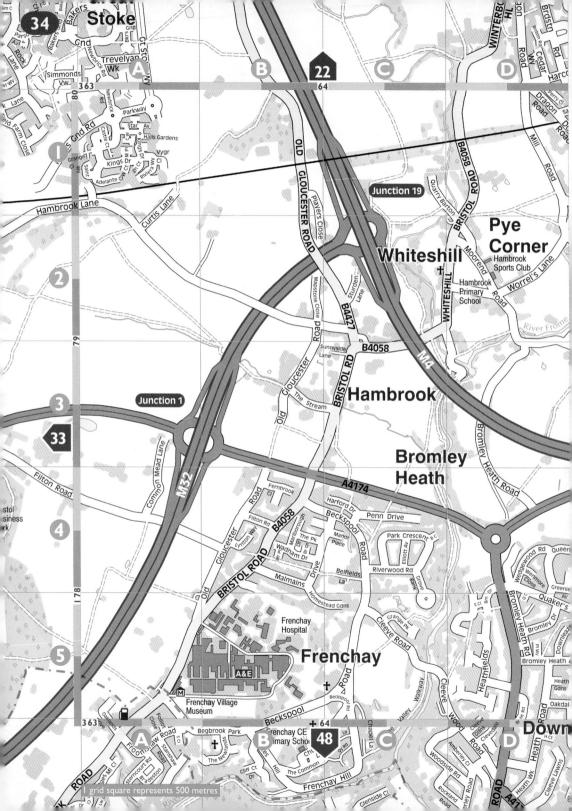

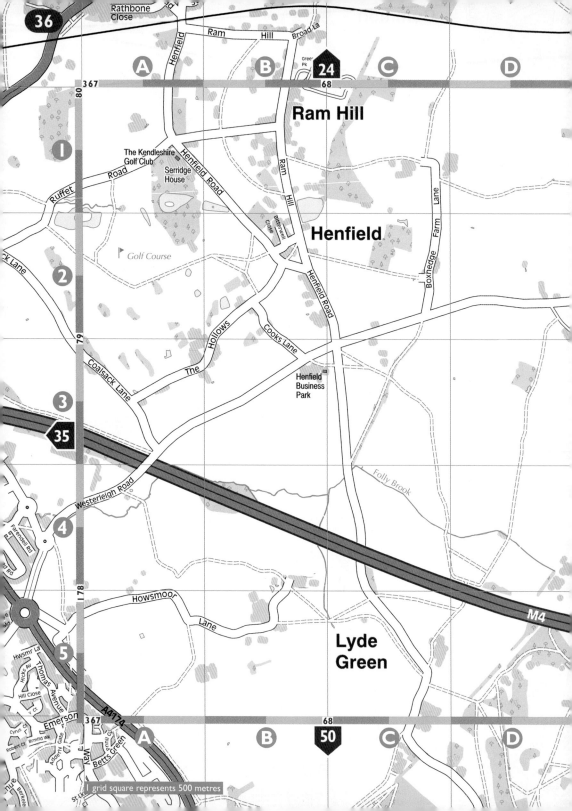

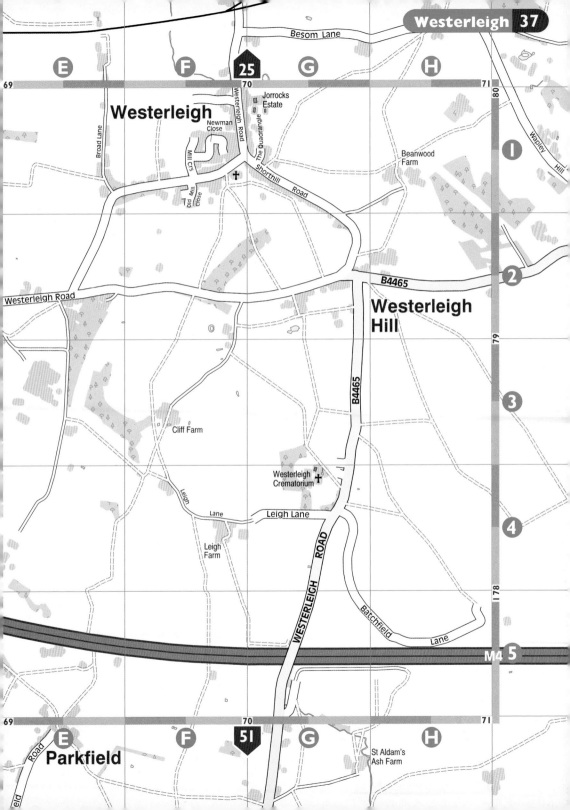

Besom Lane

E   F   **25**   G   H

69   70   71

I

Westerleigh Road

Westerleigh

Jorrocks Estate

Broad Lane

Newman Close

Mill Crs

Beanwood Farm

Wapley Hill

Pit Mill Close

The Quadrangle

Shorthill Road

B4465

Westerleigh Hill

2

Westerleigh Road

79

3

B4465

Cliff Farm

Leigh Lane

Westerleigh Crematorium

Leigh Lane

4

Leigh Farm

WESTERLEIGH ROAD

178

Batchfield Lane

M4 **5**

69   70   71

E   F   **51**   G   H

Parkfield

St Aldam's Ash Farm

Road

80

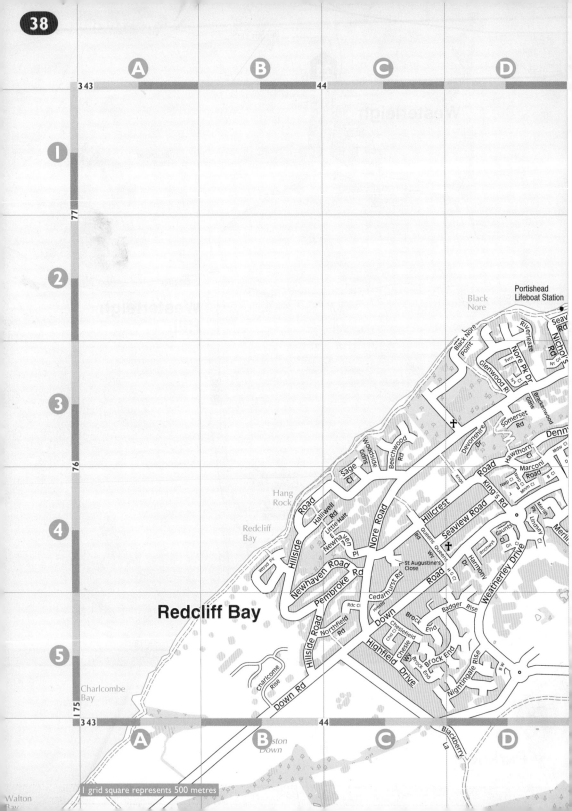

A   B   C   D

3 43   44

1

77

2

Black
Nore

Portishead
Lifeboat Station

3

Seav
Nichol's
Rd

Riverleaze

Black Nore
Point

Nore Pk Dr

Glenwood Rd

Brackenwood

Somerset
Rd

Denn

Woodside
Gdns

Beechwood
Rd

Devonshire
Dr

Hawthorn
Cl

76

Marconi
Road

Sage
Cl

Hillcrest

King's Rd

Hang
Rock

Road

Halliwell
Rd

Little Halt

Nore Road

Seaview Road

Merlin

4

Redcliff
Bay

Hillside

Newha ven
Pl

Queens
Rd

Weatherley Drive

St Augustine's
Close

Newhaven Road

Pembroke
Rd

Cedarhurst Rd

Harmony

Badger Rise

Redcliff Bay

Hillside Road

Northfield
Rd

Down

Brock
End

Brock End

Nightingale Rise

5

Highfield
Drive

Chestle
Wy

175

Charlcombe
Bay

charlcome
Rise

Down Rd

3 43   44

A   B   C   D

ston
Down

Blackberry
La

Walton
Bay

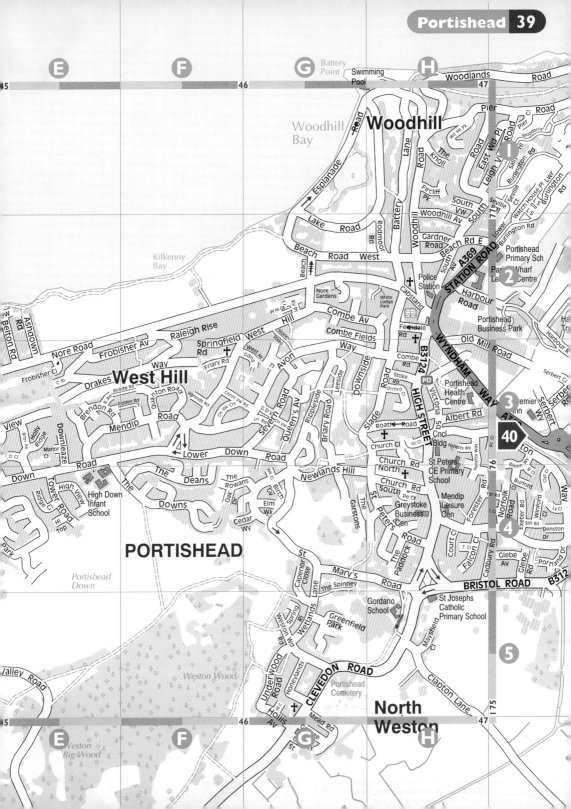

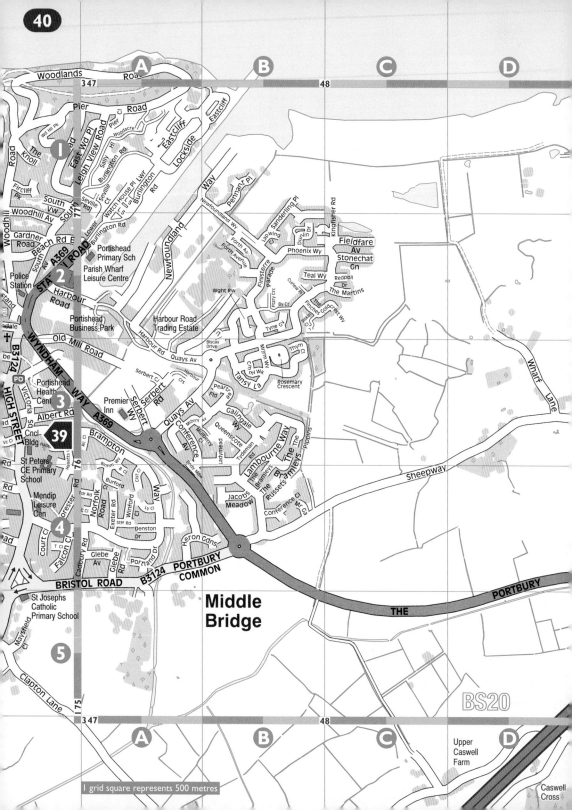

The Royal
Portbury Dock

E   F   G   H

49   50   51

St George's Road

Gordano Road

Normans Wy

Portbury Sawmills
Industrial Estate

1

77

Royal Portbury Dock Road

Marsh Lane

Redland Av

2

The Drove

Portbury Way

First Avenue

Garonor Way

Gordano Way

3

42

Marsh Lane

Bradley Road

Banvard Road

The Dro

Royal Portbury Dock Dock Road

Junction 19

16

M5

4

Sheepway

Station Road

A369 THE PORTBURY HUNDRED

Days Inn

Gordano Service Area

A369

M5

Priory Rd

Priory Farm
Trading Estate

St Marys CE VA
Primary School

Church La

Church

High   Street

St George's

A369

5

175

Portbury

High St

Gordano RFC

Hillside

Forge
End

Brittan
Place

Mill Close

Mill Lane

Portbur

9   50   51

E   F   G   H

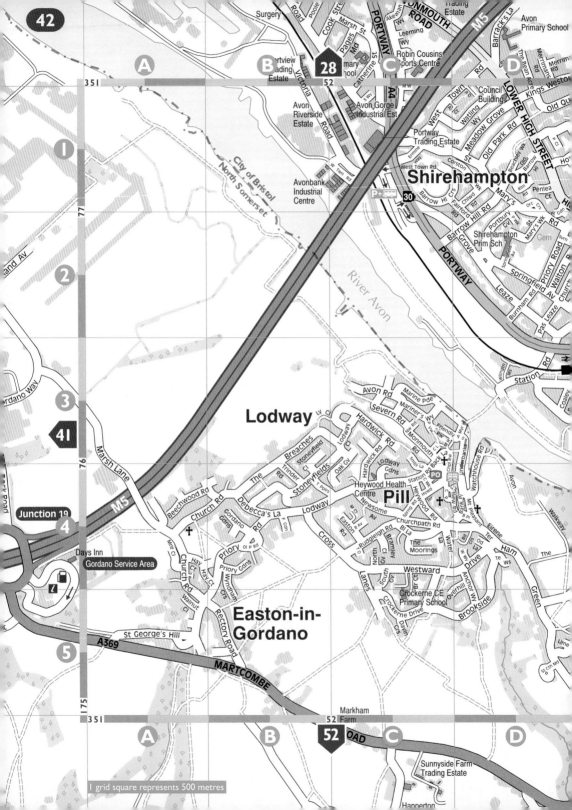

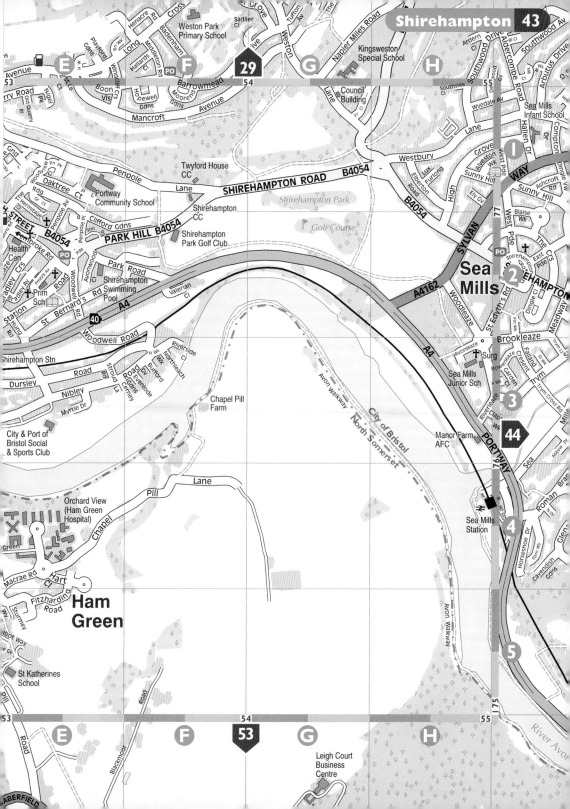

Weston Park Primary School

Sadlier Cl

Henacre Rd

Long

Cross

Playford Gdns

Middleton Rd

Badenham

Hallards Cl

Windcliff Crs

PO

F

Boon Vls

Hopewell Gdns

Moorend Gdns

E

Avenue

W H

53

Avenue

Mancroft

29
54

G

The

Grove

Tufton Av

Napier Miles Road

Kingsweston Special School

Council Building

Lane

Southside

Ardern Cl

Southwood Drive

Aldercombe Road

Southwood Cl

Arbutus Grove

Hallen Dr

Wyedale Av

Sea Mills Infant School

Compton

H

77

55

I

WAY

West Pde

Ardmore Cl

Lane

Penpole

Twyford House CC

Portway Community School

SHIREHAMPTON ROAD B4054

Lane

Shirehampton Park

Shirehampton CC

Golf Course

Westbury

Lux Furlong

Elberton Road

High

Ilveston Wk

Sunny Hill

Grove

Blaise Wk

Sunny Hill

Ashcroft Rd

The Crs

Ely Gv

2

PO

HEHAMPTON

Oaktree Ct

The Hermitage

Penpole Av

Penpole Pl

Clifford Gdns

Shirehampton Park Golf Club

B4054

A4162

Sea Mills

Woodleaze

Meadow

STREET

Health Cen

Pembroke Rd

Prmbrk Av

Park Road

Avonwood

Shirehampton Swimming Pool

Valerian Cl

A4

Avonleaze

Brookleaze

Bowsdeaze Crescent

Trym Cl

Falland

3

Trym Cross Rd

Bradley Crs

Prim Sch

St Bernard's Rd

Avonmouth Rd

Woodwell Rd

A4

40

Woodwell Road

Riverside Cl

Northleach

Burford Cl

Riverleaze

Surg

Sea Mills Junior Sch

Riverleaze

Clap

Trym

PORTWAY

44

Dursley

Shirehampton Stn

Road

Stroud La

Evenlode Gdns

Cerney

Road

Chapel Pill Farm

Avon Walkway

North Somerset

City of Bristol

Manor Farm AFC

Roman

Nibley

Myrtle Dr

City & Port of Bristol Social & Sports Club

Pill

Lane

Chapel

Green

Orchard View (Ham Green Hospital)

Macrae Rd

Hart Cl

Fitzharding Road

Ham Green

Sturmey

Cabot Way

St Katherines School

76

Sea Mills Station

4

Horseshoe Dr

Bpln Wk

Cavendish Gdns

Glen

175

Avon Walkway

5

Roman

Glen

54

53

E

F

G

H

Road

Blackmoor

Leigh Court Business Centre

River Avon

55

ABERFIELD

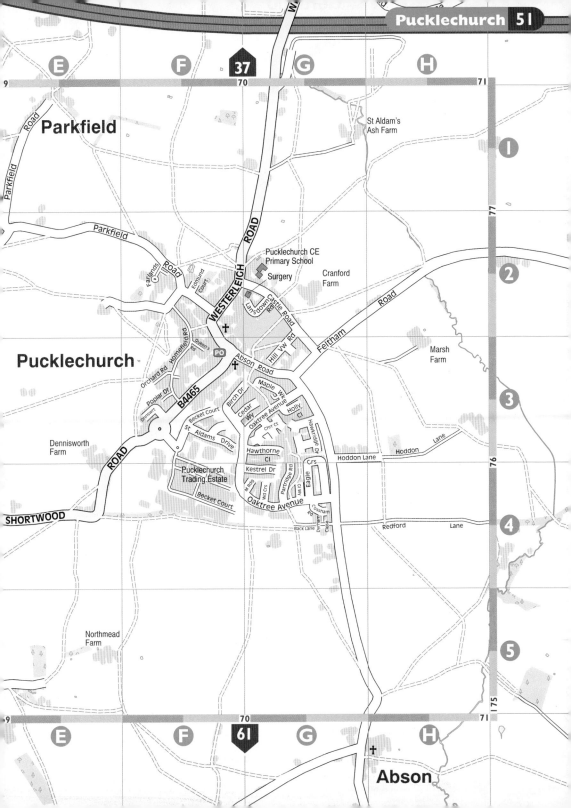

E F 37 70 G H
9 70 71 77

I

2

Parkfield

St Aldam's
Ash Farm

Parkfield Road

Parkfield Road

Eaklands Road

Pucklechurch CE
Primary School

Surgery

Cranford
Farm

Feltham Road

Marsh
Farm

WESTERLEIGH ROAD

Castle Road

Lansdown Road

Edmund
Court

Queen's Rd

PO

Abson Road

Hill Vw Rd

Orchard Rd

Homefield Rd

Poplar Dr

Brinswrt

B4465

Pucklechurch

Birch Dr

Cedar Wy

Maple Wk

Oaktree Avenue

Holly Cl

Chrr Ct

Hawbridge Dr

3

76

Dennisworth
Farm

ROAD

St Aldams Drive

Becket Court

Hawthorne Cl

Kestrel Dr

Eagle Wk

Partridge Rd

Hoddon Lane

Hoddon Lane

Hoddon

Pucklechurch
Trading Estate

Becket Court

Oaktree Avenue

Crs

Cossham

Back Lane

Dvrham Close

Redford Lane

4

SHORTWOOD

Northmead
Farm

5

175

9 70 71

E F 61 70 G H

Abson

St Katherines
School

E   F   **43**   G   H

53   54   55   75

Aberfield
Road

Blackmoor
Road

River Avon

I

ABERFIELD HILL

A369 PILL ROAD

Leigh Court
Business
Centre

Haberfield
Park Farm

2

74

Abbots Leigh

Dennyview Road

Church Road

Monarch's Way

Knightcott Rd

Harris Lane

Glen
Av

Sandy Lane

Manor Lane

Manor Road

The Mnr Cl

A369

Home Farm Road

Monarch's Way

3

54

Manor
House

Glen
Farm

30 ABBOTS LEIGH

Asparove Av

4

Clifton
College
Sports Club

173

BS8

Manor Road

Upper
Farm

BEGGAR BUSH LANE   B3129

5   Leig

Cotham Park
RFC

53   54   55

E   Weir Lane   F   **70**   G   H

▷ *Golf Course*

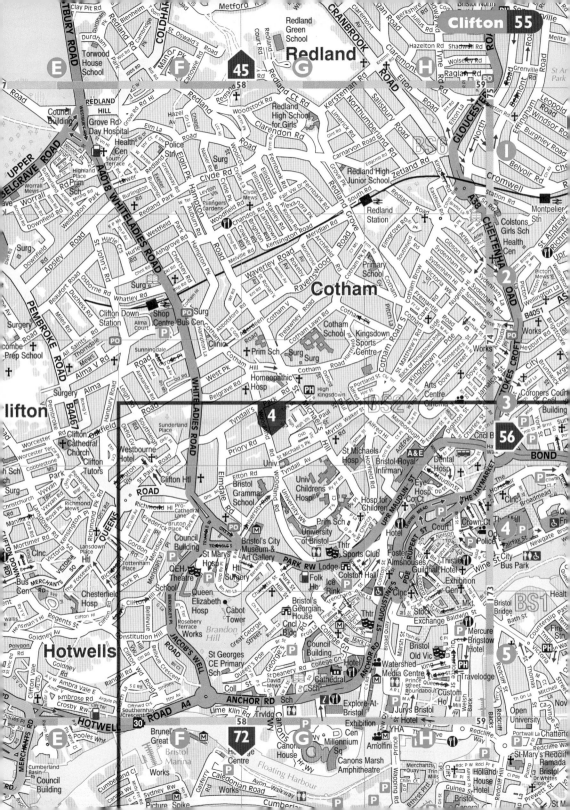

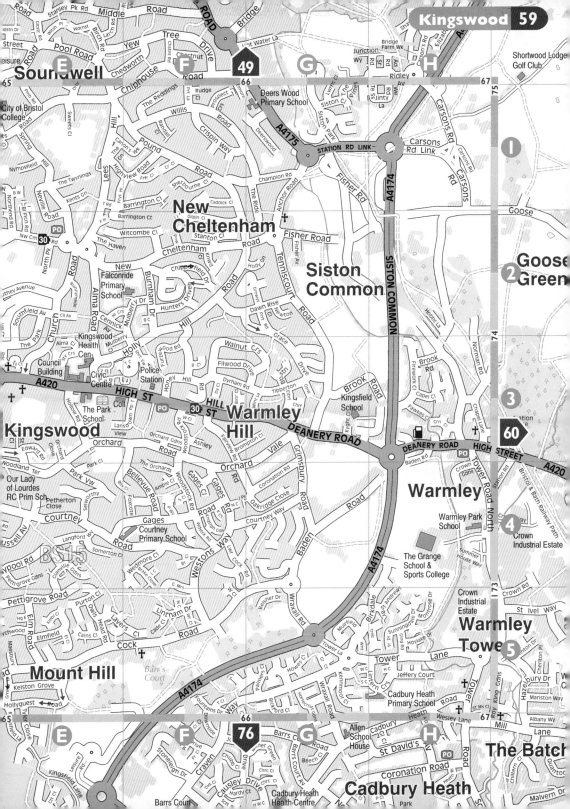

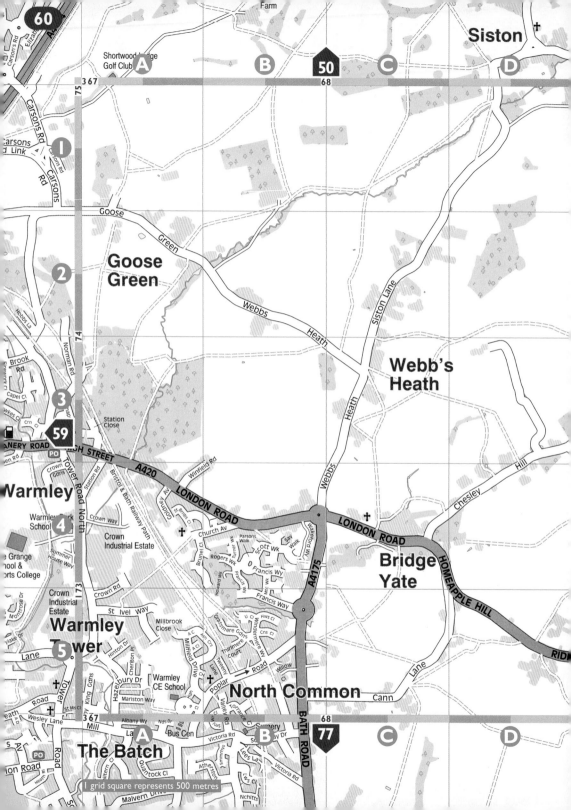

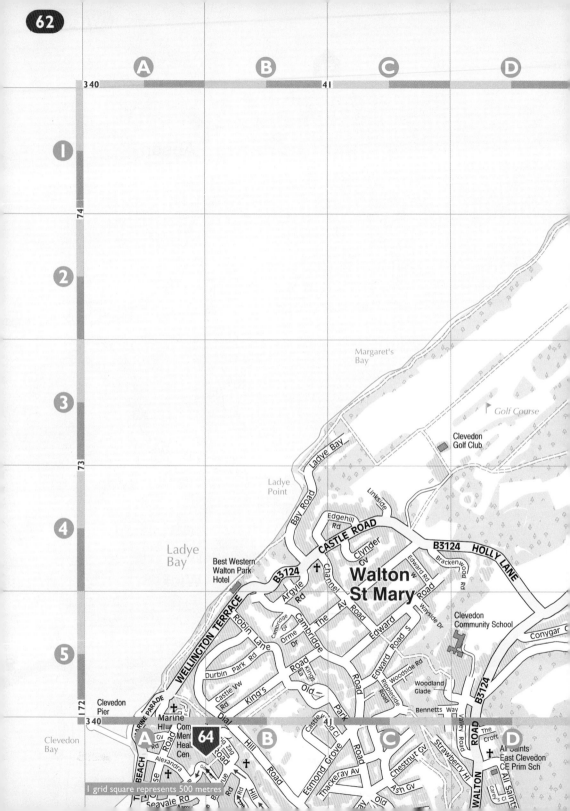

Margaret's Bay

Golf Course

Clevedon Golf Club

Ladye Bay

Ladye Point

Linkside

Edgehill Rd

CASTLE ROAD

Clynder Gv

B3124 HOLLY LANE

Best Western Walton Park Hotel

Ladye Bay

Bay Road

B3124

Channel Road

Brackenwood Rd

Walton St Mary

Argyle Rd

The Av

Edward Rd

Edward Road S

Clevedon Community School

WELLINGTON TERRACE

Cambridge Gv

Cambridge Road

Orme Dr

Edward Road

Wayside Dr

Conygar C

Robin Lane

Kings

Woodside Rd

Durbin Park Rd

Castle Vw Rd

King's

Old

Park

Rippleside

Woodland Glade

B3124

Clevedon Pier

Marine Hl

MARINE PARADE

Dial Hill Road

Bennetts Way

VALLEY ROAD

The Croft

Clevedon Bay

Com Men Heal Cen

Castle

Hill Road

Esmond Grove

Chestnut Gv

Strawberry Hl

All Saints East Clevedon CE Prim Sch

BEACH

GV Rd

Alexandra

Thackeray Av

Ash Gv

Old

WALTON ROAD

All Saints

Carey's

Seavale Rd

1 grid square represents 500 metres

Ladye Bay

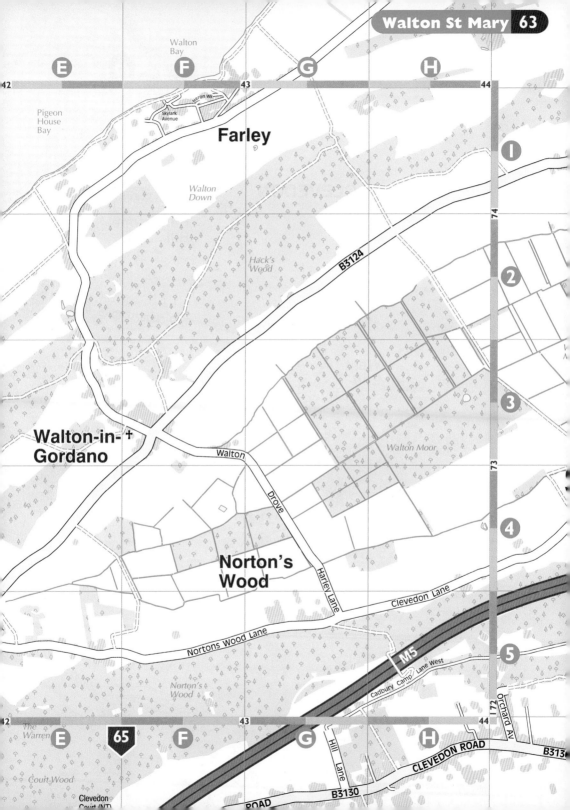

E   F   G   H

42   43   44

I

Walton
Bay

Pigeon
House
Bay

Skylark
Avenue

Heron Wk

Farley

Walton
Down

74

2

Hack's
Wood

B3124

3

Walton-in-
Gordano

Walton

Walton Moor

73

4

Drove

Norton's
Wood

Harley Lane

Clevedon Lane

5

Nortons Wood Lane

M5

Norton's
Wood

Cadbury Camp Lane West

Orchard Av

72

The
Warren

42   43   44

E   **65**   F   G   H

Hill Lane

CLEVEDON ROAD

B313

Court Wood

ROAD   B3130

Clevedon
Court (NT)

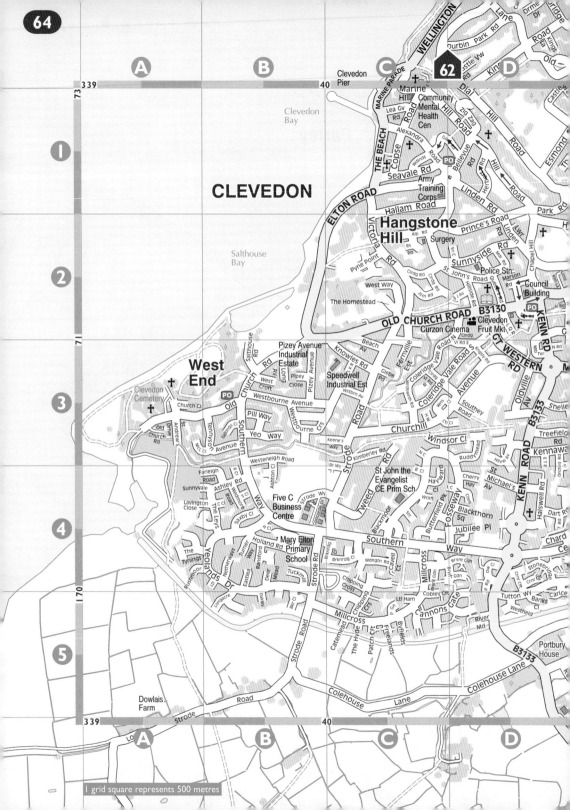

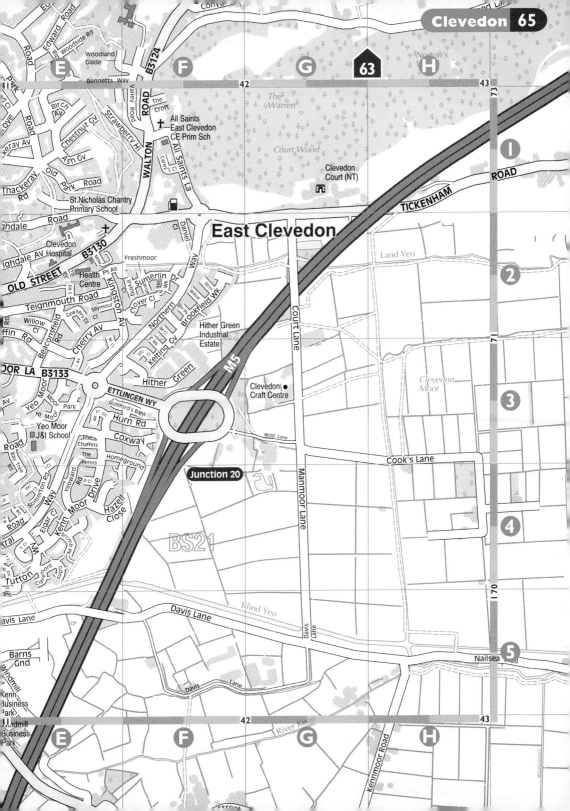

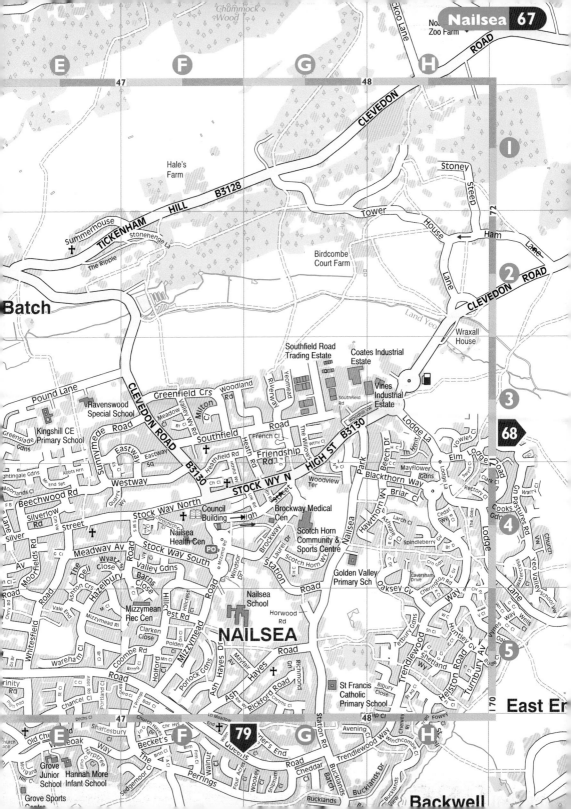

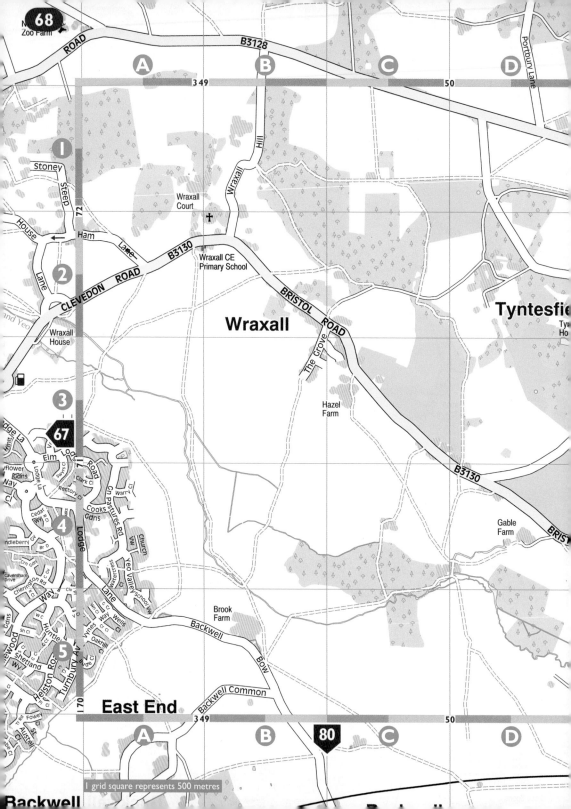

Zoo Farm

68

ROAD

B3128

Portbury Lane

A

B

C

D

349

50

Stoney

I

Steep

72

Wraxall Court

Wraxall Hill

House Lane

Ham Lane

B3130

CLEVEDON ROAD

2

Wraxall CE Primary School

Wraxall House

and Yeo

Wraxall

BRISTOL ROAD

The Grove

Tyntesfie

Ty Ho

3

67

Elm

Lodge La

Lodge Rd

Swn C

Clark Cl

Warr Cl

Cn Pastures Rd

Rectory Cl

Cooks Gdns

Church

Hazel Farm

Cedar Wy

Lodge Lane

Way

Cherington Rd

Caversham Drive

Crn Gdn

Ci Ox

4

Watercress

Yeo Valley school Wy

VW

B3130

Gable Farm

BRIST

ndleberry Gv

Br Cl

W C

Yeo Valley Lane

Wells Cl

Brook Farm

5

Helston Rd

Turnbury Av

Hintle

Oakhill

Vynes Way

Backwell

BOW

Shetland Wy

170

Fowey

Austell

East End

Backwell Common

349

50

A

B

80

C

D

1 grid square represents 500 metres

Backwell

E F 52 G H

Failand Hill House

Failand Farm

CLEVEDON ROAD

B3128

Failand Lodge Farm

I

PO

Flax

Jubilee Dr

Bourton

Road

Woodland Wy

Owen Wy

Short Wy

Bwdn Wy

Sixty Acres Cl

Old Chelsea La

Woodland Cl

Belmont Dr

Belmont Dr

Belmont Dr

Belmont Dr

Manor Way

Hill Dr

Fix Brdge Rd

P

Green Lane

CLEVEDON ROAD

Longwood House

Bri Spr

2

WESTON ROAD

B3129

Failand

3

70

Tyntesfield Plantation

Belmont House

B3129

HILL

BELMONT

B3130

ROAD

Ashton Hill Plantation

4

5

Tyntesfield
e (NT)

ld

OL

E F 81 G H

Station Road

CLEVEDON ROAD

B3130

Flax Bourton CE

Flax Bourton

Weston R

Cambridge

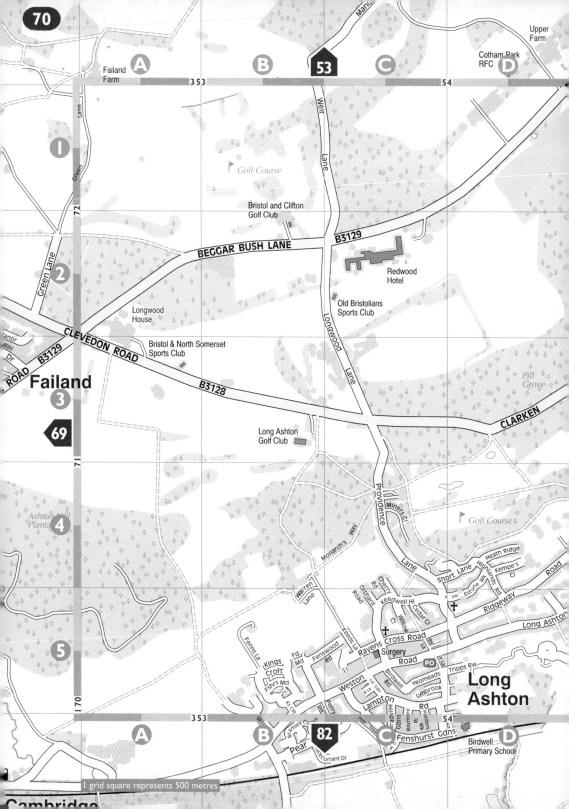

A **B** **53** **C** Cotham Park RFC **D**

Upper Farm

Failand Farm

I

Golf Course

Bristol and Clifton Golf Club

B3129

2

BEGGAR BUSH LANE

Redwood Hotel

Old Bristolians Sports Club

Longwood House

CLEVEDON ROAD

Bristol & North Somerset Sports Club

Failand

3

B3128

69

Long Ashton Golf Club

CLARKEN

Pill Grove

4

Ashton Hill Planta

Golf Course

Providence Lane

Miners Cl

Monarch's Way

Warren Lane

Heath Ridge

Short Lane

Highlands Rd

Kempe's Cl

Ridgeway

Long Ashton Road

5

Cherry Rd

Orchard

Keedwell Hi

Cedar Cl

Willow

Fenswood Rd

Ravens Cross Road

Surgery

Road

PO

Tripps Rw

Birdwell

Yeomeads

Lynbrook

Long Ashton

Kings Croft

Weston

Lampton

Fadville Gdns

Raymore Rd

Fenshurst Gdns

Birdwell Primary School

A **B** **82** **C** **D**

Pear

Cambridge

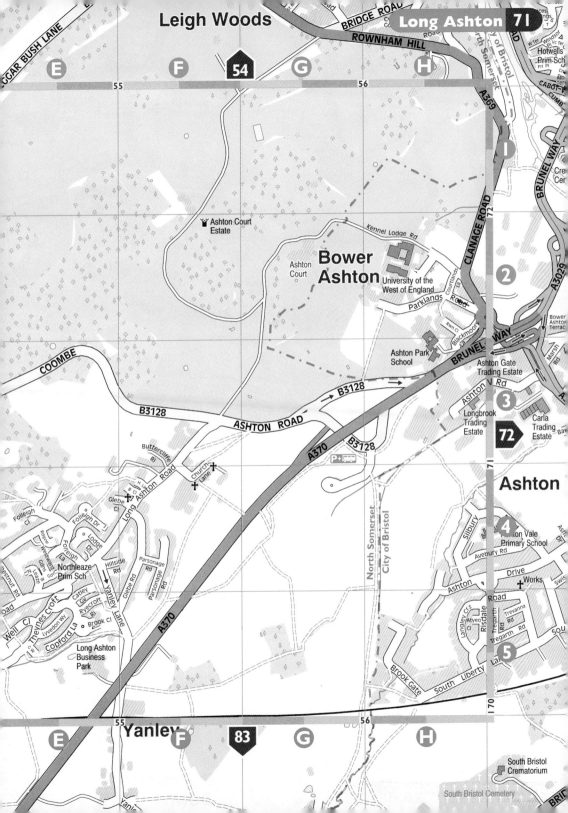

BRIDGE ROAD

ROWNHAM HILL

E F **54** G H

55 56

I

2

Ashton Court Estate

Kennel Lodge Rd

Bower Ashton

Ashton Court

University of the West of England

Parklands Road

Ashton Park School

BRUNEL WAY

Ashton Gate Trading Estate

COOMBE

B3128

Ashton V Rd

3

Longbrook Trading Estate

Carla Trading Estate

B3128

ASHTON ROAD

B3128

72

Buttercliffe Rd

Church Lane

A370

Ashton

Folleigh Cl

Glebe Cl

Long Ashton Road

P+

North Somerset

City of Bristol

Silbury

4

Ashton Vale Primary School

Folleigh Dr

Lodge Dr

Parsonage Rd

Avebury Rd

Northleaze Prim Sch

Hillside Rd

Glebe Rd

Parsonage Rd

Ashton Road

Drive

Works

Yanley Lane

Riscale

Tregarth Rd

Trevanna Rd

Theynes Croft

Copford La

5

Long Ashton Business Park

Brook Gate

South Liberty

Tregarth La

55 56

A370

E F **83** G H

Yanley

South Bristol Crematorium

South Bristol Cemetery

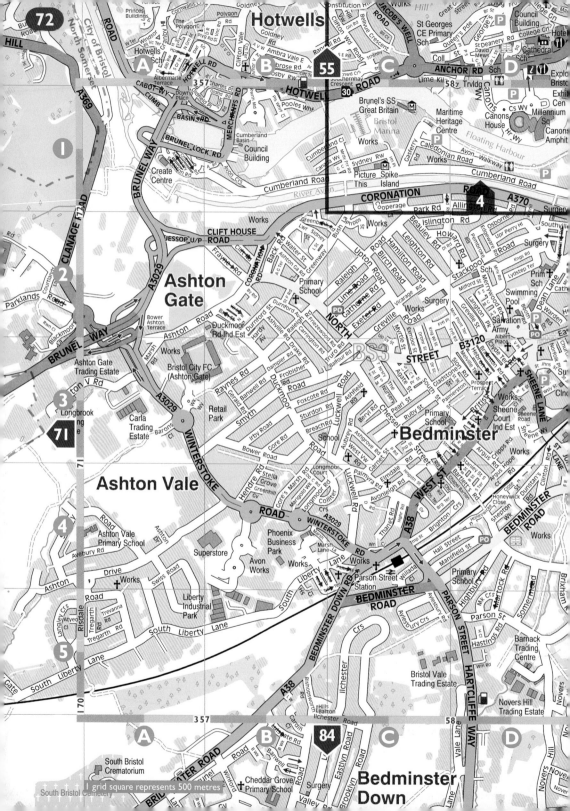

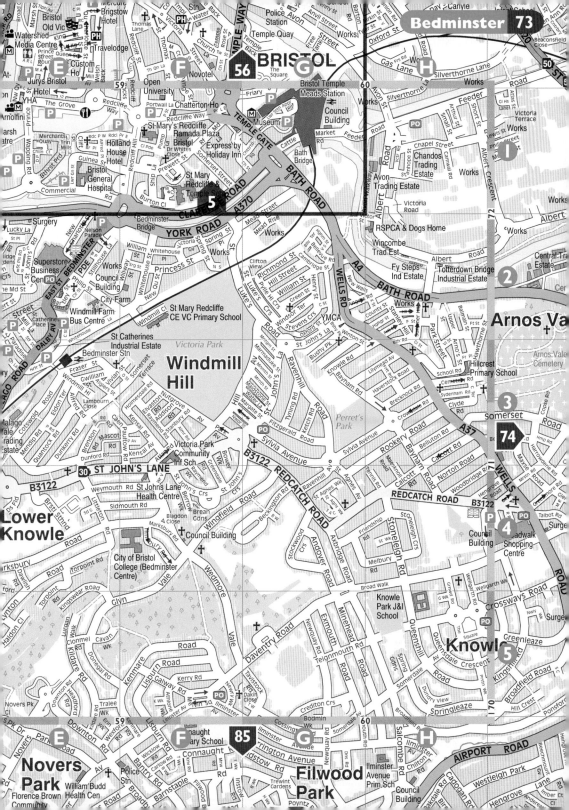

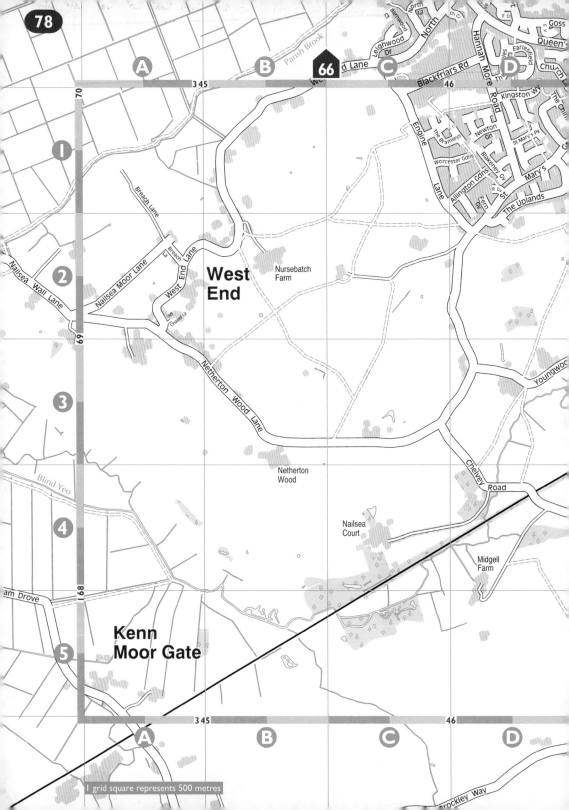

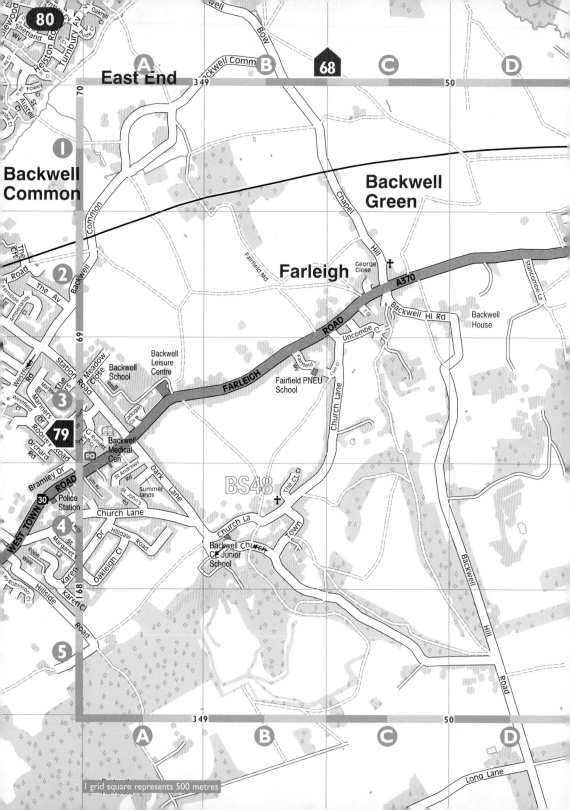

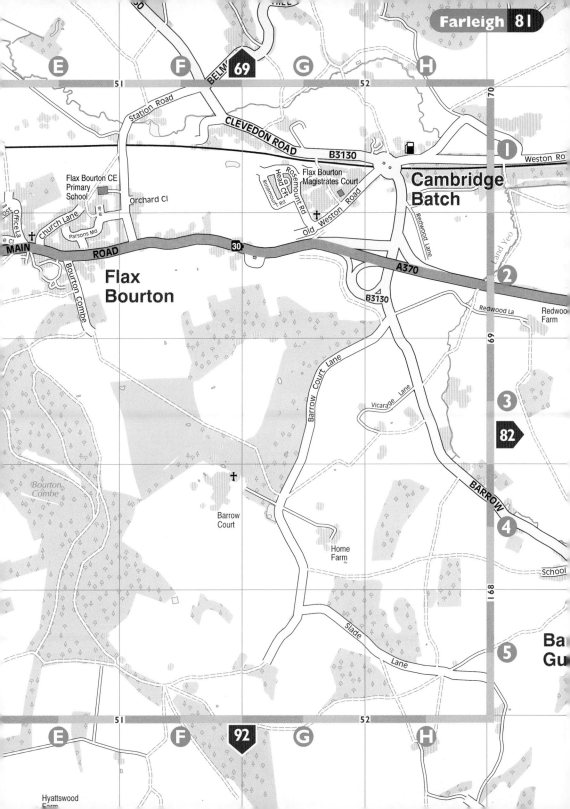

E 51 F BELM 69 G 52 H 70 I

Station Road
CLEVEDON ROAD B3130
Weston Ro

Flax Bourton CE Primary School
Orchard Cl
Br M
Church Lane
Parsons Md
Rosemount Rd
Head Cft
Rosemount Ct
Rosemount Rd
Flax Bourton Magistrates Court
Old Weston Road
Redwood Lane

Cambridge Batch

Office La
e Cl
Post
MAIN ROAD 30
A370

Flax Bourton

Bourton Combe
B3130
Land Yeo

2

Redwood La
Redwoo
Farm

Barrow Court Lane
Vicarage Lane

3

82

Bourton Combe

Barrow Court

Home Farm

BARROW

4

School

Slade Lane

5

Ba
Gu

E 51 F 92 G 52 H

Hyattswood
Farm

E   F   **71**   G   H

55   **56**   **70**

Yanley

Long Ashton Business Park

Copfol

Brook Cot   South Liberty   Lo

South Bristol Crematorium

BRIG

South Bristol Cemetery

Yanley Lane

A38

Yanley Lane

Poplar Road

Marguerite Rd

Donald Road

Tugela Rd   Head

King's

Martha's Orch   Oldmead Wk

Marfield Wk

Kings Walk

Highridge Wk

Lock Gdns

2

Greylands Road

Gardner Av

Westward Road

Lamin

Watchill Av

BRIDGWATER ROAD

Highridge

Golf Course

Woodspring Golf & Country Club

Yanleigh

Cincey Rd

Hayes   Elm   Sn Wk

Spartley

Road

Mr Gw

Geoffrey   Cl   Mov

Elsbert   Dr

Rye   Clese

Barton

Acorn Gv

Sparterfield

3

Lakemead   Av

Cutter

Highridge

Infant S

Highrid

84

Road

Wyatt   Cl

Av

Highridge   Crs

Wyatt   Av

BS41

North Somerset   City of Bristol

Highridge Green

Highridge Road

4   King George's

Keble Av

Wit

Barrow Common

Collier's Brook

Oaktree Gdns

Coldpark Gdns

Coldpark Rd

Pearl Cl

Acres

Elmtree Drive

Millground

Waterbridge Rd   Rd

Paybridge Rd   Three

Leyland Wk

WATER ROAD

Dundry Lane

Monarch's Wn

Turtlegate Av   Four Acres

Highmead Gdns

Turtlegate Wk

Stillman Cl

The Coppice

Huntingham

Rd

Four Acres Primary Sch

PO

Acres

5

Four Acres

Bearb

Peart Dr

Peart Cl

The Ridings

M Wks

Chalcroft Wk   Farmer Rd

Four Way

Horsepool Rd

E   **F**   **94**   **G**   **H**

55   **56**

Redford Crs

Hersey Gdns

Sherrin   W

Billand Cl

een's Road

Highridge

Dundry Lane

Way

I grid square represents 500 metres

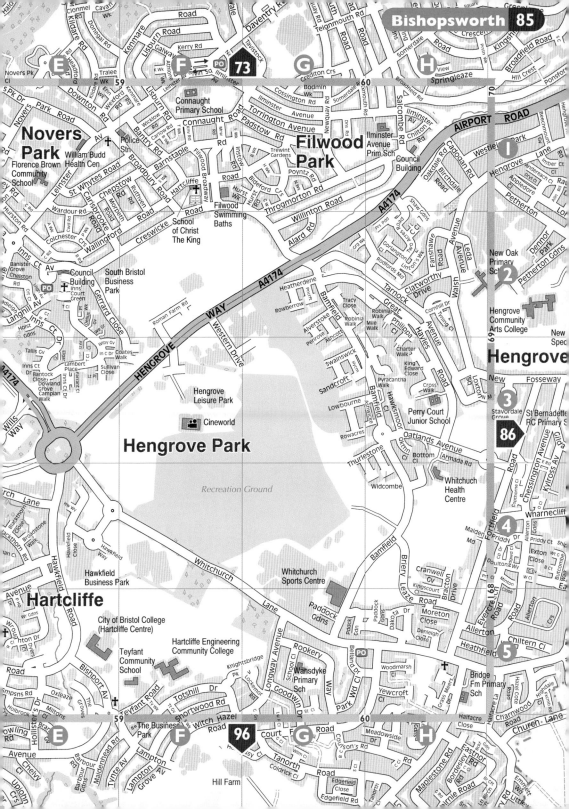

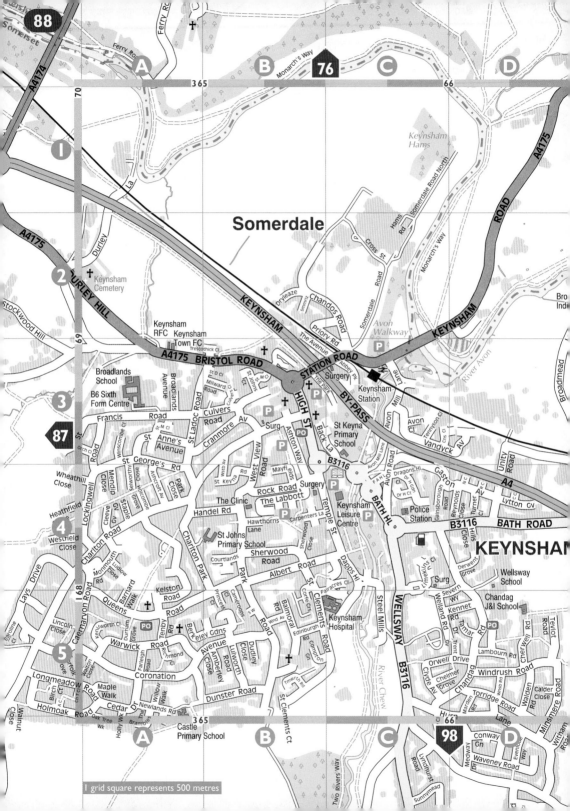

88

A   B   76   C   D

365   70   66

Somerset
A4174

I

A4175

Keynsham Hams

Somerdale

Keynsham Road North

Somerdale Road

Keynsham Hams

2
Durley
✝ Keynsham
Cemetery
DURLEY HILL
Stockwood Hill
69

KEYNSHAM ROAD

Dryleaze
Chandos Road
Cross St
Monarch's Way
KEYNSHAM ROAD A4175
Bro
Ind

Keynsham
RFC   Keynsham
Town FC
Trescothick Cl
A4175 BRISTOL ROAD
STATION ROAD

Smmtt
Priory Rd
The Avenue
Somerdale Road
Avon
Walkway
River Avon
Broadmead

P

3
Broadlands
School
B6 Sixth
Form Centre
Francis   Road
Broadlands Avenue
St D Cl
St Johns
Milward
Road
Culvers
St Johns M Cl

Surgery
Abbey Pk
The Park
Keynsham
Station
Avon Mill Lane

Lane

87
St
Birch Road
Mendip Close
Lockingwell
St Ladoc Road
Cranmore   Av
Culvers
Road
Surg
P
Ashton Way
HIGH ST
PO
Back La
St Keyna
Primary
School
Avon
Cl
Avon Rd
Vandyck Av
A4
Unity Road

Wheathill
Close
Heathfield
Close
St George's Rd
St
Anne's
Avenue
Winscombe Av
Selworthy
Holcombe
Staple
Cleeve
Grove
Park
Close
West View Rd
WestB Av
St Keyna
Rd
Mayfields
Rock Road   Surgery
FA H I
P
Dragons Hl
Tennyson Cl
Gaston
Lytton GV
Lambrook
Gainsborough
Reynolds
Turner
Constable Cl
Lytton GV

4
Westfield
Close
Charlton
Road
Monmouth
Rd
Ludlow
Rd
The Clinic
Handel Rd
Courtlands
St Johns
Primary School
Hawthorns
Lane
Carpenters La
Sherwood
Close
The Labbott
Temple St
Keynsham
Leisure
Centre
P
BATH HL.
Police
Station
B3116   BATH ROAD

KEYNSHAM

Lays Drive
168
Caernarvon Road
Barnard Walk
Kelston
Road
Charlton Park
Sherwood
Road
Albert Road
St Clements
Road
Falacres Rd
Dapps Hi
Steel Mills
Linkeins Cl
Severn
WY
Welland Rd
Welland Rd
Derwent Grove
Surg
Wellsway
School

5
Lincoln
Close
Caroline
Kenilworth Cl
Durham Rd
Queens
PO
Tenby
Berkeley Gdns
Princess
Cnr
Warwick   Road
Farleigh Rd
Ormond Cl
Avenue
Amberley
Close
Lilworth
Close
Dudley
Close
Road
Wnd Av
Edinburgh
Road
Coke Crt
Comp Cl
Keynsham
Hospital
WELLSWAY
B3116
River Chew
Welland Rd
Kennet
Tamar
Grove
Clyde Av
Chelmer
Grove
Chandag
Lambourn Rd
Cherwell Rd
PO
Chandag
J&I School
Trent Dr
Trent Cl
Windrush Road
Teviot Road

Longmeadow Road
Birch Grove
Suffolk Cl
Walton Cl
Coronation
Maple
Walk
Dunster Road
Tmwr sm Gn
Orwell Drive
Torridge
Road
Walden Rd
Calder
Close
Minsmere Road
Witham Cl

Holmoak   Road
Wainut
Close
Cedar   Cl
Willow Walk
Holly Wk
Oak Tree
Wk
Newlands Rd
Bramble
365
Castle
Primary School
St Clements Ct
Two Rivers' Way
66

A   B   C   98   D

Conway
Medway
Waveney Road
Lyndhurst
Sunnymead
Eveniode
Way
Marden
Hur
Lane

A431
BATH RD
CHERRY
The Park
KEYNSHAM ROAD
Cherry Gdns
Br Cl
Cl
Clay

E
F
77
G
H

67
68
70

A431 BATH ROAD
Bitton
Monarch's Wa

Meadow School
Tayman Rdg
Gold

I
Monarch's Wa

Kings Sq
Croft Cl
Mill La
Baron Close
PO
Aubrey Meads
HIGH STREET

Field Grove Farm
Monarch's Way
Harrington Close
Edwin Short Cl
Church Road
Church Lane

Monarch's Way

2
ROMAN RD A43

mead Lane
rial Estate
South Gloucestershire
Bath and North East Somerset
Bristol & Bath Railway Path

69

Avon Walkway

3
River

Avon Riverside Station
Avon Farm

Avon Valley Country Park

Avon Lane

Ashmead
Ashmead Ind Est
Business Centre
Road
Pixash Lane
World's End Lane
Bristol & Bath Railway Path

4

Bath Rd
Ellsbridge Close

BATH ROAD A4

88

5

Copse Road
Kelston Cl
Wedmore Rd
Chelwood Rd
Wick House
Queen Sq
C Cl

67
68

E
F
G
99
H
tton
Road
Norman
Iford Ct
High Street
Homefield Rd
Homefield
Jena Ct
Iford Close
Beech Road
Chest

Claverton Rd W
Boyd Road
Roundmoor
Lansdown
Victoria

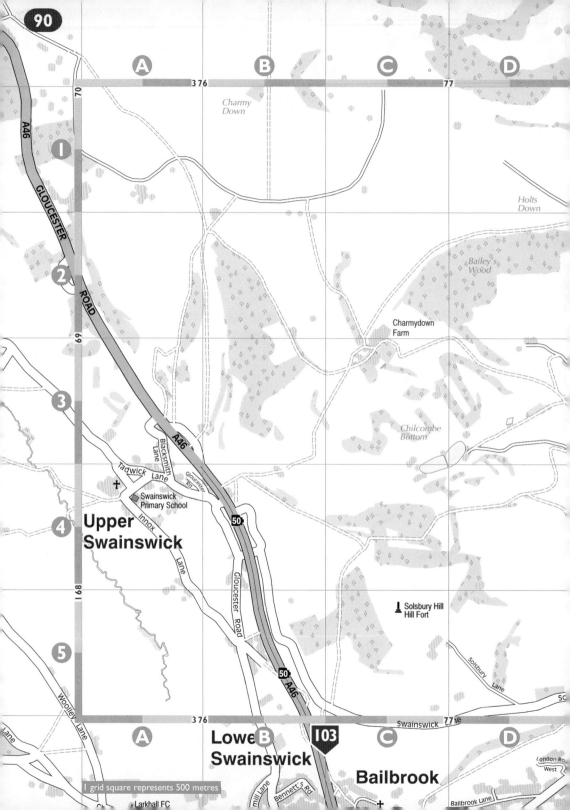

90

A **3 76** B C **77** D

I

A46

Charmy
Down

GLOUCESTER

Holts
Down

2

Bailey's
Wood

ROAD

69

Charmydown
Farm

3

Blacksmith Lane

A46

Gloucester Rd

Chilcombe
Bottom

Tadwick Lane

✝

Swainswick
Primary School

4 **Upper
Swainswick**

Innox Lane

50

Gloucester Road

168

🏛 Solsbury Hill
Hill Fort

5

Solsbury Lane

Sc

Woolley Lane

50 A46

Lane

A **3 76** B **103** C **77**ie D

Swainswick

London Roa
West

Lower **B**

Swainswick

mill Lane

Bennett's Rd

Bailbrook

Bailbrook Lane

Larkhall FC

✝

1 grid square represents 500 metres

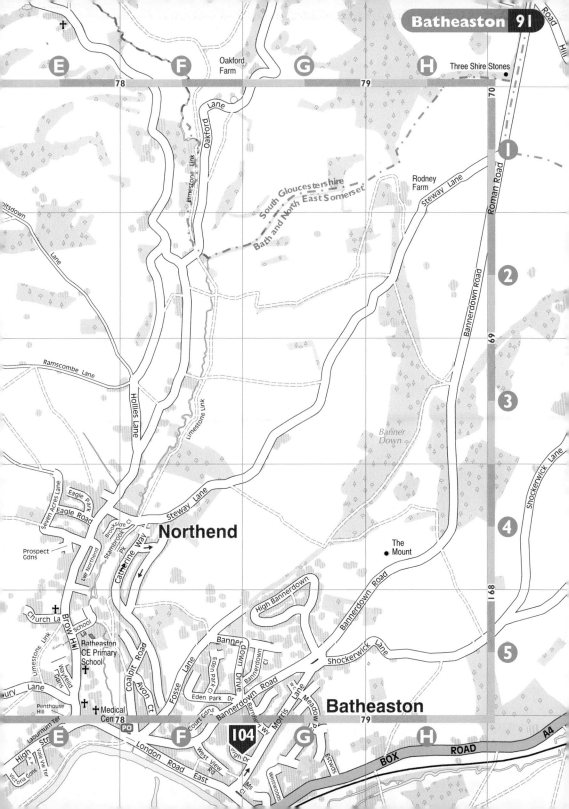

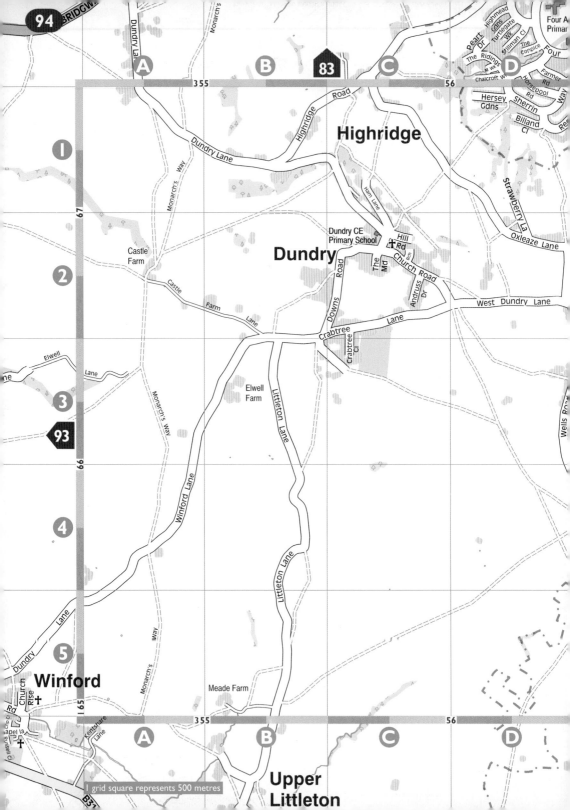

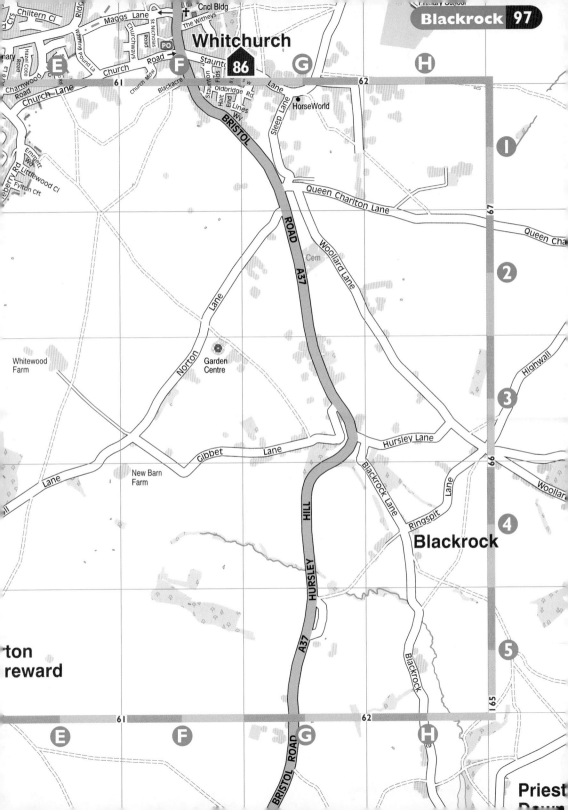

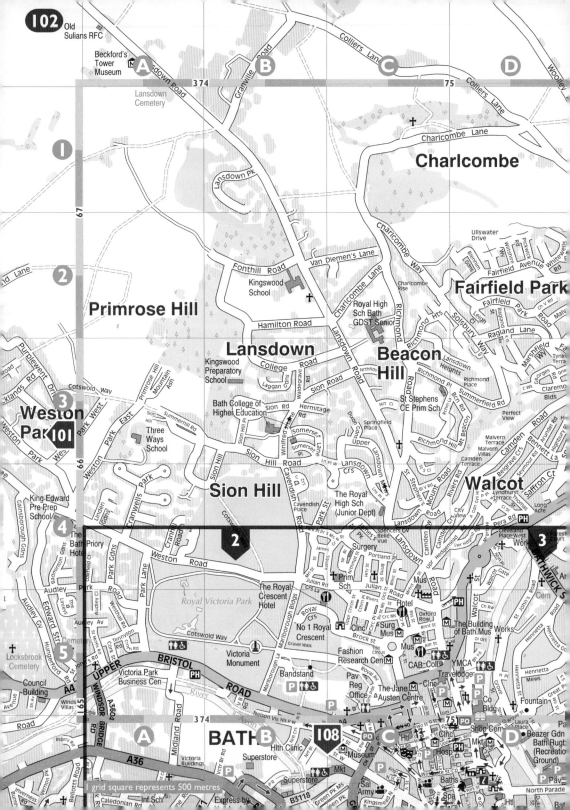

Box
Bridge

BOX ROAD

E   80   F   G   81   H

A4

Ashley   Road

▶ *Golf Course*

Kingsdown

I

Lower Kingsdown Road

Kingsdown GV

Kingsdown
Golf Club

Road

Carstons

Street

67

2

Farleigh Rise

Link Lane

3

Farleigh   Rise

Brown's Folly

66

Link Lane

4

PH

Monkton Farleigh
& South Wraxall
CE Primary School

PO

5

✝

**Monkton
Farleigh**

0

Broad Stones

Butt's Lane

165

Rushm
Farm

E   80   F   G   81   H

SALT

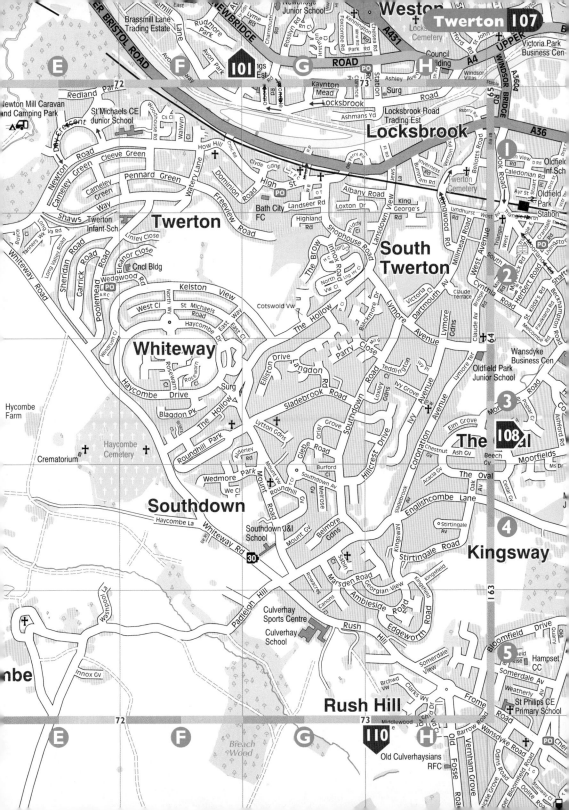

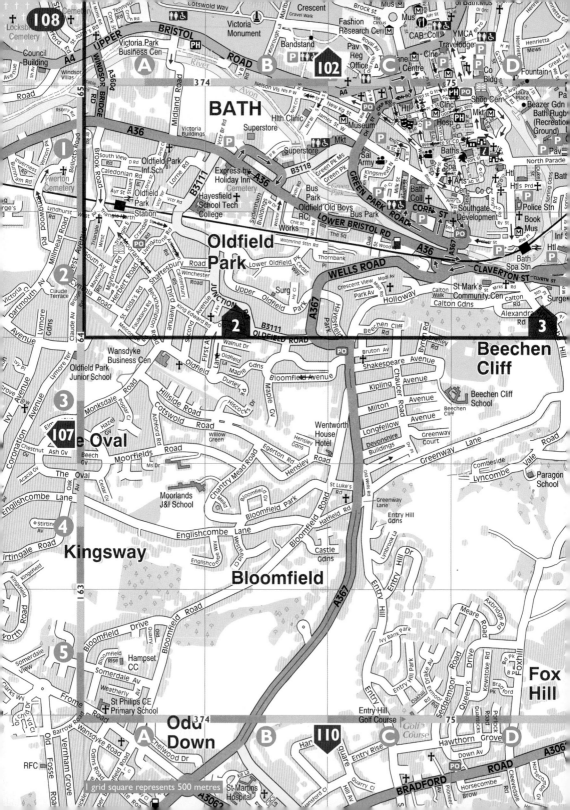

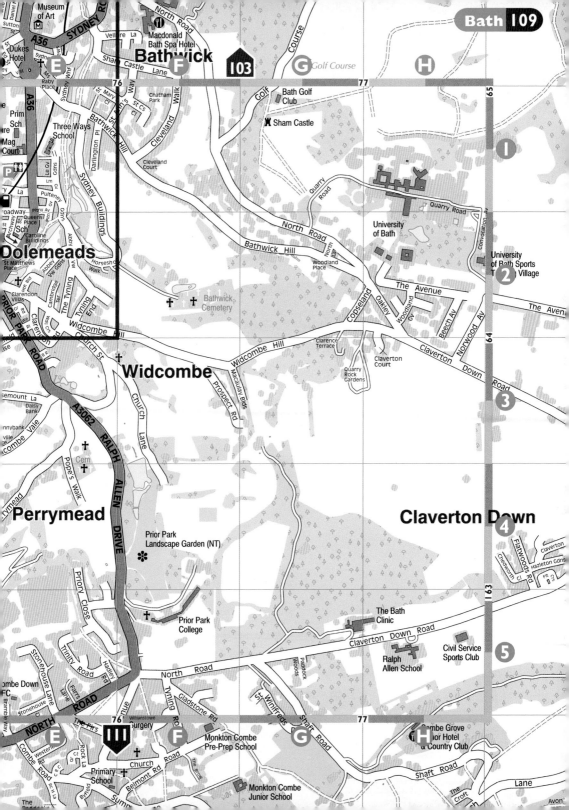

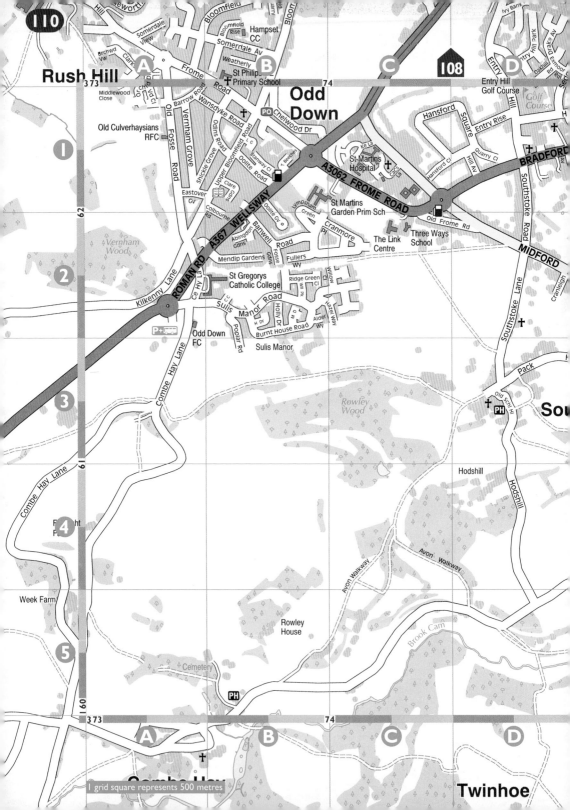

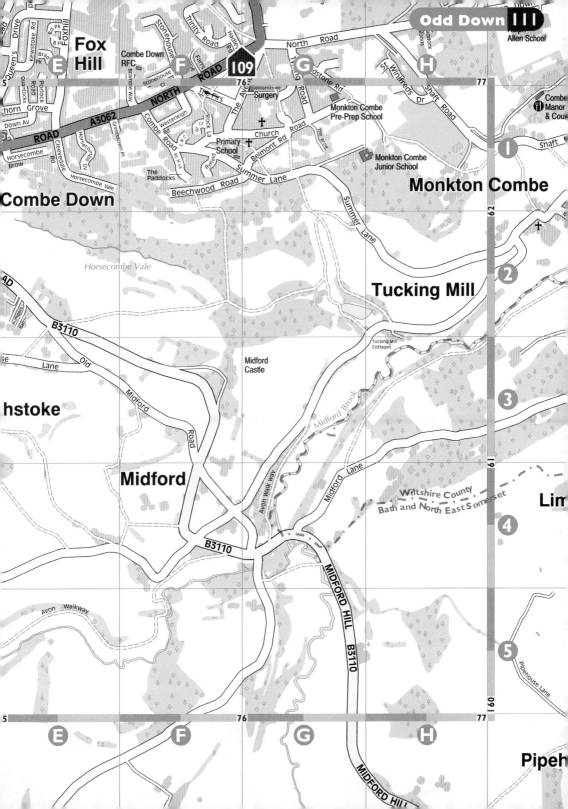

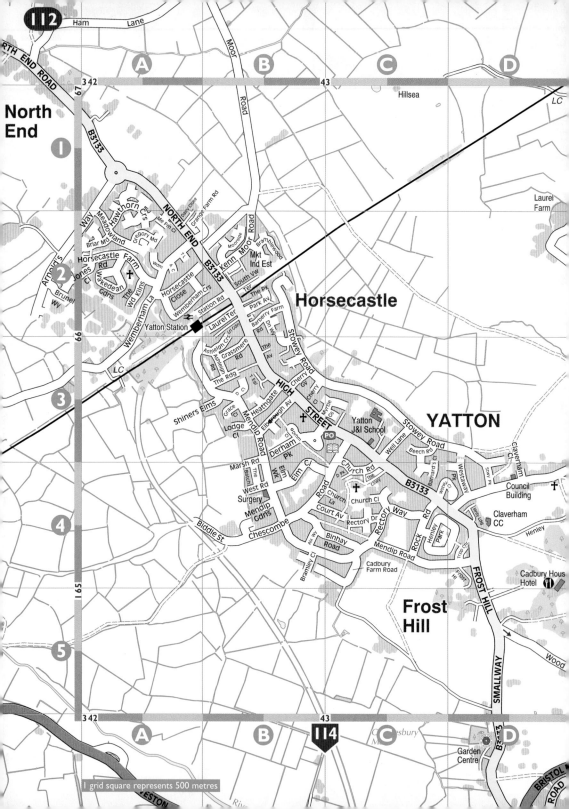

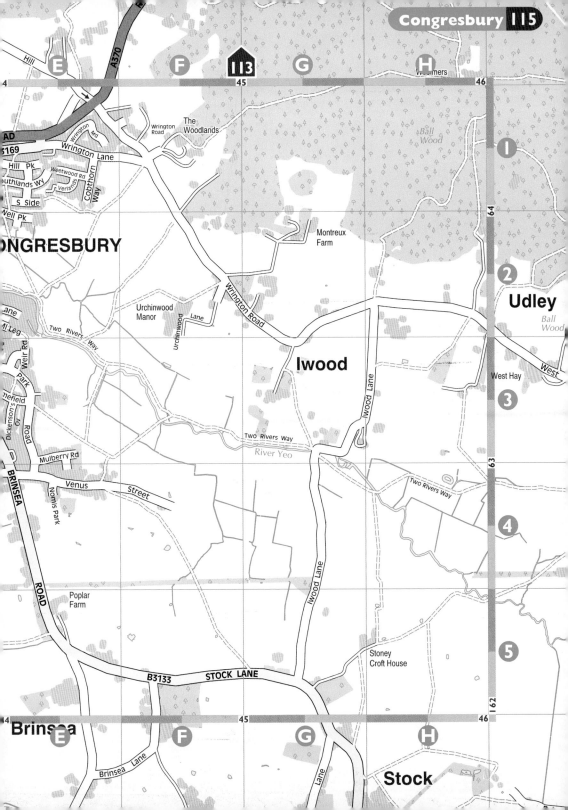

Hill

E

A370

3169
AD

Wrington Rd
Wrington Road

Wrington Lane

Hill Pk
Southlands WY
Weetwood Rd
Verlands
S Side
Cobthorn Way
Well Pk

ONGRESBURY

F

113
45

The
Woodlands

G

Montreux
Farm

Ball
Wood

Wedmers

H

46

I

64

Lane
M Leg

Two Rivers Way

Weir Rd
Park

Dickenson's

Road

enefield
Way

Mulberry Rd

Venus
Street

Nomis Park

BRINSEA

Urchinwood
Manor

Urchinwood Lane

Wrington Road

Iwood

Iwood Lane

River Yeo

Two Rivers Way

Two Rivers Way

2

Udley

Ball
Wood

West Hay

West

3

63

4

62

ROAD

Poplar
Farm

B3133   **STOCK LANE**

Stoney
Croft House

5

Brinsea

E

Brinsea Lane

F

Iwood Lane

G

4
45

46

H

Stock

A 333 B C 34 D

1

65

2

Sand Bay 3

64

4

5

163 333

A B **121** C 34 D

Sandbay Farm

Sand Farm Lane

Sand Farm

St. Bridges Close

Myrtle Tree Crescent

Country View Holiday Park

Elmsley Lane

Beach Road

Court Road

Beach Rd

Sand Road

Lower Norton Lane

Kewstoke

Sth Cls

Crookes Lane

PO

Kewside

Kewside Gardens

Manor Gardens

Orchard Close

Norton La

Commodore Hotel

P

Beach Road

Kewstoke Road

Kewstoke Primary School

Monks

Golf Course

Woodspring Crescent

Woodspring Av

Worlebury Golf Club

Worlebury

Toll

Furze Road

Worlebury Park Road

W Lnk Cl

Greenacre

High

Worlebury

Worlebury Road

Cliff Road

Furz Cl

St Pauls CE VA First Sch

lebury St

Milton Gdns

Milbury

The Gln

Penrice Close

Naunton Wy

The Crs

Tirley Wy

Powis Cl

Windsor Road

I grid square represents 500 metres

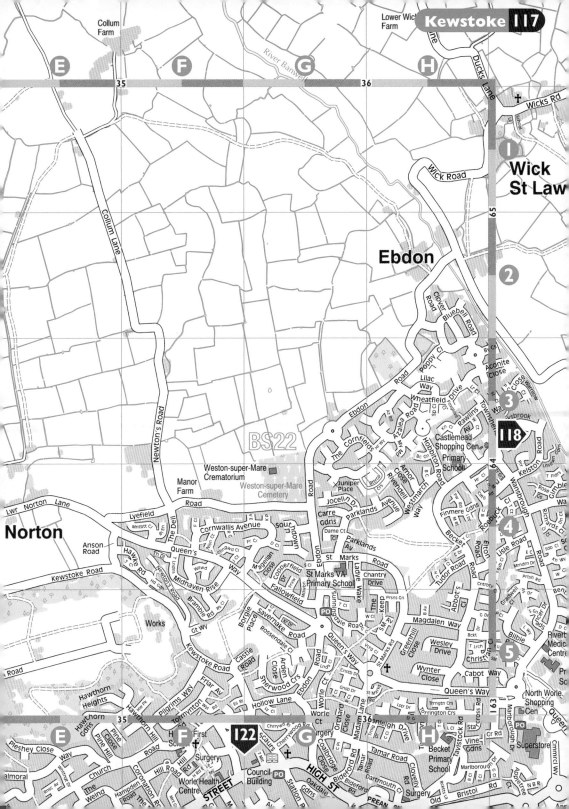

Birnbeck
Island

Life Boat
Station

Pier

Anchor
Head

Kewstoke Road

Worlebury Hill

Westcliff College
of Further Education

South Road

South Road

Shrubbery Avenue

Cecil

Road

Peter's Av

6

Atlantic
Bus Pk

New Birchfield
Hotel

New Ocean
Hotel

Anchor
Head Hotel

Daunceys
Hotel

St John's
Close

All Saints' Rd

Tichborne

Kew
Road

St Jsphs Rd

Upper

Church

St Peter's Av

Grove Pk Rd

Queen's Road

Coombe Rd

Arundell Road

Road-Lower

Bristol

Park Pl

Royal Crs

Weston
College

South Crs

Road

Grove
Lane

Southside

Lambretta
Scooter
Mus

Marine
Lake

Old Knightstone
Theatre

Knightstone
Causeway

Knightstone
Road

The
Arosfa
Hotel

Playhouse

Surgery

Waterloo

Somerset
Museum

Nrth

Time
Machine Mus

Baker Street

**WESTON-
SUPER-MARE**

Model
Yacht
Pond

The
Royal Hotel

Royal Parade

Winter
Gardens
& Pavilion

Sovereign
Shop Cen

North St

Palmer St

Alfred Ct

Orchard St

Regent Street

Jubilee Road

George St

Little George St

Grand
Pier

MARINE PIER

A370

Alexandra Parade

Co Court
Works

Cinema
Superstore

Oxford St

Dolphin Square
Shopping Centre

Carlton St

Town Hall

CAB

Mag
Crts

Station Road

P

Salvation
Army

Prim
Sch

Police Stn

Graham

Weston-s
Mare Stn

Ashbrook
House
Sch

Surgery

Neva

Health &
Fitness
Club

SeaQuarium

Ellenborough Pk N

Ellenborough Park

Albert Avenue

Ridgeway Av

Sunnyside Rd

Weston
Bay

Ellenborough Park S

Corpus
Christi RC
Primary School

Clevedon

Albert

Road

Road

Clifton

Dickenson Rd

124

Parade

A370

Clarence Road North

Severn Road

Wallscote

Exeter Rd

Clarence Park

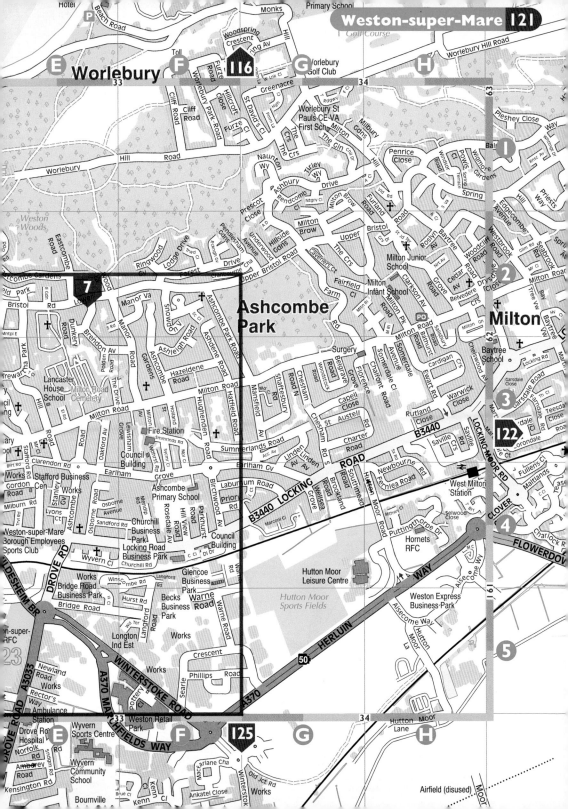

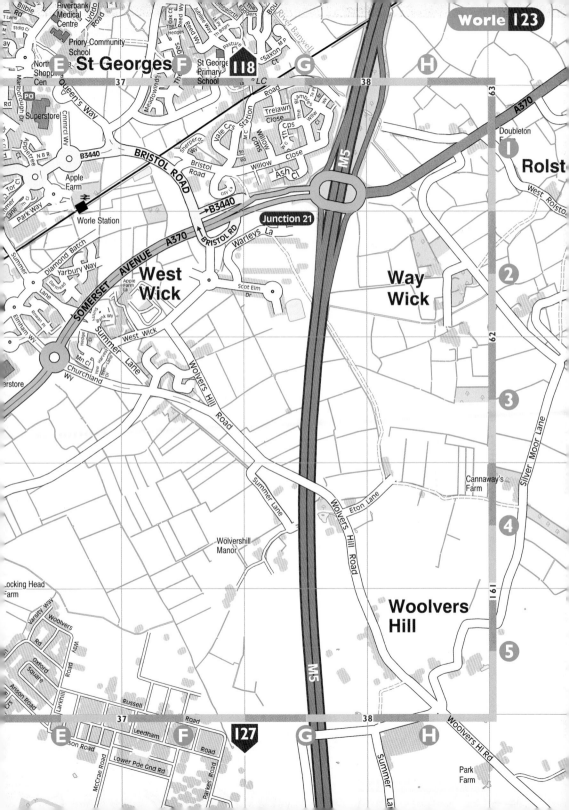

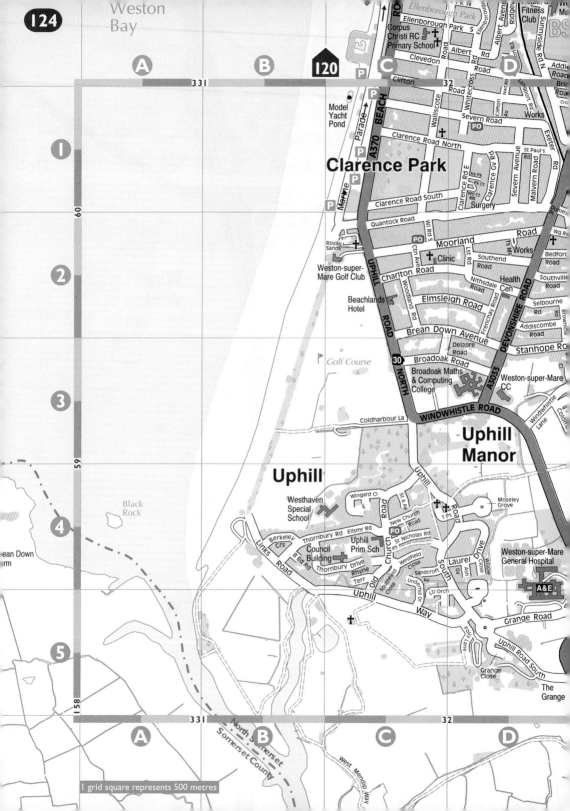

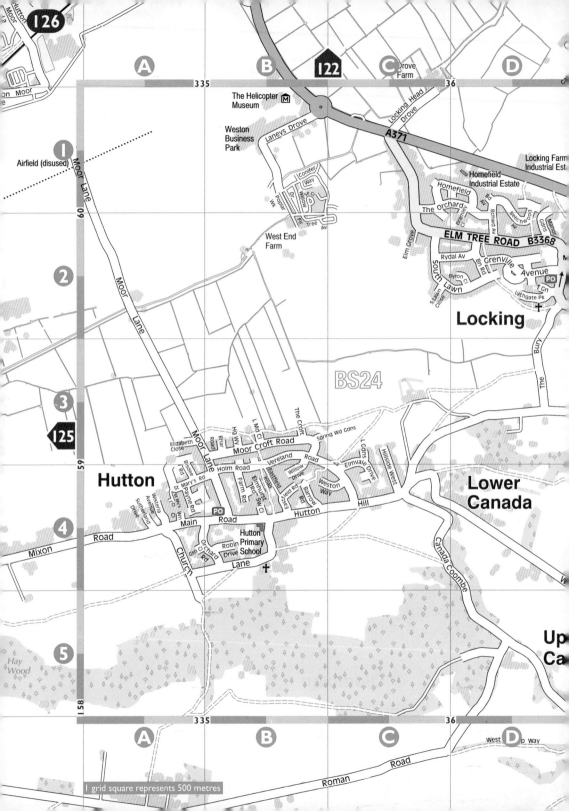

126

A 335 **B** **122** **C** Drove Farm 36 **D**

1

The Helicopter Museum Ⓜ

Locking Head Drove

Weston Business Park

Laneys Drove

A371

Airfield (disused)

Moor Lane

Locking Farm Industrial Est

Homefield Industrial Estate

Homefield Av

The orchard

Bramley

Bchwd Av

Beechwood

Manor Gdns

Conifer Way

Willow C

Poplar Dr

Willow Wk

Tree Av

ELM TREE ROAD B3368

Elm Grove

Rydal Av

Bn Rd

Grenville

Byron Cl

Avenue

PO

2

West End Farm

South Lawn

S Lawn Close

Tn Gn

Lychgate Pk

Locking

The Bury

3

125

BS24

Elizabeth Close

Moor Lane

Hg Wy

L Md Cl

The Croft

Spring Wd Gdns

Moor Croft Road

Bfar

Road

Bisc hre

Rd

St Mary's Rd

Holm Road

Vereland Road

Elmhurst Road

Willow Drive

Eastfield Road

Weston Way

Road

Barrow

L Cans Drive

Elmvale Drive

Hillside West

The

Hutton

St Payne Rd

Wisteria Avenue

Sutherland Drive

Mixon

Road

Main

Road

St John's Wn

Farm Rd

Field Rd

B3583

Hutton Hill

Lower Canada

4

PO

Gsn Cl

Orchard Rd

Church

Robin Drive

Hutton Primary School

Lane

✝

Canada Coombe

Up
Ca

5

Hay Wood

A 335 **B** **C** 36 **D**

West p Way

Roman Road

I grid square represents 500 metres

Abbots Leigh	53 H3	
Abson	61 H1	
Almondsbury	10 C2	
Arnos Vale	74 A2	
Ashcombe Park	7 K1	
Ashley Down	46 B4	
Ashton Gate	72 A2	
Ashton Vale	72 A4	
Avonmouth	28 C2	
Aztec West	10 C5	
Backwell	79 C5	
Backwell Common	79 H1	
Backwell Green	80 C1	
Bailbrook	103 G1	
Barrow Common	83 E4	
Barrow Gurney	82 A5	
Barton Hill	57 E5	
The Batch	77 E1	
Bath	3 H5	
Bathampton	103 H4	
Batheaston	91 G5	
Bathford	104 D2	
Bathwick	103 F5	
Bathwick	3 K3	
Beacon Hill	102 C3	
Bedminster	72 C3	
Bedminster Down	84 C1	
Beechen Cliff	3 G7	
Berwick	18 B4	
Bishopston	45 H4	
Bishopsworth	84 A4	
Bitton	89 H1	
Blackhorse	49 F1	
Blackrock	97 H4	
Blaise Hamlet	30 B3	
Bloomfield	108 B4	
Bourton	118 D3	
Bower Ashton	71 G2	
Bradley Stoke	21 H2	
Brentry	31 F2	
Bridge Yate	60 C4	
Brislington	73 H4	
Bristol	4 B4	
Bromley Heath	34 C3	
Broom Hill	75 F2	
Broomhill	47 G2	
Buckover	9 H5	
Burnett	98 C5	
Cadbury Heath	76 D1	
Cambridge Batch	81 H1	
Catbrain	19 F4	
Charlcombe	102 C1	
Chelvey	79 E4	
Chipping Sodbury	27 F1	
Clarence Park	124 C1	
Claverham	113 F2	
Claverton Down	109 H4	
Clay Hill	57 H1	
Clays End	106 C1	
Cleeve	113 H3	
Clevedon	64 B1	
Clifton	54 D3	
Coalpit Heath	24 B4	
Colt's Green	27 G2	
Combe Down	111 E1	
Compton Greenfield	18 C2	
Congresbury	114 D2	
Conham	75 F1	
Coombe Dingle	30 A5	
Corston	99 H4	
Cotham	55 G2	
Cowhorn Hill	77 F2	
Crew's Hole	57 H4	
Cribbs Causeway	18 D4	
Crossways	9 F2	
Dodington	27 G5	
Dolemeads	3 H6	
Downend	48 D1	
Dundry	94 B2	
East Clevedon	65 F2	
East Dundry	95 G3	
East End	68 A5	
Easter Compton	18 D1	
Eastfield	45 F1	
Easton	57 E2	
Easton-in-Gordano	42 B5	
Eastville	47 G3	
Ebdon	117 H2	
Elborough	127 E3	
Emerson's Green	49 H2	
Engine Common	13 F2	
Englishcombe	106 D5	
Failand	69 H5	
Fairfield Park	102 D2	
Farleigh	80 B2	
Farley	63 F1	
Felton	93 G4	
Filton	32 D2	
Filwood Park	85 G1	
Fishponds	47 H3	
Flax Bourton	81 E2	
Fox Hill	108 D5	
Frampton Cotterell	23 G1	
Frampton End	24 A2	
Frenchay	34 B5	
Frost Hill	112 C5	
Golden Hill	45 H2	
Goose Green	60 A2	
Goose Green	13 H4	
Great Stoke	22 A5	
Grovesend	9 G5	
The Hacket	9 G4	
Halien	18 A5	
Hambrook	34 C3	
Ham Green	43 E5	
Hangstone Hill	64 C2	
Hanham	75 H1	
Hanham Green	75 H5	
Harry Stoke	33 G3	
Hartcliffe	85 E5	
Headley Park	84 C2	
Henbury	30 C3	
Henfield	36 B2	
Hengrove	85 H3	
Hengrove Park	85 F3	
Henleaze	45 G2	
Hewish	119 H3	
Hicks Common	23 F5	
Hicks Gate	87 G1	
Highridge	94 C1	
Hillend	127 G4	
Hillfields	48 B5	
Holbrook Common	61 E3	
Horfield	46 B2	
Horsecastle	112 B2	
Hotwells	55 E5	
Hutton	126 A4	
Iron Acton	12 B3	
Iwood	115 G3	
Kelston	100 D1	
Kendleshire	35 G2	
Kenn Moor Gate	78 A5	
Kewstoke	116 B4	
Keynsham	88 D4	
Kingsdown	105 G1	
Kingsway	107 H4	
Kingswood	59 E3	
The Knapp	9 G1	
Knowle	73 H5	
Lambridge	103 F2	
Lansdown	102 B3	
Larkhall	103 E2	
Lawrence Weston	29 F4	
Leigh Woods	54 A5	
Little Sodbury End	15 H5	
Little Stoke	21 E3	
Locking	126 D2	
Lockleaze	47 E1	
Lodway	42 B3	
Long Ashton	70 D5	
Longwell Green	76 B3	
Lower Canada	126 D4	
Lower Failand	52 A4	
Lower Knowle	73 E4	
Lower Swainswick	103 F1	
Lower Weston	101 H5	
Lulsgate Bottom	92 A4	
Lyde Green	36 C5	
Maiden Head	95 E3	
Mangotsfield	49 F3	
May's Green	119 G5	
Mayshill	24 C1	
Mead Riding	14 C3	
Middle Bridge	80 B5	
Midford	111 F4	
Milton	122 A2	
Monkton Combe	111 H1	
Monkton Farleigh	105 G5	
Montpelier	56 A1	
Moorend	35 E3	
Morton	9 E2	
Mount Hill	59 E5	
Nailsea	67 F5	
Netham	57 E5	
Newbridge	101 F4	
New Cheltenham	59 F2	
Newton St Loe	106 C1	
Nibley	25 E1	
North Common	60 D5	
North Corner	23 F1	
Northend	91 F4	
North Weston	39 H5	
North Wick	95 H4	
Norton	117 E4	
Norton Malreward	96 D5	
Norton's Wood	63 F4	
Novers Park	85 E1	
Odd Down	110 B1	
Oldfield Park	2 B6	
Oldland	76 D3	
Oldland Common	77 G3	
Oldmixon	125 F5	
The Oval	107 H3	
Parkfield	51 E1	
Patchway	20 C1	
Perrymead	109 E4	
Pill	42 C4	
Portbury	41 E5	
Portishead	39 F4	
Potters Hill	92 B3	
Primrose Hill	102 A2	
Pucklechurch	51 E3	
Pye Corner	34 D2	
Ram Hill	36 B1	
Redcliff Bay	38 A5	
Redland	45 G5	
Ridgeway	47 H5	
The Rocks	14 B2	
Rush Hill	107 G5	
St Anne's Park	57 G5	
St George	58 A4	
St Georges	118 A5	
Saltford	99 E2	
Sea Mills	43 H2	
Sheepway	41 E3	
Shirehampton	42 C1	
Shortwood	50 B4	
Sion Hill	102 B4	
Siston	50 D5	
Siston Common	50 A5	
Sneyd Park	44 B5	
Somerdale	88 B2	
Soundwell	49 E5	
Southdown	107 F4	
Southmead	31 F4	
Southville	110 D3	
South Twerton	107 H2	
Speedwell	58 A1	
Staple Hill	49 E4	
Stapleton	47 F4	
Stockwood	86 C3	
Stockwood Vale	87 G3	
Stoke Bishop	44 C4	
Stoke Gifford	21 F5	
Stone-edge Batch	66 D2	
Stone Hill	76 B2	
Stub Riding	14 D4	
Thornbury	8 C3	
Tickenham	66 A2	
Totteroak	15 G2	
Tuckling Mill	111 H2	
Twerton	107 F2	
Two Mile Hill	58 B2	
Tyntesfield	68 D2	
Uphill	124 B4	
Uphill Manor	124 D3	
Upper Canada	126 D5	
Upper Swainswick	90 A4	
Upper Town	92 D4	
Upper Weston	101 G1	
Vinney Green	49 G1	
Walcot	102 D4	
Walton-in-Gordano	63 E3	
Walton St Mary	62 C4	
Warmley	59 H4	
Warmley Hill	59 F3	
Warmley Tower	59 H5	
Watley's End	23 G3	
Way Wick	123 H2	
Webb's Heath	60 C5	
Westbury on Trym	44 C1	
Westbury Park	45 F4	
West End	64 A3	
West End	78 B2	
Westerleigh	37 E1	
Westerleigh Hill	37 H2	
West Hewish	119 F3	
West Hill	39 E5	
Weston	101 F5	
Weston Park	101 H3	
Weston-super-Mare	6 A5	
West Town	79 G4	
West Wick	123 F2	
Whitchurch	86 B5	
Whitehall	57 E2	
Whiteshill	34 C2	
Whiteway	107 F5	
Wick	61 H4	
Wick St Lawrence	118 A1	
Widcombe	109 F3	
Willsbridge	77 E4	
Windmill Hill	73 F5	
Winford	93 H5	
Winterbourne	22 D4	
Winterbourne Down	35 F1	
Withywood	84 A4	
Woodhill	39 G1	
Woolvers Hill	123 H5	
Worle	122 B2	
Worlebury	116 A5	
Wraxall	68 B2	
Yanley	83 F1	
Yate	14 A5	
Yate Rocks	14 B1	
Yatton	112 C3	

USING THE STREET INDEX

Street names are listed alphabetically. Each street name is followed by its postal town or area locality, the Postcode District, the page number, and the reference to the square in which the name is found.

Standard index entries are shown as follows:

Abbey Gn *CBATH/BATHN* BA1........**3** G5

Street names and selected addresses not shown on the map due to scale restrictions are shown in the index with an asterisk:

Abbey St *CBATH/BATHN* BA1 * **3** G4

GENERAL ABBREVIATIONS

ACC....ACCESS	CTYD....COURTYARD	HLS....HILLS	MWY....MOTORWAY	SE....SOUTH EAST
ALY....ALLEY	CUTT....CUTTINGS	HO....HOUSE	N....NORTH	SER....SERVICE AREA
AP....APPROACH	CV....COVE	HOL....HOLLOW	NE....NORTH EAST	SH....SHORE
AR....ARCADE	CYN....CANYON	HOSP....HOSPITAL	NW....NORTH WEST	SHOP....SHOPPING
ASS....ASSOCIATION	DEPT....DEPARTMENT	HRB....HARBOUR	O/P....OVERPASS	SKWY....SKYWAY
AV....AVENUE	DL....DALE	HTH....HEATH	OFF....OFFICE	SMT....SUMMIT
BCH....BEACH	DM....DAM	HTS....HEIGHTS	ORCH....ORCHARD	SOC....SOCIETY
BLDS....BUILDINGS	DR....DRIVE	HVN....HAVEN	OV....OVAL	SP....SPUR
BND....BEND	DRO....DROVE	HWY....HIGHWAY	PAL....PALACE	SPR....SPRING
BNK....BANK	DRY....DRIVEWAY	IMP....IMPERIAL	PAS....PASSAGE	SQ....SQUARE
BR....BRIDGE	DWGS....DWELLINGS	IN....INLET	PAV....PAVILION	ST....STREET
BRK....BROOK	E....EAST	IND EST....INDUSTRIAL ESTATE	PDE....PARADE	STN....STATION
BTM....BOTTOM	EMB....EMBANKMENT	INF....INFIRMARY	PH....PUBLIC HOUSE	STR....STREAM
BUS....BUSINESS	EMBY....EMBASSY	INFO....INFORMATION	PK....PARK	STRD....STRAND
BVD....BOULEVARD	ESP....ESPLANADE	INT....INTERCHANGE	PKWY....PARKWAY	SW....SOUTH WEST
BY....BYPASS	EST....ESTATE	IS....ISLAND	PL....PLACE	TDG....TRADING
CATH....CATHEDRAL	EX....EXCHANGE	JCT....JUNCTION	PLN....PLAIN	TER....TERRACE
CEM....CEMETERY	EXPY....EXPRESSWAY	JTY....JETTY	PLNS....PLAINS	THWY....THROUGHWAY
CEN....CENTRE	EXT....EXTENSION	KG....KING	PLZ....PLAZA	TNL....TUNNEL
CFT....CROFT	F/O....FLYOVER	KNL....KNOLL	POL....POLICE STATION	TOLL....TOLLWAY
CH....CHURCH	FC....FOOTBALL CLUB	L....LAKE	PR....PRINCE	TPK....TURNPIKE
CHA....CHASE	FK....FORK	LA....LANE	PREC....PRECINCT	TR....TRACK
CHYD....CHURCHYARD	FLD....FIELD	LDG....LODGE	PREP....PREPARATORY	TRL....TRAIL
CIR....CIRCLE	FLDS....FIELDS	LGT....LIGHT	PRIM....PRIMARY	TWR....TOWER
CIRC....CIRCUS	FLS....FALLS	LK....LOCK	PROM....PROMENADE	U/P....UNDERPASS
CL....CLOSE	FM....FARM	LKS....LAKES	PRS....PRINCESS	UNI....UNIVERSITY
CLFS....CLIFFS	FT....FORT	LNDG....LANDING	PRT....PORT	UPR....UPPER
CMP....CAMP	FTS....FLATS	LTL....LITTLE	PT....POINT	V....VALE
CNR....CORNER	FWY....FREEWAY	LWR....LOWER	PTH....PATH	VA....VALLEY
CO....COUNTY	FY....FERRY	MAG....MAGISTRATE	PZ....PIAZZA	VIAD....VIADUCT
COLL....COLLEGE	GA....GATE	MAN....MANSIONS	QD....QUADRANT	VIL....VILLA
COM....COMMON	GAL....GALLERY	MD....MEAD	QU....QUEEN	VIS....VISTA
COMM....COMMISSION	GDN....GARDEN	MDW....MEADOWS	QY....QUAY	VLG....VILLAGE
CON....CONVENT	GDNS....GARDENS	MEM....MEMORIAL	R....RIVER	VLS....VILLAS
COT....COTTAGE	GLD....GLADE	MKT....MARKET	RBT....ROUNDABOUT	VW....VIEW
COTS....COTTAGES	GLN....GLEN	MKTS....MARKETS	RD....ROAD	W....WEST
CP....CAPE	GN....GREEN	ML....MALL	RDG....RIDGE	WD....WOOD
CPS....COPSE	GND....GROUND	MNR....MANOR	REP....REPUBLIC	WHF....WHARF
CR....CREEK	GRA....GRANGE	MS....MEWS	RES....RESERVOIR	WK....WALK
CREM....CREMATORIUM	GRG....GARAGE	MSN....MISSION	RFC....RUGBY FOOTBALL CLUB	WKS....WALKS
CRS....CRESCENT	GT....GREAT	MT....MOUNT	RI....RISE	WLS....WELLS
CSWY....CAUSEWAY	GTWY....GATEWAY	MTN....MOUNTAIN	RP....RAMP	WY....WAY
CT....COURT	GV....GROVE	MTS....MOUNTAINS	RW....ROW	YD....YARD
CTRL....CENTRAL	HGR....HIGHER	MUS....MUSEUM	S....SOUTH	YHA....YOUTH HOSTEL
CTS....COURTS	HL....HILL		SCH....SCHOOL	

POSTCODE TOWNS AND AREA ABBREVIATIONS

ALMDB...................Almondsbury	CLVDN...................Clevedon	LGASH...................Long Ashton
AVONM...................Avonmouth	COR/BOX...................Corsham/Box	MANG/FISH...............Mangotsfield/
BATHSE............Bath south & east	EVILLE/WHL.........Eastville/Whitehall	Fishponds
BLAG/CWMG/WR............Blagdon/	FRCTL/WBN......Frampton Cotterell/	MTN/WRL........Milton/Worle
Chew Magna/	Winterbourne	NAIL...................Nailsea
Wrington	HGRV/WHIT......Hengrove/Whitchurch	OLD/WMLY/WICK............Oldland/
BMSTR...................Bedminster	HNBRY/STHM.......Henbury/Southmead	Warmley/Wick
BMSTRD/HC/WWD............Bedminster	HNLZ/SM/SNYPK/WT.......Henleaze/	OMX/HUT/LCK............Oldmixon/
Down/Hartcliffe/	Sea Mills/Sneyd Park/	Hutton/Locking
Withywood	Westbury on Trym	PLTN/PENS..........Paulton/Pensford
BNWL...................Banwell	HORF/LLZ............Horfield/Lockleaze	PTSHD/EG...................Portishead/
BOAV............Bradford-on-Avon	KEYN...................Keynsham	Easton-in-Gordano
BOS...................Burnham-on-Sea	KGWD/HNM...........Kingswood/Hanham	RDLND/MONT......Redland/Montpelier

BRSG/KWL/STAPK...........Brislington/	THNB/SVB...Thornbury/Severn Beach
Knowle/St Anne's Park	WSM...............Weston-super-Mare
BRSTK/PCHW...............Bradley Stoke/	WUE...............Wotton-under-Edge
Patchway	YATE/CS...........Yate/Chipping Sodbury
CBATH/BATHN...............Central Bath/	YTN/CONG...........Yatton/Congresbury
Bath north	
CBRIS/FH...............Central Bristol/	
Floating Harbour	
CBRISNE...............Central Bristol	
north & east	
CFTN/FAIL...............Clifton/Failand	
CHPMW/MSHF......Chippenham west/	
Marshfield	

Index - streets

Abb - Avo

A

Abbey Churchyard
CBATH/BATHN BA1 ....3 G5
Abbey Ct
BRSG/KWL/STAPK BS4..........75 E1
Abbeydale FRCTL/WBN BS36 ...23 E4
Abbey Gdns
OMX/HUT/LCK BS24 ....122 B3
Abbey Rd
CBATH/BATHN BA1 ....3 G5
Abbey Gn CBATH/BATHN BA1 ...3 G5
Abbey Pk KEYN BS31..............88 C3
Abbey Rd
HNLZ/SM/SNYPK/WT BS9 .....44 D2
Abbey St CBATH/BATHN BA1 * ...3 G4
Abbey Vw BATHSE BA2 ....3 K6
Abbey View Gdns BATHSE BA2 ....3 J6
Abbeywood Dr
HNLZ/SM/SNYPK/WT BS9 ....44 A3
Abbots Av KGWD/HNM BS15 ...75 H2
Abbotsbury Rd NAIL BS48 ......67 E5
Abbots Cl HGRV/WHIT BS14....96 D1
Abbot's Ct MTN/WRL BS22 ....117 H5
Abbotsford Rd
RDLND/MONT BS6..............55 F2
Abbots Horn NAIL BS48..........67 E4
Abbots Leigh Rd
CFTN/FAIL BS8 ....53 H4
Abbots Rd
KGWD/HNM BS15..............75 H4
Abbots Wy
HNLZ/SM/SNYPK/WT BS9 .....45 H2
Abbotswood KGWD/HNM BS15 ...58 D4
YATE/CS BS37 ....25 H3
Aberdeen Rd
RDLND/MONT BS6..............55 F2
Abingdon Gdns BATHSE BA2 ...110 B2
Abingdon Rd MANG/FISH BS16 ...48 C2
Ableton La HNBRY/STHM BS10 ...17 F2
Ableton Wk
HNLZ/SM/SNYPK/WT BS9 .....43 H5
Abraham Cl EVILLE/WHL BS5 ...56 D3
Abson Rd HGRV/WHIT BS16 ....51 F3
OLD/WMLY/WICK BS30 ....61 G2
Acacia Av MANG/FISH BS16 .....49 E4
WSM BS23.......................121 G3
Acacia Cl MANG/FISH BS16 .....48 C5
Acacia Ct KEYN BS31..............87 H5
Acacia Gv BATHSE BA2 ....107 H4
Acacia Ms MANG/FISH BS16 * ...48 D4
Acacia Rd MANG/FISH BS16 .....48 D4
Acer Village HGRV/WHIT BS14 ...86 B2
Acid Rd AVONM BS11 ....28 C1
Aconite Cl MTN/WRL BS22 ....117 H3
Acorn Gv
BMSTRD/HC/WWD BS13.......83 H3
Acraman's Rd BMSTR BS3 ....72 D2
Acresbush Cl
BMSTRD/HC/WWD BS13.......84 B4
Acton Rd MANG/FISH BS16 ....48 A5
Adams Hay
BRSG/KWL/STAPK BS4..........74 C5
Adams Land FRCTL/WBN BS36 ...24 A3
Adastral Rd
OMX/HUT/LCK BS24 ....127 G2
Adderly Ga MANG/FISH BS16 ....49 H1
Addicott Rd WSM BS23............7 F7
Addiscombe Rd
HGRV/WHIT BS14...............86 A4
RDLND/MONT BS6..............124 D2
Addison Rd BMSTR BS3..........73 E3
Adelaide Pl EVILLE/WHL BS5 ....56 D3
MANG/FISH BS16...............47 H4
Adelaide Ter
MANG/FISH BS16 * 48 A4
Adelante Cl BRSTK/PCHW BS34 ...34 A1
Admiral Cl MANG/FISH BS16 ....47 F1
Agate St BMSTR BS3 ....72 C3
Aiken St EVILLE/WHL BS5 ....56 D5
Ainslies Belvedere
CBATH/BATHN BA1 * 3 F1
Aintree Dr MANG/FISH BS16 ....35 F4
Air Balloon Rd EVILLE/WHL BS5 ...58 A4
Airport Rd HGRV/WHIT BS14 ...85 H1
Aisecome Wy MTN/WRL BS22 ...121 H5
Akeman Wy AVONM BS11........28 C5
Alanscourt
OLD/WMLY/WICK BS30 ....77 E1
Alard Rd BRSG/KWL/STAPK BS4 ...85 G2
Albany Ga BRSTK/PCHW BS34 ...21 G5
Albany Rd BATHSE BA2...........107 G1
RDLND/MONT BS6..............56 B2
Albany St KGWD/HNM BS15 ....58 C3
Albany Wy
OLD/WMLY/WICK BS30 ....77 F1
Albemarle Rw CFTN/FAIL BS8 ...54 D5
Albermarle Rd CFTN/FAIL BS8 ...54 D5
Albert Av WSM BS23...............6 E7
Albert Crs CBRISNE BS2 ....73 H1
Albert Gv
EVILLE/WHL BS5.................57 H3
Albert Gv South
EVILLE/WHL BS5.................57 H3

Alberton Rd MANG/FISH BS16 ...47 H2
Albert Pde EVILLE/WHL BS5.....57 E3
Albert Pk RDLND/MONT BS6 ....56 B1
Albert Park Pl
RDLND/MONT BS6..............56 A2
Albert Pl BMSTR BS3.............72 D2
HNLZ/SM/SNYPK/WT BS9.....45 E1
Albert Qd WSM BS23...............6 D2
Albert Rd CBRISNE BS2..........73 H2
CLVDN BS21.....................64 C2
KEYN BS31.......................88 B4
KGWD/HNM BS15...............76 A1
MANG/FISH BS16...............49 E4
PTSHD/EG BS20.................39 H3
WSM BS23.........................7 H6
Albert Ter BATHSE BA2 * 107 H1
MANG/FISH BS16...............47 H4
Albion Cl MANG/FISH BS16.....49 F3
Albion Dockside Est
CBRIS/FH BS1 *...................4 B6
Albion Pl CBATH/BATHN BA1 ....2 C3
Albion Rd EVILLE/WHL BS5......56 D2
Albion St EVILLE/WHL BS5......57 E3
Albion Ter CBATH/BATHN BA1....2 C3
Alcove Rd MANG/FISH BS16 ....49 E2
Aldercombe Rd
HNLZ/SM/SNYPK/WT BS9.....30 A5
Alderdown Cl AVONM BS11......29 G5
Alder Dr EVILLE/WHL BS5.......57 G2
Alderley Rd BATHSE BA2.........107 F3
Aldermoor Wy
OLD/WMLY/WICK BS30 ....76 B2
Aldernay Av
BRSG/KWL/STAPK BS4..........75 G2
Alderton Rd HORF/LLZ BS7.....32 A5
Alder Wy BATHSE BA2 ....110 B2
Aldwick Av
BMSTRD/HC/WWD BS13.......95 H1
Alec Ricketts Cl BATHSE BA2 ...107 E2
Alexander Blds
CBATH/BATHN BA1 * 103 E3
Alexander Wy
YTN/CONG BS49 ....112 B4
Alexandra Cl MANG/FISH BS16 ...48 D4
Alexandra Gdns
MANG/FISH BS16...............48 D4
Alexandra Pde WSM BS23.........7 E4
Alexandra Pk MANG/FISH BS16 ...47 H4
RDLND/MONT BS6..............55 G1
Alexandra Rd CFTN/FAIL BS8 ...54 D5
BMSTRD/HC/WWD BS13.......84 A2
CFTN/FAIL BS8...................54 D5
CLVDN BS21.....................64 C1
FRCTL/WBN BS36...............25 H1
HNBRY/STHM BS10.............31 G5
MANG/FISH BS16...............47 H4
WSM BS23 * 75 H1
Alexandra Wy THNB/SVB BS35 ...8 C1
Alford Rd
BRSG/KWL/STAPK BS4..........74 B4
Alfred Cl WSM BS23................6 E4
Alfred Hl CBRISNE BS2 ....4 E1
Alfred Pde CBRISNE BS2 ....4 E1
Alfred Pl CBRIS/FH BS1............5 F7
CBRISNE BS2.....................5 G3
Alfred Rd BMSTR BS3.............73 E3
RDLND/MONT BS6..............45 E4
Alfred St CBATH/BATHN BA1 .....3 F2
CBRISNE BS2......................5 G3
EVILLE/WHL BS5.................57 E3
WSM BS23.........................7 F4
Algiers St BMSTR BS3............72 D4
Alison Gdns NAIL BS48...........79 H2
Allanmead Rd
HGRV/WHIT BS14...............86 A4
Allans Wy OMX/HUT/LCK BS24 ...122 C4
Allerton Crs HGRV/WHIT BS14 ...86 A5
Allerton Gdns
HGRV/WHIT BS14...............86 A4
Allerton Rd HGRV/WHIT BS14 ...85 H5
Allfoxton Rd HORF/LLZ BS7......46 D5
All Hallows Rd EVILLE/WHL BS5 ...56 D3
Allington Dr
OLD/WMLY/WICK BS30 ....76 C2
Allington Gdns NAIL BS48.......78 D1
Allington Rd BMSTR BS3..........4 C7
Allison Av
BRSG/KWL/STAPK BS4..........74 D2
Allison Rd
BRSG/KWL/STAPK BS4..........74 D3
All Saints Cl
OLD/WMLY/WICK BS30 ....76 A3
All Saints Gdns CFTN/FAIL BS8 * ...55 E5
All Saints La CLVDN BS21.........65 F1
All Saints La CBRIS/FH BS1 ......5 F3
All Saints Rd
CBATH/BATHN BA1 * 102 C4
All Saints' Rd CFTN/FAIL BS8 ....55 E5
All Saints St CBRIS/FH BS1 ....5 F3
Alma Cl KGWD/HNM BS15 ......59 E3
Alma Ct CFTN/FAIL BS8...........55 E2
Alma Rd EVILLE/WHL BS5........55 F3

Alma Road Av CFTN/FAIL BS8...55 F3
Alma St WSM BS23.................6 E4
Alma Vale Rd CFTN/FAIL BS8 ...55 F3
Almeda Rd EVILLE/WHL BS5....58 A5
Almond Cl MTN/WRL BS22......125 E2
Almond Wy MANG/FISH BS16 ...49 F3
Almorah Rd BMSTR BS3 ....73 F3
Alpha Rd BMSTR BS3 ....73 E2
Alpine Gdns
CBATH/BATHN BA1 *...........102 D4
Alpine Rd EVILLE/WHL BS5 .....57 E2
Alsop Rd KGWD/HNM BS15....58 D3
Alton Rd HORF/LLZ BS7..........46 B2
Altringham Rd
EVILLE/WHL BS5.................55 F5
Alverstoke HGRV/WHIT BS14 ...85 G2
Alveston Wk
HNLZ/SM/SNYPK/WT BS9.....43 H1
Alwins Ct
OLD/WMLY/WICK BS30 ....76 C2
Amberey Rd WSM BS23..........125 E1
Amberlands Cl NAIL BS48........79 H2
Amberley Cl KEYN BS31..........88 B5
MANG/FISH BS16...............48 D1
Amberley Rd
BRSTK/PCHW BS34.............20 D2
MANG/FISH BS16...............48 D1
Amble Cl KGWD/HNM BS15 ....59 F4
Ambleside Av
HNBRY/STHM BS10.............31 F4
Ambleside Rd BATHSE BA2 .....107 G5
Ambra Ter CFTN/FAIL BS8 * 55 E5
Ambra V CFTN/FAIL BS8 * 55 E5
Ambra V East CFTN/FAIL BS8 ...55 E5
Ambra V West CFTN/FAIL BS8 ...55 E5
Ambrose Rd CFTN/FAIL BS8.....55 E5
Ambury CBATH/BATHN BA1......3 F6
Amercombe Wk
HGRV/WHIT BS14...............86 C2
Amery La CBATH/BATHN BA1 ....3 G5
Anchor Cl
BRSG/KWL/STAPK BS4..........57 H5
Anchor Rd CBATH/BATHN BA1 ...101 G3
CBRIS/FH BS1 * 4 C4
KGWD/HNM BS15...............59 G2
Anchor Wy PTSHD/EG BS20....42 A4
Andereach Cl HGRV/WHIT BS14 ...86 A1
Andover Rd
BRSG/KWL/STAPK BS4..........73 G4
Andruss Dr LGASH BS41 ....94 C2
Angers Rd
BRSG/KWL/STAPK BS4..........73 G2
Angiesea Pl CFTN/FAIL BS8.....55 E1
Anglo Ter
CBATH/BATHN BA1 *...........102 D4
Ankatel Cl WSM BS23.............6 A2
Annandale Av MTN/WRL BS22 ...122 D2
Anson Cl KEYN BS31...............99 E2
Anson Rd MTN/WRL BS22......117 E4
OMX/HUT/LCK BS24 ....122 D5
Ansteys Cl KGWD/HNM BS15 ...75 G1
Anstey's Rd KGWD/HNM BS15 ...75 G1
Anstey St EVILLE/WHL BS5 .....56 D2
Anthea Rd EVILLE/WHL BS5 ....56 A5
Antona Ct AVONM BS11..........42 C1
Antona Dr AVONM BS11..........42 C1
Antrim Rd
HNLZ/SM/SNYPK/WT BS9.....45 F2
Anvil Rd YTN/CONG BS49 * 113 F2
Anvil St CBRISNE BS2..............5 K4
Apex Ct ALMDB BS32.............11 F4
Apperley Cl YATE/CS BS37 ....25 H2
Appleby Wk
BRSG/KWL/STAPK BS4..........86 A1
Appledore Cl HGRV/WHIT BS14 ...86 A1
Apple Farm La
OMX/HUT/LCK BS24 ....123 F2
Applegate HNBRY/STHM BS10 ...31 F2
Appletree Ct MTN/WRL BS22 * ...123 F1
Applin Gn MANG/FISH BS16 ....50 A2
Approach Rd CBRIS/FH BS1 *.....5 H5
Apsley Cl MTN/WRL BS22......117 G1
Apsley Ms ALMDB BS32..........11 E5
Apsley Ms CFTN/FAIL BS8 * 55 E2
Apsley Rd CBATH/BATHN BA1 ...101 F5
CFTN/FAIL BS8...................55 E2
Apsley St EVILLE/WHL BS5......57 E1
Arbutus Dr
HNLZ/SM/SNYPK/WT BS9.....44 A1
The Arcade CBRIS/FH BS1 *......5 G2
Archer Ct
OLD/WMLY/WICK BS30 ....76 C3
Archfield Rd RDLND/MONT BS6...55 H5
Archway St BATHSE BA2...........3 J6
Ardagh Ct HORF/LLZ BS7 *......46 B3
Arden Cl ALMDB BS32.............21 G4
MTN/WRL BS22.................117 G5
Ardenton Wk
HNBRY/STHM BS10.............31 E2
Ardern Cl
HNLZ/SM/SNYPK/WT BS9.....29 H5

Argus Ct BMSTR BS3.............72 D4
Argus Rd BMSTR BS3.............72 D3
Argyle Av WSM BS23.............125 E2
Argyle Dr YATE/CS BS37..........14 A3
Argyle Pl CFTN/FAIL BS8.........55 E5
Argyle Rd CBRISNE BS2..........56 A3
CLVDN BS21.....................62 B5
MANG/FISH BS16...............58 B1
Argyle St BRSG/KWL/STAPK BS4 ...3 G4
BMSTR BS3......................72 D2
EVILLE/WHL BS5.................57 E1
Argyle Ter BATHSE BA2 *........107 H1
Arley Cots RDLND/MONT BS6 ...55 H2
Arley Hl RDLND/MONT BS6 .....55 H2
Arley Pk RDLND/MONT BS6.....55 H2
Arley Ter EVILLE/WHL BS5.......57 G2
Arlingham Wy
BRSTK/PCHW BS34.............20 A2
Arlington Rd
BRSG/KWL/STAPK BS4..........57 F5
Arlington Vls CFTN/FAIL BS8 ....55 E4
Armada Pl CBRISNE BS2..........56 A3
Armada Rd HGRV/WHIT BS14 ...85 H3
Armes Ct BATHSE BA2.............3 H7
Armidale Av RDLND/MONT BS6...56 A2
Armoury Sq EVILLE/WHL BS5 ...56 C3
Armstrong Cl THNB/SVB BS35 ....9 E5
Armstrong Dr
OLD/WMLY/WICK BS30 ....77 E1
Armstrong Wy YATE/CS BS37 ...13 G4
Arnall Dr HNBRY/STHM BS10 ...30 D4
Arneside Rd
HNBRY/STHM BS10.............31 G4
Arnold Rd MANG/FISH BS16 ....49 H5
Arnor Cl MTN/WRL BS22........117 H4
Arno's St
BRSG/KWL/STAPK BS4..........73 H2
Arrowfield Cl HGRV/WHIT BS14 ...85 H5
Artemesia Av MTN/WRL BS22 ...122 B3
Arthurs Cl MANG/FISH BS16 ....50 A2
Arthur Skemp Cl
EVILLE/WHL BS5.................56 D4
Arthur St CBRISNE BS2 ....73 H1
EVILLE/WHL BS5.................57 E3
Arthurswood Rd
BMSTRD/HC/WWD BS13.......84 B5
Arundel Cl
BMSTRD/HC/WWD BS13.......84 C5
Arundell Rd WSM BS23 ....7 F2
Arundel Rd
CBATH/BATHN BA1 ....102 D3
BMSTR BS3......................72 D2
HORF/LLZ BS7...................45 H5
Ascot Cl MANG/FISH BS16 ......35 F4
Ascot Rd MANG/FISH BS16 .....31 H3
Ashbourne Cl
OLD/WMLY/WICK BS30 ....60 A5
Ashcombe Crs
OLD/WMLY/WICK BS30 ....60 A5
Ashcombe Gdns WSM BS23 * 7 J2
Ashcombe Park Rd WSM BS23 ...7 H3
Ashcott BMSTRD/HC/WWD BS13 ...83 G4
Ashcott Rd HGRV/WHIT BS14 ...85 G3
Ashcroft Av KEYN BS31...........88 A4
Ashcroft Rd
HNLZ/SM/SNYPK/WT BS9.....44 A1
Ashcombe Crs
OLD/WMLY/WICK BS30 ....60 A5
Ashdene Av EVILLE/WHL BS5 ...47 F5
Ashdene Rd WSM BS23............7 K2
Ashdown Rd PTSHD/EG BS20 ...39 E2
Asher La CBRISNE BS2 ....5 J2
Ashfield Pl RDLND/MONT BS6 ...56 B2
Ashfield Rd BMSTR BS3..........72 C3
Ashfield Ter BMSTR BS3 * 72 D3
Ashford Dr
OMX/HUT/LCK BS24 ....125 F5
Ashford Rd BATHSE BA2 ....108 A3
BRSTK/PCHW BS34.............20 C3
Ash Gv BATHSE BA2 ....107 H3
CLVDN BS21.....................65 E1
MANG/FISH BS16...............48 C1
Ash Gv WSM BS23.................124 D4
Ashgrove Av CFTN/FAIL BS8 ....53 H4
Ash Gv WSM BS23.................53 H4
Ashgrove Av HORF/LLZ BS7 * ...46 B4
Ashgrove Rd BMSTR BS3........72 C5
CFTN/FAIL BS8...................55 F2
HORF/LLZ BS7...................46 B4
Ash Hayes Dr NAIL BS48........67 F5
Ash Hayes Rd NAIL BS48........67 F5
Ashland Rd
BMSTRD/HC/WWD BS13.......84 B5
Ashleigh Crs YTN/CONG BS49 ...113 E3
Ashleigh Rd WSM BS23............7 J2

Ashley KGWD/HNM BS15........59 F3
Ashley Av CBATH/BATHN BA1 ...101 H5
Ashley Cl HORF/LLZ BS7.........46 B4
Ashley Court Rd HORF/LLZ BS7 * ...56 B2
Ashley Down Rd HORF/LLZ BS7 ...46 A3
Ashley Grove Rd CBRISNE BS2 ...56 B1
Ashley Hl HORF/LLZ BS7........46 B3
Ashley Pde CBRISNE BS2........56 B1
Ashley Rd CBATH/BATHN BA1 ...104 D2
CLVDN BS21.....................64 B4
COR/BOX SN13.................105 G1
RDLND/MONT BS6..............56 A2
Ashley St CBRISNE BS2..........56 C2
Ashley Ter
CBATH/BATHN BA1 ....101 H5
Ashmans Yd
CBATH/BATHN BA1 ....107 G1
Ashmead Pk KEYN BS31 * 89 E4
Ashmead Rd KEYN BS31.........89 E4
Ashmead Wy CBRIS/FH BS1.....72 A1
Ash Ridge Rd ALMDB BS32 .....10 D4
Ashton
HORF/LLZ BS7...................46 A3
Ashton Av CBRIS/FH BS1........72 B1
Ashton Cl CLVDN BS21...........64 B4
Ashton Crs NAIL BS48............67 E5
Ashton Dr BMSTR BS3...........71 H5
Ashton Gate Rd BMSTR BS3 ....72 B2
Ashton Gate Ter BMSTR BS3 ....72 B2
Ashton Hl BATHSE BA2...........99 E4
Ashton Rd LGASH BS41..........71 F3
Ashton Vale Rd BMSTR BS3.....71 H3
Ashton Wy KEYN BS31...........88 B3
Ashvale Cl NAIL BS48............67 H4
Ashville Rd BMSTR BS3..........72 B2
Ash Wk HNBRY/STHM BS10 ....31 F2
Ashwell Cl HGRV/WHIT BS14 ...86 D3
Ashwicke HGRV/WHIT BS14.....85 G3
Aspen Park Rd
MTN/WRL BS22.................122 B3
Aspley Cl CBATH/BATHN BA1 ...101 G5
Assembly Rooms La
CBRIS/FH BS1 * 4 E4
Astry Cl AVONM BS11............29 G4
Atchley St EVILLE/WHL BS5.....56 D4
Atherston
OLD/WMLY/WICK BS30 ....77 F1
Athlone Wk
BRSG/KWL/STAPK BS4..........73 F5
Atholl Cl MTN/WRL BS22.......117 G5
Atkins Cl HGRV/WHIT BS14.....86 D3
Atlantic Rd AVONM BS11........28 C5
WSM BS23.......................120 B2
Atlantic Rd South WSM BS23.....6 A1
Atlas Cl EVILLE/WHL BS5........58 B5
Atlas Rd BMSTR BS3.............73 F5
Atlas St CBRISNE BS2 ....74 A1
Atwell Dr ALMDB BS32...........20 D1
Atwood Dr AVONM BS11........29 H3
Atyeo Cl BMSTR BS3.............71 H3
Aubrey Meads
OLD/WMLY/WICK BS30 ....89 H1
Aubrey Rd BMSTR BS3 ....72 C3
Auburn Av
OLD/WMLY/WICK BS30 ....77 E3
Auburn Rd RDLND/MONT BS6 ...56 S1
Auckland Cl WSM BS23.........125 E3
Auden Md HORF/LLZ BS7........32 C5
Audley Av CBATH/BATHN BA1 ...101 F5
Audley Cl CBATH/BATHN BA1 ....2 A2
Audley Gv CBATH/BATHN BA1 ...101 F5
Audley Park Rd
CBATH/BATHN BA1 ....101 F5
Audrey Wk
HNLZ/SM/SNYPK/WT BS9.....45 H2
Augusta Pl CBATH/BATHN BA1 * ...A3
Austen Dr MTN/WRL BS22.....118 A4
Austen Gv HORF/LLZ BS7.......32 C5
Autumn Ms
OMX/HUT/LCK BS24 ....122 D3
Avalon Cl YTN/CONG BS49 ....112 A2
Avalon La EVILLE/WHL BS5.....58 B5
Avalon Rd EVILLE/WHL BS5 ....58 B5
Avebury Rd BMSTR BS3..........71 H4
Avening Cl NAIL BS48............79 G1
Avening Rd KGWD/HNM BS15 ...75 F1
The Avenue BATHSE BA2.........111 F1
BRSTK/PCHW BS34.............21 E4
BRSTK/PCHW BS34.............10 D5
CFTN/FAIL BS8...................55 E3
CLVDN BS21.....................62 B5
HNLZ/SM/SNYPK/WT BS9.....44 B5
HORF/LLZ BS7...................46 A5
KEYN BS31.......................88 C3
MANG/FISH BS16...............33 G4
WSM BS23.........................7 H5
YATE/CS BS37...................25 H1
YTN/CONG BS49 ....112 B3
Averay Rd MANG/FISH BS16 ....47 E4
Avon Cl EVILLE/WHL BS5........57 H5

KEYN BS31 .... 88 C3
WSM BS23 .... 125 E4
Avon Ct CBATH/BATHN BA1 .... 91 F5
Avon Crs CBRIS/FH BS1 .... 72 B1
Avondale Blds
  CBATH/BATHN BA1 .... 103 E2
Avondale Ct
  OLD/WMLY/WICK BS30 * 76 C4
Avondale Pl
  CBATH/BATHN BA1 .... 104 A1
Avondale Rd
  KGWD/HNM BS15 * 58 C1
Avondale Works
  KGWD/HNM BS15 * 58 C1
Avondown Cl
  HNBRY/STHM BS10 .... 31 H3
Avondown Ct BMSTR BS3 .... 73 F4
Avon Gv
  HNLZ/SM/SNYPK/WT BS9 .... 54 B1
Avonlea KGWD/HNM BS15 .... 75 H1
Avonleaze
  HNLZ/SM/SNYPK/WT BS9 .... 43 H3
Avonleigh Rd BMSTR BS3 .... 72 C4
Avon Meads CBRISNE BS2 .... 74 B1
Avon Mill La WSM BS23 .... 7 F3
Avonmouth Rd AVONM BS11 .... 28 B4
Avonmouth Wy AVONM BS11 .... 28 C4
  HNBRY/STHM BS10 .... 30 C2
Avonmouth Wy West
  AVONM BS11 .... 28 B3
Avon Pk CBATH/BATHN BA1 .... 101 F5
  EVILLE/WHL BS5 .... 57 F4
Avon Rd
  BMSTRD/HC/WWD BS13 .... 84 B3
  KEYN BS31 .... 88 C4
Avonside Rd CBRISNE BS2 .... 57 E5
Avonside Wy
  BRSG/KWL/STAPK BS4 .... 57 H5
Avon St BATHSE BA2 .... 3 F6
  CBRISNE BS2 .... 5 J4
Avon V
  HNLZ/SM/SNYPK/WT BS9 .... 44 A4
Avonvale Rd EVILLE/WHL BS5 .... 57 E4
Avon Vw KGWD/HNM BS15 .... 75 G3
Avon Walkway BATHSE BA2 .... 110 C4
  BATHSE BA2 .... 2 A1
  CBATH/BATHN BA1 .... 100 D4
  CBRIS/FH BS1 .... 4 D7
  CBRISNE BS2 .... 5 K7
  KEYN BS31 .... 99 H3
  PTSHD/EC BS20 .... 42 D4
Avon Wy EVILLE/WHL BS5 .... 57 G1
  HNBRY/STHM BS10 .... 31 H5
  HNLZ/SM/SNYPK/WT BS9 .... 44 A3
  PTSHD/EC BS20 .... 39 G3
  THNB/SVB BS35 .... 8 D4
Avonwood Cl AVONM BS11 .... 43 E2
Awdelett Cl AVONM BS11 .... 29 F4
Axbridge Cl NAIL BS48 .... 79 F1
Axbridge Rd BATHSE BA2 .... 108 D5
  BRSG/KWL/STAPK BS4 .... 73 G4
Axe Cl WSM BS23 .... 125 F1
Aycote Cl MTN/WRL BS22 .... 121 H1
Aylesbury Crs BMSTR BS3 .... 72 C5
Aylesbury Rd BMSTR BS3 .... 72 C5
Aylmer Crs HGRV/WHIT BS14 .... 86 A5
Aylminton Wk AVONM BS11 .... 29 H5
Ayr St BATHSE BA2 .... 2 A5
Azaria Rd MTN/WRL BS22 .... 117 H3
Azelin Av
  BMSTRD/HC/WWD BS13 .... 84 C4

B

Backfields CBRISNE BS2 .... 5 G1
Backfields La CBRISNE BS2 .... 56 A3
Back La KEYN BS31 .... 88 B5
  MANG/FISH BS16 .... 51 G4
  PTSHD/EC BS20 .... 42 C4
Back of Kingsdown Pde
  RDLND/MONT BS6 .... 55 H3
Back St BMSTR BS3 .... 72 B2
Back Stoke La
  HNLZ/SM/SNYPK/WT BS9 .... 44 D2
Back St WSM BS23 .... 6 E4
Backwell Bow NAIL BS48 .... 68 A5
Backwell Common NAIL BS48 .... 79 H2
Backwell Hill Rd NAIL BS48 .... 80 C2
Backwell Vw NAIL BS48 * 68 B2
Backwell Wk
  BMSTRD/HC/WWD BS13 .... 84 A1
Badenham Gv AVONM BS11 .... 29 F5
Baden Rd EVILLE/WHL BS5 .... 57 E4
  KGWD/HNM BS15 .... 59 G4
Bader Cl YATE/CS BS37 .... 13 H4
Badger Ri PTSHD/EC BS20 .... 38 D5
Badgers Cl ALMDB BS32 .... 11 F4
Badger Sett EVILLE/WHL BS5 .... 58 B4
Badgers Holt HGRV/WHIT BS14 .... 86 B3
The Badgers MTN/WRL BS22 .... 118 D5
Badgers Wk
  OMX/HUT/LCK BS24 .... 122 C3
Badgeworth YATE/CS BS37 .... 25 H4
Badminton Rd
  MANG/FISH BS16 .... 35 F5
Badminton Ct YATE/CS BS37 * 13 G5
Badminton Gdns
  CBATH/BATHN BA1 .... 101 H4
  FRCTL/WBN BS36 .... 35 G2
  MANG/FISH BS16 .... 35 F5
  YATE/CS BS37 .... 27 F2
  YATE/CS BS37 .... 13 G5
Baglyn Av KGWD/HNM BS15 .... 49 F5
Bagnell Cl HGRV/WHIT BS14 .... 86 D4
Bagnell Rd HGRV/WHIT BS14 .... 86 D4
Bagworth Dr
  OLD/WMLY/WICK BS30 .... 76 C3
Bailbrook Gv
  CBATH/BATHN BA1 .... 103 F1
Bailbrook La
  CBATH/BATHN BA1 .... 103 G1
Baildon Rd WSM BS23 .... 125 E2
Bailey Cl MTN/WRL BS22 .... 122 B3

Bailey Ct PTSHD/EC BS20 .... 40 B2
Baileys Ct ALMDB BS32 .... 21 H4
Baileys Court Rd ALMDB BS32 .... 21 G4
Baileys Mead Rd
  MANG/FISH BS16 .... 47 E3
Baker Cl CLVDN BS21 .... 64 B5
Bakersfield
  OLD/WMLY/WICK BS30 .... 76 D3
Bakers Gnd BRSTK/PCHW BS34 .... 21 H5
Baker St WSM BS23 .... 7 F3
Balaclava Rd MANG/FISH BS16 .... 47 H5
Baldwin St CBRIS/FH BS1 .... 5 F4
Balfour Rd BMSTR BS3 .... 72 C3
Ballance St CBATH/BATHN BA1 .... 3 F1
Ballast La AVONM BS11 .... 28 D3
Balmain St
  BRSG/KWL/STAPK BS4 .... 73 H2
Balmoral Cl BRSTK/PCHW BS34 .... 33 F1
Balmoral Ct MANG/FISH BS16 .... 49 G3
Balmoral Rd HORF/LLZ BS7 .... 56 B1
  KEYN BS31 .... 88 B5
Balmoral Wy MTN/WRL BS22 .... 121 H1
Baltic Pl PTSHD/EC BS20 .... 42 D4
Bamfield HGRV/WHIT BS14 .... 85 G2
Bampton Cl
  BMSTRD/HC/WWD BS13 .... 84 C2
  MANG/FISH BS16 .... 50 A2
Bampton Cft MANG/FISH BS16 .... 50 A2
Bampton Dr MANG/FISH BS16 .... 34 D5
Banfield Cl AVONM BS11 .... 29 G5
Bangor Gv
  BRSG/KWL/STAPK BS4 .... 75 E1
Bangrove Wk AVONM BS11 .... 29 E5
Banister Gv
  BRSG/KWL/STAPK BS4 .... 85 E2
Bank Pl PTSHD/EC BS20 .... 42 D4
Bank Rd AVONM BS11 .... 16 D5
  KGWD/HNM BS15 .... 58 D3
Banks Cl CLVDN BS21 .... 64 D5
Bankside MANG/FISH BS16 .... 49 F4
Bankside Rd
  BRSG/KWL/STAPK BS4 .... 74 C3
Bannerdown Cl
  CBATH/BATHN BA1 .... 91 G5
Bannerdown Dr
  CBATH/BATHN BA1 .... 91 G5
Bannerdown Rd
  CBATH/BATHN BA1 .... 104 B1
Bannerleigh La CFTN/FAIL BS8 .... 54 C4
Bannerleigh Rd CFTN/FAIL BS8 .... 54 C4
Bannerman Rd
  EVILLE/WHL BS5 .... 56 D3
Banner Rd RDLND/MONT BS6 .... 56 A2
Bantock Cl
  BRSG/KWL/STAPK BS4 .... 85 E3
Bantry Rd
  BRSG/KWL/STAPK BS4 .... 85 F1
Banwell Cl
  BMSTRD/HC/WWD BS13 .... 84 B1
  KEYN BS31 .... 98 B2
Banwell Rd BATHSE BA2 .... 110 B2
  BMSTR BS3 .... 72 B3
  OMX/HUT/LCK BS24 .... 127 E3
Banyard Rd PTSHD/EC BS20 .... 41 G3
Baptist St EVILLE/WHL BS5 .... 56 C2
Barberry Farm Rd
  YTN/CONG BS49 .... 112 B2
Barbour Gdns
  BMSTRD/HC/WWD BS13 .... 96 A1
Barbour Rd
  BMSTRD/HC/WWD BS13 .... 96 A1
Barcroft Cl KGWD/HNM BS15 .... 58 C3
Barkers Md YATE/CS BS37 .... 14 A4
Barker Wk EVILLE/WHL BS5 .... 56 C2
Barkleys Hi MANG/FISH BS16 .... 47 E3
Barley Cl FRCTL/WBN BS36 .... 23 H2
  MANG/FISH BS16 .... 49 G2
Barley Cft
  HNLZ/SM/SNYPK/WT BS9 .... 44 D4
Barley Cross MTN/WRL BS22 .... 117 H5
Barnabas St CBRISNE BS2 .... 56 B1
Barnard's Cl YTN/CONG BS49 .... 112 C4
Barnard Wk KEYN BS31 .... 88 A5
Barnes St EVILLE/WHL BS5 .... 57 F3
Barnfield Wy
  CBATH/BATHN BA1 .... 91 G5
Barnhill Rd YATE/CS BS37 .... 26 D1
Barn Owl Wy
  BRSTK/PCHW BS34 .... 21 H5
Barns Cl NAIL BS48 .... 82 B5
  NAIL BS48 .... 67 F4
Barns Gnd CLVDN BS21 .... 65 E5
Barnstaple Rd
  BRSG/KWL/STAPK BS4 .... 85 F1
Barnstaple Wk
  BRSG/KWL/STAPK BS4 .... 85 F1
Barnwell Cl HNBRY/STHM BS10 .... 31 E1
Barnwood Ct NAIL BS48 .... 66 C5
Barnwood Rd YATE/CS BS37 .... 25 G3
Baron Cl
  OLD/WMLY/WICK BS30 .... 89 H1
Barons Cl BMSTR BS3 .... 72 A3
Barossa Pl CBRIS/FH BS1 .... 5 F7
Barrack's La AVONM BS11 .... 28 D5
Barratt St EVILLE/WHL BS5 .... 57 E1
Barrington Ct
  KGWD/HNM BS15 .... 59 F1
Barrington Rd
  MANG/FISH BS16 .... 59 E2
Barrow Court La NAIL BS48 .... 81 G3
Barrow Ct
  OLD/WMLY/WICK BS30 .... 61 F5
Barrow Hill Crs AVONM BS11 .... 42 C1
Barrow Hill Rd AVONM BS11 .... 42 C1
Barrow La
  BLAG/CWMG/WR BS40 .... 93 G3
Barrowmead Dr AVONM BS11 .... 29 F5
Barrow Rd BATHSE BA2 .... 110 A1
  CBRISNE BS2 .... 56 C4
  EVILLE/WHL BS5 .... 56 C4
The Barrows MTN/WRL BS22 .... 121 H4
Barrow St NAIL BS48 .... 81 H4
Barrs Ct CBRIS/FH BS1 * 5 G2
Barrs Court Av
  EVILLE/WHL BS5 .... 76 D1
Barrs Court Rd
  OLD/WMLY/WICK BS30 .... 76 D1
Barry Cl OLD/WMLY/WICK BS30 .... 77 F5

Rarry Rd
  OLD/WMLY/WICK BS30 .... 77 F4
Barter Cl KGWD/HNM BS15 * 58 D3
Bartholomew Sq
  HORF/LLZ BS7 .... 46 B1
Bartlett Cl BRSTK/PCHW BS34 .... 72 D4
Bartlett St CBATH/BATHN BA1 .... 3 F3
Bartletts Wy
  OMX/HUT/LCK BS24 .... 127 E2
Bartley St BMSTR BS3 .... 73 E2
Barton Blds
  CBATH/BATHN BA1 * 3 F3
Barton Cl
  BRSG/KWL/STAPK BS4 .... 57 H5
  FRCTL/WBN BS36 .... 23 E5
Barton Ct EVILLE/WHL BS5 .... 57 E5
Barton Gn EVILLE/WHL BS5 * 56 D4
Barton Hill Rd EVILLE/WHL BS5 .... 56 D4
Bartonia Gv
  BRSG/KWL/STAPK BS4 .... 74 C5
Barton Mnr CBRISNE BS2 .... 56 C5
Barton Rd CBRISNE BS2 .... 5 K4
Barton St CBATH/BATHN BA1 .... 3 F4
  CBRIS/FH BS1 * 5 F1
  EVILLE/WHL BS5 * 57 E5
The Barton BATHSE BA2 .... 99 H5
  MANG/FISH BS16 .... 75 C2
Barton V CBRISNE BS2 .... 5 K4
Barwick AVONM BS11 * 43 E1
Barwood Cl KGWD/HNM BS15 .... 59 F3
Batchfield La MANG/FISH BS16 .... 37 G5
Bates Cl EVILLE/WHL BS5 .... 56 C2
Bathampton La BATHSE BA2 .... 103 H3
Bath Br BMSTR BS3 .... 5 J7
Bath Blds RDLND/MONT BS6 .... 55 H3
Bathford Hi
  CBATH/BATHN BA1 .... 104 C2
Bath Hi KEYN BS31 .... 88 C4
Bath Rd BMSTR BS3 .... 5 K7
  BRSG/KWL/STAPK BS4 .... 73 H2
  KEYN BS31 .... 88 D4
  MTN/WRL BS22 .... 117 H4
Bath Road Brislington Hi
  BRSG/KWL/STAPK BS4 .... 74 D4
Bath St BMSTR BS3 .... 72 B2
  CBRIS/FH BS1 * 5 G4
  MANG/FISH BS16 .... 49 E4
Bathurst Pde CBRIS/FH BS1 .... 4 E7
Bathurst Rd MTN/WRL BS22 .... 121 H2
Bathwell Rd
  BRSG/KWL/STAPK BS4 .... 73 H5
Bathwick Hi BATHSE BA2 .... 3 K4
Bathwick Ri BATHSE BA2 .... 3 K2
Bathwick St BATHSE BA2 .... 3 H1
Batley Ct
  OLD/WMLY/WICK BS30 .... 77 G2
Batstone Cl
  CBATH/BATHN BA1 .... 102 D2
Battenburg Rd
  EVILLE/WHL BS5 .... 58 A3
Batten's La EVILLE/WHL BS5 .... 57 G5
Batten's La EVILLE/WHL BS5 .... 58 A5
Battens Rd EVILLE/WHL BS5 .... 58 A5
Battersby Wy
  HNBRY/STHM BS10 .... 30 C3
Battersea Rd EVILLE/WHL BS5 .... 57 E3
Battery La PTSHD/EC BS20 .... 39 H2
Battson Rd HGRV/WHIT BS14 .... 86 B5
Baugh Gdns MANG/FISH BS16 .... 35 E4
Baxter Cl KGWD/HNM BS15 .... 59 G3
Bay Gdns EVILLE/WHL BS5 .... 57 E1
Bayham Rd
  BRSG/KWL/STAPK BS4 .... 73 G3
Bayleys Dr KGWD/HNM BS15 .... 58 D5
Baynton Meadow
  MANG/FISH BS16 .... 50 A2
Baynton Rd BMSTR BS3 .... 72 B2
Bay Rd CLVDN BS21 .... 64 D1
Bayswater Av
  RDLND/MONT BS6 .... 45 F4
Bayswater Rd HORF/LLZ BS7 .... 46 B1
Bay Tree Cl BRSTK/PCHW BS34 .... 20 B5
Bay Tree Rd
  CBATH/BATHN BA1 .... 103 E2
  CLVDN BS21 .... 65 E3
Baytree Rd MTN/WRL BS22 .... 121 H2
Bay Tree Vw MTN/WRL BS22 .... 122 A2
Baytree Vw MTN/WRL BS22 .... 122 A2
Bay Willow Dr
  RDLND/MONT BS6 .... 55 F1
Beach Av CLVDN BS21 .... 64 C3
Beach End Rd WSM BS23 .... 124 B4
Beachgrove Gdns
  MANG/FISH BS16 .... 48 C4
Beachgrove Rd
  MANG/FISH BS16 .... 48 C4
Beach Hi PTSHD/EC BS20 .... 40 A2
Beach Mns CBRISNE BS2 * 56 C5
Beach Rd MTN/WRL BS22 .... 116 A5
  WSM BS23 .... 124 B1
Beach Rd East PTSHD/EC BS20 .... 39 H2
Beach Rd West
  PTSHD/EC BS20 .... 39 G2
The Beach CLVDN BS21 .... 64 C1
Beacon La FRCTL/WBN BS36 .... 23 H1
Beaconlea KGWD/HNM BS15 .... 58 D5
Beacon Rd
  CBATH/BATHN BA1 .... 102 D3
Beaconsfield Cl
  EVILLE/WHL BS5 * 57 H2
Beaconsfield Rd
  BRSG/KWL/STAPK BS4 .... 74 A3
  CFTN/FAIL BS8 .... 55 E3
  CLVDN BS21 .... 65 E3
  EVILLE/WHL BS5 .... 57 H2
  WSM BS23 .... 6 E5
Beaconsfield St
  EVILLE/WHL BS5 * 57 E3
Beale Cl HGRV/WHIT BS14 .... 86 D3
Beam St EVILLE/WHL BS5 .... 57 E4
The Bean Acre AVONM BS11 .... 28 D5
Bean St EVILLE/WHL BS5 * 56 D2
Bearbridge Rd
  BMSTRD/HC/WWD BS13 .... 84 A5
Bear Yard Ms CFTN/FAIL BS8 * 55 E5
Beatrix Pl HORF/LLZ BS7 .... 32 C5

Beauchamp Rd HORF/LLZ BS7 .... 45 H4
Beauford Sq CBATH/BATHN BA1 .... 3 F4
Beaufort Cl EVILLE/WHL BS5 .... 57 F4
Beaufort Crs
  BRSTK/PCHW BS34 .... 33 G1
Beaufort East
  CBATH/BATHN BA1 .... 103 F3
Beaufort Ms
  CBATH/BATHN BA1 .... 103 E3
  CFTN/FAIL BS8 * 54 D4
Beaufort Pl
  CBATH/BATHN BA1 .... 103 F3
  EVILLE/WHL BS5 .... 34 B4
Beaufort Ter
  CBATH/BATHN BA1 * 103 F3
  EVILLE/WHL BS5 * 57 E1
Beaufort Rd
  BRSG/KWL/STAPK BS4 .... 55 E2
  EVILLE/WHL BS5 .... 57 F4
  FRCTL/WBN BS36 .... 23 G2
  HORF/LLZ BS7 .... 46 B2
  KGWD/HNM BS15 .... 58 B1
  MANG/FISH BS16 .... 49 E4
  WSM BS23 .... 7 G4
  YATE/CS BS37 .... 13 H5
Beaufort St BMSTR BS3 .... 72 D4
  EVILLE/WHL BS5 .... 56 C3
Beaufort Vs
  CBATH/BATHN BA1 .... 103 E3
Beauley Rd BMSTR BS3 .... 72 C2
Beaumont
  OLD/WMLY/WICK BS30 .... 76 D3
  WSM BS23 .... 125 E2
Beaumont St EVILLE/WHL BS5 .... 56 C3
Beaumont Ter EVILLE/WHL BS5 .... 56 C3
Beau St CBATH/BATHN BA1 .... 3 F5
Beaver Cl FRCTL/WBN BS36 .... 23 F3
Beazer Cl MANG/FISH BS16 .... 48 D5
Beck Cl MANG/FISH BS16 .... 50 A2
Becket Dr MTN/WRL BS22 .... 117 F3
Becket Rd MTN/WRL BS22 .... 117 H4
Becket's La NAIL BS48 .... 79 F1
Beckford Ct BATHSE BA2 * 3 J4
Beckford Gdns BATHSE BA2 .... 3 K1
  HGRV/WHIT BS14 .... 96 D1
Beckhampton Rd BATHSE BA2 .... 2 B7
Beckington Rd BMSTR BS3 .... 73 G4
Beckington Wk BMSTR BS3 .... 73 G4
Beckspool Rd MANG/FISH BS16 .... 34 C5
Bedford Crs HORF/LLZ BS7 .... 46 B3
Bedford Rd WSM BS23 .... 124 D2
Bedminster Down Rd
  BMSTRD/HC/WWD BS13 .... 72 B5
Bedminster Pde BMSTR BS3 .... 73 E2
Bedminster Pde BMSTR BS3 .... 73 E2
Bedminster Rd BMSTR BS3 .... 72 C5
Bedwin Cl PTSHD/EC BS20 .... 38 D4
Beech Av BATHSE BA2 .... 109 H3
Beech Cl
  OLD/WMLY/WICK BS30 .... 76 D1
Beechcroft LGASH BS41 .... 94 C2
Beechcroft Wk HORF/LLZ BS7 .... 32 C5
Beech Dr NAIL BS48 .... 67 H4
Beechen Cliff BATHSE BA2 .... 2 E7
Beechen Cliff Rd BATHSE BA2 .... 2 E7
Beechen Cliff Rd BATHSE BA2 .... 58 B1
Beeches Gv
  BRSG/KWL/STAPK BS4 .... 74 C4
The Beeches ALMDB BS32 .... 21 F2
  BATHSE BA2 .... 110 B1
  BRSG/KWL/STAPK BS4 .... 74 D1
  OLD/WMLY/WICK BS30 .... 60 A3
Beechfield Cl LGASH BS41 .... 71 F4
Beechfield Gv
  HNLZ/SM/SNYPK/WT BS9 .... 30 A5
Beech Gv BATHSE BA2 .... 107 H3
Beechmont Dr
  OMX/HUT/LCK BS24 .... 125 E5
Beechmount Cl
  OMX/HUT/LCK BS24 .... 125 E5
Beechmount Gv
  HGRV/WHIT BS14 .... 86 A1
Beech Rd HORF/LLZ BS7 .... 46 A3
  KEYN BS31 .... 99 F1
  YTN/CONG BS49 .... 112 C3
Beechwood Av
  KGWD/HNM BS15 .... 76 A1
Beechwood Cl
  HGRV/WHIT BS14 .... 86 D2
Beechwood Rd BATHSE BA2 .... 111 F1
  MANG/FISH BS16 .... 48 C4
  NAIL BS48 .... 67 E4
  PTSHD/EC BS20 .... 42 A4
  PTSHD/EC BS20 .... 38 C4
Beehive Yd CBATH/BATHN BA1 .... 3 G3
Begbrook Dr MANG/FISH BS16 .... 47 H2
Begbrook La MANG/FISH BS16 .... 47 H2
Begbrook Pk MANG/FISH BS16 .... 48 A1
Beggar Bush La CFTN/FAIL BS8 .... 70 A2
Beggarswell Cl CBRISNE BS2 .... 56 B3
Belfast Wk
  BRSG/KWL/STAPK BS4 .... 85 E1
Belfields La MANG/FISH BS16 .... 34 C4
Belfry OLD/WMLY/WICK BS30 .... 76 D3
Belgrave Crs
  CBATH/BATHN BA1 .... 102 D4
Belgrave Hi CFTN/FAIL BS8 .... 55 E1
Belgrave Pl
  CBATH/BATHN BA1 * 102 D4
  CFTN/FAIL BS8 .... 55 E5
Belgrave Rd
  CBATH/BATHN BA1 .... 103 E4
  CFTN/FAIL BS8 .... 55 F5
  MANG/FISH BS16 .... 121 G5
Bellamy Av
  BMSTRD/HC/WWD BS13 .... 84 D5
Bellamy Cl KGWD/HNM BS15 .... 75 H3
Belland Dr HGRV/WHIT BS14 .... 85 G5
Bella Vista Rd
  CBATH/BATHN BA1 .... 102 C4
Bell Barn Rd
  HNLZ/SM/SNYPK/WT BS9 .... 44 B2
Bell Cl HNBRY/STHM BS10 .... 46 A1

Bellevue CFTN/FAIL BS8 .... 4 A7
Bellevue Cl KGWD/HNM BS15 .... 59 E4
Bellevue Crs CFTN/FAIL BS8 .... 4 A4
Bellevue Pk
  BRSG/KWL/STAPK BS4 .... 74 C1
Bellevue Rd
  BRSG/KWL/STAPK BS4 .... 73 G2
  CLVDN BS21 .... 64 D1
  EVILLE/WHL BS5 .... 58 A3
Belle Vue Rd EVILLE/WHL BS5 .... 57 E2
Bellevue Rd KGWD/HNM BS15 .... 59 F4
Bellevue Ter
  BRSG/KWL/STAPK BS4 .... 73 G2
Bell Hi MANG/FISH BS16 .... 47 E4
Bell Hill Rd EVILLE/WHL BS5 .... 57 H5
Bellhouse Wk AVONM BS11 .... 29 H4
Bellotts Rd BATHSE BA2 .... 107 H1
Bell Rd FRCTL/WBN BS36 .... 24 A5
Belluton Rd
  BRSG/KWL/STAPK BS4 .... 73 H3
Belmont CBATH/BATHN BA1 .... 3 F2
Belmont Dr BRSTK/PCHW BS34 .... 21 G5
Belmont Hill NAIL BS48 .... 69 F5
Belmont Pk HORF/LLZ BS7 * 32 B4
Belmont Rd BATHSE BA2 .... 74 B2
  RDLND/MONT BS6 .... 45 H4
Belmont St EVILLE/WHL BS5 .... 56 C2
Belmore Gdns BATHSE BA2 .... 107 G4
Beloe Rd HORF/LLZ BS7 .... 45 H3
Belroyal Av
  BRSG/KWL/STAPK BS4 .... 75 E3
Belsher Dr KGWD/HNM BS15 .... 59 G5
Belstone Wk
  BRSG/KWL/STAPK BS4 .... 84 D2
Belton Rd EVILLE/WHL BS5 .... 56 D2
  PTSHD/EC BS20 .... 39 E3
Belvedere CBATH/BATHN BA1 .... 3 F1
Belvedere Crs MTN/WRL BS22 .... 121 H2
Belvedere Rd
  RDLND/MONT BS6 .... 45 E5
Belvoir Rd BATHSE BA2 * 2 A7
  RDLND/MONT BS6 .... 56 A1
Bence Ct KGWD/HNM BS15 .... 58 D5
Benford Cl MANG/FISH BS16 .... 48 C2
Bennett La
  CBATH/BATHN BA1 .... 102 D3
Bennett Rd EVILLE/WHL BS5 .... 57 G4
Bennetts Rd CBATH/BATHN BA1 .... 26 B1
Bennett's Rd
  CBATH/BATHN BA1 .... 103 F1
Bennett St CBATH/BATHN BA1 .... 3 F2
Bensaunt Gv
  HNBRY/STHM BS10 .... 31 H1
Bentley Cl HGRV/WHIT BS14 .... 96 C1
Bentley Rd MTN/WRL BS22 .... 118 A5
Benville Av
  HNLZ/SM/SNYPK/WT BS9 .... 30 A5
Berenda Dr
  OLD/WMLY/WICK BS30 .... 77 E3
Beresford Cl
  CBATH/BATHN BA1 .... 101 F1
Berkeley Av CFTN/FAIL BS8 .... 4 C3
  HORF/LLZ BS7 .... 45 H5
Berkeley Crs CFTN/FAIL BS8 .... 4 B3
Berkeley Gdns KEYN BS31 .... 88 A5
  WSM BS23 .... 124 B4
Berkeley Gn EVILLE/WHL BS5 .... 57 E1
Berkeley Gn MANG/FISH BS16 .... 34 B4
Berkeley Green Rd
  EVILLE/WHL BS5 .... 57 E1
Berkeley Pl
  CBATH/BATHN BA1 * 102 D4
  CFTN/FAIL BS8 .... 4 A4
Berkeley Md ALMDB BS32 .... 21 H4
Berkeley Rd MANG/FISH BS16 .... 58 A1
Berkeley Sq CFTN/FAIL BS8 .... 4 B3
Berkeley St EVILLE/WHL BS5 .... 47 E5
Berkeley Wy MANG/FISH BS16 .... 49 H1
Berkshire Rd HORF/LLZ BS7 .... 45 H5
Berners Cl
  BRSG/KWL/STAPK BS4 * 85 E2
Berrow Wk BMSTR BS3 .... 73 F4
Berry Hill Cl
  HNBRY/STHM BS10 .... 31 H4
Berry La HORF/LLZ BS7 .... 46 C2
Berwick Cl THNB/SVB BS35 .... 18 B2
Berwick Dr HNBRY/STHM BS10 .... 17 H5
Berwick La HNBRY/STHM BS10 .... 18 A5
Berwick Rd EVILLE/WHL BS5 .... 56 D1
Beryl Gv HGRV/WHIT BS14 .... 86 B1
Beryl Rd BMSTR BS3 .... 72 C3
Besom La YATE/CS BS37 .... 25 G5
Bethel Rd EVILLE/WHL BS5 .... 57 H3
Betjeman Ct
  OLD/WMLY/WICK BS30 .... 76 D1
Betts Gn MANG/FISH BS16 .... 50 A1
Bevan Ct BRSTK/PCHW BS34 .... 32 B3
Beverley Av MANG/FISH BS16 .... 35 F4
Beverley Cl EVILLE/WHL BS5 .... 58 D4
Beverley Gdns
  HNLZ/SM/SNYPK/WT BS9 .... 44 B1
Beverley Rd HORF/LLZ BS7 .... 32 B5
Beverstone KGWD/HNM BS15 .... 58 C3
Beverston Gdns AVONM BS11 .... 29 H3
Bevington Cl
  BRSTK/PCHW BS34 .... 20 A1
Bevington Wk
  BRSTK/PCHW BS34 .... 20 A1
Bewdley Rd BATHSE BA2 .... 109 E3
Bexley Rd MANG/FISH BS16 .... 48 B3
Bibstone KGWD/HNM BS15 .... 59 G3
Bibury Av BRSTK/PCHW BS34 .... 20 D2
Bibury Cl
  HNLZ/SM/SNYPK/WT BS9 .... 45 H1
  HORF/LLZ BS7 .... 67 H5
Bibury Crs
  HNLZ/SM/SNYPK/WT BS9 .... 45 H1
  KGWD/HNM BS15 .... 75 H1
Bickerton Cl
  HNBRY/STHM BS10 .... 30 D2
Bickford Cl
  OLD/WMLY/WICK BS30 .... 59 G5
Bickley Cl KGWD/HNM BS15 .... 75 G3

Biddestone Rd *HORF/LLZ* BS7......32 A4
Biddisham Cl *NAIL* BS48......67 F5
Biddle St *YTN/CONG* BS49......112 A4
Bideford Crs
  BRSG/KWL/STAPK BS4......85 C1
Bideford Rd *MTN/WRL* BS22......122 C1
Bidwell Cl *HNBRY/STHM* BS10......31 F2
Bifield Cl *HGRV/WHIT* BS14......87 F4
Bifield Gdns *HGRV/WHIT* BS14......86 D4
Bifield Rd *HGRV/WHIT* BS14......87 E4
Bigwood La *CBRIS/FH* BS1......4 C4
Bilberry Cl
  HNLZ/SM/SNYPK/WT BS9......30 A5
Bilbie Cl *HNBRY/STHM* BS10......45 H2
Bilbie Rd *MTN/WRL* BS22......118 A5
Bilbury La *CBATH/BATHN* BA1......3 F5
Billand Cl
  BMSTRD/HC/WWD BS13......94 D1
Bindon Dr *HNBRY/STHM* BS10......31 H1
Binhay Rd *YTN/CONG* BS49......112 C4
Binley Gv *HGRV/WHIT* BS14......86 C4
Binmead Gdns
  BMSTRD/HC/WWD BS13......84 C5
Birbeck Rd
  HNLZ/SM/SNYPK/WT BS9......44 C3
Birchall Rd *RDLND/MONT* BS6......45 G4
Birch Av *CLVDN* BS21......65 E1
Birch Cl *BRSTK/PCHW* BS34......20 A5
  OMX/HUT/LCK BS24......100 A1
Birch Ct *KEYN* BS31......87 H5
  YATE/CS BS37......13 H5
Birch Cft *HNBRY/STHM* BS10......96 D1
Birchdale Rd *HGRV/WHIT* BS14......87 E4
Birch Dene *NAIL* BS48......67 H4
Birch Dr *MANG/FISH* BS16......51 F3
The Birches *NAIL* BS48 *......67 H4
Birch Gv *PTSHD/EG* BS20......39 G4
Birch Rd *BMSTR* BS3......72 C2
  YATE/CS BS37......13 H5
Birchwood Av *WSM* BS23......7 K4
Birchwood Ct
  BRSG/KWL/STAPK BS4......57 H5
Birchwood Rd
  BRSG/KWL/STAPK BS4......74 D2
Birdale Cl *HNBRY/STHM* BS10......30 C2
Birdcombe Cl *NAIL* BS48......67 F3
Birdlip Cl *NAIL* BS48......79 C1
Birdwell La *LGASH* BS41......70 C5
Birdwell Rd *LGASH* BS41......70 C5
Birdwood *KGWD/HNM* BS15......58 D5
Birkbeck Ct *WSM* BS23......6 D5
Birkdale
  OLD/WMLY/WICK BS30......59 H5
  YATE/CS BS37......26 A2
Birkett Rd *WSM* BS23......120 A2
Birkin St *CBRISNE* BS2......5 K4
Birnbeck Rd *WSM* BS23......6 A1
Biscay Dr *PTSHD/EG* BS20......40 B3
Biscoe Rd
  OMX/HUT/LCK BS24......126 A3
Bishop Av *MTN/WRL* BS22......117 H5
Bishop La *HORF/LLZ* BS7 *......46 A4
Bishop Manor Rd
  HNBRY/STHM BS10......45 H1
Bishop Ms *CBRISNE* BS2 *......56 A3
Bishop Rd *HORF/LLZ* BS7......45 G4
  MANG/FISH BS16......50 A2
Bishops Cl
  HNLZ/SM/SNYPK/WT BS9......44 C5
Bishops Cove
  BMSTRD/HC/WWD BS13......84 A4
Bishops Knoll
  HNLZ/SM/SNYPK/WT BS9......44 A5
Bishops Rd *YTN/CONG* BS49......113 C3
Bishop St *CBRISNE* BS2......56 A3
Bishop's Wd *ALMDB* BS32......11 E1
Bishopsworth Rd
  BMSTRD/HC/WWD BS13......84 B2
Bishop Ter *CBRISNE* BS2 *......56 A3
Bishopthorpe Rd
  HNBRY/STHM BS10......45 H1
Bishport Av
  BMSTRD/HC/WWD BS13......95 H1
Bishport Cl
  BMSTRD/HC/WWD BS13......84 C5
Bisley *YATE/CS* BS37......25 C3
Bissex Md *MANG/FISH* BS16......49 H3
Bittern Cl *MTN/WRL* BS22......122 C2
Bitterwell Cl *FRCTL/WBN* BS36......36 B2
Blackacre *HGRV/WHIT* BS14......97 F1
Blackberry Av
  MANG/FISH BS16......47 G3
Blackberry Dr
  MANG/FISH BS16......23 H4
  MTN/WRL BS22......122 D2
Blackberry HI *MANG/FISH* BS16......47 C3
Blackcurrant Dr *LGASH* BS41......82 B1
Blackdown Ct
  HGRV/WHIT BS14......86 A4
Blackdown Rd *PTSHD/EG* BS20......39 E3
Blackfriars Rd *NAIL* BS48......78 C1
Blackhorse HI *THNB/SVB* BS35......19 F2
Blackhorse La
  MANG/FISH BS16......35 C5
Blackhorse Pl
  MANG/FISH BS16......49 C2
Blackhorse Rd
  KGWD/HNM BS15......58 D4
  MANG/FISH BS16......49 C2
Blackmoor *CLVDN* BS21......64 C4
Blackmoor La *BMSTR* BS5......53 E1
Blackmoors La *BMSTR* BS3......71 H3
Blackmore Dr *BATHSE* BA2......107 C2
Black Nore Point
  PTSHD/EG BS20......38 C5
Blackrock La *HGRV/WHIT* BS14......97 C4
Blacksmith La
  CBATH/BATHN BA1......90 A3
Blackswarth Rd
  EVILLE/WHL BS5......57 F4
Blackthorn Cl
  BMSTRD/HC/WWD BS13......85 E4
Blackthorn Dr *ALMDB* BS32......21 F3
Blackthorn Gdns
  MTN/WRL BS22......122 D2
Blackthorn Rd
  BMSTRD/HC/WWD BS13......85 E4
Blackthorn Sq *CLVDN* BS21......64 D4

Blackthorn Wk
  KGWD/HNM BS15......59 E1
Blackthorn Wy *NAIL* BS48......65 D3
Bladen Cl *PTSHD/EG* BS20......40 A4
Bladud's Blds
  CBATH/BATHN BA1......3 C3
Blagdon Cl *BMSTR* BS3......73 F4
  OMX/HUT/LCK BS24......125 E5
Blagdon Pk *BATHSE* BA2......107 F5
Blagrove Cl
  BMSTRD/HC/WWD BS13......95 H1
Blagrove Crs
  BMSTRD/HC/WWD BS13......95 H1
Blaisdon *MTN/WRL* BS22......122 A4
  YATE/CS BS37......26 A1
Blaisdon Cl *HNBRY/STHM* BS10......30 D4
Blaisedell Vw
  HNBRY/STHM BS10......30 B2
Blaise Hamlet
  HNBRY/STHM BS10 *......30 B2
Blaise Wk
  HNLZ/SM/SNYPK/WT BS9......44 A2
Blake End *MTN/WRL* BS22......117 F4
Blakeney Cv *NAIL* BS48......67 C4
Blakeney Mills *YATE/CS* BS37......25 H1
Blakeney Rd
  BRSTK/PCHW BS34......20 A1
  HORF/LLZ BS7......46 A2
Blakes Rd *THNB/SVB* BS35......8 D5
Blanchards *YATE/CS* BS37......27 E2
Blandamour Wy
  HNBRY/STHM BS10......31 H3
Blandford Cl
  HNLZ/SM/SNYPK/WT BS9......44 A4
  NAIL BS48......67 E5
Blenheim Cl *EVILLE/WHL* BS5......56 C2
Blenheim Dr
  BRSTK/PCHW BS34......32 D1
  YATE/CS BS37......13 C4
Blenheim Gdns
  CBATH/BATHN BA1......102 D2
Blenheim Rd
  RDLND/MONT BS6......45 F5
Blenheim St *EVILLE/WHL* BS5......56 C2
Blenheim Wy *PTSHD/EG* BS20......40 A4
Blenman Cl *MANG/FISH* BS16......48 A1
Blethwin Cl *HNBRY/STHM* BS10......30 D4
Blind La *CBATH/BATHN* BA1......101 H2
  YTN/CONG BS49......113 E4
Bloomfield Av *BATHSE* BA2......108 B3
Bloomfield Dr *BATHSE* BA2......108 A4
Bloomfield Gv *BATHSE* BA2......108 B4
Bloomfield Pk *BATHSE* BA2......108 B4
Bloomfield Ri *BATHSE* BA2......108 A5
Bloomfield Rd North
  BATHSE BA2 *......108 A5
Bloomfield Rd *BATHSE* BA2......108 A5
Bloomfield Road Link
  BRSG/KWL/STAPK BS4......74 B2
Bloy St *EVILLE/WHL* BS5......57 E2
Bluebell Rd *MTN/WRL* BS22......122 D2
The Bluebells *ALMDB* BS32......21 C3
Blueberry Wy *MTN/WRL* BS22......122 C2
Blue Falcon Rd
  KGWD/HNM BS15......59 E1
Blue Water Dr
  OMX/HUT/LCK BS24......127 C3
Blythe Gdns *MTN/WRL* BS22 *......117 H5
Boat Stall La *CBATH/BATHN* BA1......3 C4
Bockenem Cl *THNB/SVB* BS35......9 E5
Bodley Wy
  BRSG/KWL/STAPK BS4......122 B4
Bodmin Wk
  BRSG/KWL/STAPK BS4......74 D5
Bolton Rd *HORF/LLZ* BS7......46 A5
Bond St *CBRISNE* BS2......5 H1
Bonnington Wk *HORF/LLZ* BS7......46 D1
Bonville Rd
  BRSG/KWL/STAPK BS4......74 D5
Boon Vis *AVONM* BS11......43 E1
Booth Rd *BMSTR* BS5......72 D2
Boot La *BMSTR* BS3......72 D3
Bordesley Rd *HGRV/WHIT* BS14......96 D1
Boreal Wy
  OMX/HUT/LCK BS24......122 C3
Borgie Pl *MTN/WRL* BS22......117 F5
Borleyton Wk
  BMSTRD/HC/WWD BS13......84 C5
Borver Gv
  BMSTRD/HC/WWD BS13......84 C5
Boscombe Crs *MANG/FISH* BS16......35 F5
Boston Rd *HORF/LLZ* BS7......32 B5
Boswell St *EVILLE/WHL* BS5......57 F2
Botham Cl *MTN/WRL* BS22......117 H4
Botham Dr
  BRSG/KWL/STAPK BS4......74 D5
Bottom La *HGRV/WHIT* BS14......85 H3
Bottom Rd *BMSTR* BS3 *......56 C1
Boulevard *WSM* BS23......6 E3
Boulters Rd
  BMSTRD/HC/WWD BS13......84 D5
Boulton's Rd *KGWD/HNM* BS15......58 D3
Boundary Cl *WSM* BS23......124 D5
Boundary Rd *AVONM* BS11......28 D2
  FRCTL/WBN BS36......24 B5
  OMX/HUT/LCK BS24......122 D4
Bourchier Gdns
  BMSTRD/HC/WWD BS13......95 C1
Bourne Cl *FRCTL/WBN* BS36......23 E5
  KGWD/HNM BS15......58 B3
Bourne Rd *KGWD/HNM* BS15......58 A3
Bourneville Rd
  EVILLE/WHL BS5......57 F3
Bournville Rd *WSM* BS23......125 E2
Boursland Cl *ALMDB* BS32......11 F5
Bourton Av *BRSTK/PCHW* BS34......21 E2
Bourton Cl *BRSTK/PCHW* BS34......21 E2
Bourton Combe *NAIL* BS48......81 E1
Bourton La *MTN/WRL* BS22......118 C4
Bourton Md *LGASH* BS41 *......81 E1
  NAIL BS48......81 E1
Bourton Wk
  BMSTRD/HC/WWD BS13......84 B1
Boverton Rd
  BRSTK/PCHW BS34......32 D2
Bowden Cl
  HNLZ/SM/SNYPK/WT BS9......30 A5

Bowden Pl *MANG/FISH* BS16......49 F1
Bowden Rd *EVILLE/WHL* BS5......57 C2
Bowden Wy *CFTN/FAIL* BS8......69 C3
Bowen Rd
  OMX/HUT/LCK BS24......127 E2
Bower Ashton Ter *BMSTR* BS3......72 A2
Bowerleaze
  HNLZ/SM/SNYPK/WT BS9......43 H3
Bower Rd *BMSTR* BS3......72 B3
Bower Wk *BMSTR* BS3......73 F3
Bowling HI *YATE/CS* BS37......26 C1
Bowling Rd *YATE/CS* BS37......26 D2
Bow Md
  BRSG/KWL/STAPK BS4 *......74 C5
Bowring Cl
  BMSTRD/HC/WWD BS13......95 H1
Bowsland Wy *ALMDB* BS32......11 F5
Bowstreet La *THNB/SVB* BS35......19 E2
Boxhedge Farm La
  FRCTL/WBN BS36......36 C2
Box Rd *CBATH/BATHN* BA1......104 D1
Boyce Cl *BATHSE* BA2......107 E2
Boyce Dr *CBRISNE* BS2......56 C1
Boyce's Av *CFTN/FAIL* BS8......55 E4
Boyd Cl
  OLD/WMLY/WICK BS30......61 F4
Boyd Rd *KEYN* BS31......99 E1
Brabazon Rd
  BRSTK/PCHW BS34......32 D3
Bracewell Gdns
  HNBRY/STHM BS10......31 C1
Bracey Dr *MANG/FISH* BS16......48 C2
Brackenbury Dr
  BRSTK/PCHW BS34......21 C5
Brackendene *ALMDB* BS32......21 E1
Brackenwood Gdns
  PTSHD/EG BS20......38 D3
Brackenwood Rd *CLVDN* BS21......62 C4
Bracton Dr *HGRV/WHIT* BS14......96 D1
Bradeston Gv *MANG/FISH* BS16......48 A1
Bradford Cl *CLVDN* BS21......64 C4
Bradford Pk *BATHSE* BA2......108 D5
Bradford Rd *BATHSE* BA2......110 D1
Bradley Av *EVILLE/WHL* BS5......56 D5
  FRCTL/WBN BS36......23 E5
Bradley Crs *AVONM* BS11......43 E2
Bradley Pavilions
  BRSTK/PCHW BS34......20 B2
  PTSHD/EG BS20......20 B2
Bradley Stoke Wy *ALMDB* BS32......21 C2
Bradley Stoke Wy *BRSTK/PCHW* BS34......21 C2
Bradville Gdns *LGASH* BS41......82 C1
Bradwell Gv
  HNBRY/STHM BS10......31 C5
Bracton Rd *HGRV/WHIT* BS14......96 D1
Braemar Av *HORF/LLZ* BS7......32 B4
Braemar Crs *HORF/LLZ* BS7......32 B4
Bragg's La *CBRISNE* BS2......5 K2
Braikenridge Cl *CLVDN* BS21......64 D4
Braikenridge Rd
  BRSG/KWL/STAPK BS4......74 C2
Brainsfield
  HNLZ/SM/SNYPK/WT BS9......44 D2
Brake Cl *ALMDB* BS32......21 C4
  KGWD/HNM BS15......59 F4
The Brake *FRCTL/WBN* BS36......24 A5
  YATE/CS BS37......14 A2
Bramble Dr
  HNLZ/SM/SNYPK/WT BS9......44 A5
Bramble La
  HNLZ/SM/SNYPK/WT BS9......44 A5
Bramble Rd *MTN/WRL* BS22......117 F5
The Brambles
  BMSTRD/HC/WWD BS13......84 D5
  MTN/WRL BS22......123 C1
Bramble Wy *BATHSE* BA2......109 E5
Bramblewood
  YTN/CONG BS49......112 B2
Brambling Wk
  MANG/FISH BS16......47 H2
Bramley Cl
  OMX/HUT/LCK BS24......126 D2
  PTSHD/EG BS20......42 C4
  YTN/CONG BS49......112 B4
Bramley Copse *LGASH* BS41......82 B1
Bramley Ct
  OLD/WMLY/WICK BS30......76 C2
Bramley Dr *NAIL* BS48......79 H4
Bramley Sq *YTN/CONG* BS49 *......115 E3
The Bramleys *NAIL* BS48......79 H4
Brampton Wy *PTSHD/EG* BS20......40 A3
Branche Gv
  BMSTRD/HC/WWD BS13......96 A1
Brandash Rd *YATE/CS* BS37......27 E1
Brandon Hill La *CFTN/FAIL* BS8......4 D3
Brandon Steep *CBRIS/FH* BS1......4 C4
Brandon St *CBRIS/FH* BS1......4 D4
Brangwyn Gv *HORF/LLZ* BS7......46 D2
Brangwyn Sq *MTN/WRL* BS22......122 C1
Branksome Dr
  BRSTK/PCHW BS34......32 D2
  FRCTL/WBN BS36......23 E4
Branksome Rd
  RDLND/MONT BS6......45 F5
Bransby Wy
  OMX/HUT/LCK BS24......122 D3
Branscombe Rd
  HNLZ/SM/SNYPK/WT BS9......44 A4
Branscombe Wk
  PTSHD/EG BS20......38 D5
Branwhite Cl *HORF/LLZ* BS7......46 D1
Brassmill La
  CBATH/BATHN BA1......101 F5
Bratton Rd
  BRSG/KWL/STAPK BS4......85 E2
Braunton Rd *BMSTR* BS3......72 C4
Braydon Av *BRSTK/PCHW* BS34......21 F2
Brayne Ct
  OLD/WMLY/WICK BS30......76 C3
Breaches Ga *ALMDB* BS32......21 H4
The Breaches *PTSHD/EG* BS20......42 B4
Breach Rd *BMSTR* BS3......72 A4
Breach La *NAIL* BS48......78 A1
Breach Rd *BMSTR* BS3......72 B3
Breachwood Vw *BATHSE* BA2......107 H5
Bream Down Av
  HNLZ/SM/SNYPK/WT BS9......45 F3
  WSM BS23......124 C2

Brean Gdns *BMSTR* BS3......73 F4
Brecknock Rd
  BRSG/KWL/STAPK BS4......73 H3
Brecon Cl
  HNLZ/SM/SNYPK/WT BS9......45 F2
Brecon Rd
  HNLZ/SM/SNYPK/WT BS9......45 F2
Brecon Vw
  OMX/HUT/LCK BS24......125 F5
Bredon *YATE/CS* BS37......25 H3
Bredon Cl *KGWD/HNM* BS15......59 F4
Bredon Nook Rd
  HNBRY/STHM BS10......45 C1
Bree Cl *MTN/WRL* BS22......117 H4
Brendon Av *WSM* BS23......7 H1
Brendon Cl
  OLD/WMLY/WICK BS30......77 E2
Brendon Rd *BMSTR* BS3......73 E3
  PTSHD/EG BS20......39 E3
Brenner St *EVILLE/WHL* BS5......56 D1
Brent Rd *HORF/LLZ* BS7......46 B3
Brentry Av *EVILLE/WHL* BS5......56 D4
Brentry La *HNBRY/STHM* BS10......31 E3
Brentry Rd *MANG/FISH* BS16......47 C4
Brereton Wy
  OLD/WMLY/WICK BS30......77 E2
Brewerton Cl
  HNBRY/STHM BS10......31 C2
Brewhouse *CBRIS/FH* BS1 *......5 C4
Briar Cl *NAIL* BS48......67 H4
Briar Ct *PTSHD/EG* BS20......42 C4
Briarfield Av *KGWD/HNM* BS15......59 E5
Briar Md *YTN/CONG* BS49......112 A2
Briar Rd *OMX/HUT/LCK* BS24......126 B3
Briars Ct *BATHSE* BA2......107 F5
Briarside Rd
  HNBRY/STHM BS10......31 C2
The Briars *NAIL* BS48......79 C2
Briar Wk *MANG/FISH* BS16......48 C5
Briar Wy *MANG/FISH* BS16......48 B4
Briarwood
  HNLZ/SM/SNYPK/WT BS9......44 D2
Briary Rd *PTSHD/EG* BS20......39 C3
Bravels Gv *RDLND/MONT* BS6......56 B1
Brick St *CBRISNE* BS2......5 K2
Bridewell La *CBATH/BATHN* BA1......3 F4
  OMX/HUT/LCK BS24......127 E5
Bridewell St *CBRIS/FH* BS1......5 E4
Bridge Cl *HGRV/WHIT* BS14......86 B5
Bridge Farm Cl
  HGRV/WHIT BS14 *......96 D1
Bridge Farm Sq
  YTN/CONG BS49......114 D2
Bridge Farm Wk
  MANG/FISH BS16......49 H5
Bridgeleap Rd
  MANG/FISH BS16......35 F5
Bridge Rd *BATHSE* BA2......107 H2
  CFTN/FAIL BS8......54 D4
  EVILLE/WHL BS5......46 D5
  KGWD/HNM BS15......49 F5
  WSM BS23......7 H6
Bridge St *CBRIS/FH* BS1......5 E5
Bridges Ct *MANG/FISH* BS16......48 C2
Bridges Dr *MANG/FISH* BS16......48 B2
Bridge St *CBRIS/FH* BS1......5 F4
  EVILLE/WHL BS5......57 E1
Bridge Valley Rd
  CFTN/FAIL BS8......54 C3
Bridge Wk *HORF/LLZ* BS7......32 C5
Bridge Wy *FRCTL/WBN* BS36......23 H2
Bridgman Gv
  BRSTK/PCHW BS34......32 D2
Bridgwater Ct
  OMX/HUT/LCK BS24......125 C5
Bridgwater Rd *LGASH* BS41......82 D5
  NAIL BS48......93 E2
Briercliffe Rd
  HNLZ/SM/SNYPK/WT BS9......44 B1
Brierly Furlong
  BRSTK/PCHW BS34......33 F2
Briery Leaze Rd
  HGRV/WHIT BS14......85 H4
Brighton Crs *BMSTR* BS3......72 C4
Brighton Ms *CFTN/FAIL* BS8......55 F3
Brighton Pk *EVILLE/WHL* BS5......56 D3
Brighton Pl *KGWD/HNM* BS15......58 D2
Brighton Rd
  BRSTK/PCHW BS34......20 B2
  RDLND/MONT BS6......55 C2
  WSM BS23......7 F7
Brighton St *CBRISNE* BS2......56 A2
Brighton Ter *BMSTR* BS3......72 C4
Bright St *EVILLE/WHL* BS5......56 D4
Brigstocke Rd *CBRISNE* BS2......56 A2
The Brimbles *HORF/LLZ* BS7......32 D3
Brimbleworth La
  MTN/WRL BS22......118 B5
Brinkworthy Rd
  MANG/FISH BS16......47 F2
Brinmead Wk
  BMSTRD/HC/WWD BS13......95 E1
Brins Cl *BRSTK/PCHW* BS34......33 H1
Brinsea Rd *YTN/CONG* BS49......114 D2
Brinsham La *FRCTL/WBN* BS36......14 C1
Brinsmead Crs
  PTSHD/EG BS20......42 D4
Briscoes Av
  BMSTRD/HC/WWD BS13......84 D5
Bristol & Bath Railway Pth
  BATHSE BA2......100 C4
  EVILLE/WHL BS5......57 F2
  KEYN BS31......99 H2
  MANG/FISH BS16......48 A4
  OLD/WMLY/WICK BS30......60 A4
Bristol Br *CBRIS/FH* BS1 *......5 C4
Bristol HI
  BRSG/KWL/STAPK BS4......74 C4
Bristol Pkwy North
  BRSTK/PCHW BS34......34 A1
Bristol Rd *BATHSE* BA2......100 A4
  FRCTL/WBN BS36......23 F2
  HGRV/WHIT BS14......97 F1
  KEYN BS31......88 A3
  MANG/FISH BS16......48 B3
  NAIL BS48......68 B2
  PTSHD/EG BS20......39 H4

  THNB/SVB BS35......8 C5
  YTN/CONG BS49......114 D1
Bristol Road Lower *WSM* BS23......6 E1
Bristow Broadway
  AVONM BS11......28 C4
Britannia Cl *MANG/FISH* BS16......35 F4
Britannia Crs
  BRSTK/PCHW BS34......21 F5
Britannia Rd
  BRSTK/PCHW BS34......19 H3
  EVILLE/WHL BS5......56 D2
  KGWD/HNM BS15......58 C3
Britannia Wy *CLVDN* BS21......64 C4
British Rd *BMSTR* BS3......72 D5
Brittan Pl *PTSHD/EG* BS20......41 C5
Britten Ct
  OLD/WMLY/WICK BS30......76 C2
Britton Gdns *KGWD/HNM* BS15......58 C2
Brixham Rd *BMSTR* BS3......72 D5
Brixton Rd *EVILLE/WHL* BS5......56 D3
Brixton Road Ms
  EVILLE/WHL BS5 *......56 D3
Broadbury Rd
  BRSG/KWL/STAPK BS4......85 F1
Broad Cft *ALMDB* BS32......11 E5
Broadcroft Av
  YTN/CONG BS49......113 F2
Broadcroft Cl
  YTN/CONG BS49......113 F2
Broadfield Av
  KGWD/HNM BS15......58 C3
Broadfield Rd
  BRSG/KWL/STAPK BS4......73 H5
Broadlands Av *KEYN* BS31......65 F2
Broadlands Dr *AVONM* BS11......29 C2
Broad La *FRCTL/WBN* BS36......24 B5
  YATE/CS BS37......37 E1
  YATE/CS BS37......13 C3
Broadleas
  BMSTRD/HC/WWD BS13......84 B1
Broadleaze *AVONM* BS11......42 D1
Broadleys Av
  HNLZ/SM/SNYPK/WT BS9......45 F1
Broadmead *CBRIS/FH* BS1......5 C2
Broadmead La *KEYN* BS31......88 D3
Broadmoor La
  CBATH/BATHN BA1......101 F1
Broadmoor Pk
  CBATH/BATHN BA1......101 C2
Broadmoor V
  CBATH/BATHN BA1......101 F1
Broadoak HI *LGASH* BS41......95 E2
Broad Oak Rd
  BMSTRD/HC/WWD BS13......84 A5
Broadoak Rd *WSM* BS23......124 C5
Broad Oaks *CFTN/FAIL* BS8......54 C5
Broadoak Wk *MANG/FISH* BS16......48 A4
Broad Pln *CBRISNE* BS2......5 J4
Broad Quay *CBATH/BATHN* BA1......3 F6
  CBRIS/FH BS1......4 E4
Broad Rd *KGWD/HNM* BS15......58 C2
Broad Stones *BOAV* BA15......105 F5
Broadstone Wk
  BMSTRD/HC/WWD BS13......85 E4
Broad St *CBATH/BATHN* BA1......3 C3
  CBRIS/FH BS1......5 E4
  MANG/FISH BS16......49 E4
  YATE/CS BS37......26 D1
  YTN/CONG BS49......114 D2
Broad Wk
  BRSG/KWL/STAPK BS4......73 C4
Broadway *BATHSE* BA2......3 J6
  KEYN BS31......89 C5
  OMX/HUT/LCK BS24......127 C2
  YATE/CS BS37......125 E5
  YATE/CS BS37......14 C5
Broadway Av
  HNLZ/SM/SNYPK/WT BS9......45 H2
Broadway Ct *BATHSE* BA2 *......3 H6
Broadway Rd
  BMSTRD/HC/WWD BS13......84 A4
  HORF/LLZ BS7......45 H5
Broadways Dr
  MANG/FISH BS16......47 H1
Broad Weir *CBRIS/FH* BS1......5 H3
Brock End *PTSHD/EG* BS20......38 C4
Brockhurst Gdns
  KGWD/HNM BS15......58 A3
Brockhurst Rd
  KGWD/HNM BS15......58 A3
Brockley Cl
  BRSTK/PCHW BS34......19 E3
  NAIL BS48......67 E5
  OMX/HUT/LCK BS24......125 E5
Brockley Crs
  OMX/HUT/LCK BS24......125 E5
Brockley La *NAIL* BS48......79 E5
Brockley Rd *KEYN* BS31......99 E1
Brockley Wk
  BMSTRD/HC/WWD BS13......84 B1
Brockridge La
  FRCTL/WBN BS36......23 H3
Brocks La *LGASH* BS41......70 C5
Brocks Rd
  BMSTRD/HC/WWD BS13......95 H1
Brock St *CBATH/BATHN* BA1......2 E2
Brockway *NAIL* BS48......67 H4
Brockworth *YATE/CS* BS37......25 C4
Brockworth Crs
  MANG/FISH BS16......47 H2
Bromfield Wk
  MANG/FISH BS16......34 D5
Bromley Dr *MANG/FISH* BS16......34 D5
Bromley Heath Av
  MANG/FISH BS16......34 D5
Bromley Heath Rd
  MANG/FISH BS16......34 D5
Bromley Rd *HORF/LLZ* BS7......46 B3
Brompton Cl
  KGWD/HNM BS15......59 F3
Brompton Rd
  OMX/HUT/LCK BS24......125 F4
Broncksea Rd *HORF/LLZ* BS7......32 B4
Bronte Cl *WSM* BS23......125 F5
Bronte Wk *HORF/LLZ* BS7......32 C5
Brook Cl *LGASH* BS41......82 B1
Brookcote Dr
  BRSTK/PCHW BS34......21 F4

Brookdale Rd
BMSTRD/HC/WWD BS13 84 C3
Brookfield Av HORF/LLZ BS7 45 H5
Brookfield Cl YATE/CS BS37 27 E1
Brookfield La
RDLND/MONT BS6 55 H1
Brookfield Pk
CBATH/BATHN BA1 101 G2
Brookfield Rd
BRSTK/PCHW BS34 20 D2
RDLND/MONT BS6 55 H2
Brookfield Wk CLVDN BS21 65 F2
OLD/WMLY/WICK BS30 77 F3
Brook Ga BMSTR BS3 71 H5
Brook Hl RDLND/MONT BS6 56 A2
Brookland Rd
RDLND/MONT BS6 45 H3
WSM BS23 121 G4
Brook La MANG/FISH BS16 47 G2
RDLND/MONT BS6 56 B2
Brooklea
OLD/WMLY/WICK BS30 77 E2
Brookleaze
HNLZ/SM/SNYPK/WT BS9 44 A3
Brookleaze Blds
CBATH/BATHN BA1 103 E2
Brook Lintons
BRSG/KWL/STAPK BS4 74 C3
Brooklyn Rd
BMSTRD/HC/WWD BS13 84 C1
CBATH/BATHN BA1 103 F2
Brookmead THNB/SVB BS35 9 E5
Brook Rd BMSTR BS3 73 E2
KGWD/HNM BS15 59 G3
MANG/FISH BS16 48 A4
RDLND/MONT BS6 56 B2
Brookside
BLAG/CWMG/WR BS40 93 G5
PTSHD/EG BS20 42 D5
Brookside Cl
CBATH/BATHN BA1 91 E4
Brookside Dr
FRCTL/WBN BS36 23 H2
Brookside Rd
BRSG/KWL/STAPK BS4 74 D4
Brook St EVILLE/WHL BS5 57 E4
YATE/CS BS37 26 C1
Brookthorpe YATE/CS BS37 25 H2
Brookthorpe Av AVONM BS11 29 G5
Brookthorpe Ct YATE/CS BS37 25 H2
Brookview Wk
BMSTRD/HC/WWD BS13 84 C2
Brook Wy ALMDB BS32 21 E1
Broom Farm Cl NAIL BS48 79 F1
Broom Hl MANG/FISH BS16 47 G3
Broomhill Rd
BRSG/KWL/STAPK BS4 75 E5
The Brooms MANG/FISH BS16 35 G3
Brotherswood Ct ALMDB BS32 11 F4
Brougham Hayes BATHSE BA2 2 B5
Brougham Pl
CBATH/BATHN BA1 103 F2
Brow Hl CBATH/BATHN BA1 91 E5
Browning Ct HORF/LLZ BS7 32 D4
Brownlow Rd WSM BS23 124 D2
The Brow BATHSE BA2 111 G1
BATHSE BA2 107 G2
Broxholme Wk AVONM BS11 29 F5
Bruce Av EVILLE/WHL BS5 57 E2
Bruce Rd EVILLE/WHL BS5 57 E2
Brue Cl WSM BS23 125 E1
Brunel Cl
OLD/WMLY/WICK BS30 60 A4
Brunel Lock Development
CBRIS/FH BS1 * 72 A1
Brunel Lock Rd CBRIS/FH BS1 72 A1
Brunel Rd
BMSTRD/HC/WWD BS13 84 A1
NAIL BS48 66 C5
Brunel Wy BMSTR BS3 71 H3
CBRIS/FH BS1 72 A1
THNB/SVB BS35 8 C5
Brunswick Pl
CBATH/BATHN BA1 * 3 F2
CBRIS/FH BS1 * 72 A1
Brunswick Sq CBRISNE BS2 5 G1
Brunswick St
CBATH/BATHN BA1 103 E3
CBRISNE BS2 56 A3
Bruton Av BATHSE BA2 108 C3
PTSHD/EG BS20 39 E3
Bruton Cl EVILLE/WHL BS5 57 H3
NAIL BS48 79 F1
Bruton Pl CFTN/FAIL BS8 4 A3
Bryansons Cl MANG/FISH BS16 47 F2
Bryant Gdns CLVDN BS21 64 C4
Bryants Cl MANG/FISH BS16 34 C4
Bryant's Hl EVILLE/WHL BS5 58 B5
Brynland Av HORF/LLZ BS7 46 A4
Buchanans Whf North
CBRIS/FH BS1 * 5 F5
Buchanans Whf South
CBRIS/FH BS1 * 5 F5
Buckingham Dr
BRSTK/PCHW BS34 33 F1
Buckingham Gdns
MANG/FISH BS16 49 E2
Buckingham Pl
MANG/FISH BS16 49 E2
Buckingham Rd
BRSG/KWL/STAPK BS4 74 C1
OMX/HUT/LCK BS24 125 G4
Buckingham St BMSTR BS3 72 D4
Buckingham V
CFTN/FAIL BS8 55 E3
Buckland Gn MTN/WRL BS22 117 H3
Bucklands Batch NAIL BS48 79 G1
Bucklands Dr NAIL BS48 79 G1
Bucklands Gv NAIL BS48 79 G1
Bucklands La NAIL BS48 79 G1
Bucklands Vw NAIL BS48 79 H1
Bude Av EVILLE/WHL BS5 58 A3
Bude Cl NAIL BS48 67 H5
Bude Rd BRSTK/PCHW BS34 32 D2
Buller Rd
BRSG/KWL/STAPK BS4 74 B4
Bull La EVILLE/WHL BS5 57 H5
PTSHD/EG BS20 42 C4
Bumpers Batch BATHSE BA2 111 E2
Bunting Ct MTN/WRL BS22 122 B2
Burbank Cl
OLD/WMLY/WICK BS30 76 D3
Burchells Green Cl
KGWD/HNM BS15 58 B3
Burchells Green Rd
KGWD/HNM BS15 58 B2
Burcombe Cl FRCTL/WBN BS36 24 B3
Burcott Rd AVONM BS11 16 C5
Burden Cl ALMDB BS32 21 G4
Burfoote Gdns
HGRV/WHIT BS14 86 D5
Burfoot Rd HGRV/WHIT BS14 86 D5
Burford Av BRSTK/PCHW BS34 21 E2
Burford Cl BATHSE BA2 107 G4
PTSHD/EG BS20 40 A4
Burford Gv AVONM BS11 43 F3
Burgage Cl YATE/CS BS37 26 D2
Burghill Rd HNBRY/STHM BS10 31 E4
Burghley Ct FRCTL/WBN BS36 23 E5
Burghley Rd RDLND/MONT BS6 56 A1
Burgis Rd HGRV/WHIT BS14 86 C3
Burleigh Gdns
CBATH/BATHN BA1 101 F4
Burley Av MANG/FISH BS16 49 F3
Burley Crest MANG/FISH BS16 49 F2
Burley Gv MANG/FISH BS16 49 F2
Burlington Rd PTSHD/EG BS20 40 A1
RDLND/MONT BS6 55 F1
Burlington St
CBATH/BATHN BA1 2 E1
WSM BS23 6 E3
Burnbush Cl HGRV/WHIT BS14 86 D3
Burnell Dr CBRISNE BS2 56 B3
Burneside Cl
HNBRY/STHM BS10 31 G3
Burnett Hl KEYN BS31 98 B4
Burney Wy
OLD/WMLY/WICK BS30 76 D3
Burnham Cl KGWD/HNM BS15 59 F2
Burnham Dr KGWD/HNM BS15 59 F2
OMX/HUT/LCK BS24 125 E5
Burnham Rd AVONM BS11 42 D2
BATHSE BA2 107 H1
Burnt House Rd BATHSE BA2 110 B2
Burrington Av
OMX/HUT/LCK BS24 125 E5
Burrington Cl NAIL BS48 67 F5
Burrington Wk
BMSTRD/HC/WWD BS13 84 B1
Burrough Wy
FRCTL/WBN BS36 23 E5
Burton Cl CBRIS/FH BS1 5 G7
Burton Ct CFTN/FAIL BS8 * 4 A3
Burton St CBATH/BATHN BA1 3 F4
Burwalls Rd CFTN/FAIL BS8 54 C5
Burycourt Cl AVONM BS11 29 G4
Bury Hl MANG/FISH BS16 35 E2
Bury Hill Vw MANG/FISH BS16 35 E4
The Bury OMX/HUT/LCK BS24 126 D3
Bush Av BRSTK/PCHW BS34 21 E5
Bushy Pk
BRSG/KWL/STAPK BS4 73 G3
Butcombe Wk
HGRV/WHIT BS14 86 A4
Butlers Cl EVILLE/WHL BS5 57 H4
Butlers Wk EVILLE/WHL BS5 57 H5
Buttercliffe Ri LGASH BS41 71 F3
Buttercup Crs MTN/WRL BS22 117 H4
Butterfield Cl FRCTL/WBN BS36 23 H4
HNBRY/STHM BS10 46 A1
Butterfield Pk CLVDN BS21 64 C4
Butterfield Rd
HNBRY/STHM BS10 46 A1
Buttermere Rd WSM BS23 125 F1
Butterworth Ct
BRSG/KWL/STAPK BS4 85 E2
Butt La THNB/SVB BS35 8 D1
Buxton Wk HORF/LLZ BS7 32 C5
Bye Md MANG/FISH BS16 35 G5
Byfield BATHSE BA2 111 F1
Byfields CLVDN BS21 64 C5
Byron Cl OMX/HUT/LCK BS24 126 C2
Byron Pl CFTN/FAIL BS8 4 B3
MANG/FISH BS16 49 E4
Byron Rd BATHSE BA2 108 C3
WSM BS23 125 F2
Byron St CBRISNE BS2 56 B2

C

Cabot Cl KEYN BS31 99 E2
KGWD/HNM BS15 58 C4
YATE/CS BS37 26 B1
Cabot Ri PTSHD/EG BS20 39 E3
Cabot Wy CFTN/FAIL BS8 54 D5
MTN/WRL BS22 117 H5
PTSHD/EG BS20 42 D5
Cabstand PTSHD/EG BS20 39 H2
Cadbury Camp La West
CLVDN BS21 63 H5
Cadbury Farm Rd
YTN/CONG BS49 112 C4
Cadbury Heath Rd
OLD/WMLY/WICK BS30 77 E1
Cadbury Rd KEYN BS31 98 B2
PTSHD/EG BS20 39 H4
Cadbury Sq YTN/CONG BS49 * 115 E3
Caddick Cl KGWD/HNM BS15 59 F1
Cade Cl BRSTK/PCHW BS34 21 G5
KGWD/HNM BS15 59 F5
Cadmium Rd AVONM BS11 28 C2
Cadogan Gv NAIL BS48 80 A3
Cadogan Rd HGRV/WHIT BS14 85 H1
Caen Rd BMSTR BS3 73 E3
Caernarvon Rd KEYN BS31 87 H5
Caine Rd HORF/LLZ BS7 46 B1
Cains Cl KGWD/HNM BS15 59 E5
Cairn Cl NAIL BS48 67 H5
Cairn Gdns FRCTL/WBN BS36 35 E1
Cairns' Crs CBRISNE BS2 56 B2
Cairns Rd RDLND/MONT BS6 45 F3
Calcott Rd
BRSG/KWL/STAPK BS4 73 H3
Caldbeck Cl
HNBRY/STHM BS10 31 H3
Calder Cl KEYN BS31 88 D5
Caldicot Cl AVONM BS11 30 A3
OLD/WMLY/WICK BS30 77 E4
Caledonian Rd BATHSE BA2 2 A5
CBRIS/FH BS1 4 B6
Caledonia Pl CFTN/FAIL BS8 54 D5
California Rd
OLD/WMLY/WICK BS30 76 D3
Callicroft Rd
BRSTK/PCHW BS34 20 C3
Callington Rd
BRSG/KWL/STAPK BS4 74 B5
Callowhill Ct CBRIS/FH BS1 5 G2
Calton Gdns BATHSE BA2 3 F7
Calton Rd BATHSE BA2 3 G7
Calton Wk BATHSE BA2 3 F7
Camberley Dr
FRCTL/WBN BS36 23 F2
Camberley Rd
BRSG/KWL/STAPK BS4 84 D1
Camberley Wk
MTN/WRL BS22 122 B4
Camborne Rd HORF/LLZ BS7 46 C1
Cambrian Dr YATE/CS BS37 14 A4
Cambridge Crs
HNLZ/SM/SNYPK/WT BS9 45 E1
Cambridge Gv CLVDN BS21 62 B5
Cambridge Pk
RDLND/MONT BS6 45 F5
Cambridge Pl BATHSE BA2 3 J7
WSM BS23 6 D3
Cambridge Rd CLVDN BS21 62 B5
HORF/LLZ BS7 45 H4
Cambridge St BMSTR BS3 73 G2
EVILLE/WHL BS5 57 E4
Cambridge Ter BATHSE BA2 3 J7
Camden Crs CBATH/BATHN BA1 3 F1
Camden Rd
CBATH/BATHN BA1 102 D3
Camden Rw CBATH/BATHN BA1 3 F1
Camden Ter
CBATH/BATHN BA1 102 D3
CFTN/FAIL BS8 55 E5
WSM BS23 7 F4
Cameley Gn BATHSE BA2 107 E1
Camelford Rd EVILLE/WHL BS5 57 F2
Cameron Wk HORF/LLZ BS7 47 E2
Cameroons Cl KEYN BS31 88 B4
Camerton Cl KEYN BS31 99 F1
Camerton Rd EVILLE/WHL BS5 57 F2
Camomile Wk PTSHD/EG BS20 40 B3
Campbell Farm Dr
AVONM BS11 29 F4
Campbell St CBRISNE BS2 56 A2
Campian Wk
BRSG/KWL/STAPK BS4 85 E3
Campion Cl MTN/WRL BS22 122 A4
THNB/SVB BS35 9 E2
Campion Dr ALMDB BS32 11 F5
Camp Rd CFTN/FAIL BS8 54 D4
Camp Rd North WSM BS23 120 A2
Camp Vw FRCTL/WBN BS36 35 E1
NAIL BS48 67 E4
Camwal Rd CBRISNE BS2 73 H1
Canada Coombe
OMX/HUT/LCK BS24 126 C4
Canada Wy CBRIS/FH BS1 72 B1
Canal Br BATHSE BA2 * 3 J7
Canberra Crs
OMX/HUT/LCK BS24 122 D5
Canberra Gv
BRSTK/PCHW BS34 32 D1
Canford La
HNLZ/SM/SNYPK/WT BS9 44 C1
Canford Rd
HNLZ/SM/SNYPK/WT BS9 44 D1
Cannans Cl FRCTL/WBN BS36 23 E3
Cann La OLD/WMLY/WICK BS30 60 C5
Cannons Ga CLVDN BS21 64 C5
Cannon St CBRIS/FH BS1 5 F2
Canons Cl BATHSE BA2 107 G5
Canon's Rd CBRIS/FH BS1 4 E5
Canon's Wk KGWD/HNM BS15 59 E1
Canons Wy CBRIS/FH BS1 4 C5
Canowie Rd RDLND/MONT BS6 45 F5
Cantell Gv HGRV/WHIT BS14 87 E4
Canterbury Cl MTN/WRL BS22 117 H4
YATE/CS BS37 14 A4
Canterbury Rd BATHSE BA2 2 B6
Canterbury St EVILLE/WHL BS5 56 D5
Cantock's Cl CFTN/FAIL BS8 4 C3
Canvey Cl HNBRY/STHM BS10 46 A1
Canynge Rd CFTN/FAIL BS8 54 D3
Canynge Sq CFTN/FAIL BS8 54 D3
Canynge St CBRIS/FH BS1 5 G5
Capel Cl KGWD/HNM BS15 59 H3
Capell Cl MTN/WRL BS22 121 G3
Capel Rd AVONM BS11 29 H4
Capenor Cl PTSHD/EG BS20 39 G4
Capgrave Cl
BRSG/KWL/STAPK BS4 75 F3
Capgrave Crs
BRSG/KWL/STAPK BS4 75 F3
Caraway Gdns EVILLE/WHL BS5 57 E1
Carberry Vw
OMX/HUT/LCK BS24 122 D3
Cardigan Crs MTN/WRL BS22 121 H3
Cardigan Rd
HNLZ/SM/SNYPK/WT BS9 45 F2
Cardill Cl
BMSTRD/HC/WWD BS13 84 B1
Cardinal Cl BATHSE BA2 110 B2
Carey's Cl CLVDN BS21 65 F1
Careys Wy
OMX/HUT/LCK BS24 122 B4
Carice Gdns CLVDN BS21 64 D4
Carisbrooke Rd
BRSG/KWL/STAPK BS4 85 E1
Carlow Rd
BRSG/KWL/STAPK BS4 85 F1
Carlton Ct
HNLZ/SM/SNYPK/WT BS9 * 45 E1
Carlton Man North WSM BS23 * 6 D5
Carlton Man South WSM BS23 * 6 D5
Carlton Pk EVILLE/WHL BS5 57 E3
Carlton St WSM BS23 6 D5
Carlyle Rd EVILLE/WHL BS5 57 E2
Carmarthen Cl YATE/CS BS37 14 B3
Carmarthen Gv
OLD/WMLY/WICK BS30 77 E5
Carmarthen Rd
HNLZ/SM/SNYPK/WT BS9 45 E2
Carnarvon Rd
RDLND/MONT BS6 55 G1
Caroline Blds BATHSE BA2 3 J6
Caroline Cl KEYN BS31 87 H5
YATE/CS BS37 14 D5
Caroline Pl CBATH/BATHN BA1 * 3 F1
Carpenter Cl WSM BS23 7 K5
Carpenters La KEYN BS31 88 B4
Carpenter's Shop La
MANG/FISH BS16 48 D2
Carre Gdns MTN/WRL BS22 117 G4
Carrington Rd BMSTR BS3 72 B2
Carrs Cl BATHSE BA2 107 F1
Carsons Rd MANG/FISH BS16 59 H1
Carson's Rd MANG/FISH BS16 49 H5
Carsons Road Link
MANG/FISH BS16 59 H1
Carter Wk ALMDB BS32 21 F2
Cartledge Rd EVILLE/WHL BS5 57 E2
Cassell Rd MANG/FISH BS16 48 C3
Cassey Bottom La
EVILLE/WHL BS5 58 A4
Casson Dr MANG/FISH BS16 33 G5
Castle Cl HNBRY/STHM BS10 30 C3
NAIL BS48 80 D2
Castle Coombe THNB/SVB BS35 8 D2
Castle Ct BRSG/KWL/STAPK BS4 74 B2
BRSTK/PCHW BS34 34 A1
THNB/SVB BS35 8 C3
Castle Farm La LGASH BS41 94 A2
Castle Farm Rd
KGWD/HNM BS15 75 G4
Castle Gdns BATHSE BA2 108 B4
Castle Rd CLVDN BS21 62 B4
KGWD/HNM BS15 58 C1
MANG/FISH BS16 51 G2
MTN/WRL BS22 117 F5
OLD/WMLY/WICK BS30 77 F3
Castle St CBRIS/FH BS1 5 H3
THNB/SVB BS35 8 B2
Castle Vw
OMX/HUT/LCK BS24 122 C3
Castle View Rd CLVDN BS21 62 B5
Castlewood Cl CLVDN BS21 64 D1
Catbrain Hl HNBRY/STHM BS10 19 F4
Catbrain La HNBRY/STHM BS10 19 F4
Catemead CLVDN BS21 64 C5
Cater Rd
BMSTRD/HC/WWD BS13 84 C3
Catharine Pl CBATH/BATHN BA1 2 E2
Catherine Mead St BMSTR BS3 72 D2
Catherine St AVONM BS11 42 C1
Catherine Wy
CBATH/BATHN BA1 91 E4
Catley Gv LGASH BS41 71 E5
Cattistock Dr EVILLE/WHL BS5 58 A5
Cattle Market Rd CBRIS/FH BS1 5 J6
Cattybrook Rd
MANG/FISH BS16 50 B3
Cattybrook Rd North
MANG/FISH BS16 50 B2
Cattybrook St EVILLE/WHL BS5 56 D3
Caulfield Rd MTN/WRL BS22 117 H4
Causeway CLVDN BS21 66 C3
The Causeway
FRCTL/WBN BS36 24 A3
YTN/CONG BS49 114 D2
Causeway Vw NAIL BS48 66 D4
Causley Dr
OLD/WMLY/WICK BS30 76 C1
Cavan Wk
BRSG/KWL/STAPK BS4 73 E5
Cave Cl MANG/FISH BS16 48 D2
Cave Dr MANG/FISH BS16 48 D2
Cave Gv MANG/FISH BS16 49 H1
Cavell Ct CLVDN BS21 64 C4
Cavendish Cl KEYN BS31 99 E2
Cavendish Crs
CBATH/BATHN BA1 102 B4
Cavendish Gdns
HNLZ/SM/SNYPK/WT BS9 44 A4
Cavendish Pl
CBATH/BATHN BA1 102 B4
Cavendish Rd
BRSTK/PCHW BS34 20 B2
CBATH/BATHN BA1 102 B4
HNLZ/SM/SNYPK/WT BS9 45 E3
Caveners Ct MTN/WRL BS22 121 G2
Caversham Dr NAIL BS48 67 H4
Cave St CBRISNE BS2 56 A3
Cecil Av EVILLE/WHL BS5 57 H2
Cecil Rd CFTN/FAIL BS8 54 D3
KGWD/HNM BS15 58 D3
WSM BS23 7 G1
Cedar Av MTN/WRL BS22 121 H2
Cedar Cl BRSTK/PCHW BS34 20 B3
LGASH BS41 70 C5
OLD/WMLY/WICK BS30 77 E2
Cedar Dr KEYN BS31 88 A5
Cedar Gv BATHSE BA2 108 A4
HNLZ/SM/SNYPK/WT BS9 44 B3
Cedarhurst Rd PTSHD/EG BS20 38 C5
Cedar Pk
HNLZ/SM/SNYPK/WT BS9 44 B3
Cedar Rw AVONM BS11 * 43 F2
Cedar Wy BATHSE BA2 2 D6
FRCTL/WBN BS36 22 D5
MANG/FISH BS16 51 F3
NAIL BS48 67 H4
PTSHD/EG BS20 39 F4
Cedern Av
OMX/HUT/LCK BS24 127 F3
Cedric Cl CBATH/BATHN BA1 101 H5
Cedric Rd CBATH/BATHN BA1 101 H4
Celandine Cl THNB/SVB BS35 9 E2
Celestine Rd YATE/CS BS37 13 G4
Celia Ter BRSG/KWL/STAPK BS4 57 H5
Cemetery Rd
BRSG/KWL/STAPK BS4 73 H3
Cennick Av KGWD/HNM BS15 59 E2
Centaurus Rd
BRSTK/PCHW BS34 19 G3
Central Av KGWD/HNM BS15 75 H1
Central Wy CLVDN BS21 64 D4
Centre Dr BNWL BS29 127 H2
Ceres Cl
OLD/WMLY/WICK BS30 76 C4
Cerimon Ga BRSTK/PCHW BS34 21 G5
Cerney Gdns NAIL BS48 67 H4
Cerney La AVONM BS11 43 E3
Cesson Cl YATE/CS BS37 27 E1
Chadleigh Gv
BRSG/KWL/STAPK BS4 84 D2
The Chaffins CLVDN BS21 65 E3
Chaingate La YATE/CS BS37 12 D1
Chakeshill Cl
HNBRY/STHM BS10 31 G2
Chakeshill Dr
HNBRY/STHM BS10 31 G2
Chalcombe Cl
BRSTK/PCHW BS34 21 E2
Chalcroft Wk
BMSTRD/HC/WWD BS13 83 H5
Chalfield Cl KEYN BS31 98 B2
Chalfont Rd MTN/WRL BS22 121 H3
Chalford Cl YATE/CS BS37 25 H2
Chalk Farm Cl PLTN/PENS BS39 96 D5
Chalks Rd EVILLE/WHL BS5 57 F3
Challender Av
HNBRY/STHM BS10 30 D3
Challoner Ct CBRIS/FH BS1 4 E7
Challow Dr MTN/WRL BS22 121 G1
Champion Rd
KGWD/HNM BS15 59 G1
Champneys Av
HNBRY/STHM BS10 30 D2
Champs Sur Marne
ALMDB BS32 21 G2
Chancel Cl
HNLZ/SM/SNYPK/WT BS9 44 B5
NAIL BS48 67 E5
Chancery St EVILLE/WHL BS5 56 D4
Chandag Rd KEYN BS31 88 D5
Chandler Cl
CBATH/BATHN BA1 101 G3
Chandos Rd KEYN BS31 88 B2
RDLND/MONT BS6 55 F2
Channel Hts
OMX/HUT/LCK BS24 125 E5
Channell's Hl
HNLZ/SM/SNYPK/WT BS9 31 E5
Channel Rd CLVDN BS21 62 B4
Channel View Crs
PTSHD/EG BS20 39 F3
Channel View Rd
PTSHD/EG BS20 39 F3
Channon's Hl MANG/FISH BS16 47 H4
Chantry Cl NAIL BS48 66 C5
Chantry Dr MTN/WRL BS22 117 G4
Chantry Gv AVONM BS11 30 A3
Chantry La MANG/FISH BS16 35 F4
Chantry Mead Rd
BATHSE BA2 108 B4
Chantry Rd CFTN/FAIL BS8 55 F2
THNB/SVB BS35 8 C2
Chapel Barton BMSTR BS3 72 C4
NAIL BS48 66 D5
Chapel Cl NAIL BS48 67 F4
Chapel Ct CBATH/BATHN BA1 * 3 F5
Chapel Gdns
HNBRY/STHM BS10 31 E4
Chapel Green La
RDLND/MONT BS6 55 F1
Chapel Hl CLVDN BS21 64 D2
NAIL BS48 80 C1
Chapel La AVONM BS11 29 H3
EVILLE/WHL BS5 57 G1
KGWD/HNM BS15 59 H3
MANG/FISH BS16 48 C1
OLD/WMLY/WICK BS30 77 E3
WUE GL12 9 H3
YTN/CONG BS49 113 F3
Chapel Orch YATE/CS BS37 13 G5
Chapel Pill La PTSHD/EG BS20 43 E4
Chapel Rd
BMSTRD/HC/WWD BS13 84 B3
EVILLE/WHL BS5 56 D2
KGWD/HNM BS15 75 H1
Chapel Rw CBATH/BATHN BA1 104 D2
CBATH/BATHN BA1 2 E4
PTSHD/EG BS20 42 C4
Chapel St CBRISNE BS2 73 H1
THNB/SVB BS35 8 C4
Chapel Wy
BRSG/KWL/STAPK BS4 57 G5
HNBRY/STHM BS10 31 H5
Chaplin Rd EVILLE/WHL BS5 56 D2
Chapter St CBRISNE BS2 56 A3
Chapter Wk RDLND/MONT BS6 55 F1
Charborough Rd
BRSTK/PCHW BS34 32 B3
Chard Cl NAIL BS48 79 G1
Chard Rd CLVDN BS21 64 D4
Chardstock Av
HNLZ/SM/SNYPK/WT BS9 30 A5
Charfield KGWD/HNM BS15 59 G3
Charfield Rd
HNBRY/STHM BS10 31 G4
Chargrove
OLD/WMLY/WICK BS30 60 A5
YATE/CS BS37 25 H3
Charis Av HNBRY/STHM BS10 45 G1
Charlcombe La
CBATH/BATHN BA1 102 C2
Charlcombe Ri
CBATH/BATHN BA1 102 C2
Charlcombe View Rd
CBATH/BATHN BA1 102 D2
Charlcombe Wy
CBATH/BATHN BA1 102 C2
Charlcome Ri PTSHD/EG BS20 38 B5
Charlecombe Ct
HNLZ/SM/SNYPK/WT BS9 * 44 D2
Charlecombe Rd
HNLZ/SM/SNYPK/WT BS9 44 D2
Charles Av BRSTK/PCHW BS34 33 G1
Charles Cl THNB/SVB BS35 8 D1
Charles Ct CFTN/FAIL BS8 * 55 E5
Charles Pl CFTN/FAIL BS8 55 E5
Charles Rd BRSTK/PCHW BS34 32 D2
Charles St CBATH/BATHN BA1 2 E4
CBRIS/FH BS1 5 F1
Charles Wesley Ct
EVILLE/WHL BS5 58 A5
Charlock Rd
MTN/WRL BS22 122 A4
Charlotte St CBATH/BATHN BA1 2 E4
CBRIS/FH BS1 4 C4
Charlotte St South
CBRIS/FH BS1 4 C4

Charlton Av
BRSTK/PCHW BS34 32 B3
WSM BS23 124 C2
Charlton Gdns
HNBRY/STHM BS10 31 H1
Charlton La
HNBRY/STHM BS10 31 E2
Charlton Leaze
HNBRY/STHM BS10 19 E4
Charlton Mead Dr
HNBRY/STHM BS10 31 H1
Charlton Pk KEYN BS31 88 A4
Charlton Pl HNBRY/STHM BS10 31 H2
Charlton Rd
HNBRY/STHM BS10 31 F4
KEYN BS31 88 A4
KGWD/HNM BS15 58 B2
WSM BS23 124 C2
Charlton St EVILLE/WHL BS5 56 D4
Charlton Vw PTSHD/EG BS20 39 G3
Charminster Rd
MANG/FISH BS16 48 B5
Charmouth Rd
CBATH/BATHN BA1 101 G5
Charnell Rd MANG/FISH BS16 49 E4
Charnhill Brow
MANG/FISH BS16 49 G4
Charnhill Crs MANG/FISH BS16 49 F4
Charnhill Dr MANG/FISH BS16 49 F4
Charnhill Rdg MANG/FISH BS16 49 G4
Charnhill V MANG/FISH BS16 49 F4
Charnwood MANG/FISH BS16 49 G4
Charnwood Rd
HGRV/WHIT BS14 97 E1
Charterhouse Cl NAIL BS48 67 G5
Charterhouse Rd
EVILLE/WHL BS5 57 F3
Charter Rd MTN/WRL BS22 121 G3
Charter Wk HGRV/WHIT BS14 85 H3
Chasefield La MANG/FISH BS16 48 B4
Chase Rd KGWD/HNM BS15 58 D1
The Chase MANG/FISH BS16 48 C5
Chatcombe YATE/CS BS37 26 A3
Chatham Pk BATHSE BA2 109 F1
Chatham Rw CBATH/BATHN BA1 3 G2
Chatsworth Pk THNB/SVB BS35 8 D2
Chatsworth Rd
BRSG/KWL/STAPK BS4 74 B2
MANG/FISH BS16 48 B5
Chatterton Gn
HGRV/WHIT BS14 85 G5
Chatterton Rd YATE/CS BS37 25 H1
Chatterton Sq CBRIS/FH BS1 5 H7
Chaucer Rd BATHSE BA2 108 C3
WSM BS23 125 F2
Chaundey Gv
BMSTRD/HC/WWD BS13 84 C4
Cheapside CBRISNE BS2 56 B3
Cheapside St BMSTR BS3 73 G2
Cheap St CBATH/BATHN BA1 3 G4
Cheddar Cl NAIL BS48 79 G1
Cheddar Gv
BMSTRD/HC/WWD BS13 84 B1
Chedworth KGWD/HNM BS15 49 E5
YATE/CS BS37 25 F3
Chedworth Rd HORF/LLZ BS7 46 C2
Cheese La CBRISNE BS2 5 H4
Chelford Gv BRSTK/PCHW BS34 20 D2
Chelmer Gv KEYN BS31 88 C5
Chelmsford Wk
BRSG/KWL/STAPK BS4 75 E1
Chelsea Cl KEYN BS31 88 D4
Chelsea Pk EVILLE/WHL BS5 57 E3
Chelsea Rd
CBATH/BATHN BA1 101 H5
EVILLE/WHL BS5 56 D2
Chelston Rd
BRSG/KWL/STAPK BS4 85 E2
Chelswood Av
MTN/WRL BS22 121 H3
Cheltenham Crs
RDLND/MONT BS6 * 55 H2
Cheltenham Rd
RDLND/MONT BS6 55 H2
Cheltenham St BATHSE BA2 2 D6
Chelvey Est NAIL BS48 * 79 F5
Chelvey La NAIL BS48 79 F5
Chelvey Ri NAIL BS48 79 H1
Chelvey Rd NAIL BS48 78 D3
Chelvy Cl
BMSTRD/HC/WWD BS13 96 A1
Chelwood Dr BATHSE BA2 110 B1
Chelwood Rd AVONM BS11 42 D1
KEYN BS31 89 H5
Chepstow Pk MANG/FISH BS16 35 F4
Chepstow Rd
BRSG/KWL/STAPK BS4 85 E1
Chequers Cl
OLD/WMLY/WICK BS30 77 F3
Cherington KGWD/HNM BS15 75 G1
YATE/CS BS37 25 H4
Cherington Rd
HNBRY/STHM BS10 45 G1
NAIL BS48 67 H5
Cheriton Pl
HNLZ/SM/SNYPK/WT BS9 45 F1
OLD/WMLY/WICK BS30 60 A5
Cherry Av CLVDN BS21 65 E3
Cherry Cl YTN/CONG BS49 112 B3
Cherry Garden La
OLD/WMLY/WICK BS30 77 E4
Cherry Garden Rd
OLD/WMLY/WICK BS30 77 F5
Cherry Gdns
OLD/WMLY/WICK BS30 77 F5
Cherry Gv MANG/FISH BS16 49 G2
YTN/CONG BS49 112 B3
Cherry Hay CLVDN BS21 64 D4
Cherry La CBRIS/FH BS1 5 F1
Cherry Rd LGASH BS41 70 C4
NAIL BS48 67 E5
YATE/CS BS37 26 C1
Cherry Tree Cl KEYN BS31 87 H5
Cherrytree Ct MANG/FISH BS16 51 G3
Cherrytree Crs
MANG/FISH BS16 58 C1
Cherrytree Rd
MANG/FISH BS16 58 C1
Cherry Wd
OLD/WMLY/WICK BS30 77 E4
Cherrywood Ri
MTN/WRL BS22 122 C1
Cherrywood Rd
MTN/WRL BS22 122 C1
Chertsey Rd RDLND/MONT BS6 55 F2
Cherwell Cl THNB/SVB BS35 8 D5
Cherwell Rd KEYN BS31 88 D5
Chescombe Rd
YTN/CONG BS49 112 B4
Chesham Rd North
MTN/WRL BS22 121 G3
Chesham Rd South
MTN/WRL BS22 121 G3
Chesham Wy KGWD/HNM BS15 58 D2
Cheshire Cl YATE/CS BS37 14 A4
Chesle Cl PTSHD/EG BS20 38 C5
Cheslefield PTSHD/EG BS20 38 C5
Chesle Wy PTSHD/EG BS20 38 C5
Chesley Hl
OLD/WMLY/WICK BS30 60 D4
Chessel Cl ALMDB BS32 11 E5
Chessel Ct BMSTR BS3 * 72 C4
Chessel St BMSTR BS3 72 C3
Chessington Av
HGRV/WHIT BS14 86 A4
Chesterfield Av
RDLND/MONT BS6 56 A1
Chesterfield Rd
MANG/FISH BS16 49 E3
RDLND/MONT BS6 56 A1
Chestermaster Cl ALMDB BS32 10 C2
Chester Park Rd
MANG/FISH BS16 58 B1
Chester Rd EVILLE/WHL BS5 57 G2
Chesters
OLD/WMLY/WICK BS30 76 D2
Chester St EVILLE/WHL BS5 56 D1
Chesterton Dr NAIL BS48 67 H4
The Chestertons BATHSE BA2 104 A4
Chestnut Av MTN/WRL BS22 122 D2
Chestnut Cha NAIL BS48 67 H4
Chestnut Cl HGRV/WHIT BS14 86 D4
YTN/CONG BS49 114 D2
Chestnut Ct MANG/FISH BS16 49 G3
Chestnut Dr THNB/SVB BS35 8 D3
YATE/CS BS37 26 C1
YTN/CONG BS49 113 E2
Chestnut Gv BATHSE BA2 107 H3
CLVDN BS21 65 E1
Chestnut Rd KGWD/HNM BS15 49 F5
LGASH BS41 71 E4
MANG/FISH BS16 48 D2
Chestnut Springs
YATE/CS BS37 13 F2
Chestnut Wk
BMSTRD/HC/WWD BS13 84 B3
KEYN BS31 99 F1
Chestnut Wy KGWD/HNM BS15 49 F5
Chetwode Cl
HNBRY/STHM BS10 31 H2
Chevening Cl
BRSTK/PCHW BS34 33 F1
Cheviot Dr THNB/SVB BS35 9 F4
Cheviot Wy
OLD/WMLY/WICK BS30 77 F1
Chewton Cl MANG/FISH BS16 48 B5
Cheyne Rd
HNLZ/SM/SNYPK/WT BS9 44 B2
Chichester Wy
OMX/HUT/LCK BS24 122 D3
YATE/CS BS37 13 H4
Chillington Ct
BRSTK/PCHW BS34 20 A1
Chillwood Cl YATE/CS BS37 12 C4
Chiltern Cl HGRV/WHIT BS14 86 A5
OLD/WMLY/WICK BS30 77 F1
Chiltern Pk THNB/SVB BS35 9 E4
Chilton Rd
BRSG/KWL/STAPK BS4 85 H1
CBATH/BATHN BA1 103 E3
The Chimes NAIL BS48 78 D1
The Chine MANG/FISH BS16 47 F3
Chine Vw MANG/FISH BS16 35 F5
Chiphouse Rd
KGWD/HNM BS15 59 E1
Chipperfield Dr
KGWD/HNM BS15 59 F2
Chipping Cross CLVDN BS21 64 C4
The Chippings
MANG/FISH BS16 47 F3
Chisbury St EVILLE/WHL BS5 47 E5
Chittening Rd AVONM BS11 17 E3
Chock La
HNLZ/SM/SNYPK/WT BS9 45 E1
Christchurch Av
MANG/FISH BS16 48 D3
Christchurch Cl NAIL BS48 67 F4
Christchurch La
MANG/FISH BS16 48 D2
Christchurch Pth South
WSM BS23 * 7 F3
Christchurch Rd
CFTN/FAIL BS8 55 E4
Christian Cl MTN/WRL BS22 117 H5
Christina Ter CFTN/FAIL BS8 * 72 B1
Christmas St CBRIS/FH BS1 4 E3
Chubb Cl
OLD/WMLY/WICK BS30 76 C1
Church Av EVILLE/WHL BS5 56 D2
HNLZ/SM/SNYPK/WT BS9 44 C4
OLD/WMLY/WICK BS30 60 A4
Church Cl BATHSE BA2 104 A2
CBATH/BATHN BA1 104 C2
CLVDN BS21 64 A3
FRCTL/WBN BS36 23 H2
PTSHD/EG BS20 39 H3
YTN/CONG BS49 112 C4
Church Dr YTN/CONG BS49 114 D2
Churchfarm Cl YATE/CS BS37 14 B4
Church Farm Rd
MANG/FISH BS16 49 H2
Church Hayes Cl NAIL BS48 79 F1
Church Hayes Dr NAIL BS48 79 F1
Church Hl
BRSG/KWL/STAPK BS4 74 D4
Churchill Av CLVDN BS21 64 C3
Churchill Cl CLVDN BS21 64 C3
OLD/WMLY/WICK BS30 76 D1
Churchill Dr
HNLZ/SM/SNYPK/WT BS9 44 B1
Churchill Rd
BRSG/KWL/STAPK BS4 74 B2
WSM BS23 7 J5
Churchland Wy
OMX/HUT/LCK BS24 123 E3
Church La BATHSE BA2 109 F3
BMSTR BS3 72 D2
CBATH/BATHN BA1 91 E5
CBRIS/FH BS1 5 H5
CFTN/FAIL BS8 4 A5
CLVDN BS21 66 C2
EVILLE/WHL BS5 57 F3
FRCTL/WBN BS36 24 A4
FRCTL/WBN BS36 22 C4
HGRV/WHIT BS14 97 E1
HNBRY/STHM BS10 30 C3
LGASH BS41 71 F4
MANG/FISH BS16 35 E3
NAIL BS48 80 A4
NAIL BS48 66 D5
OLD/WMLY/WICK BS30 89 H2
OMX/HUT/LCK BS24 126 A4
PTSHD/EG BS20 41 G5
YTN/CONG BS49 112 C4
Church Leaze AVONM BS11 42 D2
Church Mdw HGRV/WHIT BS14 97 F1
Church Pde
BRSG/KWL/STAPK BS4 74 D4
Churchpath Rd
PTSHD/EG BS20 42 C4
Church Pl PTSHD/EG BS20 42 C4
Church Ri
BLAG/CWMG/WR BS40 93 H5
Church Rd ALMDB BS32 10 C2
BATHSE BA2 111 G1
BLAG/CWMG/WR BS40 93 H5
BMSTR BS3 72 D3
BMSTRD/HC/WWD BS13 84 B4
BRSTK/PCHW BS34 32 C2
CBATH/BATHN BA1 101 H3
CFTN/FAIL BS8 53 G3
EVILLE/WHL BS5 57 F3
FRCTL/WBN BS36 35 E1
HGRV/WHIT BS14 86 A5
HNLZ/SM/SNYPK/WT BS9 44 B5
HORF/LLZ BS7 46 A2
KGWD/HNM BS15 75 G1
LGASH BS41 94 C2
MANG/FISH BS16 58 D1
MTN/WRL BS22 122 A1
OLD/WMLY/WICK BS30 89 H1
OLD/WMLY/WICK BS30 61 F5
PLTN/PENS BS39 96 D5
PTSHD/EG BS20 42 A4
THNB/SVB BS35 19 E1
THNB/SVB BS35 8 C2
YATE/CS BS37 14 A5
YTN/CONG BS49 112 C4
Church Rd North
PTSHD/EG BS20 39 H3
Church Rd South
PTSHD/EG BS20 39 H4
Churchside MANG/FISH BS16 48 B1
Church St CBATH/BATHN BA1 104 C2
CBATH/BATHN BA1 101 G3
CBRIS/FH BS1 5 H5
EVILLE/WHL BS5 56 D5
Church Town NAIL BS48 80 B4
Church Vw ALMDB BS32 10 B3
NAIL BS48 68 A4
Church Wk PTSHD/EG BS20 42 C4
Churchward Cl
KGWD/HNM BS15 75 G1
Churchward Rd
MTN/WRL BS22 118 A5
YATE/CS BS37 13 F4
Churchways HGRV/WHIT BS14 86 B5
Churchways Av HORF/LLZ BS7 46 A2
Churchways Crs HORF/LLZ BS7 46 A2
Churclands Rd BMSTR BS3 72 C4
Churston Cl HGRV/WHIT BS14 96 D1
The Circle BATHSE BA2 107 G4
Circular Rd
HNLZ/SM/SNYPK/WT BS9 54 C1
Circus Ms CBATH/BATHN BA1 2 E2
Circus Pl CBATH/BATHN BA1 2 E2
The Circus CBATH/BATHN BA1 2 E2
City Rd CBRISNE BS2 56 A3
City Vw CBATH/BATHN BA1 102 D4
The Clamp
OLD/WMLY/WICK BS30 77 F3
Clanage Rd BMSTR BS3 71 H2
Clapton La PTSHD/EG BS20 39 H5
Clapton Wk
HNLZ/SM/SNYPK/WT BS9 43 H3
Clara Cross La BATHSE BA2 110 C1
Clare Av HORF/LLZ BS7 45 G5
Clare Gdns BATHSE BA2 110 B1
Claremont Av HORF/LLZ BS7 45 G5
Claremont Blds
CBATH/BATHN BA1 102 D3
Claremont Gdns CLVDN BS21 65 E4
Claremont Rd
CBATH/BATHN BA1 103 E3
HORF/LLZ BS7 45 H5
Claremont St EVILLE/WHL BS5 56 C2
Claremont Ter
CBATH/BATHN BA1 * 102 D3
Claremont Wk
CBATH/BATHN BA1 102 D3
Clarence Av MANG/FISH BS16 49 E3
Clarence Gdns
MANG/FISH BS16 49 E3
Clarence Grove Rd WSM BS23 124 D1
Clarence Pl
CBATH/BATHN BA1 101 G5
CBRISNE BS2 4 D1
Clarence Rd CBRIS/FH BS1 73 F2
CBRISNE BS2 56 C4
KGWD/HNM BS15 58 B2
MANG/FISH BS16 48 D3
Clarence Rd East WSM BS23 124 D1
Clarence Rd North WSM BS23 124 C1
Clarence Rd South WSM BS23 124 C1
Clarence St
CBATH/BATHN BA1 102 D4
Clarence Ter BATHSE BA2 109 G3
Clarendon Rd BATHSE BA2 3 J7
RDLND/MONT BS6 55 G1
WSM BS23 7 G3
Clarendon Vls BATHSE BA2 3 J7
Clare Rd EVILLE/WHL BS5 56 D1
KGWD/HNM BS15 58 C1
RDLND/MONT BS6 55 H2
Clare St CBRIS/FH BS1 4 E4
EVILLE/WHL BS5 57 E3
Clare Wk THNB/SVB BS35 8 C2
Clark Cl NAIL BS48 67 H4
Clark Dr MANG/FISH BS16 47 H2
Clarken Cl NAIL BS48 67 F5
Clarken Coombe LGASH BS41 70 D3
Clarke St BMSTR BS3 73 E2
Clarkson Av MTN/WRL BS22 121 H2
Clark St EVILLE/WHL BS5 56 C3
Clarks Wy BATHSE BA2 107 H5
Clatworthy Dr
HGRV/WHIT BS14 85 H2
Claude Av BATHSE BA2 107 H3
Claude Ter BATHSE BA2 107 H2
Clavell Rd HNBRY/STHM BS10 30 D3
Claverham Cl YTN/CONG BS49 112 D3
Claverham Pk
YTN/CONG BS49 113 F2
Claverham Rd
MANG/FISH BS16 48 A3
YTN/CONG BS49 113 E3
Claverton Blds BATHSE BA2 * 3 H7
Claverton Ct BATHSE BA2 109 H3
Claverton Down Rd
BATHSE BA2 109 G5
Claverton Rd KEYN BS31 99 E2
Claverton Rd West KEYN BS31 99 E1
Claverton St BATHSE BA2 3 G6
Clay Bottom EVILLE/WHL BS5 57 F1
Clayfield YATE/CS BS37 14 A2
Clayfield Rd
BRSG/KWL/STAPK BS4 74 D3
Clay Hl EVILLE/WHL BS5 57 G1
Clay La BRSTK/PCHW BS34 21 E3
OLD/WMLY/WICK BS30 77 G5
WUE GL12 9 F3
Claymore Cresent
KGWD/HNM BS15 58 B2
Claypiece Rd
BMSTRD/HC/WWD BS13 84 A5
Claypit Hl YATE/CS BS37 26 D3
Clay Pit Rd RDLND/MONT BS6 45 E5
Claypool Rd KGWD/HNM BS15 58 D4
Clayton Cl PTSHD/EG BS20 40 A4
Clayton St AVONM BS11 28 A4
EVILLE/WHL BS5 56 D3
Cleave St CBRISNE BS2 56 C1
Cleeve Av MANG/FISH BS16 49 E1
Cleeve Ct MANG/FISH BS16 48 D1
Cleevedale Rd BATHSE BA2 111 E1
Cleeve Dr YTN/CONG BS49 113 G3
Cleeve Gdns MANG/FISH BS16 48 D1
Cleeve Gn BATHSE BA2 107 E1
Cleeve Gv KEYN BS31 88 A4
Cleeve Hl MANG/FISH BS16 48 D1
Cleeve Hill Extension
MANG/FISH BS16 49 E2
Cleeve Hill Rd
YTN/CONG BS49 113 H4
Cleeve La
OLD/WMLY/WICK BS30 61 H2
Cleeve Lawns MANG/FISH BS16 48 D1
Cleeve Lodge Rd
MANG/FISH BS16 49 E1
Cleeve Park Rd
MANG/FISH BS16 48 D1
Cleeve Pl NAIL BS48 67 H5
Cleeve Rd
BRSG/KWL/STAPK BS4 74 A3
MANG/FISH BS16 49 E2
YATE/CS BS37 26 A1
Cleeves Ct
OLD/WMLY/WICK BS30 76 C4
Cleevewood Pk
MANG/FISH BS16 * 34 D5
Cleeve Wood Rd
MANG/FISH BS16 34 C5
Clement St CBRISNE BS2 5 J1
Clermont Cl BRSTK/PCHW BS34 20 B2
Clevedale MANG/FISH BS16 48 D1
Clevedon La CLVDN BS21 63 H5
Clevedon Rd CFTN/FAIL BS8 69 E1
CLVDN BS21 66 B2
HORF/LLZ BS7 45 H4
NAIL BS48 81 F1
NAIL BS48 67 F3
PTSHD/EG BS20 39 G5
WSM BS23 6 D7
Clevedon Ter
RDLND/MONT BS6 55 H3
Cleveland Cl THNB/SVB BS35 9 F4
Cleveland Ct BATHSE BA2 109 F1
Cleveland Pl East
CBATH/BATHN BA1 3 H1
Cleveland Pl West
CBATH/BATHN BA1 3 G1
Cleveland Rw BATHSE BA2 * 103 E4
Cleveland Wk BATHSE BA2 109 F1
Cleve Rd BRSTK/PCHW BS34 32 C1
Clewson Ri HGRV/WHIT BS14 96 C1
Cliff Court Dr
MANG/FISH BS16 48 B1
Clifford Gdns AVONM BS11 43 E2
Clifford Rd MANG/FISH BS16 48 C4
Cliff Rd MTN/WRL BS22 121 F1
Clift House Rd BMSTR BS3 72 B2
Clifton Av WSM BS23 124 D1
Clifton Cl CFTN/FAIL BS8 54 D4
Clifton Down CFTN/FAIL BS8 54 D3
Clifton Down Rd
CFTN/FAIL BS8 55 E4
Clifton High Gv
HNLZ/SM/SNYPK/WT BS9 44 C3
Clifton Hl CFTN/FAIL BS8 55 E5
Clifton Pk CFTN/FAIL BS8 54 D4
Clifton Park Rd CFTN/FAIL BS8 54 D3
Clifton Pl EVILLE/WHL BS5 56 C3
Clifton Rd CFTN/FAIL BS8 55 E5
Clifton St BMSTR BS3 72 D3
EVILLE/WHL BS5 56 C3
Clifton V CFTN/FAIL BS8 55 E5
Clifton Vale Cl CFTN/FAIL BS8 55 E5
Clifton Vw BMSTR BS3 73 G2
Cliftonwood Crs CFTN/FAIL BS8 4 A5
Clifton Wood Rd CFTN/FAIL BS8 4 A4
Cliftonwood Ter
CFTN/FAIL BS8 55 E5
Clift Pl CBRIS/FH BS1 5 F6
Clift Rd BMSTR BS3 72 B2
Clinton Rd BMSTR BS3 72 D4
Clive Rd HGRV/WHIT BS14 86 B2
Cloisters Rd FRCTL/WBN BS36 23 E4
Clonmel Rd
BRSG/KWL/STAPK BS4 73 E5
Closemead CLVDN BS21 64 D4
The Close BRSTK/PCHW BS34 21 E4
FRCTL/WBN BS36 24 A4
HNBRY/STHM BS10 18 D5
MANG/FISH BS16 48 D5
THNB/SVB BS35 8 C4
Clothier Rd
BRSG/KWL/STAPK BS4 75 E4
Clouds Hill Av EVILLE/WHL BS5 57 G3
Clouds Hill Rd EVILLE/WHL BS5 57 H3
Clovelly Cl EVILLE/WHL BS5 57 H3
Clovelly Rd EVILLE/WHL BS5 57 H3
MTN/WRL BS22 122 D1
Clover Cl CLVDN BS21 65 F2
Clover Ct MTN/WRL BS22 122 A4
Cloverdale Dr
OLD/WMLY/WICK BS30 76 D3
Clover Gnd
HNLZ/SM/SNYPK/WT BS9 31 F5
Cloverlea Rd
OLD/WMLY/WICK BS30 77 F1
Clover Leaze ALMDB BS32 21 F4
Clover Rd MTN/WRL BS22 117 H2
Clyde Av KEYN BS31 88 C5
Clyde Gdns BATHSE BA2 107 G1
EVILLE/WHL BS5 58 B5
Clyde Gv BRSTK/PCHW BS34 32 B3
Clyde La RDLND/MONT BS6 55 F1
Clyde Ms RDLND/MONT BS6 55 G1
Clyde Rd BRSG/KWL/STAPK BS4 73 H3
FRCTL/WBN BS36 23 H2
RDLND/MONT BS6 55 F1
Clyde Ter BMSTR BS3 72 D3
BRSG/KWL/STAPK BS4 73 H3
Clynder Gv CLVDN BS21 62 C4
Coalbridge Cl MTN/WRL BS22 122 C1
Coaley Rd AVONM BS11 42 D3
Coalpit Rd CBATH/BATHN BA1 91 F5
Coalsack La FRCTL/WBN BS36 35 H2
Coalville Rd FRCTL/WBN BS36 24 B3
Coape Rd HGRV/WHIT BS14 87 E4
Coates Gv NAIL BS48 67 H4
Coates Wk
BRSG/KWL/STAPK BS4 85 E3
Cobblestone Ms CFTN/FAIL BS8 55 E4
Cobden St EVILLE/WHL BS5 57 E4
Coberley KGWD/HNM BS15 58 C5
Cobhorn Dr
BMSTRD/HC/WWD BS13 84 A5
Cobley Cft CLVDN BS21 64 C5
Cobourg Rd RDLND/MONT BS6 56 B2
Cobthorn Wy YTN/CONG BS49 115 E1
Cock Rd KGWD/HNM BS15 59 E5
Codrington Pl CFTN/FAIL BS8 55 E4
Codrington Rd HORF/LLZ BS7 45 H5
Cogan Rd MANG/FISH BS16 49 E5
Cogsall Rd HGRV/WHIT BS14 87 E3
Coker Rd MTN/WRL BS22 122 D1
Colbourne Rd BATHSE BA2 110 A2
Colchester Crs
BRSG/KWL/STAPK BS4 85 E2
Coldharbour La
MANG/FISH BS16 33 G4
WSM BS23 124 C3
Coldharbour Rd
RDLND/MONT BS6 45 F5
Coldpark Gdns
BMSTRD/HC/WWD BS13 83 H4
Coldpark Rd
BMSTRD/HC/WWD BS13 83 H4
Coldrick Cl HGRV/WHIT BS14 96 C1
Colebrook Rd
KGWD/HNM BS15 58 C3
Coleford Rd
HNBRY/STHM BS10 31 H5
Colehouse La CLVDN BS21 64 C5
Colemead
BMSTRD/HC/WWD BS13 84 C4
Coleridge Rd CLVDN BS21 64 C2
EVILLE/WHL BS5 47 E5
WSM BS23 125 F3
Coleridge Vale Rd East
CLVDN BS21 64 D2
Coleridge Vale Rd North
CLVDN BS21 64 C3
Coleridge Vale Rd South
CLVDN BS21 64 C3
Coleridge Vale Rd West
CLVDN BS21 64 C3
Cole Rd CBRISNE BS2 56 D5
Colesborne Cl YATE/CS BS37 25 H2
Coleshill Dr
BMSTRD/HC/WWD BS13 84 C4
Colin Cl THNB/SVB BS35 8 C3
College Av MANG/FISH BS16 48 A3
College Ct MANG/FISH BS16 48 A3
College Flds CFTN/FAIL BS8 54 D3
College Gn CBRIS/FH BS1 4 D4
College Park Dr
HNBRY/STHM BS10 30 D4
College Rd CBATH/BATHN BA1 102 B3
CFTN/FAIL BS8 54 D3
HNLZ/SM/SNYPK/WT BS9 45 E1
MANG/FISH BS16 48 A3
College Sq CBRIS/FH BS1 4 C5
College St CBRIS/FH BS1 4 C4
College Vw
CBATH/BATHN BA1 * 102 D3
College Wy BRSTK/PCHW BS34 32 D1
Collet Cl MTN/WRL BS22 118 B4
Collett Cl KGWD/HNM BS15 75 G1
Collett Wy YATE/CS BS37 13 G4
Colliers Break MANG/FISH BS16 49 H3
Collingwood Av
KGWD/HNM BS15 59 E2
Collingwood Cl KEYN BS31 99 F2
MTN/WRL BS22 117 F4
Collingwood Rd
RDLND/MONT BS6 55 F2
Collin Rd BRSG/KWL/STAPK BS4 74 C2
Collins Av BRSTK/PCHW BS34 21 E4

Collinson Rd
BMSTRD/HC/WWD BS13 84 C4
Collins St AVONM BS11 28 B5
Colliter Crs BMSTR BS3 72 B4
Collum La MTN/WRL BS22 117 E1
Coln Sq THNB/SVB BS35 8 D4
Colombo Crs WSM BS23 124 D3
Colston Av CBRIS/FH BS1 4 E4
Colston Cl FRCTL/WBN BS36 35 E1
MANG/FISH BS16 48 D5
Colston Dl MANG/FISH BS16 47 G4
Colston Fort CBRISNE BS2 * 55 H3
Colston Hl MANG/FISH BS16 47 F4
Colston Pde CBRIS/FH BS1 5 G6
Colston Rd EVILLE/WHL BS5 57 E2
Colston St CBRIS/FH BS1 4 E3
MANG/FISH BS16 48 D5
Colston Yd CBRISNE BS2 4 E2
Colthurst Dr KGWD/HNM BS15 76 A1
Colts Gn YATE/CS BS37 27 G2
Colwyn Rd EVILLE/WHL BS5 57 E2
Combe Av PTSHD/EG BS20 39 G2
Combe Flds PTSHD/EG BS20 39 G2
Combe Gv CBATH/BATHN BA1 101 G5
Combe Hay La BATHSE BA2 110 A3
Combe Pk CBATH/BATHN BA1 101 H4
Combermere THNB/SVB BS35 9 E4
Combe Rd BATHSE BA2 111 F1
PTSHD/EG BS20 39 H3
Combe Road Cl BATHSE BA2 111 F1
Combeside BATHSE BA2 108 D4
Combe Side NAIL BS48 79 H2
Combfactory La
EVILLE/WHL BS5 56 D3
Comb Paddock
HNLZ/SM/SNYPK/WT BS9 45 F1
Comfortable Pl
CBATH/BATHN BA1 2 B3
Commercial Rd CBRIS/FH BS1 4 E7
Commercial Wy
MTN/WRL BS22 123 E1
The Common (East)
ALMDB BS32 21 E1
Commonfield Rd AVONM BS11 29 H4
Common Ga YATE/CS BS37 * 15 G3
Common La PTSHD/EG BS20 52 B2
Common Mead La
MANG/FISH BS16 34 A4
Commonmead La
YATE/CS BS37 27 H1
Common Rd FRCTL/WBN BS36 23 F3
KGWD/HNM BS15 75 G3
The Common
BRSTK/PCHW BS34 20 D1
MANG/FISH BS16 48 B1
Compton Dr
HNLZ/SM/SNYPK/WT BS9 44 A1
OMX/HUT/LCK BS24 122 B4
Compton Gn KEYN BS31 88 B5
Compton Md NAIL BS48 * 82 A5
Compton St EVILLE/WHL BS5 57 E4
Comyn Wk MANG/FISH BS16 48 A3
Concorde Dr CLVDN BS21 64 B4
HNBRY/STHM BS10 31 F3
Concorde Rd
BRSTK/PCHW BS34 20 A3
The Concourse
BRSG/KWL/STAPK BS4 74 C4
Condor Cl MTN/WRL BS22 122 A3
Condover Rd
BRSG/KWL/STAPK BS4 75 E3
Conduit Pl CBRISNE BS2 56 C2
Conduit Rd CBRISNE BS2 56 C2
Conference Av PTSHD/EG BS20 40 A3
Conference Cl PTSHD/EG BS20 40 B4
Congleton Rd EVILLE/WHL BS5 57 F3
Conham Hl KGWD/HNM BS15 75 F1
Conham Rd KGWD/HNM BS15 75 E1
Conifer Cl FRCTL/WBN BS36 23 G1
MANG/FISH BS16 48 D2
Conifer Wy
OMX/HUT/LCK BS24 126 B1
Coniston Av
HNLZ/SM/SNYPK/WT BS9 44 C2
Coniston Cl
OLD/WMLY/WICK BS30 60 B5
Coniston Crs WSM BS23 125 E2
Coniston Rd
BRSTK/PCHW BS34 20 A2
Connaught Pl WSM BS23 6 D2
Connaught Rd
BRSG/KWL/STAPK BS4 85 F1
Connection Rd BATHSE BA2 107 F1
Constable Cl KEYN BS31 88 C3
Constable Dr MTN/WRL BS22 117 G5
Constable Rd HORF/LLZ BS7 46 C2
Constantine Av
BRSTK/PCHW BS34 21 G5
Constitution Hl CFTN/FAIL BS8 4 A4
Convent Cl HNBRY/STHM BS10 30 B2
Convocation Av BATHSE BA2 109 H2
Conway Gn KEYN BS31 98 B1
Conway Rd
BRSG/KWL/STAPK BS4 74 B2
Conygar Cl CLVDN BS21 62 D5
Conygre Rd BRSTK/PCHW BS34 32 D2
Cook Cl OLD/WMLY/WICK BS30 77 F2
Cooke's Dr THNB/SVB BS35 19 E1
Cooks Cl ALMDB BS32 11 E4
Cook's Folly Rd
HNLZ/SM/SNYPK/WT BS9 54 B1
Cooks Gdns NAIL BS48 68 A4
Cooks La FRCTL/WBN BS36 36 B2
Cook's La CLVDN BS21 65 H3
Cooksley Rd EVILLE/WHL BS5 57 E3
Cook St AVONM BS11 28 B5
Cookworthy Cl
EVILLE/WHL BS5 56 D5
Coombe Av THNB/SVB BS35 8 C2
Coombe Bridge Av
HNLZ/SM/SNYPK/WT BS9 44 B2
Coombe Brook Cl
KGWD/HNM BS15 58 B2
Coombe Cl HNBRY/STHM BS10 30 B2
Coombe Dl
HNLZ/SM/SNYPK/WT BS9 44 A2
NAIL BS48 92 B4
Coombe Gdns
HNLZ/SM/SNYPK/WT BS9 44 C2
Coombe Hay La BATHSE BA2 110 A2
Coombe La CFTN/FAIL BS8 52 A1
HNLZ/SM/SNYPK/WT BS9 44 B2
Coombe Rd EVILLE/WHL BS5 57 E1
NAIL BS48 67 E5
WSM BS23 6 E2
Coombe Rocke
HNLZ/SM/SNYPK/WT BS9 * 44 B2
Coombes Wy
OLD/WMLY/WICK BS30 77 G2
Coombe Wy
HNBRY/STHM BS10 30 D4
Cooperage La BMSTR BS3 4 A7
Cooperage Rd EVILLE/WHL BS5 57 E4
Co-Operation Rd
EVILLE/WHL BS5 57 E2
Cooper Rd
HNLZ/SM/SNYPK/WT BS9 44 D1
THNB/SVB BS35 8 C5
Coopers Dr YATE/CS BS37 14 B2
The Coots HGRV/WHIT BS14 86 D3
Copeland Dr HGRV/WHIT BS14 86 A4
Cope Pk ALMDB BS32 11 E2
Copford La LGASH BS41 71 E5
Copley Ct KGWD/HNM BS15 76 B1
Copley Gdns HORF/LLZ BS7 46 D2
MTN/WRL BS22 122 C1
Copperfield Dr
MTN/WRL BS22 117 G4
The Coppice ALMDB BS32 21 G3
BMSTRD/HC/WWD BS13 83 H5
Copse Cl OMX/HUT/LCK BS24 125 F5
Copseland BATHSE BA2 109 G2
Copse Rd
BRSG/KWL/STAPK BS4 74 A3
CLVDN BS21 64 C1
KEYN BS31 89 F5
The Copse MTN/WRL BS22 123 G1
Copthorne Cl HGRV/WHIT BS14 86 A4
Coralberry Dr MTN/WRL BS22 122 C2
Corbet Cl AVONM BS11 29 H3
Corbett Cl YATE/CS BS37 14 B3
Cordwell Wk
HNBRY/STHM BS10 45 H1
Corey Cl CBRISNE BS2 56 B2
Corfe Cl NAIL BS48 67 E5
Corfe Crs KEYN BS31 88 B4
Corfe Pl OLD/WMLY/WICK BS30 77 E5
Corfe Rd
BRSG/KWL/STAPK BS4 85 E2
Coriander Dr ALMDB BS32 22 A3
Coriander Wk EVILLE/WHL BS5 57 E1
Corinum Cl MANG/FISH BS16 50 A2
Cork Pl CBATH/BATHN BA1 * 2 A3
Cork St CBATH/BATHN BA1 2 A2
Cork Ter CBATH/BATHN BA1 2 A2
Cormorant Cl MTN/WRL BS22 122 C2
Corner Cft CLVDN BS21 64 D4
Cornfield Cl ALMDB BS32 21 E1
The Cornfields
MTN/WRL BS22 117 G3
Cornhill Dr HGRV/WHIT BS14 85 H2
Cornish Gv HGRV/WHIT BS14 86 D3
Cornish Rd HGRV/WHIT BS14 86 D3
Cornish Wk HGRV/WHIT BS14 86 D3
Cornleaze
BMSTRD/HC/WWD BS13 84 B4
Corn St CBATH/BATHN BA1 3 F5
CBRIS/FH BS1 5 F4
Cornwall Crs YATE/CS BS37 14 B4
Cornwallis Av CFTN/FAIL BS8 54 D5
MTN/WRL BS22 117 F4
Cornwallis Crs CFTN/FAIL BS8 54 D5
Cornwallis Gv CFTN/FAIL BS8 54 D5
Cornwall Rd HORF/LLZ BS7 45 H4
Coronation Av BATHSE BA2 107 H4
KEYN BS31 88 A5
MANG/FISH BS16 48 A4
Coronation Cl
OLD/WMLY/WICK BS30 76 D1
Coronation Pl CBRIS/FH BS1 * 5 F4
Coronation Rd BMSTR BS3 72 B2
CBATH/BATHN BA1 2 A2
KGWD/HNM BS15 59 F4
MANG/FISH BS16 49 E3
MTN/WRL BS22 122 B1
OLD/WMLY/WICK BS30 77 E1
Corondale Rd MTN/WRL BS22 122 A3
The Corridor
CBATH/BATHN BA1 * 3 G4
Corsley Wk
BRSG/KWL/STAPK BS4 85 G1
Corston Dr BATHSE BA2 106 A1
Corston La BATHSE BA2 99 H4
Corston Wk AVONM BS11 42 C1
Cossham Cl THNB/SVB BS35 8 D2
Cossham Rd EVILLE/WHL BS5 57 F3
MANG/FISH BS16 51 G4
Cossham Wk EVILLE/WHL BS5 58 A2
Cossington Rd
BRSG/KWL/STAPK BS4 85 G1
Cossins Rd RDLND/MONT BS6 45 F5
Costiland Dr
BMSTRD/HC/WWD BS13 84 A3
Cote Dr
HNLZ/SM/SNYPK/WT BS9 45 E4
Cote House La
HNLZ/SM/SNYPK/WT BS9 45 E3
Cote La
HNLZ/SM/SNYPK/WT BS9 45 E3
Cote Lea Pk
HNLZ/SM/SNYPK/WT BS9 45 E1
Cote Paddock
HNLZ/SM/SNYPK/WT BS9 44 D4
Cote Pk
HNLZ/SM/SNYPK/WT BS9 44 C2
Cote Rd
HNLZ/SM/SNYPK/WT BS9 45 E4
Cotham Brow
RDLND/MONT BS6 55 H1
Cotham Gdns
RDLND/MONT BS6 55 F2
Cotham Gv RDLND/MONT BS6 55 H2
Cotham Hl RDLND/MONT BS6 55 F2
Cotham Lawn Rd
RDLND/MONT BS6 55 G3
Cotham Pk RDLND/MONT BS6 55 G2
Cotham Park Man
RDLND/MONT BS6 * 55 G2
Cotham Pk North
RDLND/MONT BS6 55 G2
Cotham Pl RDLND/MONT BS6 * 55 G3
Cotham Rd RDLND/MONT BS6 55 G3
Cotham Rd South
RDLND/MONT BS6 55 H3
Cotham Side
RDLND/MONT BS6 55 H2
Cotham V RDLND/MONT BS6 55 G2
Cotman Wk HORF/LLZ BS7 46 D2
MTN/WRL BS22 122 C1
Cotrith Gv HNBRY/STHM BS10 30 C2
Cotswold Cl PTSHD/EG BS20 39 H4
Cotswold Rd BATHSE BA2 108 A3
BMSTR BS3 73 E3
YATE/CS BS37 26 D2
Cotswold Vw BATHSE BA2 107 G2
KGWD/HNM BS15 58 D1
Cotswold Wy
CBATH/BATHN BA1 2 C2
Cottage Gdns EVILLE/WHL BS5 58 A4
Cottage Pl CBRISNE BS2 4 E1
Cottington Ct
KGWD/HNM BS15 76 B1
Cottisford Rd EVILLE/WHL BS5 46 D4
Cottle Gdns HGRV/WHIT BS14 87 E3
Cottle Rd HGRV/WHIT BS14 87 E3
Cotton Mill La EVILLE/WHL BS5 57 E5
Cottonwood Dr
OLD/WMLY/WICK BS30 76 D3
Cottrell Av KGWD/HNM BS15 58 B3
Cottrell Rd EVILLE/WHL BS5 47 E5
Coulson Dr MTN/WRL BS22 118 A5
Coulson's Cl HGRV/WHIT BS14 96 D1
Coulson's Rd HGRV/WHIT BS14 96 C1
Coulson Wk KGWD/HNM BS15 58 C1
Counterpool Rd
KGWD/HNM BS15 58 C4
Counterslip CBRIS/FH BS1 5 G4
Counterslip Gdns
HGRV/WHIT BS14 86 B3
Countess Wk MANG/FISH BS16 47 F2
County St
BRSG/KWL/STAPK BS4 73 H2
County Wy BRSTK/PCHW BS34 34 A1
Court Av BRSTK/PCHW BS34 21 H5
YTN/CONG BS49 112 B4
Court Cl HORF/LLZ BS7 46 A1
PTSHD/EG BS20 39 H4
The Court Cl NAIL BS48 80 B4
Courtenay Rd KEYN BS31 98 B2
Courteney Cresent
BRSG/KWL/STAPK BS4 85 E2
Court Farm Rd
HGRV/WHIT BS14 96 C1
KGWD/HNM BS15 76 A5
Courtfield Gv MANG/FISH BS16 48 A4
Court Gdns
CBATH/BATHN BA1 104 B1
YATE/CS BS37 * 26 A2
Courtlands ALMDB BS32 21 E1
KEYN BS31 88 B4
Courtlands La BMSTR BS3 71 H2
Court La CBATH/BATHN BA1 104 C2
CLVDN BS21 65 G2
Courtney Rd KGWD/HNM BS15 59 E4
Courtney Wy KGWD/HNM BS15 59 G4
Court Pl MTN/WRL BS22 122 C1
Court Rd FRCTL/WBN BS36 23 F2
HORF/LLZ BS7 46 B2
KGWD/HNM BS15 58 D4
MTN/WRL BS22 116 B3
Courtside Ms
RDLND/MONT BS6 55 G2
Court Vw
OLD/WMLY/WICK BS30 61 G5
Court View Cl ALMDB BS32 10 C2
Cousins Cl HNBRY/STHM BS10 30 B2
Cousins La EVILLE/WHL BS5 57 H4
Cousins Ms
BRSG/KWL/STAPK BS4 57 H5
Cousins Wy MANG/FISH BS16 35 G5
Couzens Cl YATE/CS BS37 14 D5
Couzens Pl BRSTK/PCHW BS34 21 H5
Coventry Wk
BRSG/KWL/STAPK BS4 57 H5
Cowdray Rd
BRSG/KWL/STAPK BS4 85 E2
Cowhorn Hl
OLD/WMLY/WICK BS30 77 F2
Cowler Wk
BMSTRD/HC/WWD BS13 84 A5
Cowling Dr HGRV/WHIT BS14 86 B4
Cowling Rd HGRV/WHIT BS14 86 B4
Cowper Rd RDLND/MONT BS6 55 F2
Cowper St EVILLE/WHL BS5 57 E4
Cox Ct OLD/WMLY/WICK BS30 76 C2
Coxley Dr CBATH/BATHN BA1 103 E2
Coxway CLVDN BS21 65 E3
Crabtree Cl LGASH BS41 94 C3
Crabtree La LGASH BS41 94 B3
Crabtree Pk CLVDN BS21 * 64 C4
Crabtree Wk EVILLE/WHL BS5 57 F1
Cradock Cl
OLD/WMLY/WICK BS30 76 D2
Cranberry Wk
HNLZ/SM/SNYPK/WT BS9 30 A5
Cranbourne Cha WSM BS23 7 K1
Cranbourne Rd
BRSTK/PCHW BS34 20 B3
Cranbrook Rd
RDLND/MONT BS6 45 G5
Crandale Rd BATHSE BA2 2 A6
Crandell Cl HNBRY/STHM BS10 30 D1
Crane Cl KGWD/HNM BS15 59 H3
Cranford Cl MTN/WRL BS22 122 A2
Cranham YATE/CS BS37 25 G3
Cranham Cl KGWD/HNM BS15 59 F1
Cranham Dr
BRSTK/PCHW BS34 21 E1
Cranham Rd
HNBRY/STHM BS10 31 G5
Cranhill Rd CBATH/BATHN BA1 2 B1
Cranleigh BATHSE BA2 110 D2
Cranleigh Court Rd
YATE/CS BS37 13 H5
Cranleigh Gdns
HNLZ/SM/SNYPK/WT BS9 44 C4
Cranleigh Rd HGRV/WHIT BS14 86 A4
Cranmore Av KEYN BS31 88 B3
Cranmore Crs
HNBRY/STHM BS10 31 H4
Cranmore Pl BATHSE BA2 110 B2
Cranside Av RDLND/MONT BS6 45 G5
Cransley Crs
HNLZ/SM/SNYPK/WT BS9 45 G1
Crantock Av
BMSTRD/HC/WWD BS13 84 C1
Crantock Dr ALMDB BS32 10 D2
Crantock Rd YATE/CS BS37 25 H1
Cranwell Gv HGRV/WHIT BS14 85 H4
Cranwell Rd
OMX/HUT/LCK BS24 127 F1
Crates Cl KGWD/HNM BS15 * 59 E3
Craven Cl
OLD/WMLY/WICK BS30 76 C1
Craven Wy
OLD/WMLY/WICK BS30 76 C1
Crawford Cl CLVDN BS21 64 B4
Craydon Gv HGRV/WHIT BS14 86 C5
Craydon Rd HGRV/WHIT BS14 86 C4
Craydon Wk HGRV/WHIT BS14 86 C4
Crediton Crs
BRSG/KWL/STAPK BS4 73 G5
Crescent Gdns
CBATH/BATHN BA1 2 D3
Crescent Rd MANG/FISH BS16 48 C2
The Crescent
HNLZ/SM/SNYPK/WT BS9 44 A2
MANG/FISH BS16 48 D5
MANG/FISH BS16 33 G4
MTN/WRL BS22 121 G2
NAIL BS48 79 H3
OLD/WMLY/WICK BS30 61 F4
Crescent Vw BATHSE BA2 2 E7
Cresswell Cl MTN/WRL BS22 122 D1
The Crest
BRSG/KWL/STAPK BS4 74 B4
Creswicke Av
KGWD/HNM BS15 75 H1
Creswicke Rd
BRSG/KWL/STAPK BS4 85 F2
Crewkerne Cl NAIL BS48 68 A5
Crew's Hole Rd
EVILLE/WHL BS5 57 G4
Cribbs Cswy
HNBRY/STHM BS10 19 E5
Cricket Field Gn NAIL BS48 * 67 E4
Cricket La HNBRY/STHM BS10 31 E5
Cricklade Ct NAIL BS48 67 H5
Cricklade Rd HORF/LLZ BS7 46 A4
Cripps Rd BMSTR BS3 72 D3
Crispin La THNB/SVB BS35 8 C3
Crispin Wy KGWD/HNM BS15 59 F1
Crockerne Dr PTSHD/EG BS20 42 C5
Croft Av MANG/FISH BS16 47 E4
Croft Cl OLD/WMLY/WICK BS30 89 G1
Crofters Wk ALMDB BS32 21 F2
Crofton Av HORF/LLZ BS7 46 A2
Crofton Flds FRCTL/WBN BS36 23 E4
Croft Rd CBATH/BATHN BA1 103 E3
Crofts End Rd EVILLE/WHL BS5 57 G2
The Croft CLVDN BS21 65 F1
MANG/FISH BS16 49 F3
NAIL BS48 79 H2
OLD/WMLY/WICK BS30 * 77 F3
OMX/HUT/LCK BS24 126 B3
Croft Vw
HNLZ/SM/SNYPK/WT BS9 45 G1
Crokeswood Wk AVONM BS11 29 G4
Crome Rd HORF/LLZ BS7 46 D1
Cromer Rd EVILLE/WHL BS5 57 E1
WSM BS23 124 D1
Cromwell Ct KGWD/HNM BS15 76 B1
Cromwell Dr MTN/WRL BS22 117 H4
Cromwell Rd EVILLE/WHL BS5 58 A3
RDLND/MONT BS6 55 H1
Cromwells Hide
MANG/FISH BS16 47 G3
Cromwell St BMSTR BS3 72 D3
Crookes La MTN/WRL BS22 116 B4
Croomes Hl MANG/FISH BS16 48 D2
Cropthorne Rd HORF/LLZ BS7 32 C4
Cropthorne Rd South
HORF/LLZ BS7 32 C5
Crosby Rw CFTN/FAIL BS8 55 E5
Crosscombe Dr
BMSTRD/HC/WWD BS13 95 G1
Crosscombe Wk
BMSTRD/HC/WWD BS13 95 G1
Cross Elms La
HNLZ/SM/SNYPK/WT BS9 44 C3
Crossfield Rd MANG/FISH BS16 49 E5
Cross Lanes PTSHD/EG BS20 42 B4
Crossleaze Rd
KGWD/HNM BS15 75 H3
Crossley Cl FRCTL/WBN BS36 23 F3
Crossman Av FRCTL/WBN BS36 23 E5
Crossman Wk CLVDN BS21 65 F2
Cross St KEYN BS31 88 C2
KGWD/HNM BS15 58 C2
WSM BS23 6 E4
Cross Tree Gv ALMDB BS32 21 F2
Cross Wk HGRV/WHIT BS14 85 H3
Crossways La THNB/SVB BS35 9 F2
Crossways Rd
BRSG/KWL/STAPK BS4 73 H5
THNB/SVB BS35 9 E3
Crow La CBRIS/FH BS1 5 F4
HNBRY/STHM BS10 30 D3
Crowley Wy AVONM BS11 28 B4
Crowndale Rd
BRSG/KWL/STAPK BS4 73 H3
Crown Gdns
OLD/WMLY/WICK BS30 59 H4
Crown Hl CBATH/BATHN BA1 101 H3
EVILLE/WHL BS5 59 H3
Crown Hill Wk EVILLE/WHL BS5 57 H2
Crownleaze MANG/FISH BS16 48 D5
Crown Rd CBATH/BATHN BA1 101 G3
KGWD/HNM BS15 58 D1
OLD/WMLY/WICK BS30 60 A5
Crown Wy
OLD/WMLY/WICK BS30 60 A4
Crows Gv ALMDB BS32 11 F4
Crowther Pk HORF/LLZ BS7 46 C4
Crowther Rd HORF/LLZ BS7 46 C4
Crowthers Av YATE/CS BS37 14 A4
Crowther St BMSTR BS3 72 C3
Croydon St EVILLE/WHL BS5 56 D3
The Crunnis ALMDB BS32 21 G4
Crusty La PTSHD/EG BS20 42 C3
Crystal Wy ALMDB BS32 21 G2
Cuckoo La FRCTL/WBN BS36 35 F2
Cuffington Av
BRSG/KWL/STAPK BS4 74 C2
Culverhill Rd YATE/CS BS37 26 C1
Culvers Cl KEYN BS31 88 B3
Culvers Rd KEYN BS31 88 B3
Culver St CBRIS/FH BS1 4 D4
The Culvert ALMDB BS32 21 F2
Culverwell Rd
BMSTRD/HC/WWD BS13 84 B5
Cumberland Basin
CBRIS/FH BS1 72 B1
Cumberland Basin Rd
CFTN/FAIL BS8 72 A1
Cumberland Cl CBRIS/FH BS1 72 B1
Cumberland Gv
RDLND/MONT BS6 56 B1
Cumberland Pl CFTN/FAIL BS8 54 D5
Cumberland Rd CBRIS/FH BS1 72 A1
Cumberland Rw
CBATH/BATHN BA1 2 E4
Cumberland St CBRISNE BS2 5 G1
Cumbria Cl THNB/SVB BS35 9 F3
Cunningham Gdns
MANG/FISH BS16 48 B3
Cunnington Cl
OLD/WMLY/WICK BS30 76 D5
Curland Gv HGRV/WHIT BS14 86 A4
Curlew Cl MANG/FISH BS16 * 47 H2
Curlew Gdns MTN/WRL BS22 122 C2
Curlew Pl PTSHD/EG BS20 40 B2
Currells La
BLAG/CWMG/WR BS40 92 C3
Curtis La BRSTK/PCHW BS34 34 A2
Custom Cl HGRV/WHIT BS14 85 H2
Cutler Rd
BMSTRD/HC/WWD BS13 84 A3
Cuttsheath Rd WUE GL12 9 H3
Cygnet Crs MTN/WRL BS22 122 C2
Cylde Pk RDLND/MONT BS6 55 F1
Cynder Wy MANG/FISH BS16 35 G4
Cynthia Rd BATHSE BA2 107 H2
Cypress Gdns CFTN/FAIL BS8 54 C5
Cypress Gv
HNLZ/SM/SNYPK/WT BS9 45 G2
Cyrus Ct MANG/FISH BS16 49 H1

D

Dafford's Blds
CBATH/BATHN BA1 103 E2
Dafford St CBATH/BATHN BA1 103 F2
Dahlia Gdns BATHSE BA2 3 K2
Dairy Cl YTN/CONG BS49 112 A2
Daisy Bank BATHSE BA2 109 E3
Daisy Rd EVILLE/WHL BS5 57 E1
Dakin Cl BRSG/KWL/STAPK BS4 73 G5
Dakota Dr HGRV/WHIT BS14 85 H5
Dalby Av BMSTR BS3 73 E3
Dale St EVILLE/WHL BS5 57 H3
Daley Cl MTN/WRL BS22 118 A5
Dalkeith Av KGWD/HNM BS15 58 C2
Dalrymple Rd CBRISNE BS2 56 A2
Dalston Rd BMSTR BS3 72 C2
Dalton Sq CBRISNE BS2 56 A3
Dame Court Cl
MTN/WRL BS22 117 G4
Dampier Rd BMSTR BS3 72 B3
Damson Rd MTN/WRL BS22 122 A3
Danbury Crs
HNBRY/STHM BS10 31 G4
Danbury Wk
HNBRY/STHM BS10 31 G4
Dancey Md
BMSTRD/HC/WWD BS13 83 H3
Dandy's Meadow
PTSHD/EG BS20 40 A3
Danesbury KGWD/HNM BS15 76 A2
Dangerfield Av
BMSTRD/HC/WWD BS13 83 H3
Daniel Cl CLVDN BS21 65 F2
Daniel Ms BATHSE BA2 3 J2
Daniel St BATHSE BA2 3 J2
Dapps Hl KEYN BS31 88 C4
Dark La BATHSE BA2 104 A3
NAIL BS48 80 A4
Darley Cl HNBRY/STHM BS10 30 B2
Darlington Pl BATHSE BA2 3 K5
Darlington Rd BATHSE BA2 3 K2
Darlington St BATHSE BA2 3 J3
Darmead OMX/HUT/LCK BS24 123 E2
Darnley Av HORF/LLZ BS7 46 B2
Dart Cl THNB/SVB BS35 8 C4
Dartmoor St BMSTR BS3 72 C2
Dartmouth Av BATHSE BA2 107 H2
Dartmouth Cl MTN/WRL BS22 122 C1
Dart Rd CLVDN BS21 64 D4
Daubeny Cl MANG/FISH BS16 48 B3
Daventry Rd
BRSG/KWL/STAPK BS4 73 G5
Davey St CBRISNE BS2 56 B2
Davey Ter CBRISNE BS2 * 56 B2
David's Rd HGRV/WHIT BS14 86 B3
David St CBRISNE BS2 5 J3
Davies Dr
BRSG/KWL/STAPK BS4 75 E1
Davin Crs PTSHD/EG BS20 42 C5
Davis Cl OLD/WMLY/WICK BS30 76 C1
Davis Ct THNB/SVB BS35 8 D2
Davis La CLVDN BS21 64 D5
Davis St AVONM BS11 28 B5
Dawes Cl CLVDN BS21 64 D4
Dawley Cl FRCTL/WBN BS36 23 E3
Dawlish Rd BMSTR BS3 73 E4
Dawn Ri KGWD/HNM BS15 59 G2
Daws Ct MANG/FISH BS16 48 B4
Day Crs BATHSE BA2 107 E1
Day's Rd CBRISNE BS2 56 C5
Deacon Cl FRCTL/WBN BS36 23 E5
Deacons Cl MTN/WRL BS22 122 B1
Deadmill La
CBATH/BATHN BA1 103 F1
Dean Av THNB/SVB BS35 8 D2
Dean Cl KGWD/HNM BS15 75 F2
MTN/WRL BS22 118 A5
Dean Crs BMSTR BS3 72 D2

Deanery Rd *CBRIS/FH* BS1 .... 4 C5
Deanhill La *BMSTR* BS3 .... 59 G3
Deanhill La
  CBATH/BATHN BA1 .... 101 E2
Dean La *BMSTR* BS3 .... 72 D2
Dean Rd *AVONM* BS11 .... 16 C5
Dean's Dr *EVILLE/WHL* BS5 ...... 58 A1
Deans Md *AVONM* BS11 .... 29 C5
The Deans *PTSHD/EG* BS20 ...... 39 F4
Dean St *BMSTR* BS3 .... 72 D2
  CBRISNE BS2 .... 56 A5
Debecca's La *PTSHD/EG* BS20 .... 42 B4
De Clifford Rd *AVONM* BS11 ..... 30 A3
Deep Coombe Rd *BMSTR* BS3 ... 72 B4
Deep Pit Rd *EVILLE/WHL* BS5 .... 57 H2
Deep St *CBRIS/FH* BS1 .... 5 F2
Deerhurst *KGWD/HNM* BS15 ..... 59 E1
  YATE/CS BS37 .... 25 C2
Deering Cl *AVONM* BS11 .... 29 H4
Deer Md *CLVDN* BS21 .... 64 B4
Deerswood *KGWD/HNM* BS15 ... 59 C1
Delabere Av *MANG/FISH* BS16 ... 48 B3
Delapre Rd *WSM* BS23 .... 124 D3
De la Warre Ct
  BRSG/KWL/STAPK BS4 .... 57 H5
Delius Gv
  BRSG/KWL/STAPK BS4 .... 85 E2
The Dell *ALMDB* BS32 .... 21 C3
  HNLZ/SM/SNYPK/WT BS9 ... 44 D3
  MTN/WRL BS22 .... 117 F4
  NAIL BS48 .... 67 G4
Delvin Rd *HNBRY/STHM* BS10 ... 31 G5
Denbigh St *CBRISNE* BS2 .... 56 A2
Dene Cl *KEYN* BS31 .... 98 A1
Dene Rd *HGRV/WHIT* BS14 ...... 86 B5
Denleigh Cl *HGRV/WHIT* BS14 ... 85 H5
Denmark Pl *HORF/LLZ* BS7 ...... 46 A5
Denmark Rd *BATHSE* BA2 .... 3 K2
Denmark St *CBRIS/FH* BS1 ...... 4 D4
Denning Ct *MTN/WRL* BS22 ..... 118 A4
Dennisworth *MANG/FISH* BS16 .. 51 F3
Denmor Pk *HGRV/WHIT* BS14 ... 86 A2
Denny Cl *PTSHD/EG* BS20 .... 39 E5
Denny Vw *PTSHD/EG* BS20 ..... 38 D3
Dennyview Rd *CFTN/FAIL* BS8 ... 53 F5
Denston Dr *PTSHD/EG* BS20 .... 40 A4
Denston Wk
  BMSTRD/HC/WWD BS13 .... 84 B2
Denton Patch
  MANG/FISH BS16 .... 49 H1
Dentwood Gv
  HNLZ/SM/SNYPK/WT BS9 ... 43 H1
Derby Rd *HORF/LLZ* BS7 .... 46 A5
Derby St *EVILLE/WHL* BS5 .... 57 F4
Derham Ct *YTN/CONG* BS49 .... 112 B3
Derham Pk *YTN/CONG* BS49 .... 112 B3
Derham Rd
  BMSTRD/HC/WWD BS13 .... 84 B4
Dermot St *CBRISNE* BS2 * 56 C2
Derricke Rd *HGRV/WHIT* BS14 ... 87 E5
Derrick Rd *KGWD/HNM* BS15 ... 58 D5
Derry Rd *BMSTR* BS3 .... 72 C4
Derwent Cl *BRSTK/PCHW* BS34 .. 20 B2
Derwent Gv *KEYN* BS31 .... 88 D4
Derwent Rd *EVILLE/WHL* BS5 ... 57 H2
  WSM BS23 .... 125 F2
Devaney Cl
  BRSG/KWL/STAPK BS4 .... 75 E1
De Veroise Ct *KGWD/HNM* BS15 . 73 E4
Devon Gv *EVILLE/WHL* BS5 ...... 57 E3
Devon Rd *EVILLE/WHL* BS5 ...... 57 E2
Devonshire Blds *BATHSE* BA2 ... 108 C3
Devonshire Dr *PTSHD/EG* BS20 .. 38 D2
Devonshire Rd *BATHSE* BA2 .... 108 C5
Devonshire Rd *BATHSE* BA2 .... 103 H5
  RDLND/MONT BS6 .... 45 F4
  WSM BS23 .... 124 D5
Dewfalls Dr *ALMDB* BS32 .... 21 F1
Dial Hill Rd *CLVDN* BS21 .... 62 B5
Dial La *BLAG/CWMG/WR* BS40 .. 93 E3
  MANG/FISH BS16 .... 48 D2
Diamond Batch
  OMX/HUT/LCK BS24 .... 123 E2
Diamond Rd *EVILLE/WHL* BS5 ... 57 H4
Diamond St *BMSTR* BS3 .... 72 D3
Diana Gdns *ALMDB* BS32 .... 21 G2
Dibden Cl *MANG/FISH* BS16 ..... 35 C5
Dibden La *MANG/FISH* BS16 .... 49 C1
Dibden Rd *MANG/FISH* BS16 .... 35 C5
Dickens Cl *HORF/LLZ* BS7 .... 32 C5
Dickenson Rd *WSM* BS23 .... 6 E7
Dickenson's Gv
  YTN/CONG BS49 .... 115 E3
Dickinsons Fld *BMSTR* BS3 ..... 73 E4
Didsbury Cl *HNBRY/STHM* BS10 . 30 C3
Dighton Ga *BRSTK/PCHW* BS34 .. 21 C5
Dighton St *CBRIS/FH* BS1 .... 5 F1
Dingle Cl
  HNLZ/SM/SNYPK/WT BS9 ... 44 A2
Dingle Rd
  HNLZ/SM/SNYPK/WT BS9 ... 44 A2
The Dingle *FRCTL/WBN* BS36 .... 35 E2
  HNLZ/SM/SNYPK/WT BS9 ... 44 A1
  YATE/CS BS37 .... 14 B3
Dingle Vw
  HNLZ/SM/SNYPK/WT BS9 ... 44 A1
Dinglewood Cl
  HNLZ/SM/SNYPK/WT BS9 ... 44 B1
Dings Wk *CBRISNE* BS2 .... 56 C5
Dirac Rd *HORF/LLZ* BS7 .... 46 B4
Dixon Gdns
  CBATH/BATHN BA1 .... 102 C3
Dixon Rd
  BRSG/KWL/STAPK BS4 .... 75 E4
Dock Gate La *CFTN/FAIL* BS8 * .. 72 E1
Dodington Rd *YATE/CS* BS37 .... 26 D4
Dodington St *YATE/CS* BS37 .... 26 D3
Dodisham Wk
  MANG/FISH BS16 .... 48 B2
Dog La *HNBRY/STHM* BS10 ..... 30 A4
Dolecroft La *MTN/WRL* BS22 ... 118 D2
Dolemoor La *YTN/CONG* BS49 .. 114 A2
Dolman Cl *HNBRY/STHM* BS10 .. 30 C2
Dominion Rd *BATHSE* BA2 ...... 107 F1
  MANG/FISH BS16 .... 47 H5
Donald Rd
  BMSTRD/HC/WWD BS13 .... 84 A2
Donal Early Wy *HORF/LLZ* BS7 .. 32 A5

Doncaster Rd
  HNBRY/STHM BS10 .... 31 F4
Donegal Rd
  BRSG/KWL/STAPK BS4 .... 73 E5
Dongola Av *HORF/LLZ* BS7 ...... 46 A4
Dongola Rd *HORF/LLZ* BS7 ..... 46 A4
Doone Rd *HORF/LLZ* BS7 .... 32 B5
Dorcas Av *BRSTK/PCHW* BS34 ... 21 H5
Dorchester Cl *NAIL* BS48 .... 79 E1
Dorchester Rd *HORF/LLZ* BS7 ... 46 C1
Dorchester St
  CBATH/BATHN BA1 .... 3 G6
Dorester Cl *HNBRY/STHM* BS10 . 31 G1
Dorian Cl *HORF/LLZ* BS7 .... 46 A1
Dorian Rd *HORF/LLZ* BS7 .... 46 A1
Dorian Wy *HORF/LLZ* BS7 ...... 32 A5
Dormeads Vw
  OMX/HUT/LCK BS24 .... 122 C4
Dormer Cl *FRCTL/WBN* BS36 .... 24 B3
Dormer Rd *EVILLE/WHL* BS5 .... 46 C5
Dorset Cl *BATHSE* BA2 .... 2 A3
Dorset Gv *CBRISNE* BS2 .... 56 C2
Dorset Rd
  HNLZ/SM/SNYPK/WT BS9 ... 45 F2
  KGWD/HNM BS15 .... 58 D2
Dorset St *BATHSE* BA2 .... 2 A3
  BMSTR BS3 .... 72 C3
Dorset Wy *YATE/CS* BS37 ...... 14 C4
Douglas Rd *HORF/LLZ* BS7 ..... 46 A1
  KGWD/HNM BS15 .... 59 E4
  WSM BS23 .... 125 E1
Doulton Wy *HGRV/WHIT* BS14 .. 85 H4
Dovecote *YATE/CS* BS37 .... 26 A3
Dovedale *PTSHD/EG* BS20 ...... 39 E4
Dove La *CBRISNE* BS2 .... 56 B4
Dovercourt Rd *HORF/LLZ* BS7 ... 46 C3
Dover Pl *CBATH/BATHN* BA1 * .. 102 D3
  CFTN/FAIL BS8 * 4 B3
Dovers La *CBATH/BATHN* BA1 .. 104 D2
Dovers Pk *CBATH/BATHN* BA1 .. 104 D2
Dove St *CBRISNE* BS2 .... 55 H3
Dove St South *CBRISNE* BS2 .... 5 F1
Dovetail Dr *WSM* BS23 .... 7 K5
Dovey Ct
  OLD/WMLY/WICK BS30 ..... 77 F1
Dowdeswell Cl
  HNBRY/STHM BS10 .... 30 D2
Dowding Cl *YATE/CS* BS37 ...... 15 E5
Dowding Rd
  CBATH/BATHN BA1 .... 103 E3
Dowland Gv
  BRSG/KWL/STAPK BS4 .... 85 E3
Dowling Rd
  BMSTRD/HC/WWD BS13 .... 96 A1
Down Av *BATHSE* BA2 .... 111 E1
Down Cl *PTSHD/EG* BS20 .... 38 D3
Downend Pk *HORF/LLZ* BS7 .... 46 C3
Downend Park Rd
  MANG/FISH BS16 .... 48 D3
Downend Rd *HORF/LLZ* BS7 .... 46 C5
  KGWD/HNM BS15 .... 58 D2
Downfield *KEYN* BS31 * 88 A4
Downfield Dr *FRCTL/WBN* BS36 . 23 H2
Downfield Rd *CFTN/FAIL* BS8 ... 55 E2
Down La *BATHSE* BA2 .... 104 A3
Downleaze
  HNLZ/SM/SNYPK/WT BS9 ... 56 A1
  MANG/FISH BS16 .... 34 D5
  PTSHD/EG BS20 .... 39 E3
Downman Rd *HORF/LLZ* BS7 ... 46 C5
Down Rd *FRCTL/WBN* BS36 ..... 34 D1
  PTSHD/EG BS20 .... 38 D5
Downs Cote Av
  HNLZ/SM/SNYPK/WT BS9 ... 44 D2
Downs Cote Dr
  HNLZ/SM/SNYPK/WT BS9 ... 44 D2
Downs Cote Gdns
  HNLZ/SM/SNYPK/WT BS9 ... 44 D2
Downs Cote Pk
  HNLZ/SM/SNYPK/WT BS9 ... 45 E2
Downs Cote Vw
  HNLZ/SM/SNYPK/WT BS9 ... 45 E2
Downs Pk East
  HNLZ/SM/SNYPK/WT BS9 ... 45 E3
Downs Pk West
  RDLND/MONT BS6 .... 45 E3
Downs Rd
  HNLZ/SM/SNYPK/WT BS9 ... 45 E2
  LGSH BS41 .... 94 D5
The Downs *PTSHD/EG* BS20 .... 39 E4
Downton Rd
  BRSG/KWL/STAPK BS4 .... 73 E5
Dowry Pl *CFTN/FAIL* BS8 .... 72 A1
Dowry Rd *CFTN/FAIL* BS8 ...... 55 E5
Dowry Sq *CFTN/FAIL* BS8 ...... 71 H1
Dragon Ct *EVILLE/WHL* BS5 .... 57 G2
Dragon Rd *FRCTL/WBN* BS36 ... 35 E3
Dragons Hill Cl *KEYN* BS31 ..... 88 C4
Dragons Hill Ct *KEYN* BS31 ..... 88 C4
Dragons Hill Gdns *KEYN* BS31 .. 88 C4
Dragonswell Rd
  HNBRY/STHM BS10 .... 31 E3
Dragon Wk *EVILLE/WHL* BS5 ... 57 H2
Drainsfield Rd *BATHSE* BA2 .... 107 H5
Drake Av *BATHSE* BA2 .... 108 C5
Drake Cl *KEYN* BS31 .... 99 E2
  MTN/WRL BS22 .... 117 G2
Drake Rd *BMSTR* BS3 .... 72 B5
Drakes Wy *PTSHD/EG* BS20 .... 39 E3
Dram La *EVILLE/WHL* BS5 ...... 58 A5
Draycot Pl *CBRIS/FH* BS1 * 4 E7
Draycott Rd *HORF/LLZ* BS7 .... 46 B3
Draydon Rd
  BRSG/KWL/STAPK BS4 .... 84 D2
Drayton Cl *HGRV/WHIT* BS14 ... 86 A4
Drayton Rd
  HNLZ/SM/SNYPK/WT BS9 ... 30 A5
The Drive *HGRV/WHIT* BS14 .... 86 A4
  HNLZ/SM/SNYPK/WT BS9 ... 45 F3
  WSM BS23 .... 7 H2
Drove Rd *WSM* BS23 .... 7 G5
The Drove *PTSHD/EG* BS20 .... 41 F2

Druetts Cl *HNBRY/STHM* BS10 .. 46 A2
Druid Cl
  HNLZ/SM/SNYPK/WT BS9 ... 44 C3
Druid Hl
  HNLZ/SM/SNYPK/WT BS9 ... 44 C3
Druid Rd
  HNLZ/SM/SNYPK/WT BS9 ... 44 B4
Druid Stoke Av
  HNLZ/SM/SNYPK/WT BS9 ... 44 A3
Druid Woods
  HNLZ/SM/SNYPK/WT BS9 ... 44 A3
Drummond Ct
  OLD/WMLY/WICK BS30 ..... 76 C2
Drummond Rd *CBRISNE* BS2 ... 56 A2
  MANG/FISH BS16 .... 47 H5
Dr Whites Cl *CBRIS/FH* BS1 ..... 5 C6
Dryleaze *KEYN* BS31 .... 88 B2
  YATE/CS BS37 .... 14 A2
Dryleaze Rd *MANG/FISH* BS16 .. 49 G4
Drysdale Cl *MTN/WRL* BS22 ... 121 H2
Dubbers La *EVILLE/WHL* BS5 ... 57 C1
Dublin Crs
  HNLZ/SM/SNYPK/WT BS9 ... 45 F2
Duchess Rd *CFTN/FAIL* BS8 .... 55 E2
Duchess Wy *MANG/FISH* BS16 .. 47 H4
Ducie Rd *EVILLE/WHL* BS5 ...... 56 D4
  MANG/FISH BS16 .... 49 E4
Duckmoor Rd *BMSTR* BS3 ..... 72 B3
Dudley Cl *KEYN* BS31 .... 88 B5
Dudley Ct
  OLD/WMLY/WICK BS30 ..... 76 C2
Dudley Gv *HORF/LLZ* BS7 ...... 46 B3
Dugar Wk *RDLND/MONT* BS6 ... 45 G5
Duke St *BATHSE* BA2 .... 3 G6
Dulverton Rd *HORF/LLZ* BS7 ... 45 H4
Dumaine Av
  BRSTK/PCHW BS34 .... 21 C5
Dumfries Pl *WSM* BS23 .... 124 D1
Duncan Gdns
  CBATH/BATHN BA1 .... 101 F1
Duncombe La
  KGWD/HNM BS15 .... 58 A1
Duncombe Rd
  KGWD/HNM BS15 .... 58 B2
Dundas Cl *HNBRY/STHM* BS10 .. 30 C3
Dundonald Rd
  RDLND/MONT BS6 .... 45 E5
Dundridge Gdns
  EVILLE/WHL BS5 .... 58 A5
Dundridge La *EVILLE/WHL* BS5 . 58 A5
Dundry Cl *KGWD/HNM* BS15 ... 58 D5
Dundry La
  BLAG/CWMG/WR BS40 ...... 93 H5
Dunford Rd *BMSTR* BS3 .... 73 E3
Dungarvon Rd
  OMX/HUT/LCK BS24 .... 122 C4
Dunkeld Av
  BRSTK/PCHW BS34 .... 32 B3
Dunkerry Cl *BMSTR* BS3 .... 73 E3
Dunkerry Rd *BMSTR* BS3 ...... 67 F5
Dunkery Rd *WSM* BS23 .... 122 A3
Dunkirk Rd *MANG/FISH* BS16 .. 47 H5
Dunmail Rd
  HNBRY/STHM BS10 .... 31 G3
Dunmore St *BMSTR* BS3 * 73 G2
Dunstanford Pl *BATHSE* BA2 .... 3 K4
Dunster Crs
  OMX/HUT/LCK BS24 .... 125 F4
Dunster Gdns
  OLD/WMLY/WICK BS30 ..... 77 E4
Dunster Rd
  BRSG/KWL/STAPK BS4 .... 85 G1
  KEYN BS31 .... 88 B5
Dunsters Rd *YTN/CONG* BS49 .. 113 F2
Durban Rd *BRSTK/PCHW* BS34 .. 20 B2
Durbin Park Rd *CLVDN* BS21 ... 62 A5
Durbin Wk *EVILLE/WHL* BS5 .... 56 C3
Durdham Pk
  RDLND/MONT BS6 .... 45 E5
Durham Gv *KEYN* BS31 .... 88 A5
Durham La *KEYN* BS31 .... 88 A5
Durham Pl *BATHSE* BA2 .... 108 B5
Durham Rd *BMSTR* BS3 .... 72 B2
Durnford Av *BMSTR* BS3 ...... 72 A3
Durnford St *BMSTR* BS3 .... 72 A3
Dursley Cl *BMSTR* BS3 .... 26 A1
Dursley Rd *AVONM* BS11 ...... 43 E5
Durville Rd
  BMSTRD/HC/WWD BS13 .... 84 C3
Durweston Wk
  HGRV/WHIT BS14 .... 86 B1
Dutton Cl *HGRV/WHIT* BS14 ... 86 C5
Dutton Rd *HGRV/WHIT* BS14 ... 86 C5
Dyers Cl
  BMSTRD/HC/WWD BS13 .... 85 E5
Dyer's La *YATE/CS* BS37 .... 13 E4
Dylan Thomas Ct
  OLD/WMLY/WICK BS30 * ... 76 D1
Dyrham Cl
  HNLZ/SM/SNYPK/WT BS9 ... 45 H2
  KGWD/HNM BS15 .... 59 F5
  MANG/FISH BS16 .... 51 G4
  WSM BS23 .... 8 D1
Dyrham Pde
  BRSTK/PCHW BS34 .... 21 E2
Dyrham Rd *KGWD/HNM* BS15 .. 59 F5
Dyson Cl *YTN/CONG* BS49 .... 112 B5

E

Eagle Cl *MTN/WRL* BS22 .... 122 A3
Eagle Crs *MANG/FISH* BS16 .... 51 C4
Eagle Dr *BRSTK/PCHW* BS34 ... 20 A2
Eagle Rd *BRSG/KWL/STAPK* BS4 . 74 C4
  CBATH/BATHN BA1 .... 91 J5
The Eagles *YTN/CONG* BS49 ... 112 B3
Eagles Wd *ALMDB* BS32 .... 11 F4

Earlesfield *NAIL* BS48 .... 66 D5
Earlham Gv *WSM* BS23 .... 7 H4
Earl Russell Wy
  EVILLE/WHL BS5 .... 56 D4
Earlsmead *MANG/FISH* BS16 ... 47 F4
Earlstone Cl
  OLD/WMLY/WICK BS30 ..... 76 D2
Earlstone Crs
  OLD/WMLY/WICK BS30 ..... 76 D1
Earl St *CBRIS/FH* BS1 .... 5 F1
Easedale Cl *HNBRY/STHM* BS10 . 31 H3
Eastbourne Rd
  CBATH/BATHN BA1 * 103 E3
Eastbourne Rd
  EVILLE/WHL BS5 .... 56 D3
Eastbury Cl *THNB/SVB* BS35 .... 8 D3
Eastbury Rd *MANG/FISH* BS16 .. 48 A3
Eastcliff *PTSHD/EG* BS20 .... 40 A1
Eastcombe Gdns *WSM* BS23 ... 7 H1
Eastcombe Rd *WSM* BS23 ...... 7 H1
Eastcote Pk *HGRV/WHIT* BS14 .. 86 A4
East Cft
  HNLZ/SM/SNYPK/WT BS9 ... 45 G1
East Dundry La *LGASH* BS41 ... 95 E2
East Dundry Rd
  HGRV/WHIT BS14 .... 96 C2
  YATE/CS BS37 .... 25 E1
Eastfield
  HNLZ/SM/SNYPK/WT BS9 ... 45 F1
Eastfield Av
  CBATH/BATHN BA1 .... 101 C2
Eastfield Cl *YATE/CS* BS37 ..... 14 A2
Eastfield Gdns *WSM* BS23 ...... 7 H1
Eastfield Pk *WSM* BS23 .... 7 F1
Eastfield Rd
  HNLZ/SM/SNYPK/WT BS9 ... 45 E1
  OMX/HUT/LCK BS24 .... 126 B4
  RDLND/MONT BS6 .... 55 H1
Eastfield Ter
  HNLZ/SM/SNYPK/WT BS9 ... 45 F2
Eastgate Rd *EVILLE/WHL* BS5 ... 46 D5
East Gv *RDLND/MONT* BS6 ..... 56 B2
East Hill *BATHSE* BA2 .... 102 D5
Eastlake Cl *HORF/LLZ* BS7 ..... 46 D1
Eastland Av *THNB/SVB* BS35 ... 8 D2
Eastland Rd *THNB/SVB* BS35 ... 8 D2
Eastlea *CLVDN* BS21 .... 64 B4
Eastleigh Cl *MANG/FISH* BS16 .. 49 E4
Eastleigh Rd
  HNBRY/STHM BS10 .... 31 H4
  MANG/FISH BS16 .... 49 E4
Eastlyn Rd
  BMSTRD/HC/WWD BS13 .... 84 C1
Eastmead La
  HNLZ/SM/SNYPK/WT BS9 ... 44 C4
Eastnor Rd *HGRV/WHIT* BS14 ... 96 D1
Easton Hill Rd *THNB/SVB* BS35 .. 9 E2
Easton Rd *EVILLE/WHL* BS5 .... 56 C2
  PTSHD/EG BS20 .... 42 C4
Easton Wy *EVILLE/WHL* BS5 ... 56 C2
Eastover Cl
  HNLZ/SM/SNYPK/WT BS9 ... 31 E5
Eastover Gv *BATHSE* BA2 ...... 110 A1
East Pde
  HNLZ/SM/SNYPK/WT BS9 ... 44 A1
East Priory Cl *EVILLE/WHL* BS5 .. 57 E1
East Park Dr *EVILLE/WHL* BS5 .. 57 E1
East Priory Cl
  HNLZ/SM/SNYPK/WT BS9 ... 45 E1
East Ridge Dr
  BMSTRD/HC/WWD BS13 .... 84 A4
East Shrubbery
  RDLND/MONT BS6 .... 55 F1
East St *AVONM* BS11 .... 28 A4
  BMSTR BS3 .... 72 D2
East Vw *MANG/FISH* BS16 ..... 48 D1
Eastville *CBATH/BATHN* BA1 ... 103 E3
East Wy *BATHSE* BA2 .... 107 F2
Eastway *NAIL* BS48 .... 67 E4
Eastway Sq *NAIL* BS48 .... 67 E3
Eastwood Crs
  BRSG/KWL/STAPK BS4 .... 75 E2
Eastwood Pl *PTSHD/EG* BS20 ... 39 H1
Eastwood Rd
  BRSG/KWL/STAPK BS4 .... 75 E2
Eaton Cl *MANG/FISH* BS16 .... 104 C1
Eaton Crs *CFTN/FAIL* BS8 ...... 55 E3
Eaton St *BMSTR* BS3 * 73 F2
Ebdon Rd *MTN/WRL* BS22 .... 117 C5
Ebenezer La
  HNLZ/SM/SNYPK/WT BS9 ... 44 B2
Ebenezer St *EVILLE/WHL* BS5 ... 57 F4
Eden Cv *OMX/HUT/LCK* BS24 .. 122 B5
Eden Cv *HORF/LLZ* BS7 .... 32 C4
Eden Park Cl
  CBATH/BATHN BA1 .... 91 F5
Eden Park Dr
  CBATH/BATHN BA1 .... 91 F5
Eden Ter *CBATH/BATHN* BA1 * . 103 E2
Eden Vs *CBATH/BATHN* BA1 * .. 103 E2
Edgar Blds *CBATH/BATHN* BA1 * . 3 F5
Edgecombe Av
  MTN/WRL BS22 .... 122 A1
Edgecombe Rd
  RDLND/MONT BS6 .... 55 H1
Edgefield Cl *HGRV/WHIT* BS14 .. 96 C1
Edgefield Rd *HGRV/WHIT* BS14 . 96 C1
Edgehill Rd *CLVDN* BS21 ...... 62 B4
Edgeware Rd *BMSTR* BS3 ...... 72 D2
  MANG/FISH BS16 .... 48 C4
Edgewood Cl
  HGRV/WHIT BS14 .... 86 A1
  OLD/WMLY/WICK BS30 ..... 76 D3
Edgeworth *YATE/CS* BS37 ..... 26 A2
Edgeworth Rd *BATHSE* BA2 ... 107 H5
Edinburgh Pl *WSM* BS23 .... 6 D2
Edinburgh Rd *KEYN* BS31 ...... 88 B5
Edington Gv
  HNBRY/STHM BS10 .... 31 E3
Edmund Cl *MANG/FISH* BS16 .. 48 D2
Edmund Ct *MANG/FISH* BS16 .. 51 F2
Edna Av *BRSG/KWL/STAPK* BS4 . 74 D3

Edward Rd
  BRSG/KWL/STAPK BS4 .... 74 A2
  CLVDN BS21 .... 62 C5
  KGWD/HNM BS15 .... 59 E5
Edward Rd South *CLVDN* BS21 . 62 C4
Edward Rd West *CLVDN* BS21 .. 62 C4
Edward St
  CBATH/BATHN BA1 .... 101 H5
  EVILLE/WHL BS5 .... 57 E3
Edwin Short Cl
  OLD/WMLY/WICK BS30 ..... 89 H1
Egerton Brow *HORF/LLZ* BS7 ... 45 H4
Egerton Rd *BATHSE* BA2 .... 108 B3
  HORF/LLZ BS7 .... 45 H5
Eggshill La *YATE/CS* BS37 ...... 25 H1
Eighth Av *HORF/LLZ* BS7 .... 32 C5
Eirene Ter *PTSHD/EG* BS20 ..... 42 D4
Elberton *KGWD/HNM* BS15 .... 59 C3
Elberton Rd
  HNLZ/SM/SNYPK/WT BS9 ... 43 H3
Elborough Av
  YTN/CONG BS49 .... 112 B3
Elborough Gdns
  OMX/HUT/LCK BS24 .... 127 F3
Elbury Av *KGWD/HNM* BS15 ... 58 C5
Elderberry Wk
  HNBRY/STHM BS10 .... 31 G3
Elderwood Dr
  OLD/WMLY/WICK BS30 ..... 76 D3
Elderwood Rd
  HGRV/WHIT BS14 .... 86 A2
Eldon Pl *CBATH/BATHN* BA1 .. 103 E2
Eldon Ter *BMSTR* BS3 .... 73 E3
Eldon Wy
  BRSG/KWL/STAPK BS4 .... 74 B1
Eldred Cl
  HNLZ/SM/SNYPK/WT BS9 ... 44 A3
Eleanor Cl *BATHSE* BA2 .... 107 F2
Eleventh Av *HORF/LLZ* BS7 .... 32 C4
Elfin Rd *MANG/FISH* BS16 ..... 48 A3
Elgar Cl *BRSG/KWL/STAPK* BS4 . 85 E2
Elgin Av *HORF/LLZ* BS7 .... 32 B4
Elgin Pk *RDLND/MONT* BS6 .... 55 F1
Eliot Cl *HORF/LLZ* BS7 .... 32 C5
  WSM BS23 .... 125 E4
Elizabeth Cl
  OMX/HUT/LCK BS24 .... 126 A3
  THNB/SVB BS35 .... 9 E4
Elizabeth Crs
  BRSTK/PCHW BS34 .... 33 G1
Elizabeths Ms
  BRSG/KWL/STAPK BS4 .... 57 H5
Ella Cl *MANG/FISH* BS16 .... 48 C2
Eliacombe Rd
  OLD/WMLY/WICK BS30 ..... 76 B4
Ellan Hay Rd *ALMDB* BS32 .... 22 A4
Ellbridge Cl
  HNLZ/SM/SNYPK/WT BS9 ... 44 B3
Ellenborough Crs *WSM* BS23 * . 6 E7
Ellenborough Pk North
  WSM BS23 .... 6 D6
Ellenborough Park Rd
  WSM BS23 .... 6 E6
Ellenborough Pk South
  WSM BS23 .... 6 D6
Ellesmere *THNB/SVB* BS35 ..... 8 D4
Ellesmere Rd
  BRSG/KWL/STAPK BS4 .... 74 C5
  WSM BS23 .... 124 C4
Ellfield Cl
  BMSTRD/HC/WWD BS13 .... 84 A3
Ellicks Cl *ALMDB* BS32 .... 11 G5
Ellicott Rd *HORF/LLZ* BS7 ...... 46 B2
Ellinghurst Cl
  HNBRY/STHM BS10 .... 31 E3
Elliot Av *MANG/FISH* BS16 ..... 34 C4
Ellis Av
  BMSTRD/HC/WWD BS13 .... 84 A1
Ellis Pk *MTN/WRL* BS22 .... 118 D5
Elliston Dr *BATHSE* BA2 .... 107 C3
Elliston La *RDLND/MONT* BS6 .. 55 C1
Elliston Rd *RDLND/MONT* BS6 .. 55 C1
Ellsbridge Cl *KEYN* BS31 .... 89 E4
Ellsworth Rd
  HNBRY/STHM BS10 .... 30 D3
Elm Cl *AVONM* BS11 .... 29 C2
  BNWL BS29 .... 127 H2
  BRSTK/PCHW BS34 .... 21 F3
  NAIL BS48 .... 66 C5
  YTN/CONG BS49 .... 112 D4
Elmcroft Crs *HORF/LLZ* BS7 .... 46 C4
Elmdale Crs *THNB/SVB* BS35 ... 8 D3
Elmdale Gdns
  MANG/FISH BS16 .... 48 A4
Elmdale Rd *BMSTR* BS3 .... 72 C4
  CFTN/FAIL BS8 .... 55 F3
Elmfield *KGWD/HNM* BS15 .... 59 E5
Elmfield Cl *KGWD/HNM* BS15 .. 59 E5
Elmfield Rd
  HNLZ/SM/SNYPK/WT BS9 ... 45 E3
Elm Gv *BATHSE* BA2 .... 107 H5
  CBATH/BATHN BA1 .... 103 F2
  OMX/HUT/LCK BS24 .... 126 C2
Elmgrove Av *EVILLE/WHL* BS5 .. 14 S5
Elmgrove Dr *YATE/CS* BS37 .... 14 S5
Elmgrove Pk
  RDLND/MONT BS6 .... 56 H2
Elmgrove Rd *MANG/FISH* BS16 . 47 C5
  RDLND/MONT BS6 .... 56 A2
Elmhurst Av
  OMX/HUT/LCK BS24 .... 123 G2
Elmhurst Est
  CBATH/BATHN BA1 .... 91 G3
Elmhurst Gdns *YATE/CS* BS37 .. 14 C5
Elmhurst Rd *WSM* BS23 .... 7 H3
Elming Down Cl *ALMDB* BS32 .. 21 C4
Elm La *RDLND/MONT* BS6 ..... 55 H1
Elmlea Av
  HNLZ/SM/SNYPK/WT BS9 ... 44 D3
Elmleigh Av *MANG/FISH* BS16 .. 49 H3

Elmleigh Cl MANG/FISH BS16 49 G3
Elmleigh Rd MANG/FISH BS16 49 G3
Elm Lodge Rd NAIL BS48 67 H3
Elmore KGWD/HNM BS15 49 F5
YATE/CS BS37 25 H2
Elmore Rd BRSTK/PCHW BS34 20 B1
HORF/LLZ BS7 46 C2
Elm Pk BRSTK/PCHW BS34 32 C3
Elm Rd HORF/LLZ BS7 46 A3
KGWD/HNM BS15 59 E5
Elms Gv BRSTK/PCHW BS34 20 D1
Elmsleigh Rd WSM BS23 124 C2
Elmsley La MTN/WRL BS22 116 D2
The Elms CBATH/BATHN BA1 103 G2
Elmtree Av CLVDN BS21 66 B2
MANG/FISH BS16 49 G1
Elmtree Cl KGWD/HNM BS15 58 D2
Elmtree Dr
BMSTRD/HC/WWD BS13 84 A4
Elm Tree Pk PTSHD/EG BS20 * 41 F4
Elm Tree Rd CLVDN BS21 64 D3
OMX/HUT/LCK BS24 126 C2
Elmvale Dr
OMX/HUT/LCK BS24 126 C4
Elm Wk PTSHD/EG BS20 39 G4
YTN/CONG BS49 112 B4
Elm Wd YATE/CS BS37 26 A2
Elsbert Dr
BMSTRD/HC/WWD BS13 83 H3
Elstree Rd EVILLE/WHL BS5 57 G2
Elton La HORF/LLZ BS7 55 H1
Elton Rd CFTN/FAIL BS8 4 B2
CLVDN BS21 64 C2
KGWD/HNM BS15 58 B2
MTN/WRL BS22 117 H4
RDLND/MONT BS6 45 H5
Elton St CBRISNE BS2 5 K1
Elvard Cl
BMSTRD/HC/WWD BS13 84 B5
Elvard Rd
BMSTRD/HC/WWD BS13 84 B4
Elvaston Rd BMSTR BS3 73 F3
Elwell La
BLAG/CWMG/WR BS40 93 G3
Ely Gv
HNLZ/SM/SNYPK/WT BS9 43 H1
Embassy Rd EVILLE/WHL BS5 57 G2
Embassy Wk EVILLE/WHL BS5 57 G2
Embercourt Dr NAIL BS48 79 H3
Embleton Rd
HNBRY/STHM BS10 31 F3
Emersons Green La
MANG/FISH BS16 49 H2
Emersons Wy MANG/FISH BS16 50 A1
Emerson Wy MANG/FISH BS16 49 H1
Emery Rd
BRSG/KWL/STAPK BS4 75 E4
Emet Gv MANG/FISH BS16 49 H2
Emet La MANG/FISH BS16 49 H2
Emily Pl CFTN/FAIL BS8 * 54 D4
Emlyn Cl MTN/WRL BS22 118 A4
Emlyn Rd EVILLE/WHL BS5 57 E1
Emma-Chris Wy
BRSTK/PCHW BS34 33 E3
Emmett Wd HGRV/WHIT BS14 97 E1
Empire Crs KGWD/HNM BS15 76 B2
Emra Cl EVILLE/WHL BS5 57 H2
Enfield Rd MANG/FISH BS16 48 A5
Engine Common La
YATE/CS BS37 13 G3
Engine La NAIL BS48 78 C1
England's Crs FRCTL/WBN BS36 23 E3
Englishcombe La BATHSE BA2 107 H4
Englishcombe Pk
BATHSE BA2 * 107 H3
Englishcombe Ri BATHSE BA2 107 F4
Englishcombe Rd
BMSTRD/HC/WWD BS13 95 H1
Englishcombe Wy
BATHSE BA2 108 A4
Ennerdale Cl WSM BS23 125 F1
Ennerdale Rd
HNBRY/STHM BS10 31 H3
Entry Hl BATHSE BA2 108 C5
Entry Hill Dr BATHSE BA2 108 C5
Entry Hill Gdns BATHSE BA2 108 C4
Entry Hill Pk BATHSE BA2 108 C5
Entry Ri BATHSE BA2 110 D1
Epney Cl BRSTK/PCHW BS34 20 B1
Epsom Cl MANG/FISH BS16 35 F4
Epworth Rd
HNBRY/STHM BS10 31 E3
Erin Wk BRSG/KWL/STAPK BS4 85 E1
Ermine Wy AVONM BS11 42 C1
Ermleet Rd RDLND/MONT BS6 55 G1
Ernest Barker Cl
EVILLE/WHL BS5 * 56 D4
Ernestville Rd
MANG/FISH BS16 47 H5
Ervine Ter CBRISNE BS2 56 B3
Esgar Ri MTN/WRL BS22 117 F5
Eskdale THNB/SVB BS35 9 E5
Eskdale Cl MTN/WRL BS22 122 A3
Esmond Gv CLVDN BS21 64 D1
Esplanade Rd PTSHD/EG BS20 39 G1
Essery Rd EVILLE/WHL BS5 57 E1
Esson Rd KGWD/HNM BS15 58 B2
Estcourt Gdns
MANG/FISH BS16 47 F3
Estelle Pk EVILLE/WHL BS5 * 57 E1
Estoril YATE/CS BS37 26 B1
Estune Wk LGASH BS41 70 D5
Etloe Rd RDLND/MONT BS6 45 E4
Eton La BNWL BS29 123 G4
Eton Rd BRSG/KWL/STAPK BS4 74 C3
Ettlingen Wy CLVDN BS21 65 E3
Ettricke Dr MANG/FISH BS16 48 B2
Eugene St CBRISNE BS2 4 E1
Evans Cl BRSG/KWL/STAPK BS4 75 E1
Evans Rd RDLND/MONT BS6 55 F1
Eveleigh Av
CBATH/BATHN BA1 103 G2
Evelyn Rd CBATH/BATHN BA1 101 G4
HNBRY/STHM BS10 31 G5
Evelyn Ter
CBATH/BATHN BA1 * 102 D3
Evenlode Gdns AVONM BS11 43 F3
Evenlode Wy KEYN BS31 98 B1
Evercreech Rd
HGRV/WHIT BS14 85 H5
Everest Av MANG/FISH BS16 47 G4
Everest Rd MANG/FISH BS16 47 G4
Eve Rd EVILLE/WHL BS5 56 D2
Ewart Rd MTN/WRL BS22 121 H3
Ewell Rd HGRV/WHIT BS14 86 A3
Excelsior St BATHSE BA2 3 H6
Exeter Blds RDLND/MONT BS6 55 F1
Exeter Rd BMSTR BS3 72 C2
PTSHD/EG BS20 40 A4
WSM BS23 124 D1
Exford Cl WSM BS23 125 E4
Exley Cl OLD/WMLY/WICK BS30 77 F1
Exmoor Rd BATHSE BA2 108 C5
Exmoor St BMSTR BS3 72 C2
Exmouth Rd
BRSG/KWL/STAPK BS4 73 G5
Explore La CBRIS/FH BS1 4 D5
Exton Cl HGRV/WHIT BS14 86 A4
Eyer's La CBRISNE BS2 5 J2
Eyers Rd OMX/HUT/LCK BS24 122 C4

F

Faber Gv
BMSTRD/HC/WWD BS13 84 D5
Fabian Dr BRSTK/PCHW BS34 21 G5
Factory Rd FRCTL/WBN BS36 23 F3
Failand Cresent
HNLZ/SM/SNYPK/WT BS9 44 A3
Failand Wk
HNLZ/SM/SNYPK/WT BS9 44 A2
Fairacre Cl HORF/LLZ BS7 46 D3
OMX/HUT/LCK BS24 127 E2
Fairacres Cl KEYN BS31 88 B5
Fairfax St CBRIS/FH BS1 5 G3
Fairfield Av
CBATH/BATHN BA1 102 D2
Fairfield Cl MTN/WRL BS22 121 G2
NAIL BS48 80 C2
Fairfield Md NAIL BS48 80 B2
Fairfield Pk
CBATH/BATHN BA1 * 102 D2
Fairfield Park Rd
CBATH/BATHN BA1 102 D2
Fairfield Pl BMSTR BS3 72 C2
Fairfield Rd BMSTR BS3 72 C2
CBATH/BATHN BA1 102 D3
RDLND/MONT BS6 56 B1
Fairfield Ter
CBATH/BATHN BA1 * 102 D2
Fairfield Vw
CBATH/BATHN BA1 * 102 D2
Fairfield Wy NAIL BS48 80 B3
Fairfoot Rd
BRSG/KWL/STAPK BS4 73 H3
Fairford Cl KGWD/HNM BS15 59 F1
Fairford Crs
BRSTK/PCHW BS34 20 D2
Fairford Rd AVONM BS11 42 C1
Fair Furlong
BMSTRD/HC/WWD BS13 84 B5
Fairhaven YATE/CS BS37 26 B1
Fairhaven Rd
RDLND/MONT BS6 45 G4
Fair Lawn
OLD/WMLY/WICK BS30 76 D2
Fairlawn Av
BRSTK/PCHW BS34 32 C2
Fairlawn Rd RDLND/MONT BS6 56 B1
Fairlyn Dr KGWD/HNM BS15 49 F5
Fairoaks
OLD/WMLY/WICK BS30 76 D3
Fairview MTN/WRL BS22 117 G4
Fair View Dr RDLND/MONT BS6 55 G1
Fairview Rd KGWD/HNM BS15 59 F3
Fairway BRSG/KWL/STAPK BS4 74 C5
Fairway Cl MTN/WRL BS22 121 G1
OLD/WMLY/WICK BS30 77 E2
Fairways KEYN BS31 99 F2
Falcon Cl BRSTK/PCHW BS34 20 A2
HNLZ/SM/SNYPK/WT BS9 30 D5
PTSHD/EG BS20 39 H4
Falcon Crs MTN/WRL BS22 122 A3
Falcondale Rd
HNLZ/SM/SNYPK/WT BS9 44 D1
Falcondale Wk
HNLZ/SM/SNYPK/WT BS9 31 E5
Falcon Dr BRSTK/PCHW BS34 20 A2
Falconer Rd
CBATH/BATHN BA1 101 F1
Falcon Wk BRSTK/PCHW BS34 20 A2
Falcon Wy THNB/SVB BS35 9 E2
Falfield Rd
BRSG/KWL/STAPK BS4 74 B3
Falfield Wk HNBRY/STHM BS10 31 G5
Falkland Rd RDLND/MONT BS6 56 B1
Fallodon Ct
HNLZ/SM/SNYPK/WT BS9 45 F3
Fallodon Wy
HNLZ/SM/SNYPK/WT BS9 45 F3
Fallowfield MTN/WRL BS22 117 G4
OLD/WMLY/WICK BS30 77 F2
Falmouth Cl NAIL BS48 67 H5
Falmouth Rd HORF/LLZ BS7 45 H4
Fane Cl HNBRY/STHM BS10 31 E3
Fanshawe Rd
HGRV/WHIT BS14 85 H2
Farendell Rd MANG/FISH BS16 35 H4
Far Handstones
OLD/WMLY/WICK BS30 76 D2
Farington Rd
HNLZ/SM/SNYPK/WT BS9 45 H1
Farlands MANG/FISH BS16 51 F2
Farleigh Ri
CBATH/BATHN BA1 105 E2
Farleigh Rd CLVDN BS21 64 A4
KEYN BS31 88 A5
NAIL BS48 80 B3
Farleigh Wk
BMSTRD/HC/WWD BS13 84 B1
Farler's End NAIL BS48 79 G1
Farley Cl BRSTK/PCHW BS34 21 E3
Farm Cl MANG/FISH BS16 49 H2
MTN/WRL BS22 118 B4
Farm Ct MANG/FISH BS16 49 E1
Farmer Rd
BMSTRD/HC/WWD BS13 83 H5
Farmhouse Cl NAIL BS48 67 F4
Farmhouse Ct NAIL BS48 * 67 F5
Farm La THNB/SVB BS35 18 D1
Farm Rd MANG/FISH BS16 49 E1
MTN/WRL BS22 121 G2
OMX/HUT/LCK BS24 126 B4
Farmwell Cl
BMSTRD/HC/WWD BS13 84 C4
Farnaby Cl
BRSG/KWL/STAPK BS4 84 D2
Farnborough Rd
OMX/HUT/LCK BS24 127 F1
Farndale EVILLE/WHL BS5 58 A5
Farndale Rd MTN/WRL BS22 122 A3
Farne Cl
HNLZ/SM/SNYPK/WT BS9 45 F3
Farrant Cl
BRSG/KWL/STAPK BS4 85 E3
Farrs La BATHSE BA2 109 E5
Farr's La CBRIS/FH BS1 4 E5
Farr St AVONM BS11 28 B5
Faulkland Rd BATHSE BA2 2 A7
Faversham Dr
OMX/HUT/LCK BS24 125 F5
Fawkes Cl KGWD/HNM BS15 59 H3
Featherstone Rd
MANG/FISH BS16 47 G4
Feeder Rd CBRISNE BS2 73 H1
Felix Rd EVILLE/WHL BS5 56 D3
Felstead Rd
HNBRY/STHM BS10 32 A4
Feltham Rd MANG/FISH BS16 51 G3
Felton Gv
BMSTRD/HC/WWD BS13 84 A1
Felton La
BLAG/CWMG/WR BS40 93 E5
Felton St
BLAG/CWMG/WR BS40 92 D5
Fennel Dr ALMDB BS32 22 A3
Fennell Gv HNBRY/STHM BS10 31 E3
Fenners MTN/WRL BS22 118 A4
Fenns La LGASH BS41 70 B5
Fenshurst Gdns LGASH BS41 82 C1
Fenswood Md LGASH BS41 70 B5
Fenswood Rd LGASH BS41 70 B5
Fenton Cl KEYN BS31 99 E1
Fenton Rd HORF/LLZ BS7 45 H4
Fermaine Av
BRSG/KWL/STAPK BS4 75 E3
Fernbank Rd
RDLND/MONT BS6 55 G1
Fernbrook Cl MANG/FISH BS16 34 B4
Fern Cl HNBRY/STHM BS10 31 F2
Ferndale Av
OLD/WMLY/WICK BS30 76 C3
Ferndale Rd
CBATH/BATHN BA1 103 F1
HORF/LLZ BS7 32 C3
PTSHD/EG BS20 39 H2
Ferndene ALMDB BS32 11 E5
Ferndown YATE/CS BS37 26 A1
Ferndown Cl AVONM BS11 43 G1
Fern Gv ALMDB BS32 21 F3
NAIL BS48 78 D1
Fernhill La AVONM BS11 29 H4
Fernhurst Rd EVILLE/WHL BS5 57 H2
Fernlea Gdns PTSHD/EG BS20 42 B4
Fernlea Rd MTN/WRL BS22 121 H4
Fernleaze FRCTL/WBN BS36 24 A4
Fern Rd MANG/FISH BS16 48 D3
Fernside NAIL BS48 79 H2
Fernsteed Rd
BMSTRD/HC/WWD BS13 84 A3
Fern St CBRISNE BS2 56 B2
Fernville Est CLVDN BS21 64 C3
Ferry Ct BATHSE BA2 * 3 J5
Ferry La BATHSE BA2 3 H5
Ferry Rd KGWD/HNM BS15 76 A5
Ferry St CBRIS/FH BS1 5 G5
Fiddes Rd RDLND/MONT BS6 45 G4
Fiddlers Wood La ALMDB BS32 21 G2
The Fielders MTN/WRL BS22 118 A4
Fieldfare Av PTSHD/EG BS20 40 C2
Field Farm Cl
BRSTK/PCHW BS34 33 H1
Fielding's Rd BATHSE BA2 107 H1
Field La OLD/WMLY/WICK BS30 76 B3
Field Rd KGWD/HNM BS15 58 C2
The Fields MTN/WRL BS22 123 G1
Field View Dr MANG/FISH BS16 48 C2
Fiennes Cl MANG/FISH BS16 49 E4
Fifth Av HORF/LLZ BS7 32 C4
Fifth Wy AVONM BS11 29 E3
Filby Dr BRSTK/PCHW BS34 21 E2
Filton Av HORF/LLZ BS7 46 A2
HORF/LLZ BS7 32 C5
Filton Gv HORF/LLZ BS7 46 B2
Filton La BRSTK/PCHW BS34 33 F3
Filton Rd BRSTK/PCHW BS34 33 F3
HORF/LLZ BS7 46 B1
Filwood Broadway
BRSG/KWL/STAPK BS4 85 F1
Filwood Ct MANG/FISH BS16 48 B5
Filwood Dr KGWD/HNM BS15 59 F3
Filwood Rd MANG/FISH BS16 48 A5
Finch Cl MTN/WRL BS22 122 B3
THNB/SVB BS35 8 D2
The Finches PTSHD/EG BS20 40 B2
Finch Rd YATE/CS BS37 26 B2
Finisterre Pde PTSHD/EG BS20 40 B2
Finmere Gdns MTN/WRL BS22 117 H4
Fircliff Pk PTSHD/EG BS20 39 H1
Fireclay Rd EVILLE/WHL BS5 57 F5
Fire Engine La
FRCTL/WBN BS36 24 B3
Fire Station La AVONM BS11 28 B3
Firework Cl KGWD/HNM BS15 59 H3
Firfield St
BRSG/KWL/STAPK BS4 73 H2
Firgrove Crs YATE/CS BS37 14 B5
Fir Leaze NAIL BS48 66 C5
First Av BATHSE BA2 108 B3
BRSG/KWL/STAPK BS4 74 D1
PTSHD/EG BS20 41 G3
The Firs BATHSE BA2 111 F1
First Wy AVONM BS11 28 C4
Fir Tree Av
OMX/HUT/LCK BS24 126 B2
Fir Tree Cl BRSTK/PCHW BS34 20 A3
Fir Tree La EVILLE/WHL BS5 58 A5
Fisher Av KGWD/HNM BS15 59 G2
Fisher Rd KGWD/HNM BS15 59 G1
Fishers Md LGASH BS41 70 B5
Fishponds Rd EVILLE/WHL BS5 57 E1
Fishpool Hl HNBRY/STHM BS10 31 F1
Fitchett Wk
HNBRY/STHM BS10 30 D2
Fitzgerald Rd BMSTR BS3 73 G3
Fitzharding Rd
PTSHD/EG BS20 43 E5
Fitzroy Circ PTSHD/EG BS20 40 B2
Fitzroy Rd MANG/FISH BS16 58 B1
Fitzroy St
BRSG/KWL/STAPK BS4 73 H2
Five Acre Dr MANG/FISH BS16 47 H1
Flamingo Crs MTN/WRL BS22 122 B3
Flax Bourton Rd
CFTN/FAIL BS8 69 G3
Flaxman Cl HORF/LLZ BS7 46 D2
Flaxpits La FRCTL/WBN BS36 22 D4
Florence Gv MTN/WRL BS22 121 G3
Florence Pk ALMDB BS32 10 D2
RDLND/MONT BS6 45 F4
Florence Rd MANG/FISH BS16 49 E5
Flowerdown Br
MTN/WRL BS22 122 A4
Flowerdown Rd
OMX/HUT/LCK BS24 127 F2
Flowers Hl
BRSG/KWL/STAPK BS4 74 D5
Flowers Hill Cl
BRSG/KWL/STAPK BS4 74 D5
Flowerwell Rd
BMSTRD/HC/WWD BS13 84 C4
Folleigh Cl LGASH BS41 71 E4
Folleigh Dr LGASH BS41 71 E4
Folleigh La LGASH BS41 71 E4
Folliot Cl MANG/FISH BS16 34 A5
Folly Bridge Cl YATE/CS BS37 * 13 H5
Folly Brook Rd
MANG/FISH BS16 35 G3
Folly La CBRISNE BS2 56 C5
WSM BS23 124 D5
The Folly KEYN BS31 99 G2
MANG/FISH BS16 49 F1
Fontana Cl
OLD/WMLY/WICK BS30 77 E3
Fonthill Rd
CBATH/BATHN BA1 102 B2
HNBRY/STHM BS10 31 H3
Fontmell Ct HGRV/WHIT BS14 86 C2
Fontwell Dr MANG/FISH BS16 35 F4
Footes La FRCTL/WBN BS36 23 H3
Footshill Cl KGWD/HNM BS15 58 C5
Footshill Dr KGWD/HNM BS15 58 C4
Footshill Rd KGWD/HNM BS15 58 C5
Forde Cl
OLD/WMLY/WICK BS30 76 C1
Fordell Pl
BRSG/KWL/STAPK BS4 73 H3
Ford La MANG/FISH BS16 49 H2
Ford St EVILLE/WHL BS5 57 E5
Forefield Pl BATHSE BA2 3 H7
Forefield Ri BATHSE BA2 108 D3
Forefield Ter BATHSE BA2 3 H7
Forest Av MANG/FISH BS16 48 B5
Forest Dr HNBRY/STHM BS10 31 G2
WSM BS23 7 K1
Forest Edge KGWD/HNM BS15 75 H2
Forester Av BATHSE BA2 3 H1
Forester Ct BATHSE BA2 3 H1
Forester La BATHSE BA2 3 J1
Forester Rd BATHSE BA2 3 J2
PTSHD/EG BS20 39 H4
Forest Hills ALMDB BS32 10 D2
Forest Rd KGWD/HNM BS15 58 C5
Forest Wk MANG/FISH BS16 58 B1
Forge End PTSHD/EG BS20 41 G5
Fortfield Rd HGRV/WHIT BS14 86 A4
Forth Av PTSHD/EG BS20 40 B2
Forum Blds
CBATH/BATHN BA1 * 3 F6
Fosse Barton NAIL BS48 67 E4
Fosse Cl NAIL BS48 66 D4
Fossedale Av HGRV/WHIT BS14 86 A3
Fosse Gdns BATHSE BA2 110 B2
Fosse La CBATH/BATHN BA1 91 F5
NAIL BS48 66 D4
Fosseway CLVDN BS21 64 D4
Fosse Wy NAIL BS48 66 D4
The Fosseway CFTN/FAIL BS8 55 E5
Foster St EVILLE/WHL BS5 56 D1
Foundry La EVILLE/WHL BS5 57 H1
Fountain Blds
CBATH/BATHN BA1 3 F3
Fountaine Ct EVILLE/WHL BS5 57 E1
Fountains Dr
OLD/WMLY/WICK BS30 59 F5
Four Acre Av MANG/FISH BS16 35 E5
Four Acre Crs MANG/FISH BS16 35 E4
Four Acre Rd MANG/FISH BS16 35 E4
Four Acres
BMSTRD/HC/WWD BS13 83 H5
Four Acres Cl
BMSTRD/HC/WWD BS13 84 A5
NAIL BS48 79 F1
Fourth Av HORF/LLZ BS7 32 C3
Fourth Wy AVONM BS11 28 D4
Fowey Cl NAIL BS48 79 H1
Fowey Rd MTN/WRL BS22 117 H4
Fox And Hounds La KEYN BS31 88 C4
Fox Av YATE/CS BS37 13 H5
Foxborough Gdns
ALMDB BS32 11 F5
Fox Cl
BRSG/KWL/STAPK BS4 75 E1
Foxcombe Rd
CBATH/BATHN BA1 101 G5
HGRV/WHIT BS14 86 A5
Foxcote KGWD/HNM BS15 59 F4
Foxcote Rd BMSTR BS3 72 B3
Fox Ct OLD/WMLY/WICK BS30 76 C3
Foxcroft Cl ALMDB BS32 21 H4
Foxcroft Rd EVILLE/WHL BS5 57 F3
Fox Den Rd BRSTK/PCHW BS34 33 F2
Foxe Rd FRCTL/WBN BS36 23 G2
Foxfield Av ALMDB BS32 11 F4
Foxglove Cl MANG/FISH BS16 47 G4
MTN/WRL BS22 117 H3
THNB/SVB BS35 9 E2
Foxhill BATHSE BA2 108 D5
Fox Rd EVILLE/WHL BS5 56 C2
Fraley Rd
HNLZ/SM/SNYPK/WT BS9 45 E1
Frampton Ct
OLD/WMLY/WICK BS30 76 C2
Frampton Crs
MANG/FISH BS16 48 C4
Frampton End Rd
FRCTL/WBN BS36 24 A1
Francis Fox Rd WSM BS23 7 F5
Francis Pl
OLD/WMLY/WICK BS30 76 C2
Francis Rd BMSTR BS3 72 D4
HNBRY/STHM BS10 31 G5
Francis Wy
OLD/WMLY/WICK BS30 60 B4
Francombe Gv
HNBRY/STHM BS10 46 A2
Frankland Cl
CBATH/BATHN BA1 101 F3
Frankley Blds
CBATH/BATHN BA1 102 D3
Frankley Ter
CBATH/BATHN BA1 * 102 D3
Franklin's Wy YTN/CONG BS49 113 F2
Franklyn La CBRISNE BS2 56 B2
Franklyn St CBRISNE BS2 56 B2
Fraser Cl MTN/WRL BS22 117 G4
Fraser St BMSTR BS3 73 E3
Frayne Rd BMSTR BS3 72 B2
Frederick Pl CFTN/FAIL BS8 4 A2
Fredrick St
BRSG/KWL/STAPK BS4 73 H2
Freeland Blds EVILLE/WHL BS5 57 E1
Freeland Pl CFTN/FAIL BS8 54 D5
Freelands CLVDN BS21 64 C5
Freemans La NAIL BS48 92 C2
Freemantle Gdns
EVILLE/WHL BS5 47 E5
Freemantle Rd
EVILLE/WHL BS5 47 E5
Freestone Rd CBRISNE BS2 56 C5
Free Tank CBRIS/FH BS1 5 K5
Freeview Rd BATHSE BA2 107 F1
Fremantle La
RDLND/MONT BS6 55 H2
Fremantle Rd
RDLND/MONT BS6 55 G2
Frenchay Campus
MANG/FISH BS16 * 33 G4
Frenchay Cl MANG/FISH BS16 48 B1
Frenchay Hl MANG/FISH BS16 48 B1
Frenchay Park Rd
MANG/FISH BS16 47 H2
Frenchay Rd
MANG/FISH BS16 48 C1
WSM BS23 124 D2
French Cl NAIL BS48 67 G3
Freshland Wy
KGWD/HNM BS15 58 B3
Freshmoor CLVDN BS21 65 F2
Friar Av MTN/WRL BS22 117 F5
Friary CBRIS/FH BS1 5 J5
Friary Cl CLVDN BS21 62 A5
Friary Grange Pk
FRCTL/WBN BS36 23 E4
Friary Rd HORF/LLZ BS7 45 H5
PTSHD/EG BS20 39 F3
Friendly Rw
PTSHD/EG BS20 42 C3
Friendship Gv NAIL BS48 67 G3
Friendship Rd
BRSG/KWL/STAPK BS4 73 G4
NAIL BS48 67 G3
Friezewood Rd BMSTR BS3 72 B2
Fripp Cl EVILLE/WHL BS5 56 D5
Frobisher Av PTSHD/EG BS20 39 E3
Frobisher Cl MTN/WRL BS22 117 F4
PTSHD/EG BS20 39 E3
Frobisher Rd BMSTR BS3 72 B3
Frog La
BLAG/CWMG/WR BS40 92 D4
CBRIS/FH BS1 4 C4
FRCTL/WBN BS36 24 C2
Frogmore St CBRIS/FH BS1 4 D4
Frome Ct THNB/SVB BS35 8 D4
Frome Gln FRCTL/WBN BS36 35 E1
Frome Pl MANG/FISH BS16 47 G3
Frome Rd BATHSE BA2 110 C1
YATE/CS BS37 27 E1
Frome Ter MANG/FISH BS16 * 47 G3
Frome Valley Rd
MANG/FISH BS16 47 H2
Frome Valley Walkway
FRCTL/WBN BS36 35 E2
MANG/FISH BS16 48 C1
YATE/CS BS37 12 C5
Frome Valley Wy
YATE/CS BS37 27 G2
Frome Vw FRCTL/WBN BS36 23 H3
Frome Wy FRCTL/WBN BS36 23 E5
Froomshaw Rd
MANG/FISH BS16 48 A1
Frost Hl YTN/CONG BS49 112 D4
Fry's Cl MANG/FISH BS16 47 F4
Frys Hl BRSG/KWL/STAPK BS4 74 C4
KGWD/HNM BS15 59 E1
Fryth Wy NAIL BS48 66 D4
Fulford Rd
BMSTRD/HC/WWD BS13 84 C4
Fulford Wk
BMSTRD/HC/WWD BS13 84 C4
Fullens Cl MTN/WRL BS22 122 A4
Fuller Rd CBATH/BATHN BA1 103 F2
Fullers Wy BATHSE BA2 110 B2
Fulmar Cl THNB/SVB BS35 9 E2
Fulmar Rd MTN/WRL BS22 122 C2
Furber Ct EVILLE/WHL BS5 58 B5
Furber Rdg EVILLE/WHL BS5 58 B5
Furber Rd EVILLE/WHL BS5 58 B5
Furber V EVILLE/WHL BS5 58 B5
Furland Rd MTN/WRL BS22 121 G1
The Furlong RDLND/MONT BS6 45 G3
Furnwood EVILLE/WHL BS5 58 A5
Furze Cl MTN/WRL BS22 121 F1
Furze Rd MANG/FISH BS16 48 C5
MTN/WRL BS22 116 B5
Furzewood Rd
KGWD/HNM BS15 59 F3

Fylton Cft *HGRV/WHIT* BS14 .... 97 E1

G

Gable Rd *EVILLE/WHL* BS5 * 56 C2
Gabriel Cl
  OLD/WMLY/WICK BS30 .... 77 E1
Gadshill Dr *BRSTK/PCHW* BS34 .... 21 C5
Gadshill Rd *EVILLE/WHL* BS5 .... 47 E5
Gages Cl *KGWD/HNM* BS15 .... 59 F4
Gages Rd *KGWD/HNM* BS15 .... 59 F4
Gainsborough Dr
  MTN/WRL BS22 .... 117 C5
Gainsborough Gdns
  CBATH/BATHN BA1 .... 101 H4
Gainsborough Ms
  HNBRY/STHM BS10 * 31 F3
Gainsborough Rd *KEYN* BS31 .... 88 C4
Galingale Wy *PTSHD/EG* BS20 .... 40 B3
The Galleries *CBRIS/FH* BS1 * 5 C2
Gallivan Cl *BRSTK/PCHW* BS34 .... 20 D3
Galway Rd
  BRSG/KWL/STAPK BS4 .... 73 F5
Gander Cl
  BMSTRD/HC/WWD BS13 .... 84 C5
Gannet Rd *MTN/WRL* BS22 .... 122 C2
Garden Cl
  HNLZ/SM/SNYPK/WT BS9 .... 44 A3
  MTN/WRL BS22 .... 122 B1
Gardeners Wk *LGASH* BS41 .... 71 E5
Gardens Rd *CLVDN* BS21 .... 64 C1
The Gardens *MANG/FISH* BS16 .... 33 H4
Gardner Av
  BMSTRD/HC/WWD BS13 .... 84 A2
Gardner Rd *PTSHD/EG* BS20 .... 39 F2
Garfield Rd *EVILLE/WHL* BS5 .... 58 A5
Garner Ct *MTN/WRL* BS22 .... 118 A4
Garnet St *BMSTR* BS3 .... 72 C4
Garnett Pl *MANG/FISH* BS16 .... 49 F1
Garonor Wy *PTSHD/EG* BS20 .... 41 H3
Garrett Dr *ALMDB* BS32 .... 21 E3
Garrick Rd *BATHSE* BA2 .... 107 E2
Garsdale Cl *MTN/WRL* BS22 .... 122 A3
Garsdale Rd *MTN/WRL* BS22 .... 122 A3
Garstons *CBATH/BATHN* BA1 .... 105 E2
Garstons Cl *NAIL* BS48 .... 79 C5
The Garstons *PTSHD/EG* BS20 .... 39 C4
Garth Rd
  BMSTRD/HC/WWD BS13 .... 84 B1
Gasferry Rd *CBRIS/FH* BS1 .... 4 B7
The Gaskins *HORF/LLZ* BS7 .... 46 C5
Gas La *EVILLE/WHL* BS5 .... 56 C5
Gaston Av *KEYN* BS31 .... 88 C4
The Gastons *AVONM* BS11 .... 29 C5
Gatcombe Dr
  BRSTK/PCHW BS34 .... 33 C1
Gatcombe Rd
  BMSTRD/HC/WWD BS13 .... 84 C4
Gatehouse Av
  BMSTRD/HC/WWD BS13 .... 84 B4
Gatehouse Cl
  BMSTRD/HC/WWD BS13 .... 84 B4
Gatehouse Ct
  HGRV/WHIT BS14 .... 96 D1
Gatehouse Wy
  BMSTRD/HC/WWD BS13 .... 84 B4
Gatesby Md *BRSTK/PCHW* BS34.... 21 C5
Gathorne Crs *YATE/CS* BS37 .... 13 H5
Gathorne Rd *BMSTR* BS3 .... 72 C2
Gatton Rd *CBRISNE* BS2 .... 56 C2
Gaunts Cl *PTSHD/EG* BS20 .... 38 D4
Gaunt's La *CBRIS/FH* BS1 * 4 D4
Gaunts Rd *YATE/CS* BS37 .... 26 C2
Gay Elms Rd
  BMSTRD/HC/WWD BS13 .... 84 B5
Gayner Rd *HORF/LLZ* BS7 .... 32 C4
Gay's Hl *CBATH/BATHN* BA1 .... 102 D4
Gays Rd *KGWD/HNM* BS15 .... 75 C2
Gay St *CBATH/BATHN* BA1 .... 3 F3
Gaythorne Crs *YATE/CS* BS37 .... 13 H5
Gazelle Rd
  OMX/HUT/LCK BS24 .... 125 C3
Gazzard Cl *FRCTL/WBN* BS36 ...... 23 E3
Gee Moors *KGWD/HNM* BS15 .... 59 F4
Gefle Cl *CBRIS/FH* BS1 * 4 A7
Geoffrey Cl
  BMSTRD/HC/WWD BS13 .... 83 H3
George And Dragon La
  EVILLE/WHL BS5 .... 57 F3
George Cl *NAIL* BS48 .... 80 C2
George Jones Rd *CBRISNE* BS2 .... 56 C1
George's Pl *BATHSE* BA2 * 3 J4
George's Rd
  CBATH/BATHN BA1 .... 102 D3
Georges Sq *CBRIS/FH* BS1 .... 5 C4
George St *CBATH/BATHN* BA1 .... 3 F3
  EVILLE/WHL BS5 .... 57 E3
  WSM BS23 .... 7 F4
George Whitefield Ct
  CBRIS/FH BS1 * 5 H2
Georgian Wy *BATHSE* BA2 .... 107 C4
Gerald Rd *BMSTR* BS3 .... 72 B3
Gerard Rd *WSM* BS23 .... 7 F3
Gerrard Blds *BATHSE* BA2 * 3 J3
Gerrard Cl
  BRSG/KWL/STAPK BS4 .... 85 C2
Gerrish Av *EVILLE/WHL* BS5 .... 57 E3
  MANG/FISH BS16 .... 49 F3
Gibbet La *HGRV/WHIT* BS14 .... 97 F3
Gibbsfold Rd
  BMSTRD/HC/WWD BS13 .... 95 H1
Gibson Rd *RDLND/MONT* BS6 ...... 55 H2
Gifford Ct *BRSTK/PCHW* BS34 * 33 F3
Gifford Rd *HNBRY/STHM* BS10 .... 30 D1
Giffords Pl
  BMSTRD/HC/WWD BS13 .... 84 B2
Gilbeck Rd *NAIL* BS48 .... 66 D4
Gilbert Rd *EVILLE/WHL* BS5 .... 57 E3
  KGWD/HNM BS15 .... 58 D2
Gilberyn Dr *MTN/WRL* BS22 ...... 117 H5
Gilda Cl *HGRV/WHIT* BS14 .... 86 A4
Gilda Crs *HGRV/WHIT* BS14 .... 86 B4
Gilda Sq West
  HGRV/WHIT BS14 .... 86 A4
Gillard Cl *KGWD/HNM* BS15 .... 58 B3
Gillard Rd *KGWD/HNM* BS15 ...... 58 B3
Gill Av *MANG/FISH* BS16 .... 48 B2

Gillebank Cl *HGRV/WHIT* BS14 .... 86 C4
Gillingham Hl *EVILLE/WHL* BS5 .... 75 C1
Gillingham Ter
  CBATH/BATHN BA1 .... 103 E3
Gillingstool *THNB/SVB* BS35 .... 8 B4
Gill Ms *MTN/WRL* BS22 .... 117 H4
Gillmore Rd *MTN/WRL* BS22 ...... 122 A2
Gillray Cl *HORF/LLZ* BS7 .... 46 D2
Gillson Ct *OMX/HUT/LCK* BS24 .. 126 A4
Gilpin Cl *KGWD/HNM* BS15 .... 59 F2
Gilroy Cl *OLD/WMLY/WICK* BS30.. 77 E3
Gilslake Av *HNBRY/STHM* BS10 .. 31 F2
Gimblet Rd *MTN/WRL* BS22 ...... 118 A4
Gingells Gn *EVILLE/WHL* BS5 * 58 A3
Gipsy Patch La
  BRSTK/PCHW BS34 .... 20 D4
The Glades *EVILLE/WHL* BS5 .... 57 C1
Gladstone La *CBRISNE* BS2 .... 74 A4
Gladstone Pl *MANG/FISH* BS16 .... 48 D5
Gladstone La *FRCTL/WBN* BS36 .. 24 A3
Gladstone Rd *BATHSE* BA2 .... 109 F5
  HGRV/WHIT BS14 .... 86 A3
  KGWD/HNM BS15 .... 58 D2
Gladstone St *BMSTR* BS3 .... 72 C3
  EVILLE/WHL BS5 .... 57 F4
  MANG/FISH BS16 .... 48 D3
Glaisdale Rd *MANG/FISH* BS16 .... 48 A3
Glanville Gdns
  KGWD/HNM BS15 .... 59 E4
Glass House La *CBRISNE* BS2 ...... 74 A1
Glastonbury Cl *NAIL* BS48 .... 68 A5
  OLD/WMLY/WICK BS30 * 76 C1
Glastonbury Wy
  MTN/WRL BS22 .... 122 D1
Glebe Av *PTSHD/EG* BS20 .... 40 A4
Glebe Cl *LGASH* BS41 .... 71 E4
Glebe Fld *ALMDB* BS32 .... 10 C2
Glebelands Rd
  BRSTK/PCHW BS34 .... 32 C2
Glebe Rd *BATHSE* BA2 .... 107 C3
  CLVDN BS21 .... 64 C3
  EVILLE/WHL BS5 .... 57 C3
  LGASH BS41 .... 71 F5
  PTSHD/EG BS20 .... 40 A4
  YTN/CONG BS49 .... 7 F3
Gledemoor Dr
  FRCTL/WBN BS36 .... 24 B3
Glena Av
  BRSG/KWL/STAPK BS4 .... 74 A4
Glenarm Rd
  BRSG/KWL/STAPK BS4 .... 74 D4
Glenarm Wk
  BRSG/KWL/STAPK BS4 .... 74 D4
Glen Av *CFTN/FAIL* BS8 .... 53 F3
Glenavon Pk
  HNLZ/SM/SNYPK/WT BS9 .... 44 A4
Glen Brook
  HNLZ/SM/SNYPK/WT BS9 .... 44 A4
Glencoyne Sq
  HNBRY/STHM BS10 .... 31 C3
Glencroft Wy *MTN/WRL* BS22 .... 117 F5
Glendale *CFTN/FAIL* BS8 * 54 D5
  MANG/FISH BS16 .... 48 C5
Glendare St *EVILLE/WHL* BS5 ...... 57 E5
Glendevon Rd
  HGRV/WHIT BS14 .... 96 D1
Glen Dr
  HNLZ/SM/SNYPK/WT BS9 .... 44 D3
Gleneagles *YATE/CS* BS37 .... 26 A1
Gleneagles Cl *MTN/WRL* BS22 .... 117 C5
  NAIL BS48 .... 67 H5
Gleneagles Dr
  HNBRY/STHM BS10 .... 30 B2
Gleneagles Rd
  OLD/WMLY/WICK BS30 .... 59 H5
Glenfrome Rd *CBRISNE* BS2 .... 46 D5
Glen La *BRSG/KWL/STAPK* BS4 .... 74 C4
Glen Pk *EVILLE/WHL* BS5 .... 57 H2
Glen Park Gdns
  EVILLE/WHL BS5 .... 58 A3
Glenroy Av *EVILLE/WHL* BS5 ...... 58 B2
Glenside Campus
  MANG/FISH BS16 * 47 C3
Glenside Cl *MANG/FISH* BS16 .... 48 C1
Glenside Pk *MANG/FISH* BS16 .... 48 C1
The Glen *KEYN* BS31 .... 99 C3
  KGWD/HNM BS15 .... 75 C2
  MTN/WRL BS22 .... 121 C1
  RDLND/MONT BS6 .... 45 F5
Glentworth Rd *CFTN/FAIL* BS8 .... 4 E5
  RDLND/MONT BS6 .... 55 C1
Glenwood *MANG/FISH* BS16 ...... 48 C5
Glenwood Dr
  OLD/WMLY/WICK BS30 .... 77 E2
Glenwood Ri *PTSHD/EG* BS20 .... 38 D3
Glenwood Rd
  HNBRY/STHM BS10 .... 45 E1
Glevum Cl *MANG/FISH* BS16 ...... 50 A1
Gloster Av *EVILLE/WHL* BS5 ...... 57 E2
Gloucester Cl
  BRSTK/PCHW BS34 .... 21 F5
Gloucester La *CBRISNE* BS2 .... 5 K2
Gloucester Rd *ALMDB* BS32 ...... 10 D3
  AVONM BS11 .... 28 A4
  CBATH/BATHN BA1 .... 103 F1
  HORF/LLZ BS7 .... 55 H1
  MANG/FISH BS16 .... 49 E5
  THNB/SVB BS35 .... 8 D2
Gloucester Rd North
  HORF/LLZ BS7 .... 32 B4
Gloucester St *BATHSE* BA2 .... 54 D4
Gloucester St
  CBATH/BATHN BA1 .... 2 E2
  CBRISNE BS2 .... 5 H1
  CFTN/FAIL BS8 .... 54 D4
  EVILLE/WHL BS5 .... 57 F5
  WSM BS23 .... 6 D4
Gloucester Ter
  THNB/SVB BS35 * 8 C3
Glyn V *BMSTR* BS3 .... 73 E5
Goddard Wy
  HNBRY/STHM BS10 .... 31 E4
Godfrey Ct
  OLD/WMLY/WICK BS30 .... 76 C2
Godwin Dr *NAIL* BS48 .... 66 D4
Goffenton Dr *MANG/FISH* BS16 .. 48 B2
Goldcrest Rd *YATE/CS* BS37 .... 26 B3
Goldcrest Wy *PTSHD/EG* BS20 .... 40 B2

Golden Hl *RDLND/MONT* BS6 ...... 45 C3
Goldfinch Wy *MANG/FISH* BS16 .. 51 C4
Goldney Av *CFTN/FAIL* BS8 .... 55 E5
  OLD/WMLY/WICK BS30 .... 60 A4
Goldney Rd *CFTN/FAIL* BS8 .... 55 E5
Goldsbury Wk *AVONM* BS11 ...... 29 C4
Golf Club La *KEYN* BS31 .... 99 F2
Golf Course La
  BRSTK/PCHW BS34 .... 32 B2
  OLD/WMLY/WICK BS30 .... 77 F3
Gooch Ct
  OLD/WMLY/WICK BS30 .... 77 F3
Gooch Wy *MTN/WRL* BS22 .... 118 A5
Goodard Dr *MTN/WRL* BS22 ...... 118 A5
Goodeve Pk
  HNLZ/SM/SNYPK/WT BS9 * 44 B5
Goodeve Rd
  HNLZ/SM/SNYPK/WT BS9 .... 54 B1
Godhind St *EVILLE/WHL* BS5 ...... 56 C3
Goodeston Rd
  MANG/FISH BS16 .... 48 A5
Goodrich Cl *YATE/CS* BS37 .... 25 E1
Goodring Hl *AVONM* BS11 .... 29 C4
Good Shepherd Cl
  HORF/LLZ BS7 * 45 C4
Goodwin Dr *BMSTRD/HC/WWD* BS13 .. 85 C5
Goodwood Gdns
  MANG/FISH BS16 .... 35 F4
Goold Cl *CBATH/BATHN* BA2 ...... 99 H4
Goolden St
  BRSG/KWL/STAPK BS4 .... 73 H3
Goose Acre *ALMDB* BS32 .... 21 H4
Goosegreen *FRCTL/WBN* BS36 .... 23 H2
Goose Gn
  OLD/WMLY/WICK BS30 .... 60 A2
  YATE/CS BS37 .... 14 A4
Goose Green Wy *YATE/CS* BS37 .. 13 G3
Gooseland Cl *HGRV/WHIT* BS14 .. 96 C1
Goosey La *MTN/WRL* BS22 .... 123 F1
Cordano Gdns *PTSHD/EG* BS20 .. 42 B4
Cordano Rd *PTSHD/EG* BS20 ...... 41 F1
Gor Dano Vw *PTSHD/EG* BS20 .... 39 G3
Gordon Av *EVILLE/WHL* BS5 ...... 57 C2
Gordon Cl *EVILLE/WHL* BS5 .... 57 C2
Gordon Rd *BATHSE* BA2 .... 3 J7
  CBRISNE BS2 .... 56 B2
  EVILLE/WHL BS5 .... 57 F2
  MTN/WRL BS22 .... 118 C5
Gore Rd *BMSTR* BS3 .... 72 B5
Core's Marsh Rd *BMSTR* BS3 ...... 72 B4
Gorham Cl *AVONM* BS11 .... 30 A3
Gorlands Rd *YATE/CS* BS37 .... 27 E1
Gorlangton Cl
  HGRV/WHIT BS14 .... 85 H2
Gorse La *CFTN/FAIL* BS8 .... 48 C5
Gorse La *CFTN/FAIL* BS8 .... 5 H3
Gosforth Cl
  HNBRY/STHM BS10 .... 31 F4
Gosforth Rd
  HNBRY/STHM BS10 .... 31 F4
Goslet Rd *HGRV/WHIT* BS14 ...... 86 D4
Goss Barton *NAIL* BS48 .... 67 E5
Goss Cl *NAIL* BS48 .... 66 D5
Goss La *NAIL* BS48 .... 66 D5
Goss Vw *NAIL* BS48 .... 66 D5
Gotley Rd
  BRSG/KWL/STAPK BS4 .... 74 C4
Gott Dr *BRSG/KWL/STAPK* BS4 .... 74 C1
Goulston Rd
  BMSTRD/HC/WWD BS13 .... 84 B4
Goulston Wk
  BMSTRD/HC/WWD BS13 .... 84 B4
Gournecy Cl *AVONM* BS11 .... 29 H3
Gover Rd *KGWD/HNM* BS15 ...... 75 H3
Goving Cl *YATE/CS* BS37 .... 27 E1
  YTN/CONG BS49 .... 112 B3
Grace Cl *MANG/FISH* BS16 .... 48 D2
Grace Dr *KGWD/HNM* BS15 .... 59 C2
Grace Park Rd
  BRSG/KWL/STAPK BS4 .... 74 C5
Grace Rd *MANG/FISH* BS16 .... 48 C3
  MTN/WRL BS22 .... 118 A4
Gradwell Cl *MTN/WRL* BS22 ...... 118 A5
Graeme Cl *MANG/FISH* BS16 ...... 48 A4
Graham Rd *BMSTR* BS3 * 72 D3
  EVILLE/WHL BS5 .... 56 D2
  MANG/FISH BS16 .... 49 F2
  WSM BS23 .... 7 F2
Grainger Ct *AVONM* BS11 .... 43 E1
Grainger La *YTN/CONG* BS49 ...... 113 C3
Grampian Cl
  OLD/WMLY/WICK BS30 .... 77 F2
Granby Hl *CFTN/FAIL* BS8 .... 54 D5
Grand Pde *BATHSE* BA2 .... 3 C3
Grange Av *BRSTK/PCHW* BS34 .... 21 E4
  KGWD/HNM BS15 .... 76 A1
Grange Cl *ALMDB* BS32 .... 11 E5
  BRSTK/PCHW BS34 .... 33 H1
  THNB/SVB BS35 .... 124 D5
Grange Cl North
  HNLZ/SM/SNYPK/WT BS9 .... 45 F2
Grange Ct *KGWD/HNM* BS15 ...... 76 A1
  HNLZ/SM/SNYPK/WT BS9 .... 45 F2
Grange Court Rd
  HNLZ/SM/SNYPK/WT BS9 .... 45 F2
Grange Dr *MANG/FISH* BS16 ...... 48 C2
Grange Farm Rd
  YTN/CONG BS49 .... 112 A2
Grange Pk
  HNLZ/SM/SNYPK/WT BS9 .... 45 F2
  MANG/FISH BS16 .... 34 C5
Grange Rd
  BMSTRD/HC/WWD BS13 .... 84 A4
  CFTN/FAIL BS8 .... 55 E4
  KEYN BS31 .... 98 D1
  MANG/FISH BS16 .... 124 D5
The Grange
  HNLZ/SM/SNYPK/WT BS9 .... 44 D4
Grangeville Cl
  OLD/WMLY/WICK BS30 .... 77 E3
Grangewood Cl
  MANG/FISH BS16 .... 48 C2
Granny's La *KGWD/HNM* BS15 .... 59 E5
Grantham La
  KGWD/HNM BS15 .... 58 C2
Grantham Rd
  KGWD/HNM BS15 .... 58 C2
Grantson Cl
  BRSG/KWL/STAPK BS4 .... 74 D4

Granville Cl *KGWD/HNM* BS15 .... 75 G3
Granville Rd
  CBATH/BATHN BA1 .... 102 B1
Granville St *EVILLE/WHL* BS5 ...... 57 F5
Grasmere Cl
  HNBRY/STHM BS10 .... 31 E5
Grasmere Dr *WSM* BS23 .... 125 E2
Grassington Dr *YATE/CS* BS37 .... 26 C1
Grass Meers Dr
  HGRV/WHIT BS14 .... 85 H5
Grassmere Gdns
  OLD/WMLY/WICK BS30 .... 60 B5
Grassmere Rd
  YTN/CONG BS49 .... 112 B3
Gratitude Rd *EVILLE/WHL* BS5 .... 57 E2
Gravel Hill Rd *YATE/CS* BS37 ...... 14 B3
Gravel Hill Road (North)
  YATE/CS BS37 .... 14 C3
Gravel Wk *CBATH/BATHN* BA1 .... 2 E2
Graveney Cl
  BRSG/KWL/STAPK BS4 .... 74 C5
Gray Cl *HNBRY/STHM* BS10 .... 30 C3
Grayle Rd *HNBRY/STHM* BS10 .... 30 D2
Great Ann St *CBRISNE* BS2 .... 5 K2
Great Bedford St
  CBATH/BATHN BA1 .... 2 E1
Great Brockeridge
  HNLZ/SM/SNYPK/WT BS9 .... 44 D2
Great Dowles
  OLD/WMLY/WICK BS30 .... 76 D2
Great George St *CBRIS/FH* BS1 .... 4 C4
Great Hayles Rd
  HGRV/WHIT BS14 .... 85 H2
Great Leaze
  OLD/WMLY/WICK BS30 .... 76 D2
Great Meadow Rd
  ALMDB BS32 .... 21 H3
Great Park Rd *ALMDB* BS32 .... 11 E4
Great Pulteney St *BATHSE* BA2 .. 3 H5
Great Stanhope St
  CBATH/BATHN BA1 .... 2 D4
Great Stoke Wy
  BRSTK/PCHW BS34 .... 33 F2
Great Western La
  EVILLE/WHL BS5 .... 57 E5
Great Western Rd *CLVDN* BS21 .. 64 D2
Great Wood Cl
  BMSTRD/HC/WWD BS13 .... 84 D5
Greenacre *MTN/WRL* BS22 .... 121 C1
Greenacre Rd
  HGRV/WHIT BS14 .... 96 D1
Greenacres
  CBATH/BATHN BA1 .... 101 G1
Greenacres Pk
  FRCTL/WBN BS36 .... 24 B5
Greenbank Av East
  EVILLE/WHL BS5 .... 57 E2
Greenbank Av West
  EVILLE/WHL BS5 .... 56 D2
Greenbank Gdns
  CBATH/BATHN BA1 .... 101 C3
Greenbank Rd *BMSTR* BS3 .... 72 B2
  EVILLE/WHL BS5 .... 57 E2
  KGWD/HNM BS15 .... 76 A1
Greenbank Vw
  EVILLE/WHL BS5 .... 57 E1
Green Cft *EVILLE/WHL* BS5 .... 58 A2
Greendale Rd *BMSTR* BS3 .... 73 F3
  RDLND/MONT BS6 .... 45 F4
Green Dell Cl
  HNBRY/STHM BS10 * 30 B2
Greenditch Av
  BMSTRD/HC/WWD BS13 .... 84 D4
Greenditch Cl *NAIL* BS48 .... 58 A4
Greendown Pl *BATHSE* BA2 ...... 111 E1
Green Dragon Rd
  FRCTL/WBN BS36 .... 22 D5
Greenfield Av
  HNBRY/STHM BS10 .... 31 H5
Greenfield Crs *NAIL* BS48 .... 67 F3
Greenfield Pk
  PTSHD/EG BS20 .... 39 C5
Greenfield Pl *WSM* BS23 * 6 B2
Greenfield Rd
  HNBRY/STHM BS10 .... 31 H4
Greengage Cl
  MTN/WRL BS22 .... 122 B3
Green Hayes *YATE/CS* BS37 .... 27 E2
Greenhill Cl *MTN/WRL* BS22 ...... 117 H5
  NAIL BS48 .... 67 E4
Greenhill Gv *BMSTR* BS3 .... 72 B4
Greenhill La *AVONM* BS11 .... 29 H4
Greenland Rd
  MTN/WRL BS22 .... 122 A2
Greenlands Wy
  HNBRY/STHM BS10 .... 30 C1
Green La *AVONM* BS11 .... 28 B5
  CFTN/FAIL BS8 .... 69 H2
  FRCTL/WBN BS36 .... 22 C3
  THNB/SVB BS35 .... 18 A1
Greenleaze
  BRSG/KWL/STAPK BS4 .... 74 A5
Greenleaze Av
  MANG/FISH BS16 .... 34 D4
Greenmore Rd
  BRSG/KWL/STAPK BS4 .... 74 A4
Greenore Rd *KGWD/HNM* BS15 .. 58 C4
Green Pk *CBATH/BATHN* BA1 ...... 2 D5
Green Park Ms
  CBATH/BATHN BA1 .... 2 D5
Green Park Rd
  HNBRY/STHM BS10 .... 32 A4
Green Park Station
  CBATH/BATHN BA1 * 2 E4
Green Pastures Rd *NAIL* BS48 .... 68 A4
Greenridge Cl
  BMSTRD/HC/WWD BS13 .... 83 H5
Green's Hl *MANG/FISH* BS16 ...... 47 G5
Green Side *MANG/FISH* BS16 ...... 49 C2
Greenside Cl
  HNBRY/STHM BS10 .... 30 B2
Greenslade Gdns *NAIL* BS48 ...... 67 E3
Greensplott Rd *AVONM* BS11 .... 16 D3
Green St *BMSTR* BS3 .... 73 G2
  CBATH/BATHN BA1 .... 3 C4
Green Street *BRSTK/PCHW* BS34 .. 19 C4
  KGWD/HNM BS15 .... 59 E1
  NAIL BS48 .... 79 G4

Greenview
  OLD/WMLY/WICK BS30 .... 76 D4
Green Wk
  BRSG/KWL/STAPK BS4 .... 73 H5
Greenway Bush La *BMSTR* BS3 .. 72 B2
Greenway Ct *BATHSE* BA2 .... 108 C3
Greenway Dr
  HNBRY/STHM BS10 .... 31 H5
Greenway La *BATHSE* BA2 .... 108 C4
Greenway Pk *CLVDN* BS21 .... 65 F2
  HNBRY/STHM BS10 .... 31 H5
Greenway Rd
  RDLND/MONT BS6 .... 55 F1
Greenways *KGWD/HNM* BS15 .... 59 C2
Greenways Rd *YATE/CS* BS37 .... 13 H4
The Greenway
  MANG/FISH BS16 .... 48 C5
Greenwood Cl *HORF/LLZ* BS7 .... 46 A1
Greenwood Rd
  BRSG/KWL/STAPK BS4 .... 73 H4
  MTN/WRL BS22 .... 122 B1
Gregory Ct
  OLD/WMLY/WICK BS30 .... 77 E3
Gregory Md *YTN/CONG* BS49 .... 112 A2
Grenville Av
  OMX/HUT/LCK BS24 .... 126 D2
Grenville Cl *EVILLE/WHL* BS5 ...... 57 H3
Grenville Pl *CBRIS/FH* BS1 * 72 A1
Grenville Rd *RDLND/MONT* BS6 .. 56 A1
Greve Ct
  OLD/WMLY/WICK BS30 .... 77 E1
Greville Rd *BMSTR* BS3 .... 72 C2
Greville St *BMSTR* BS3 .... 72 D2
Greyhound Wk *CBRIS/FH* BS1 * .. 5 G2
Greylands Rd
  BMSTRD/HC/WWD BS13 .... 84 A2
Greystoke Av
  HNBRY/STHM BS10 .... 31 E5
Greystoke Gdns
  HNBRY/STHM BS10 .... 31 E5
Greystones *MANG/FISH* BS16 .... 35 E4
Griffin Cl
  OMX/HUT/LCK BS24 .... 122 B4
Griffin Cl *MTN/WRL* BS22 .... 123 E1
Griffin Rd *CLVDN* BS21 .... 64 D2
Griggfield Wk
  HGRV/WHIT BS14 .... 85 G2
Grimsbury Rd
  KGWD/HNM BS15 .... 59 G3
Grindell Rd *EVILLE/WHL* BS5 ...... 57 F4
Grinfield Av
  BMSTRD/HC/WWD BS13 .... 84 D5
Grinfield Ct
  BMSTRD/HC/WWD BS13 .... 84 D5
Grittleton Rd *HORF/LLZ* BS7 ...... 32 A5
Grosvenor Bridge Rd
  CBATH/BATHN BA1 .... 103 F3
Grosvenor Pk
  CBATH/BATHN BA1 .... 103 F3
Grosvenor Pl
  CBATH/BATHN BA1 .... 103 E3
Grosvenor Rd *CBRISNE* BS2 ...... 56 A3
Grosvenor Ter
  CBATH/BATHN BA1 * 103 F2
Grosvenor Vls
  CBATH/BATHN BA1 .... 103 E3
Grove Av *CBRIS/FH* BS1 .... 5 F6
  HNLZ/SM/SNYPK/WT BS9 .... 44 A1
Grove Bank
  MANG/FISH BS16 .... 34 C4
Grove Dr *MTN/WRL* BS22 .... 121 H2
Grove La *WSM* BS23 .... 6 D2
Grove Leaze *AVONM* BS11 .... 42 D2
Grove Pk
  BRSG/KWL/STAPK BS4 .... 74 C4
  RDLND/MONT BS6 .... 55 G1
Grove Park Av
  BRSG/KWL/STAPK BS4 .... 74 C4
Grove Park Rd
  BRSG/KWL/STAPK BS4 .... 74 C4
Grove Park Ter
  MANG/FISH BS16 .... 47 H4
Grove Rd *BNWL* BS29 .... 127 H2
  HNLZ/SM/SNYPK/WT BS9 .... 30 E5
  MANG/FISH BS16 .... 47 C4
  MTN/WRL BS22 .... 121 H2
  WSM BS23 .... 6 D2
Grovesend Rd
  THNB/SVB BS35 .... 8 C4
The Groves
  BMSTRD/HC/WWD BS13 .... 85 E5
Grove St *BATHSE* BA2 .... 3 G3
The Grove
  BRSTK/PCHW BS34 .... 20 D3
  CBATH/BATHN BA1 .... 101 H3
  CBRIS/FH BS1 .... 4 E6
  NAIL BS48 .... 68 B3
  OLD/WMLY/WICK BS30 .... 76 D2
Grove Vw *MANG/FISH* BS16 ...... 47 G2
Guernsey Av
  BRSG/KWL/STAPK BS4 .... 75 E2
Guest Av *MANG/FISH* BS16 ...... 49 H2
Guildford Rd
  BRSG/KWL/STAPK BS4 .... 57 G5
Guildhall Market
  CBATH/BATHN BA1 * 3 G3
Guinea La *CBATH/BATHN* BA1 .... 3 F2
  MANG/FISH BS16 .... 48 A3
Guinea St *CBRIS/FH* BS1 .... 5 F7
Guildford's Bank *CLVDN* BS21 .... 65 E3
Guillmores Gdns
  BRSG/KWL/STAPK BS4 .... 84 C5
Gullivers Pl *YATE/CS* BS37 .... 26 C2
Gullons Ct
  BMSTRD/HC/WWD BS13 .... 84 B3
Gullon Wk
  BMSTRD/HC/WWD BS13 .... 84 A4
Gully Brook La
  EVILLE/WHL BS5 * 56 D5
The Gully *FRCTL/WBN* BS36 .... 23 F3
Gunning Cl
  BRSG/KWL/STAPK BS4 .... 58 D5
Gunter's Hill *EVILLE/WHL* BS5 .... 58 B5
Guthrie Rd *CFTN/FAIL* BS8 .... 54 C3
Gwilliam St *BMSTR* BS3 .... 73 E3
Gwyn St *CBRISNE* BS2 .... 56 A2

Gypsy La KEYN BS31 98 C4

H

Haberfield Hl PTSHD/EG BS20 52 D1
Hacket Hl THNB/SVB BS35 9 G4
Hacket La THNB/SVB BS35 9 F3
Hadley Ct
OLD/WMLY/WICK BS30 59 H5
Hadley Rd BATHSE BA2 109 E5
Hadrian Cl
HNLZ/SM/SNYPK/WT BS9 44 A4
Hadrians Wk MANG/FISH BS16 50 A2
Halbrow Crs MANG/FISH BS16 48 C3
Haldon Cl BMSTR BS3 73 E5
Hale Cl KGWD/HNM BS15 76 A2
Hales Horn Cl ALMDB BS32 21 F4
Halfacre Cl HGRV/WHIT BS14 96 D1
Halfacre La HGRV/WHIT BS14 97 E1
Halifax Rd YATE/CS BS37 13 H3
Hallam Rd CLVDN BS21 64 C2
Hallards Cl AVONM BS11 29 F5
Hallen Cl HNBRY/STHM BS10 30 B2
MANG/FISH BS16 50 A2
Hallen Dr
HNLZ/SM/SNYPK/WT BS9 44 A1
Hallen Rd HNBRY/STHM BS10 30 A1
Halletts Wy PTSHD/EG BS20 39 H3
Halliwell Rd PTSHD/EG BS20 38 B4
Halls Gdns BRSTK/PCHW BS34 34 A1
Halls Rd KGWD/HNM BS15 58 D3
Hall St BMSTR BS3 72 C4
Halsbury Rd RDLND/MONT BS6 45 F4
Halstock Av MANG/FISH BS16 47 H5
Halston Dr CBRISNE BS2 56 B3
Halswell Gdns
BMSTRD/HC/WWD BS13 84 C5
Halswell Rd CLVDN BS21 64 D4
Halt End HGRV/WHIT BS14 97 F1
Halwyn Cl
HNLZ/SM/SNYPK/WT BS9 44 B3
Hamble Cl THNB/SVB BS35 8 D4
Hambledon Rd
MTN/WRL BS22 118 B4
Hambrook La
BRSTK/PCHW BS34 33 H1
Ham Farm La MANG/FISH BS16 49 H2
Ham Gn PTSHD/EG BS20 42 D4
Hamilton Rd BMSTR BS3 72 C2
CBATH/BATHN BA1 102 B2
EVILLE/WHL BS5 56 C3
WSM BS23 120 B2
Ham La LGASH BS41 94 C1
MANG/FISH BS16 47 G2
NAIL BS48 67 H2
The Hamlet NAIL BS48 67 H3
Hammersmith Rd
EVILLE/WHL BS5 57 F3
Hammond Cl
BRSG/KWL/STAPK BS4 74 C5
Hammond Gdns
HNLZ/SM/SNYPK/WT BS9 44 C1
Hampden Cl YATE/CS BS37 13 H3
Hampden Rd
BRSG/KWL/STAPK BS4 74 A3
MTN/WRL BS22 122 A1
Hampshire Wy YATE/CS BS37 14 B3
Hampstead Rd
BRSG/KWL/STAPK BS4 74 B3
Hampton Cl
OLD/WMLY/WICK BS30 76 D1
Hampton Cnr AVONM BS11 * 43 E2
Hampton La RDLND/MONT BS6 55 F2
Hampton Pk
RDLND/MONT BS6 55 F2
Hampton Rd
RDLND/MONT BS6 55 F1
Hampton Rw BATHSE BA2 3 K1
Hampton St KGWD/HNM BS15 58 D2
Hampton Vw
CBATH/BATHN BA1 103 E3
Hams Rd KEYN BS31 88 C2
Ham Wood Cl
OMX/HUT/LCK BS24 125 G5
Hanbury Cl KGWD/HNM BS15 76 A1
Hanbury Rd CFTN/FAIL BS8 55 E3
Handel Av EVILLE/WHL BS5 57 F4
Handel Cossham Ct
KGWD/HNM BS15 58 C2
Handel Rd KEYN BS31 88 A4
Handford Wy
OLD/WMLY/WICK BS30 77 E2
Hanford Ct HGRV/WHIT BS14 86 C2
Hanham Rd KGWD/HNM BS15 58 D5
Hanham Wy NAIL BS48 66 C4
Hannah More Rd NAIL BS48 66 D5
Hanover Cl MTN/WRL BS22 117 H4
Hanover Ct CBRIS/FH BS1 * 5 H2
Hanover Pl
CBATH/BATHN BA1 * 103 E4
CBRIS/FH BS1 4 B7
Hanover St
CBATH/BATHN BA1 103 E3
EVILLE/WHL BS5 57 E4
Hanover Ter
CBATH/BATHN BA1 * 103 E3
Hansford Cl BATHSE BA2 110 C1
Hansford Sq BATHSE BA2 110 C1
Hanson's Wy CLVDN BS21 64 C3
Hans Price Cl WSM BS23 7 F3
Hantone Hl BATHSE BA2 104 A4
Happerton La
PTSHD/EG BS20 52 C1
Hapsburg Cl MTN/WRL BS22 117 H4
Harbour Crs PTSHD/EG BS20 40 A3
Harbour Rd PTSHD/EG BS20 39 H2
Harbour Wall
HNLZ/SM/SNYPK/WT BS9 43 H4
Harbour Wy CBRIS/FH BS1 4 C6
Harbury Rd
HNLZ/SM/SNYPK/WT BS9 45 G1
Harbutts BATHSE BA2 104 A3
Harcombe Hl FRCTL/WBN BS36 35 E1
Harcombe Rd
FRCTL/WBN BS36 22 D5
Harcourt Av EVILLE/WHL BS5 58 A5
Harcourt Cl KEYN BS31 * 99 F2
Harcourt Gdns
CBATH/BATHN BA1 101 G2
Harcourt Hl RDLND/MONT BS6 45 G5
Harcourt Rd RDLND/MONT BS6 45 F4
Hardenhuish Rd
BRSG/KWL/STAPK BS4 74 C1
Harden Rd HGRV/WHIT BS14 86 D4
Hardings Ter EVILLE/WHL BS5 * 57 H3
Hardington Dr KEYN BS31 98 B2
Hardwick Cl
BRSG/KWL/STAPK BS4 74 D3
OLD/WMLY/WICK BS30 77 G1
Hardwicke YATE/CS BS37 25 G3
Hardwick Rd PTSHD/EG BS20 42 C4
Hardy Av BMSTR BS3 72 B3
Hardy Ct
OLD/WMLY/WICK BS30 76 C1
Hardy Rd BMSTR BS3 72 B4
Hareclive Rd
BMSTRD/HC/WWD BS13 84 C4
Harefield Cl KGWD/HNM BS15 75 H4
Harescombe YATE/CS BS37 26 A3
Harewood Rd EVILLE/WHL BS5 58 A2
Harford Cl
HNLZ/SM/SNYPK/WT BS9 44 A1
Harford Dr MANG/FISH BS16 34 C4
Harington Pl
CBATH/BATHN BA1 3 F4
Harlech Wy
OLD/WMLY/WICK BS30 77 E4
Harleston St EVILLE/WHL BS5 5 K1
Harley La CLVDN BS21 63 G4
Harley Ms CFTN/FAIL BS8 54 D4
Harley Pl CFTN/FAIL BS8 * 54 D4
Harley St CBATH/BATHN BA1 2 E1
Harmer Cl HNBRY/STHM BS10 30 D2
Harmony Dr PTSHD/EG BS20 38 D4
Harnhill Cl
BMSTRD/HC/WWD BS13 84 C5
Harnwood Sq HORF/LLZ BS7 46 A4
Harolds Wy KGWD/HNM BS15 58 C5
Harptree Cl NAIL BS48 79 E1
Harptree Ct
OLD/WMLY/WICK BS30 76 D2
Harptree Gv BMSTR BS3 72 C4
Harrington Av
HGRV/WHIT BS14 86 D3
Harrington Cl
OLD/WMLY/WICK BS30 89 H1
Harrington Gv
HGRV/WHIT BS14 86 D3
Harrington Rd
HGRV/WHIT BS14 86 D3
Harrington Wk
HGRV/WHIT BS14 86 D3
Harris Barton
FRCTL/WBN BS36 23 G3
Harris Ct
OLD/WMLY/WICK BS30 76 C2
Harris Gv
BMSTRD/HC/WWD BS13 95 G1
Harris La CFTN/FAIL BS8 53 F3
Harrison Cl MANG/FISH BS16 49 H2
Harrowdene Rd
BRSG/KWL/STAPK BS4 74 A3
Harrow Rd
BRSG/KWL/STAPK BS4 74 C3
Harry Stoke Rd
BRSTK/PCHW BS34 33 G2
Hartcliffe Rd
BRSG/KWL/STAPK BS4 85 F1
Hartcliffe Wk
BRSG/KWL/STAPK BS4 85 G1
Hartcliffe Wy BMSTR BS3 72 D5
BMSTRD/HC/WWD BS13 84 D2
Hart Cl PTSHD/EG BS20 43 E4
Hartfield Av
RDLND/MONT BS6 55 G3
Hartgill Cl
BMSTRD/HC/WWD BS13 95 G1
Hartington Pk
RDLND/MONT BS6 55 F1
Hartley Cl YATE/CS BS37 27 E1
Harts Cft YATE/CS BS37 14 B3
Harvest Cl ALMDB BS32 21 F1
Harvest La
OMX/HUT/LCK BS24 123 E3
Harvest Wy MTN/WRL BS22 117 H3
Harvey Cl MTN/WRL BS22 117 H4
Harveys La EVILLE/WHL BS5 57 G3
Harwood Gdns
MTN/WRL BS22 117 F4
Haselbury Gv KEYN BS31 99 F2
Haskins Ct
OLD/WMLY/WICK BS30 76 D2
Hassell Dr CBRISNE BS2 56 C4
Hastings Cl BMSTR BS3 72 D5
Hastings Rd BMSTR BS3 72 D5
Hatchet La BRSTK/PCHW BS34 33 G1
Hatchet Rd ALMDB BS32 21 F4
BRSTK/PCHW BS34 33 G1
Hatchmere THNB/SVB BS35 9 E4
Hatfield Blds BATHSE BA2 3 J7
Hatfield Rd BATHSE BA2 108 B4
WSM BS23 7 K3
Hatherley YATE/CS BS37 26 A3
Hatherley Rd HORF/LLZ BS7 46 A4
Hathway Wk EVILLE/WHL BS5 56 C3
Hatters' La YATE/CS BS37 27 E1
The Haven KGWD/HNM BS15 59 E2
Haversham Cl
MTN/WRL BS22 122 A2
Haverstock Rd
BRSG/KWL/STAPK BS4 73 H3
Haviland Gv
CBATH/BATHN BA1 101 F1
Haviland Pk
CBATH/BATHN BA1 101 G2
Havory CBATH/BATHN BA1 103 E3
Hawarden Ter
CBATH/BATHN BA1 103 E3
Hawburn Cl
BRSG/KWL/STAPK BS4 74 C4
Haweswater Cl
OLD/WMLY/WICK BS30 60 B5
Hawke Rd MTN/WRL BS22 117 F4
Hawkesbury Rd
MANG/FISH BS16 47 G5
Hawkesley Dr
BRSTK/PCHW BS34 21 F4
Hawkesworth Rd
YATE/CS BS37 13 G4
Hawkfield Cl
BMSTRD/HC/WWD BS13 85 E4
Hawkfield Rd
BMSTRD/HC/WWD BS13 85 E4
Hawkfield Wy
HGRV/WHIT BS14 85 E4
Hawkins Cl
OLD/WMLY/WICK BS30 77 F2
Hawkins Crs ALMDB BS32 21 F2
Hawkins St CBRISNE BS2 5 J3
Hawkley Dr ALMDB BS32 11 F4
Hawkridge Dr
MANG/FISH BS16 51 G3
Hawksmoor Cl
HGRV/WHIT BS14 85 H3
Hawksmoor La
MANG/FISH BS16 33 G5
Hawksworth Dr
KGWD/HNM BS15 75 G2
MTN/WRL BS22 118 A5
Hawthorn Av
KGWD/HNM BS15 75 G1
Hawthorn Cl
BRSTK/PCHW BS34 20 A3
PTSHD/EG BS20 38 D3
Hawthorn Crs THNB/SVB BS35 8 D2
YTN/CONG BS49 112 A2
Hawthorne Cl
MANG/FISH BS16 51 G3
Hawthorne Ri
HNBRY/STHM BS10 * 31 G2
The Hawthornes
MANG/FISH BS16 49 F4
Hawthorne St
BRSG/KWL/STAPK BS4 73 H3
Hawthorn Gdns
MTN/WRL BS22 122 A1
Hawthorn Gv BATHSE BA2 110 D1
Hawthorn Hts
MTN/WRL BS22 117 E5
Hawthorn Hl MTN/WRL BS22 117 F5
Hawthorn Pk MTN/WRL BS22 117 F5
Hawthorns La KEYN BS31 88 B4
Hawthorn Wy
BRSTK/PCHW BS34 21 G5
NAIL BS48 67 G4
Haycombe HGRV/WHIT BS14 85 G3
Haycombe Dr BATHSE BA2 107 F2
Haycombe La BATHSE BA2 107 F4
Hay Ct PTSHD/EG BS20 42 A4
Haycroft Rd
BRSTK/PCHW BS34 32 C2
Hayden Cl BATHSE BA2 2 D7
Haydock Cl MANG/FISH BS16 35 F4
Haydon Gdns HORF/LLZ BS7 46 D3
Hayeley Dr ALMDB BS32 21 G4
Hayes Cl CBRISNE BS2 56 C4
Hayesfield Pk BATHSE BA2 2 E7
Hayes Pl BATHSE BA2 2 E7
Hay Hl CBATH/BATHN BA1 3 F2
Hay Leaze YATE/CS BS37 13 H3
The Haymarket CBRIS/FH BS1 5 F2
Haymarket Wk CBRIS/FH BS1 5 F1
Haynes La MANG/FISH BS16 48 D3
Haythorn Ct MANG/FISH BS16 49 F3
Haytor Pk
HNLZ/SM/SNYPK/WT BS9 44 B2
Hayward Cl CLVDN BS21 64 C4
Hayward Rd EVILLE/WHL BS5 57 E4
MANG/FISH BS16 48 D5
Haywood Cl
OMX/HUT/LCK BS24 125 F5
Haywood Gdns
OMX/HUT/LCK BS24 125 F5
Hazel Av RDLND/MONT BS6 55 F1
Hazelbury Dr
OLD/WMLY/WICK BS30 60 A5
Hazelbury Rd HGRV/WHIT BS14 86 B1
NAIL BS48 67 E5
Hazel Cote Rd
HGRV/WHIT BS14 86 A5
Hazel Crs THNB/SVB BS35 9 E3
Hazeldene Rd
BRSTK/PCHW BS34 20 C3
WSM BS23 7 J2
Hazel Gv BATHSE BA2 108 A3
Hazelgrove FRCTL/WBN BS36 23 E5
Hazel Gv HORF/LLZ BS7 32 C5
Hazell Cl CLVDN BS21 65 E4
Hazelton Rd HORF/LLZ BS7 45 H5
Hazel Wy BATHSE BA2 110 B2
Hazelwood Rd
HNLZ/SM/SNYPK/WT BS9 44 B5
Head Cft NAIL BS48 81 G1
Headford Av EVILLE/WHL BS5 58 B4
Headford Rd
BRSG/KWL/STAPK BS4 73 E5
Headington Cl
KGWD/HNM BS15 76 A2
Headley Ct
BMSTRD/HC/WWD BS13 84 C3
Headley La
BMSTRD/HC/WWD BS13 84 C3
Headley Park Av
BMSTRD/HC/WWD BS13 84 C2
Headley Park Rd
BMSTRD/HC/WWD BS13 84 B2
Headley Rd
BMSTRD/HC/WWD BS13 84 B3
Headley Wk
BMSTRD/HC/WWD BS13 84 C2
Heart Meers HGRV/WHIT BS14 86 A4
Heath Cl FRCTL/WBN BS36 23 E4
Heathcote Dr
FRCTL/WBN BS36 24 B3
Heathcote Rd
MANG/FISH BS16 58 B1
Heathcote Wk
MANG/FISH BS16 58 C1
Heath Ct MANG/FISH BS16 48 D1
Heather Av FRCTL/WBN BS36 23 H4
Heather Cl KGWD/HNM BS15 58 B3
Heatherdene
HGRV/WHIT BS14 85 G2
Heather Dr BATHSE BA2 110 B2
Heathfield Cl
CBATH/BATHN BA1 101 F1
KEYN BS31 87 H4
Heathfield Crs
HGRV/WHIT BS14 85 H5
Heathfield Rd NAIL BS48 67 F4
Heathfields MANG/FISH BS16 34 D5
Heathfield Wy NAIL BS48 67 F3
Heath Gdns FRCTL/WBN BS36 24 A4
MANG/FISH BS16 34 D5
Heathgate YTN/CONG BS49 112 B3
Heath House La
EVILLE/WHL BS5 46 D4
Heath Rdg LGASH BS41 70 D4
Heath Ri
OLD/WMLY/WICK BS30 77 E1
Heath Rd EVILLE/WHL BS5 46 D5
KGWD/HNM BS15 75 G2
MANG/FISH BS16 48 D1
NAIL BS48 67 F3
Heath St EVILLE/WHL BS5 57 E1
Heath Wk MANG/FISH BS16 48 D1
Heber St EVILLE/WHL BS5 57 E4
Hebron Rd BMSTR BS3 72 D3
Hedge Cl OMX/HUT/LCK BS24 123 E3
Hedgemead Vw
MANG/FISH BS16 47 F3
The Hedgerows ALMDB BS32 21 F1
Hedgers Cl BMSTR BS3 72 B4
Hedges Cl CLVDN BS21 64 B4
The Hedges MTN/WRL BS22 118 B5
Hedwick St EVILLE/WHL BS5 57 F4
Heggard Cl
BMSTRD/HC/WWD BS13 84 B4
Hellier Wk
BMSTRD/HC/WWD BS13 95 H1
Helston Rd NAIL BS48 67 H5
Helting Ct CBATH/BATHN BA1 3 F5
Hemmings Pde
EVILLE/WHL BS5 56 D4
Hemming Wy
OMX/HUT/LCK BS24 126 B3
Hemplow Cl HGRV/WHIT BS14 86 C2
Hempton La ALMDB BS32 10 C5
Henacre Rd AVONM BS11 29 F5
Henbury Gdns
HNBRY/STHM BS10 * 30 C3
Henbury Rd
HNBRY/STHM BS10 30 C3
HNLZ/SM/SNYPK/WT BS9 31 E5
KGWD/HNM BS15 75 G1
Henbury Road Henbury Hl
HNLZ/SM/SNYPK/WT BS9 30 D5
Hencliffe Rd HGRV/WHIT BS14 86 C3
Hencliffe Wy KGWD/HNM BS15 75 G3
Henderson Rd
KGWD/HNM BS15 75 G1
Hendre Rd BMSTR BS3 72 B4
Henfield Crs
OLD/WMLY/WICK BS30 77 E2
Henfield Rd FRCTL/WBN BS36 36 B2
Hengaston St BMSTR BS3 72 C4
Hengrove Av HGRV/WHIT BS14 86 A1
Hengrove La HGRV/WHIT BS14 86 A1
Hengrove Rd
BRSG/KWL/STAPK BS4 73 H4
Hengrove Wy
BMSTRD/HC/WWD BS13 84 C4
Henleaze Av
HNLZ/SM/SNYPK/WT BS9 45 E3
Henleaze Gdns
HNLZ/SM/SNYPK/WT BS9 45 E3
Henleaze Pk
HNLZ/SM/SNYPK/WT BS9 45 G3
Henleaze Park Dr
HNLZ/SM/SNYPK/WT BS9 45 G2
Henleaze Rd
HNLZ/SM/SNYPK/WT BS9 45 E3
Henleaze Ter
HNLZ/SM/SNYPK/WT BS9 45 F1
Henley Gv
HNLZ/SM/SNYPK/WT BS9 45 F3
Henley La YTN/CONG BS49 112 D4
Henley Ldg YTN/CONG BS49 112 D4
Henley Pk YTN/CONG BS49 112 C4
Hennessy Cl HGRV/WHIT BS14 96 B1
Henrietta Gdns BATHSE BA2 3 H2
Henrietta Ms BATHSE BA2 3 H3
Henrietta Pl BATHSE BA2 3 G3
Henrietta Rd BATHSE BA2 3 H2
Henrietta St BATHSE BA2 3 H3
CBRISNE BS2 55 G3
Henry St BMSTR BS3 73 G2
CBATH/BATHN BA1 3 G5
Henry Williamson Ct
OLD/WMLY/WICK BS30 76 D1
Henshaw Cl KGWD/HNM BS15 58 C1
Henshaw Rd KGWD/HNM BS15 58 C1
Henshaw Wk KGWD/HNM BS15 58 C1
Hensley Gdns BATHSE BA2 108 B3
Hensley Rd BATHSE BA2 108 B4
Hensman's Hl CFTN/FAIL BS8 55 E5
Hepburn Rd CBRIS/FH BS1 56 A3
Herald Cl
HNLZ/SM/SNYPK/WT BS9 44 B3
Herapath St EVILLE/WHL BS5 57 E5
Herbert Crs EVILLE/WHL BS5 47 F5
Herbert Rd BATHSE BA2 2 A7
CLVDN BS21 64 D1
Herbert St BMSTR BS3 72 D2
EVILLE/WHL BS5 57 E3
Hercules Cl BRSTK/PCHW BS34 21 F4
Hereford Rd CBRISNE BS2 56 C1
Hereford St BMSTR BS3 73 E3
Herkomer Cl HORF/LLZ BS7 46 D1
Herluin Wy WSM BS23 121 G5
Hermes Cl KEYN BS31 98 D2
Hermitage Cl AVONM BS11 43 E1
Hermitage Rd
CBATH/BATHN BA1 102 B3
MANG/FISH BS16 48 D3
Hern La NAIL BS48 82 B4
Heron Cl MTN/WRL BS22 122 B2
Heron Gdns PTSHD/EG BS20 40 A4
Heron Rd EVILLE/WHL BS5 56 D2
Heron Wk CLVDN BS21 63 F1
Heron Wy YATE/CS BS37 26 B3
Herridge Cl
BMSTRD/HC/WWD BS13 84 C5
Herridge Rd
BMSTRD/HC/WWD BS13 84 C5
Hersey Gdns
BMSTRD/HC/WWD BS13 94 D1
Hesding Cl KGWD/HNM BS15 75 H3
Hestercombe Cl
OMX/HUT/LCK BS24 122 B4
Hestercombe Rd
BMSTRD/HC/WWD BS13 84 C3
Hester Wd YATE/CS BS37 14 B3
Hewland Ct AVONM BS11 30 A3
Hewlands Ct AVONM BS11 * 30 A3
Heyford Av EVILLE/WHL BS5 46 D5
Heyron Wk
BMSTRD/HC/WWD BS13 84 C5
Heywood Rd PTSHD/EG BS20 42 C4
Heywood Ter PTSHD/EG BS20 42 C4
Hicking Ct KGWD/HNM BS15 58 D2
Hickory La ALMDB BS32 11 F2
Hicks Av MANG/FISH BS16 35 H5
Hicks' Barton EVILLE/WHL BS5 57 H3
Hicks Common Rd
FRCTL/WBN BS36 23 E4
Hicks Ct
OLD/WMLY/WICK BS30 * 76 C2
Hidcote Ms
OMX/HUT/LCK BS24 122 B4
Higham St
BRSG/KWL/STAPK BS4 73 G2
High Bannerdown
CBATH/BATHN BA1 91 G5
Highbury Pde WSM BS23 * 6 B1
Highbury Pl
CBATH/BATHN BA1 102 D3
Highbury Rd BMSTR BS3 72 D5
HORF/LLZ BS7 46 B1
WSM BS23 6 B1
Highbury Ter
CBATH/BATHN BA1 102 D3
Highbury Vls
CBATH/BATHN BA1 * 102 D3
CBRISNE BS2 4 C1
Highcroft
OLD/WMLY/WICK BS30 60 A5
Highdale Av CLVDN BS21 64 D2
Highdale Cl HGRV/WHIT BS14 86 A5
Highdale Rd CLVDN BS21 64 D2
High Elm KGWD/HNM BS15 59 E5
Highett Dr EVILLE/WHL BS5 56 C2
Highfield Av KGWD/HNM BS15 76 A1
Highfield Cl BATHSE BA2 107 G2
Highfield Dr PTSHD/EG BS20 38 C5
Highfield Gdns
OLD/WMLY/WICK BS30 77 F4
Highfield Gv HORF/LLZ BS7 45 H3
Highfield Rd KEYN BS31 98 A2
OMX/HUT/LCK BS24 125 F5
YATE/CS BS37 26 C1
Highfields Cl
BRSTK/PCHW BS34 33 H2
High Gv
HNLZ/SM/SNYPK/WT BS9 43 H1
Highgrove St
BRSG/KWL/STAPK BS4 73 H2
Highgrove Wk
OMX/HUT/LCK BS24 122 D3
High Kingsdown CBRISNE BS2 55 G3
Highland Cl MTN/WRL BS22 121 G1
Highland Crs CFTN/FAIL BS8 55 E1
Highland Pl CFTN/FAIL BS8 55 E1
Highland Rd BATHSE BA2 107 G2
Highlands La
OMX/HUT/LCK BS24 122 D3
Highland Sq CFTN/FAIL BS8 * 55 E1
Highlands Rd LGASH BS41 70 D4
PTSHD/EG BS20 39 F3
Highland Ter BATHSE BA2 2 A5
High La FRCTL/WBN BS36 22 C2
Highleaze Rd
OLD/WMLY/WICK BS30 77 F2
Highmead Gdns
BMSTRD/HC/WWD BS13 83 H5
Highmore Gdns HORF/LLZ BS7 47 E1
Highnam Cl BRSTK/PCHW BS34 20 D1
High Pk HGRV/WHIT BS14 74 A5
Highridge Crs
BMSTRD/HC/WWD BS13 84 A4
Highridge Gn
BMSTRD/HC/WWD BS13 83 H3
Highridge Pk
BMSTRD/HC/WWD BS13 84 A3
Highridge Rd BMSTR BS3 72 C4
BMSTRD/HC/WWD BS13 83 H4
LGASH BS41 94 B1
Highridge Wk
BMSTRD/HC/WWD BS13 83 H2
High St AVONM BS11 42 D1
BATHSE BA2 107 G1
BATHSE BA2 104 A3
BLAG/CWMG/WR BS40 93 G5
CBATH/BATHN BA1 104 A1
CBATH/BATHN BA1 101 G2
CBATH/BATHN BA1 3 G4
CBRIS/FH BS1 5 F3
CFTN/FAIL BS8 55 E1
EVILLE/WHL BS5 56 D2
FRCTL/WBN BS36 22 D4
HNLZ/SM/SNYPK/WT BS9 31 E5
KEYN BS31 99 F1
KEYN BS31 88 B3
KGWD/HNM BS15 75 H1
MANG/FISH BS16 48 C4
MTN/WRL BS22 122 B1
NAIL BS48 67 F4
OLD/WMLY/WICK BS30 89 H1
PTSHD/EG BS20 41 F5
PTSHD/EG BS20 39 H3
THNB/SVB BS35 8 C3
WSM BS23 6 D2
YATE/CS BS37 26 D1
YATE/CS BS37 12 B3
YTN/CONG BS49 112 B3
Highview BATHSE BA2 * 2 D7
High Vw PTSHD/EG BS20 39 E4
Highview Rd
KGWD/HNM BS15 59 E1
Highway YATE/CS BS37 14 B5
Highwood La
BRSTK/PCHW BS34 19 G3
Highworth Crs YATE/CS BS37 25 H2
Highworth Rd
BRSG/KWL/STAPK BS4 74 C1
Hildesheim Br WSM BS23 7 G5
Hildesheim Cl WSM BS23 7 H6

Hildesheim Ct *WSM* BS23.............6 E5
Hill Av *BATHSE* BA2................110 D1
  BMSTR BS3....................73 F5
Hillbrook Rd *THNB/SVB* BS35......9 E4
Hill Burn
  HNLZ/SM/SNYPK/WT BS9......45 C2
Hilburn Rd *KGWD/HNM* BS15......58 A3
Hill Cl *MANG/FISH* BS16.........35 H5
Hill Crest
  BRSG/KWL/STAPK BS4.........74 A5
Hillcrest *THNB/SVB* BS35.........8 C3
Hillcrest Cl *NAIL* BS48..........67 F5
Hillcrest Dr *BATHSE* BA2........107 C4
Hillcrest Rd *NAIL* BS48..........67 F5
  PTSHD/EG BS20................38 C4
Hillcroft Cl *KGWD/HNM* BS15....76 B2
  MTN/WRL BS22................121 F1
Hilldale Rd *NAIL* BS48...........80 A4
Hill Dr *CFTN/FAIL* BS8..........69 H3
Hill End Dr *HNBRY/STHM* BS10...30 B2
Hillfields Av *MANG/FISH* BS16...48 C5
Hill Gay Cl *PTSHD/EG* BS20.......38 D4
Hill Gv
  HNLZ/SM/SNYPK/WT BS9......45 C2
Hillgrove St *CBRISNE* BS2........55 H3
Hillgrove St North
  CBRISNE BS2..................55 H3
Hill House Rd *MANG/FISH* BS16...49 F3
Hill Lawn
  BRSG/KWL/STAPK BS4.........74 C3
Hill Moor *CLVDN* BS21............65 E5
Hill Pk *YTN/CONG* BS49.........115 E1
Hill Rd *CLVDN* BS21.............64 C1
  LGASH BS41...................94 C2
  MTN/WRL BS22................122 B1
  WSM BS23.....................7 G2
Hill Rd East *MTN/WRL* BS22.....122 D1
Hills Barton
  BMSTRD/HC/WWD BS13.........72 B5
Hillsborough Rd
  BRSG/KWL/STAPK BS4.........74 B2
Hills Cl *KEYN* BS31..............88 D4
Hillsdon Rd
  HNLZ/SM/SNYPK/WT BS9......30 D5
Hillside *MANG/FISH* BS16.........49 F3
  PTSHD/EG BS20................41 F5
Hillside Av *KGWD/HNM* BS15.....58 C3
Hillside Cl *FRCTL/WBN* BS36....24 A3
Hillside Gdns *MTN/WRL* BS22....121 C2
Hillside La *FRCTL/WBN* BS36.....24 A3
Hillside Rd *BATHSE* BA2........108 A3
  CLVDN BS21...................64 D2
  EVILLE/WHL BS5...............56 D2
  LGASH BS41...................71 E4
  NAIL BS48.....................79 H4
  PTSHD/EG BS20................38 B4
Hillside St
  BRSG/KWL/STAPK BS4.........73 H2
Hillside West
  OMX/HUT/LCK BS24..........126 C3
Hill St *BMSTR* BS3...............73 C2
  CBRIS/FH BS1..................4 C3
  EVILLE/WHL BS5...............57 H3
  KGWD/HNM BS15...............58 B1
The Hill *ALMDB* BS32............10 D3
Hill Top *PTSHD/EG* BS20.........39 E4
Hilltop Gdns *EVILLE/WHL* BS5....58 A4
Hilltop Rd *MANG/FISH* BS16......58 D1
Hilltop Vw *EVILLE/WHL* BS5......58 A4
Hill Vw *CFTN/FAIL* BS8..........45 C2
  MANG/FISH BS16...............58 D1
Hillview Av *CLVDN* BS21.........64 D3
Hill View Cl
  OLD/WMLY/WICK BS30..........77 F2
Hillview Gdns
  BLAG/CWMG/WR BS40...........92 D4
Hillview Park Homes
  BLAG/CWMG/WR BS40 *.........92 C3
  MTN/WRL BS22 *..............122 A3
Hill View Rd
  BMSTRD/HC/WWD BS13.........84 B2
  CBATH/BATHN BA1.............103 E2
  MANG/FISH BS16...............51 C3
  WSM BS23.....................7 K4
Hillyfield Rd
  BMSTRD/HC/WWD BS13.........84 B3
Hinckley Cl *MTN/WRL* BS22......118 B5
Hinton Cl *KEYN* BS31.............99 F1
Hinton Dr
  OLD/WMLY/WICK BS30..........60 A5
Hinton La *CFTN/FAIL* BS8........54 D5
Hinton Rd *EVILLE/WHL* BS5.......57 E2
  MANG/FISH BS16...............48 A4
Hiscocks Dr *BATHSE* BA2.......108 B3
Hither Bath Br
  BRSG/KWL/STAPK BS4.........74 B5
Hither Gn *CLVDN* BS21...........65 F3
Hither Md *FRCTL/WBN* BS36......23 H4
Hobart Rd *WSM* BS23.............6 E7
Hobbinton Rd *MTN/WRL* BS22....117 H5
Hobbs La *NAIL* BS48.............82 B5
  OLD/WMLY/WICK BS30..........59 H2
Hobb's La *CBRIS/FH* BS1 *.......4 D4
Hobhouse Cl
  HNLZ/SM/SNYPK/WT BS9......45 G1
Hobwell La *LGASH* BS41.........71 F4
Hockeys La *MANG/FISH* BS16.....47 H5
Hodders La *MANG/FISH* BS16....118 C2
Hoddon La *MANG/FISH* BS16......51 C3
Hodshill *BATHSE* BA2...........110 D4
Hogarth Wk *HORF/LLZ* BS7.......46 D1
Hogues Wk
  BMSTRD/HC/WWD BS13.........84 C5
Holbeach Wy
  HGRV/WHIT BS14...............96 D1
Holbrook Crs
  BMSTRD/HC/WWD BS13.........85 E5
Holbrook La
  OLD/WMLY/WICK BS30..........61 E4
Holcombe Cl *BATHSE* BA2.......104 A3
Holcombe Gn
  CBATH/BATHN BA1.............101 C2
Holcombe La *BATHSE* BA2.......104 A3
Holcombe Ter
  CBATH/BATHN BA1.............101 C2
Holcombe V *BATHSE* BA2........104 A3
Holdenhurst Rd
  KGWD/HNM BS15...............58 C2

Holders Wk *LGASH* BS41.........70 C5
Holford Cl *NAIL* BS48...........67 F5
Holford Ct *HGRV/WHIT* BS14.....86 A4
Holland Rd
  CBATH/BATHN BA1.............103 E3
  CLVDN BS21...................64 B4
Holland St *WSM* BS23............7 J3
Hollidge Gdns *BMSTR* BS3........72 D2
Hollies La *CBATH/BATHN* BA1....91 F3
Hollis Av *PTSHD/EG* BS20........39 C5
Hollis Cl *LGASH* BS41...........82 D1
Hollis Crs *PTSHD/EG* BS20.......39 C5
Hollister's Dr
  BMSTRD/HC/WWD BS13.........96 A1
Holloway *BATHSE* BA2............3 F7
Hollow La *MTN/WRL* BS22.......117 G5
Hollowmead *YTN/CONG* BS49....113 E3
Hollowmead Cl
  YTN/CONG BS49..............113 E3
Hollow Rd *ALMDB* BS32..........10 C3
  KGWD/HNM BS15...............59 E3
The Hollows *FRCTL/WBN* BS36...36 A3
The Hollow *BATHSE* BA2........107 F5
Hollway Cl *HGRV/WHIT* BS14.....86 D4
Hollway Rd *HGRV/WHIT* BS14.....86 D4
Hollybrook Trading Est
  KGWD/HNM BS15...............58 B1
Hollybush La
  HNLZ/SM/SNYPK/WT BS9......44 C3
Holly Cl *EVILLE/WHL* BS5........58 A1
  MANG/FISH BS16...............51 G3
  MTN/WRL BS22................122 D2
  NAIL BS48....................67 H5
Holly Crs *BATHSE* BA2..........110 B2
Holly Dr *BATHSE* BA2...........110 B2
Holly Gn *KGWD/HNM* BS15.......59 G2
Holly Gv *MANG/FISH* BS16.......48 A5
Hollyguest Rd
  KGWD/HNM BS15...............59 E5
Holly Hill *YATE/CS* BS37.........12 C4
Holly Hill Rd *KGWD/HNM* BS15...59 F4
Holly La *CLVDN* BS21............63 G3
Hollyleigh Av
  BRSTK/PCHW BS34.............32 B3
Holly Lodge Cl *EVILLE/WHL* BS5..57 H1
Holly Lodge Rd
  EVILLE/WHL BS5...............57 H1
Hollyman Wk *CLVDN* BS21........65 F2
Hollymead La
  HNLZ/SM/SNYPK/WT BS9......44 C4
Holly Rdg *PTSHD/EG* BS20.......39 E3
Hollywood La *THNB/SVB* BS35....18 D2
Hollywood Rd
  BRSG/KWL/STAPK BS4.........74 C3
Holmdale Rd
  BRSTK/PCHW BS34.............32 D2
Holmesdale Rd *BMSTR* BS3.......73 F3
Holmes Gv
  HNLZ/SM/SNYPK/WT BS9......45 F3
Holmes Hill Rd
  EVILLE/WHL BS5...............57 H3
Holmes St *EVILLE/WHL* BS5.......56 D5
Holmoak Rd *KEYN* BS31..........87 H5
Holm Rd *OMX/HUT/LCK* BS24....126 D4
Holms Rd *WSM* BS23............125 F1
Holmwood *KGWD/HNM* BS15......75 H1
Holmwood Cl *FRCTL/WBN* BS36...22 D4
Holmwood Gdns
  HNLZ/SM/SNYPK/WT BS9......31 E5
Holsom Cl *KGWD/HNM* BS15......86 D3
Holsom Rd *HGRV/WHIT* BS14.....87 E3
Holst Gdns
  BRSG/KWL/STAPK BS4.........84 D2
Holton Rd *HORF/LLZ* BS7.........46 B1
Holtsdown La
  CBATH/BATHN BA1.............90 D1
Holyrood Cl *BRSTK/PCHW* BS34...33 F1
Holy Well Cl
  OLD/WMLY/WICK BS30..........60 C4
Homeapple Hi
  OLD/WMLY/WICK BS30..........60 C4
Home Cl *HNBRY/STHM* BS10......32 A3
Home Farm Cl *CFTN/FAIL* BS8....53 G3
Home Farm Wy
  THNB/SVB BS35................19 E1
Homefield
  OMX/HUT/LCK BS24..........126 C1
  THNB/SVB BS35................9 E4
  YATE/CS BS37.................13 G3
  YTN/CONG BS49..............114 D3
Homefield Cl *KEYN* BS31.........99 F1
Home Field Cl
  MANG/FISH BS16...............49 H2
Homefield Rd *KEYN* BS31.........99 F1
Home Gnd *AVONM* BS11...........42 D1
Homeground *CLVDN* BS21.........65 H2
Homeleaze Pk East
  CBATH/BATHN BA1.............101 F5
Homelea Pk West
  CBATH/BATHN BA1.............101 F5
Homeleaze Rd
  HNBRY/STHM BS10.............31 H2
Home Md
  BRSG/KWL/STAPK BS4 *.......85 F2
  OLD/WMLY/WICK BS30..........76 D2
Home Orch *YATE/CS* BS37........13 H5
Homestead *PTSHD/EG* BS20.......38 D5
Homestead Cl
  FRCTL/WBN BS36...............24 B3
Homestead Gdns
  MANG/FISH BS16...............34 B4
Homestead Rd
  BRSTK/PCHW BS34.............32 B3
The Homestead *CLVDN* BS21.....64 C2
  KEYN BS31....................98 A2
Honey Garston Cl
  BMSTRD/HC/WWD BS13.........84 C5
Honey Garston Rd
  BMSTRD/HC/WWD BS13.........84 C5
Home Hill Rd
  KGWD/HNM BS15...............59 F3
Honeylands *PTSHD/EG* BS20.....39 G5
Honeymead *HGRV/WHIT* BS14.....86 B3
Honeysuckle Cl *ALMDB* BS32.....11 G5

Honey Suckle La
  MANG/FISH BS16...............47 G4
Honeysuckle Pl
  OMX/HUT/LCK BS24..........122 D2
Honeywick Cl *BMSTR* BS3........72 D4
Honeywicke Cl *BMSTR* BS3.......72 D4
Honiton Rd *CLVDN* BS21.........65 E4
  MANG/FISH BS16...............48 A5
Hooper Rd *HGRV/WHIT* BS14.....86 C4
Hoover's La *YATE/CS* BS37.......12 A4
Hopechapel Hi *CFTN/FAIL* BS8...54 D5
Hope Rd *BMSTR* BS3.............73 E5
  YATE/CS BS37.................13 E5
Hope Sq *CFTN/FAIL* BS8.........54 D5
Hopetoun Rd *CBRISNE* BS2.......46 B5
Hopewell Gdns *AVONM* BS11......43 F1
Hopkin Cl *THNB/SVB* BS35........9 H3
Hopkins St *WSM* BS23............7 H3
Hopland Cl
  OLD/WMLY/WICK BS30..........77 E3
Horesham Gv
  BMSTRD/HC/WWD BS13.........84 D4
Horfield Common
  HORF/LLZ BS7.................46 A1
Horfield Rd *CBRISNE* BS2.........4 E2
  HORF/LLZ BS7.................56 C2
Horsecastle Cl
  YTN/CONG BS49..............112 A2
Horsecombe Brow
  BATHSE BA2..................111 E1
Horsecombe Gv *BATHSE* BA2.....111 E1
Horsecombe V *BATHSE* BA2......111 E1
Horscroft Gdns
  OLD/WMLY/WICK BS30..........60 D4
The Horsefair *CBRIS/FH* BS1......5 G2
Horsepool Rd
  BMSTRD/HC/WWD BS13.........83 H5
Horse Race La *CFTN/FAIL* BS8....52 A4
Horseshoe Dr
  HNLZ/SM/SNYPK/WT BS9......44 A4
Horseshoe La *YATE/CS* BS37......26 D1
Horseshoe Wk *BATHSE* BA2......3 K6
Horse St *YATE/CS* BS37..........27 E1
Horstmann Cl
  CBATH/BATHN BA1.............101 G5
Hortham La *ALMDB* BS32.........11 E1
Horton Rd *YATE/CS* BS37.........15 E5
Horton St *CBRISNE* BS2...........5 K4
Horwood Ct
  OLD/WMLY/WICK BS30..........76 D2
Horwood Rd *NAIL* BS48..........67 G5
Hosey Wk
  BMSTRD/HC/WWD BS13.........84 B4
Host St *CBRIS/FH* BS1............4 E4
Hottom Gdns *HORF/LLZ* BS7.......46 C1
Hot Water La *KGWD/HNM* BS15....49 F5
Hotwell Rd *CFTN/FAIL* BS8.......54 D5
Houlton St *CBRISNE* BS2..........5 J3
Hounds Rd *YATE/CS* BS37........27 E2
Howard Av *EVILLE/WHL* BS5......57 G3
Howard Cl *KEYN* BS31...........98 D1
Howard Rd *BMSTR* BS3...........73 E4
  MANG/FISH BS16...............48 D4
  RDLND/MONT BS6..............45 F4
  THNB/SVB BS35................8 C3
Howard St *EVILLE/WHL* BS5.......57 E1
Howard Wk
  OLD/WMLY/WICK BS30..........60 B5
Howecroft Gdns
  HNLZ/SM/SNYPK/WT BS9......44 C4
Howells Md *MANG/FISH* BS16....49 H1
Howes Cl
  OLD/WMLY/WICK BS30..........59 G5
Howett Rd *EVILLE/WHL* BS5.......57 E4
How Hl *BATHSE* BA2............107 F1
Howitt Wy
  OMX/HUT/LCK BS24..........122 C4
Howsmoor La
  MANG/FISH BS16...............35 H5
Hoylake Dr
  OLD/WMLY/WICK BS30..........59 H5
Huckford La *FRCTL/WBN* BS36....23 E5
Huckford Rd *FRCTL/WBN* BS36....23 E5
Huckley Wy *ALMDB* BS32.........11 H3
Hudd's Hill Rd *EVILLE/WHL* BS5...57 H3
Hudd's Vale Rd
  EVILLE/WHL BS5...............57 H3
Hudson Cl *YATE/CS* BS37.........26 B2
Hughenden Rd *CFTN/FAIL* BS8....55 E1
  HORF/LLZ BS7.................46 A3
  WSM BS23.....................6 C3
Hughes Gdns *HORF/LLZ* BS7......32 C5
Hulbert Cl
  BRSG/KWL/STAPK BS4.........85 E2
Hulse Rd *BRSG/KWL/STAPK* BS4..74 C5
Humberstan Wk *AVONM* BS11....29 E5
Humber Wy *AVONM* BS11.........16 D5
Humphrys Barton
  BRSG/KWL/STAPK BS4.........75 E1
Hungerford Cl
  BRSG/KWL/STAPK BS4.........86 D1
Hungerford Crs
  BRSG/KWL/STAPK BS4.........86 D1
Hungerford Gdns
  BRSG/KWL/STAPK BS4.........86 D1
Hungerford Rd
  BRSG/KWL/STAPK BS4.........74 D5
  CBATH/BATHN BA1.............101 H5
Hungerford Wk
  BRSG/KWL/STAPK BS4.........74 D5
Hung Rd *AVONM* BS11...........43 E2
Hunters Cl *KGWD/HNM* BS15.....75 H1
Hunters Dr *KGWD/HNM* BS15.....59 E3
Hunters Md *HGRV/WHIT* BS14....75 H1
Hunters Rd East
  KGWD/HNM BS15...............75 H1
Hunter's Wy
  BRSTK/PCHW BS34.............32 D2
Huntingham Rd
  BMSTRD/HC/WWD BS13.........83 H5
Huntley Gv *NAIL* BS48..........67 H5
Hunts Ground Rd
  BRSTK/PCHW BS34.............33 G2
Hunts La *HORF/LLZ* BS7..........45 G4
Hunt's La *YTN/CONG* BS49......113 E3
Hurle Crs *CFTN/FAIL* BS8........55 E2
Hurle Rd *CFTN/FAIL* BS8.........55 E2
Hurlingham Rd *HORF/LLZ* BS7....56 C1
Hurn La *KEYN* BS31.............88 C5

Hurn Rd *CLVDN* BS21............65 E3
Hursley Hl *PLTN/PENS* BS39.....97 G5
Hursley La *HGRV/WHIT* BS14.....97 H5
Hurston Rd
  BRSG/KWL/STAPK BS4.........85 E1
Hurst Rd *BRSG/KWL/STAPK* BS4..85 C1
  WSM BS23.....................7 J6
Hurst Wk
  BRSG/KWL/STAPK BS4.........85 F1
Hurstwood Rd
  MANG/FISH BS16...............48 D3
Hutton Cl
  HNLZ/SM/SNYPK/WT BS9......44 B1
  KEYN BS31....................98 B2
Hutton Hl *OMX/HUT/LCK* BS24..126 B4
Hutton Moor La
  OMX/HUT/LCK BS24..........121 H5
  OMX/HUT/LCK BS24..........125 H1
Hutton Moor Rd
  OMX/HUT/LCK BS24..........121 G4
Hutton Pk
  OMX/HUT/LCK BS24..........121 H5
Huyton Rd *EVILLE/WHL* BS5.......47 G5
Hyde Av *THNB/SVB* BS35..........8 C1
The Hyde *CLVDN* BS21...........64 C5
Hyland Gv
  HNLZ/SM/SNYPK/WT BS9......30 D5

I

Ida Rd *EVILLE/WHL* BS5..........57 E3
Iddesleigh Rd
  RDLND/MONT BS6..............45 F5
Idstone Rd *MANG/FISH* BS16.....48 B4
Iford Cl *KEYN* BS31..............99 F1
Ilchester Crs
  BMSTRD/HC/WWD BS13.........72 C5
Ilchester Rd
  BMSTRD/HC/WWD BS13.........84 C1
Iles Cl *KGWD/HNM* BS15.........76 A2
Ilex Av *CLVDN* BS21.............65 E3
Ilex Cl *BMSTRD/HC/WWD* BS13...84 A3
Ilminster Av
  BRSG/KWL/STAPK BS4.........85 H1
Ilminster Cl *CFTN/FAIL* BS8......65 E4
  NAIL BS48....................79 E1
Ilsyn Gv *HGRV/WHIT* BS14.......86 C2
Imber Court Cl
  HGRV/WHIT BS14...............86 A1
Imperial Pk
  BMSTRD/HC/WWD BS13 *......84 D3
Imperial Rd *CFTN/FAIL* BS8......55 F2
  HGRV/WHIT BS14...............86 B1
Imperial Wk *HGRV/WHIT* BS14...74 A5
The Inclosures
  OMX/HUT/LCK BS24..........122 C3
Ingleside Rd *KGWD/HNM* BS15...58 D2
Ingleton Dr *MTN/WRL* BS22.....117 H4
Ingmire Rd *EVILLE/WHL* BS5......46 D5
Inkerman Cl *HORF/LLZ* BS7.......46 A1
Innox Gdns
  BMSTRD/HC/WWD BS13.........84 B4
Innox Gv *BATHSE* BA2..........107 E5
Innox La *CBATH/BATHN* BA1.....90 A4
Innox Rd *BATHSE* BA2..........107 G2
Inns Court Av
  BRSG/KWL/STAPK BS4.........85 E2
Inns Court Dr
  BRSG/KWL/STAPK BS4.........85 E2
Inns Court Gn
  BRSG/KWL/STAPK BS4.........85 E2
Instow Rd
  BRSG/KWL/STAPK BS4.........85 F1
Instow Wk
  BRSG/KWL/STAPK BS4.........85 F1
Inverness Rd *BATHSE* BA2.......107 H1
Ipswich Dr
  BRSG/KWL/STAPK BS4.........57 G5
Irby Rd *BMSTR* BS3.............72 B3
Irena Rd *MANG/FISH* BS16......47 H5
Ireton Rd *BMSTR* BS3............72 C3
Iron Acton Wy *YATE/CS* BS37....13 E4
Ironchurch Rd *AVONM* BS11.....16 B5
Ironmould La *KEYN* BS31.........75 F5
Irving Cl *CLVDN* BS21...........65 F2
Irving Ct *MANG/FISH* BS16......48 A3
I.s.f. Rd *AVONM* BS11...........28 C4
Island Trade Pk *AVONM* BS11 *..28 C4
Isleys Ct
  OLD/WMLY/WICK BS30..........76 C3
Islington Rd *BMSTR* BS3.........72 C2
Ison Hill Rd
  HNBRY/STHM BS10 *...........30 B2
Ivo Peters Rd *BATHSE* BA2........2 D5
Ivor Rd *EVILLE/WHL* BS5.........57 E3
Ivor Ter *PTSHD/EG* BS20.........34 C5
Ivy Av *BATHSE* BA2............107 H4
Ivy Bank Pk *BATHSE* BA2......108 C5
Ivy Ct *PTSHD/EG* BS20..........38 D3
Ivy Gv *BATHSE* BA2...........107 H3
Ivy La *MANG/FISH* BS16.........48 A4
Ivy Pl *BATHSE* BA2............107 H3
Ivy Wk *BNWL* BS29............122 D3
Ivywell Rd
  HNLZ/SM/SNYPK/WT BS9......44 C5
Iwood La
  BLAG/CWMG/WR BS40.........115 G5

J

Jack Price Cl
  BMSTRD/HC/WWD BS13.........95 H1
Jacob Pl *CBRIS/FH* BS1...........5 F6
Jacobs Meadow
  PTSHD/EG BS20................40 B4
Jacob St *CBRISNE* BS2............5 H3
Jacob's Well Rd *CFTN/FAIL* BS8...4 A4
Jamaica St *CBRISNE* BS2..........55 H3
James Cl *MANG/FISH* BS16......49 E5
James Pl *CFTN/FAIL* BS8..........54 D4
James Rd *MANG/FISH* BS16......49 E5
James St *CBRISNE* BS2............56 D1
  EVILLE/WHL BS5...............5 K1

James St West
  CBATH/BATHN BA1.............2 D4
Jane St *EVILLE/WHL* BS5..........56 D4
Jarrets Rd *HNBRY/STHM* BS10....31 H3
Jarvis St *EVILLE/WHL* BS5.........5 K1
Jasmine Cl *MTN/WRL* BS22......122 D2
Jasmine Gv *AVONM* BS11.........30 A3
Jasmine La *YTN/CONG* BS49.....113 F1
Jasmine Wy
  OMX/HUT/LCK BS24..........122 D2
Jasper St *BMSTR* BS3............72 C3
Jean Rd *BRSG/KWL/STAPK* BS4..74 D4
Jefferies Hill Bottom
  KGWD/HNM BS15...............75 G1
Jeffery Ct
  OLD/WMLY/WICK BS30..........59 H5
Jekyll Cl *MANG/FISH* BS16.......47 G1
Jellicoe Av *MANG/FISH* BS16.....33 E2
Jellicoe Ct *MTN/WRL* BS22......117 F4
Jena Ct *KEYN* BS31.............99 E1
Jenner Cl *YATE/CS* BS37.........27 F2
Jenny La *HNBRY/STHM* BS10.....31 H3
Jersey Av
  BRSG/KWL/STAPK BS4.........75 E2
Jesmond Rd *CLVDN* BS21.........64 C2
  MTN/WRL BS22................118 B4
Jesse Hughes Ct
  CBATH/BATHN BA1.............103 F2
Jessop Crs *HNBRY/STHM* BS10...31 E4
Jessop Under/pass *BMSTR* BS3...72 A2
Jews La *BATHSE* BA2...........109 H1
Jinty La *KGWD/HNM* BS15.......59 E5
Jobbins Cl *YATE/CS* BS37........26 C2
Jocelin Dr *MTN/WRL* BS22......117 G4
Jocelyn Rd *HORF/LLZ* BS7.......46 B1
Jockey La *EVILLE/WHL* BS5......58 A4
John Cabot Ct *CFTN/FAIL* BS8....4 A4
Johnson Dr
  OLD/WMLY/WICK BS30..........76 C1
Johnson Rd *MANG/FISH* BS16....50 A3
Johnsons La *EVILLE/WHL* BS5....57 F2
Johnsons Rd *EVILLE/WHL* BS5....57 F2
Johnstone St *BATHSE* BA2........3 H4
John St *CBATH/BATHN* BA1.......3 F3
  CBRIS/FH BS1.................56 C1
  CBRISNE BS2..................56 C1
  KGWD/HNM BS15...............58 B5
John Wesley Rd
  EVILLE/WHL BS5...............58 B5
Jordan Wk *ALMDB* BS32.........21 F2
Joyce Cl *HORF/LLZ* BS7..........33 E4
Joy Hl *CFTN/FAIL* BS8 *.........54 D5
Jubilee Crs *MANG/FISH* BS16....49 C2
Jubilee Dr *CFTN/FAIL* BS8.......69 G2
  THNB/SVB BS35................9 E3
Jubilee Gdns *YATE/CS* BS37......14 C5
Jubilee Pl *CLVDN* BS21..........65 H5
  CFTN/FAIL BS8................59 F4
Jubilee Rd
  BRSG/KWL/STAPK BS4.........74 B5
  CBRISNE BS2..................56 C2
  KGWD/HNM BS15...............59 F3
  WSM BS23.....................7 F4
Jubilee St *CBRISNE* BS2..........5 K4
Jubilee Wy *AVONM* BS11.........28 B3
  MTN/WRL BS22................118 B5
  YATE/CS BS37.................14 B2
Julian Cl
  HNLZ/SM/SNYPK/WT BS9......44 B5
Julian Rd *CBATH/BATHN* BA1.....2 E1
  HNLZ/SM/SNYPK/WT BS9......44 C5
Julian Road Crescent La
  CBATH/BATHN BA1.............2 D1
Julius Cl *MANG/FISH* BS16......50 A2
Julius Rd *HORF/LLZ* BS7.........45 H5
Junction Av *BATHSE* BA2.........2 C7
Junction Rd *BATHSE* BA2.........2 C7
  BRSG/KWL/STAPK BS4.........74 B2
Junction Wy *KGWD/HNM* BS15...49 C5
Juniper Cl *EVILLE/WHL* BS5......58 D5
Juniper Pl *MTN/WRL* BS22.......117 G4
Juniper Wy *ALMDB* BS32.........21 H3
Jupiter Rd *BRSTK/PCHW* BS34...19 H3
Justice Av *KEYN* BS31...........99 F1
Justice Rd *MANG/FISH* BS16.....47 H5
Jutland Rd *AVONM* BS11.........28 B4

K

Karen Cl *NAIL* BS48............79 H5
Karen Dr *NAIL* BS48............79 H4
Kathdene Gdns *HORF/LLZ* BS7...46 B5
Kaynton Md
  CBATH/BATHN BA1.............101 G5
Keats Ct *HORF/LLZ* BS7.........32 C5
Keble Av
  BMSTRD/HC/WWD BS13.........83 A4
Keeds La *LGASH* BS41...........70 C5
Keedwell Hi *LGASH* BS41........70 C5
Keel Cl *EVILLE/WHL* BS5.........57 H5
Keene's Wy *CLVDN* BS21.........64 B3
Keepers La *HORF/LLZ* BS7.......46 B3
The Keep *MTN/WRL* BS22.......117 H5
  OLD/WMLY/WICK BS30..........77 G1
Keinton Wk
  HNBRY/STHM BS10.............31 H3
Kelbra Crs *FRCTL/WBN* BS36.....23 H4
Kellaway Av *HORF/LLZ* BS7......46 A2
  RDLND/MONT BS6..............46 A2
Kellaway Crs
  HNLZ/SM/SNYPK/WT BS9......45 H2
Kellways *NAIL* BS48............79 G5
Kelso Pl *CBATH/BATHN* BA1 *....2 A3
Kelston Cl *KEYN* BS31...........99 E1
  YATE/CS BS37.................13 H5
Kelston Gdns
  HNBRY/STHM BS10.............31 H5
Kelston Gv *KGWD/HNM* BS15....59 F5
Kelston Rd *CBATH/BATHN* BA1..100 D3
  HNBRY/STHM BS10.............31 H5
  KEYN BS31....................88 A4
  MTN/WRL BS22................118 B4
Kelston Vw *BATHSE* BA2........107 F2
Kelston Wk *MANG/FISH* BS16....48 C4
Kelting Gv *CLVDN* BS21..........65 F3

Kemble Cl KCWD/HNM BS15 ....59 F5
NAIL BS48.........................67 H5
Kemperleye Wy ALMDB BS32 ...21 F3
Kempe's Cl LGASH BS41.........70 D4
Kempe Wy
　OMX/HUT/LCK BS24 ....122 B4
Kempthorne La BATHSE BA2 ...110 C1
Kempton Cl THNB/SVB BS35 .....8 C1
Kencot Wk
　BMSTRD/HC/WWD BS13 .....95 G1
Kendall Gdns MANG/FISH BS16...48 D4
Kendall Rd MANG/FISH BS16 .....48 D4
Kendal Rd HORF/LLZ BS7 ....45 H1
Kendon Dr HNBRY/STHM BS10...45 H1
Kendon Wy
　HNBRY/STHM BS10 ....31 H5
Kenilworth YATE/CS BS37 ....26 B2
Kenilworth Cl KEYN BS31........88 A5
Kenilworth Ct
　CBATH/BATHN BA1 ....102 D4
Kenilworth Dr
　OLD/WMLY/WICK BS30 .....77 E5
Kenilworth Rd
　RDLND/MONT BS6 ....55 G2
Kenmare Rd
　BRSG/KWL/STAPK BS4.......73 F5
Kenmore Crs HORF/LLZ BS7 .....32 A4
Kenmore Dr HORF/LLZ BS7 ......32 A4
Kenmore Gv HORF/LLZ BS7 ......32 A4
Kennard Ri KCWD/HNM BS15 ....58 C3
Kennard Rd KCWD/HNM BS15 ...58 C3
Kennaway Rd CLVDN BS21 ......54 A3
Kenn Cl WSM BS23.............73 E2
Kennedy Wy YATE/CS BS37 ......26 A1
Kennel Lodge Rd LGASH BS41....71 H1
Kenneth Rd
　CBATH/BATHN BA1 ....101 G5
Kennion Rd EVILLE/WHL BS5.....58 A2
Kenmoor Cl
　OLD/WMLY/WICK BS30 .....59 G5
Kenn Moor Dr CLVDN BS21 ......65 E4
Kenn Moor Rd
　YTN/CONG BS49 ....112 B2
Kenn Rd CLVDN BS21...........64 D4
　EVILLE/WHL BS5.............58 A4
Kensal Av BMSTR BS3 ....73 F3
Kensal Rd BMSTR BS3 ....73 F3
Kensington Ct THNB/SVB BS35 ....8 C2
Kensington Ct
　CBATH/BATHN BA1 ....103 E3
Kensington Gdns
　CBATH/BATHN BA1 ....103 E3
Kensington Pk
　EVILLE/WHL BS5.............56 C2
Kensington Park Rd
　BRSG/KWL/STAPK BS4.......74 B4
Kensington Pl
　CBATH/BATHN BA1 * 103 E3
　CFTN/FAIL BS8..............55 E4
Kensington Rd
　EVILLE/WHL BS5.............58 A3
　MTN/WRL BS22 ....55 G2
　WSM BS23................125 E1
Kent Av YATE/CS BS37 ....14 B4
Kent Cl BRSTK/PCHW BS34 ......21 H5
Kenton Ms
　HNLZ/SM/SNYPK/WT BS9 ...45 G3
Kent Rd HORF/LLZ BS7 ....46 A5
　YTN/CONG BS49 ....114 D1
Kents Gn KCWD/HNM BS15 .....59 E1
Kent St BMSTR BS3 ....72 D3
Kent Wy MTN/WRL BS22.........55 G4
Kenwood Cl KCWD/HNM BS15...59 F2
Keppel Cl KEYN BS31 ....99 E2
Kerry Rd BRSG/KWL/STAPK BS4...73 F5
Kersteman Rd
　RDLND/MONT BS6 ....45 H5
Kestrel Cl BRSTK/PCHW BS34 ....20 A2
　THNB/SVB BS35 ....8 B2
Kestrel Dr MANG/FISH BS16 .....51 G4
　MTN/WRL BS22 ....122 B2
Keswick Wk
　HNBRY/STHM BS10 ....31 G3
Ketch Rd BMSTR BS3 ....73 G3
Kew Rd WSM BS23..............6 E1
Kewside MTN/WRL BS22........116 C4
Kewstoke Rd BATHSE BA2......108 D5
　HNLZ/SM/SNYPK/WT BS9 ...44 C4
　MTN/WRL BS22 ....116 C5
　WSM BS23................120 C1
Kew Wk
　BRSG/KWL/STAPK BS4.......86 B1
Keyes Pth MTN/WRL BS22 ......117 G4
Keynsham By-Pass KEYN BS31...88 B2
Keynsham Rd KEYN BS31 ....88 C2
　OLD/WMLY/WICK BS30 .....77 E5
Keys Av HORF/LLZ BS7 ....45 H3
Kielder Dr MTN/WRL BS22 ......117 G5
Kilbirnie Rd HGRV/WHIT BS14...96 D1
Kildare Rd
　BRSG/KWL/STAPK BS4.......73 E5
Kilkenny La BATHSE BA2 ....110 A2
Kilkenny Pl PTSHD/EG BS20 .....39 C2
Kilkenny St CBRISNE BS2 ....5 K4
Kilmersdon Rd
　BMSTRD/HC/WWD BS13....84 C5
Kilminster Cl
　BRSTK/PCHW BS34 ....21 F1
Kilminster Rd AVONM BS11 .....42 D1
Kiln Cl KCWD/HNM BS15 ....58 B2
Kilnhurst Cl
　OLD/WMLY/WICK BS30 .....76 C4
Kilvert Cl
　BRSG/KWL/STAPK BS4.......73 H1
Kimberley Av MANG/FISH BS16...48 C3
Kimberley Cl MANG/FISH BS16...49 F1
Kimberley Crs
　EVILLE/WHL BS5.............58 A2
Kimberley Rd CLVDN BS21 ......58 D2
　KCWD/HNM BS15 ....58 D2
　MANG/FISH BS16............48 C3
Kinber Cl CBATH/BATHN BA1...101 F1

King Edward Cl
　HGRV/WHIT BC14 ....85 H3
King Edward Rd BATHSE BA2 .....2 B7
Kingfisher Cl ALMDB BS32 ......11 G5
Kingfisher Dr THNB/SVB BS35 ....9 E2
Kingfisher Dr MANG/FISH BS16...47 G2
Kingfisher Rd MTN/WRL BS22...122 C3
　PTSHD/EG BS20 ....40 C2
　YATE/CS BS37 ....26 C2
King George's Rd
　BATHSE BA2 ....107 H1
　BMSTRD/HC/WWD BS13 ....84 A4
King John's Rd
　KCWD/HNM BS15 ....58 B1
King Rd BRSG/KWL/STAPK BS4 ...74 A5
King Road Av AVONM BS11 .....28 A3
Kingrove Crs YATE/CS BS37 .....27 E2
Kingrove La YATE/CS BS37 ......27 E3
Kings Av KCWD/HNM BS15 .....75 C2
King's Av EVILLE/WHL BS5 ......46 G4
Kingscote YATE/CS BS37 ....25 H4
Kingscote Pk EVILLE/WHL BS5...58 D4
Kingscourt Cl HGRV/WHIT BS14...85 H4
Kings Cft LGASH BS41 ....70 B5
Kingsdown Pde
　CBRISNE BS2 ....4 E1
Kingsdown Vw
　CBATH/BATHN BA1 * 102 D2
Kings Dr BRSTK/PCHW BS34.....34 A1
　KCWD/HNM BS15 ....75 C2
King's Dr HORF/LLZ BS7 ....45 C3
Kingsfield BATHSE BA2 ....107 H4
Kingsfield La KCWD/HNM BS15...59 E5
　OLD/WMLY/WICK BS30 .....76 B2
King's Head La
　BMSTRD/HC/WWD BS13 ....83 H2
Kingshill NAIL BS48 ....66 D4
Kingshill Rd
　BRSG/KWL/STAPK BS4.......74 A5
Kingsholme Rd
　KCWD/HNM BS15 ....58 D2
Kingsland Rd CBRISNE BS2......56 C5
Kings La CLVDN BS21 ....54 B5
King's La WSM BS23.............6 E3
Kingsleigh Ct KCWD/HNM BS15...59 F4
Kingsleigh Gdns
　KCWD/HNM BS15 ....59 F4
Kingsley Rd CLVDN BS21 ....64 D3
　EVILLE/WHL BS5.............57 E2
　RDLND/MONT BS6 ....55 H1
　WSM BS23................125 E3
Kingsmead NAIL BS48 ....66 D4
Kingsmead North
　CBATH/BATHN BA1 ....2 E5
Kingsmead Rd
　EVILLE/WHL BS5.............58 A2
Kingsmead Sq
　CBATH/BATHN BA1 * 3 F5
Kingsmead St
　CBATH/BATHN BA1 ....3 F5
Kingsmead Wk
　EVILLE/WHL BS5.............58 A2
Kingsmead West
　RDLND/MONT BS6 ....2 E5
Kingsmill
　HNLZ/SM/SNYPK/WT BS9 ...44 B3
King's Parade Av
　CFTN/FAIL BS8..............55 E2
King's Parade Ms
　CFTN/FAIL BS8..............55 E2
Kings Park Av CBRISNE BS2.....57 E5
King Sq CBRISNE BS2...........55 H3
King Square Av CBRISNE BS2...55 H3
King's Rd
　BRSG/KWL/STAPK BS4.......74 B3
　CFTN/FAIL BS8..............55 E4
　PTSHD/EG BS20 ....38 D4
Kings Sq
　OLD/WMLY/WICK BS30 .....89 G1
Kingston Av CLVDN BS21 ....65 E2
　KEYN BS31 ....98 D2
Kingston Blds
　CBATH/BATHN BA1 * 3 G5
Kingston Dr MANG/FISH BS16...49 G1
Kingston Dr MANG/FISH BS16...49 G1
Kingston La
　BLAG/CWMG/WR BS40......93 F4
Kingston Rd BMSTR BS3 ....72 D2
　CBATH/BATHN BA1 ....3 G5
Kingston Wy NAIL BS48 ....78 D1
Kingstree St
　BRSG/KWL/STAPK BS4.......73 H2
King St AVONM BS11 ....28 A4
　CBRIS/FH BS1 ....4 E5
　EVILLE/WHL BS5.............57 E2
Kings Wk
　BMSTRD/HC/WWD BS13 ....83 H2
Kingsway BATHSE BA2 ....107 H4
　BRSTK/PCHW BS34 ....34 D1
　EVILLE/WHL BS5.............58 B4
　PTSHD/EG BS20 ....39 E4
Kingsway Av KCWD/HNM BS15...58 B3
Kingsway Crs
　KCWD/HNM BS15 ....58 B3
Kings Weston Av AVONM BS11...42 D1
Kings Weston La AVONM BS11...28 C1
Kingswood Hts
　KCWD/HNM BS15 ....58 D2
Kington La THNB/SVB BS35 ......8 A5
King William Av CBRIS/FH BS1 ....4 F5
King William St BMSTR BS3 .....72 C2
Kinsale Rd HGRV/WHIT BS14....86 B2
Kinsale Wk
　BRSG/KWL/STAPK BS4.......73 F5
Kinvara Rd
　BRSG/KWL/STAPK BS4.......85 F1
Kipling Av BATHSE BA2 ....108 C3
Kipling Rd HORF/LLZ BS7 ....32 D4
Kirby Rd AVONM BS11 ....29 G4
Kirtlington Rd
　EVILLE/WHL BS5.............46 D5
Kite Hay Cl MANG/FISH BS16 * ...47 G3

Kites Cl ALMDB BS32............11 F5
Knapp Rd THNB/SVB BS55.......9 E3
Knapps La FVILLE/WHL BS5 .....57 G1
The Knapp YATE/CS BS5/ 14 A2
Knightcott Rd CFTN/FAIL BS8 ...53 F5
Knighton Rd
　HNBRY/STHM BS10 ....32 A4
Knightsbridge Pk
　BMSTRD/HC/WWD BS13.....85 F5
Knights Cl
　HNLZ/SM/SNYPK/WT BS9 ...45 F2
　MTN/WRL BS22 ....117 H5
Knightstone Cswy WSM BS23 .....6 A2
Knightstone Ct
　EVILLE/WHL BS5 * 57 E2
Knightstone Pk WSM BS23 ....124 D1
Knightstone Pl
　KCWD/HNM BS15 ....75 G3
Knightstone Rd WSM BS23 ......6 B2
Knightstone Sq
　HGRV/WHIT BS14 * 86 B4
Knightwood NAIL BS48 * 57 F4
Knightwood Rd
　BRSTK/PCHW BS34 ....21 H5
Knole Cl ALMDB BS32 ....10 B3
Knole La HNBRY/STHM BS10 ....31 E2
Knole Pk ALMDB BS32..........10 B3
Knoll HI
　HNLZ/SM/SNYPK/WT BS9 ...44 B5
The Knoll PTSHD/EG BS20......39 H1
Knovill Cl AVONM BS11.........29 H4
Knowle Rd
　BRSG/KWL/STAPK BS4.......73 G3
Knowles Rd CLVDN BS21 ....54 B5
Knowsley Rd MANG/FISH BS16...54 C5
Kyght Cl KCWD/HNM BS15 .....59 C5
Kyiross Av MANG/FISH BS16.....84 A4
Kynges Mill Cl
　MANG/FISH BS16............48 A1

L

The Labbott KEYN BS31 ....88 B4
Laburnum Ct WSM BS23......121 C4
Laburnum Gv
　BMSTRD/HC/WWD BS13.....84 A3
Laburnum Rd
　KCWD/HNM BS15 ....75 H1
　WSM BS23..................7 K4
Laburnum Ter
　CBATH/BATHN BA1 ....104 A1
Lacey Rd HGRV/WHIT BS14.....86 D3
Lacock Dr
　OLD/WMLY/WICK BS30 .....76 C4
Ladden Rd THNB/SVB BS35 ......8 D4
Ladden Ri YATE/CS BS37........59 F4
Laddon Md YATE/CS BS37 ......13 H5
Ladies Mile CFTN/FAIL BS8 .....54 D2
Ladman Gv HGRV/WHIT BS14...86 D4
Ladman Rd HGRV/WHIT BS14...86 D4
Ladycroft CLVDN BS21 ....64 B3
Ladye Bay CLVDN BS21.........62 D4
Ladye Wake MTN/WRL BS22...117 G4
Ladymead PTSHD/EG BS20......40 B3
Ladysmith Rd
　RDLND/MONT BS6 ....45 F4
Laggan Gdns
　CBATH/BATHN BA1 ....102 B3
Lakemead Gv
　BMSTRD/HC/WWD BS13.....84 A3
Lake Rd HNBRY/STHM BS10 ....31 H5
　PTSHD/EG BS20 ....39 G2
Lakeside MANG/FISH BS16 .....47 G5
Lake View Rd EVILLE/WHL BS5...57 F3
Lakewood Crs
　HNBRY/STHM BS10 ....31 F5
Lakewood Rd
　HNBRY/STHM BS10 ....31 F5
Lambert Pl
　BRSG/KWL/STAPK BS4.......85 E3
Lamb HI EVILLE/WHL BS5 ....57 G3
Lambourn Cl BMSTR BS3 ....73 F4
Lambourne Wy
　PTSHD/EG BS20 ....40 B4
Lambourn Rd KEYN BS31 ....88 D5
Lambridge
　CBATH/BATHN BA1 ....103 F3
Lambridge Blds
　CBATH/BATHN BA1 ....103 F3
Lambridge Ms
　CBATH/BATHN BA1 ....103 F3
Lambridge St
　CBATH/BATHN BA1 ....103 F3
Lambrook Rd MANG/FISH BS16...48 A4
Lamb St CBRISNE BS2...........5 J2
Lampton Ct
　BMSTRD/HC/WWD BS13.....84 A3
Lamord Ga BRSTK/PCHW BS34...21 C5
Lampards Blds
　CBATH/BATHN BA1 * 3 F3
Lampeter Rd
　HNLZ/SM/SNYPK/WT BS9 ...44 D1
Lampton Av
　BMSTRD/HC/WWD BS13.....96 B1
Lampton Gv
　BMSTRD/HC/WWD BS13.....96 B1
Lampton Rd LGASH BS41 ....70 C5
Lanaway Rd MANG/FISH BS16...48 B2
Lancashire Rd HORF/LLZ BS7 ...46 A5
Lancaster Cl
　BRSTK/PCHW BS34 ....33 F1
Lancaster Rd CBRISNE BS2 .....56 C1
　YATE/CS BS37 ....14 A4
Lancelot Rd MANG/FISH BS16...53 C5
Landemann Circ WSM BS23.....6 D2
Landemann Pth WSM BS23.....6 D3
Landrail Wk MANG/FISH BS16...47 H2
Landseer Av HORF/LLZ BS7 .....46 C4
Landseer Cl MTN/WRL BS22...117 H3
Landseer Rd BATHSE BA2......107 C1
The Land FRCTL/WBN BS36.....24 A3
Lanercost Rd
　HNBRY/STHM BS10 ....31 G3
Lanesborough Ri
　HGRV/WHIT BS14 ....86 C2

Lanes End
　BRSG/KWL/STAPK BS4.......74 B5
Laneys Dro
　OMX/HUT/LCK BS24 ....126 B1
Langdale Rd MANG/FISH BS16...47 H2
Langdale Rd BATHSE BA2......107 C5
Langfield Ct
　HNBRY/STHM BS10 ....30 C2
Langford Rd
　BMSTRD/HC/WWD BS13.....84 A1
　WSM BS23..................7 J1
Langford Wy KCWD/HNM BS15...59 G4
Langham Rd
　BRSG/KWL/STAPK BS4.......74 A4
Langhill Av
　BRSG/KWL/STAPK BS4.......85 E2
Langley Crs BMSTR BS3 ....71 H5
Langley Mow
　MANG/FISH BS16............49 H1
Langport Gdns NAIL BS48 ......79 F1
Langport Rd WSM BS23.........7 F7
Langthorn Cl FRCTL/WBN BS36...23 H3
Langton Court Rd
　BRSG/KWL/STAPK BS4.......74 C1
Langton Pk BMSTR BS3.........73 F4
Langton Rd
　BRSG/KWL/STAPK BS4.......74 C1
Langton Wy
　BRSG/KWL/STAPK BS4.......57 C5
Lansdown CI KCWD/HNM BS15...58 D1
Lansdown Cres
　CBATH/BATHN BA1 ....102 C4
Lansdown Gdns
　MTN/WRL BS22 ....118 A4
Lansdown Gv
　CBATH/BATHN BA1 ....102 C4
Lansdown Grove Ct
　CBATH/BATHN BA1 * 102 C4
Lansdown Hts
　CBATH/BATHN BA1 ....102 C4
Lansdown La
　CBATH/BATHN BA1 ....101 C1
Lansdown Pk
　CBATH/BATHN BA1 ....102 D3
Lansdown Pl CFTN/FAIL BS8 ....55 E4
Lansdown Pl East
　CBATH/BATHN BA1 ....102 C4
Lansdown Pl West
　CBATH/BATHN BA1 ....102 B3
Lansdown Rd
　CBATH/BATHN BA1 ....3 F1
　CFTN/FAIL BS8..............55 E4
　KEYN BS31 ....99 F1
　KCWD/HNM BS15 ....58 D1
　MANG/FISH BS16............51 G2
　RDLND/MONT BS6 ....55 F1
Lansdown Ter
　CBATH/BATHN BA1 ....3 F1
　RDLND/MONT BS6 ....45 H3
Lansdown Vw BATHSE BA2.....107 H2
　KCWD/HNM BS15 ....59 E3
Lanthony Cl
　OMX/HUT/LCK BS24 ....122 D3
Laphams Ct
　OLD/WMLY/WICK BS30 .....76 C2
Lapwing Cl ALMDB BS32 ....11 F5
　PTSHD/EG BS20 ....40 B2
Lapwing Gdns
　MANG/FISH BS16............47 G2
　MTN/WRL BS22 ....122 C2
Larch Cl NAIL BS48.............67 H4
The Larches MTN/WRL BS22 ...117 H5
Larchgrove Crs
　MTN/WRL BS22 ....122 C2
Larch Rd KCWD/HNM BS15 .....49 E5
Larch Wy BRSTK/PCHW BS34 ...34 C5
Larkfield FRCTL/WBN BS36......24 B3
Larkhall Pl CBATH/BATHN BA1...103 G2
Larkhall Ter
　CBATH/BATHN BA1 ....103 F2
Larkhill Rd
　OMX/HUT/LCK BS24 ....125 E5
Larkin Pl HORF/LLZ BS7 ....32 C4
Lark Pl CBATH/BATHN BA1 .....102 D2
Lark Rd MTN/WRL BS22 ....122 C2
Lark's Fld MANG/FISH BS16.....47 G3
Larksleaze Rd
　OLD/WMLY/WICK BS30 .....76 B4
Larkspur Ct THNB/SVB BS35 ....9 E3
Lasbury Gv
　BMSTRD/HC/WWD BS13.....84 D4
Latimer Cl
　BRSG/KWL/STAPK BS4.......74 C2
Latteridge Rd YATE/CS BS37 ...12 B3
Latton Rd HORF/LLZ BS7 ....32 B5
Launceston Av
　KCWD/HNM BS15 ....75 G1
Launceston Rd
　KCWD/HNM BS15 ....58 B2
Laura Pl BATHSE BA2 ....3 G4
Laurel Dr NAIL BS48 ....67 G4
　WSM BS23................124 D4
Laurel Gdns YTN/CONG BS49...112 B2
The Laurels HNBRY/STHM BS10...18 E4
　MANG/FISH BS16............51 H5
Laurel St KCWD/HNM BS15 .....58 D3
Laurel Ter YTN/CONG BS49 ....112 B2
Laurie Crs
　HNLZ/SM/SNYPK/WT BS9 ...45 H2
Laurie Lee Ct
　OLD/WMLY/WICK BS30 .....76 D1
Lavender Cl MTN/WRL BS22 ...117 H3
　THNB/SVB BS35 ....9 E3
Lavender Wy ALMDB BS32 .....21 F3
Lavenham Rd YATE/CS BS37 ....13 F5
Lavers Cl KCWD/HNM BS15 .....59 E5
Lavington Cl CLVDN BS21 ......64 A4
Lavington Rd EVILLE/WHL BS5...58 B5
Lawford Av BRSTK/PCHW BS34...21 H5
Lawfords Ga CBRISNE BS2 ....5 K2
Lawford St CBRISNE BS2 ....5 J3
Lawn Rd MANG/FISH BS16......48 B3
The Lawns MANG/FISH BS16....48 B3
　OMX/HUT/LCK BS24 ....122 A2
　YATE/CS BS37 ....14 A5
Lawnside
　HNLZ/SM/SNYPK/WT BS9 ...45 H2
Lawnwood Rd
　EVILLE/WHL BS5.............57 E1

Lawrence Cl KCWD/HNM BS15...59 G4
Lawrence Close Ms
　MTN/WRL BS22 * 122 F1
Lawrence Dr YATE/CS BS37 .....13 F5
Lawrence Gv
　HNLZ/SM/SNYPK/WT BS9 ...45 F3
Lawrence Hl EVILLE/WHL BS5...56 D4
Lawrence Ms MTN/WRL BS22...122 B1
Lawrence Weston Rd
　AVONM BS11 ....29 H3
Law's Dr OMX/HUT/LCK BS24 ...122 C4
Lawson Cl KEYN BS31 ....98 C5
Laxey Rd HORF/LLZ BS7 ....46 B1
Lays Dr KEYN BS31 ....87 H5
Leach Cl CLVDN BS21 ....64 C4
Leafy Wy OMX/HUT/LCK BS24...127 E2
Lea Grove Rd CLVDN BS21......64 C1
Leaholme Gdns
　HGRV/WHIT BS14 ....96 D1
Leaman Cl YATE/CS BS37 ....26 C1
Leap V MANG/FISH BS16 ....35 C5
Leap Valley Crs
　MANG/FISH BS16............35 F5
The Leaze YATE/CS BS37........13 H5
Leda Av HGRV/WHIT BS14......85 H2
Ledbury Rd MANG/FISH BS16...48 C4
Leechpool Wy YATE/CS BS37 ...14 A2
Lee Cl BRSTK/PCHW BS34......20 B2
Leedham Rd
　OMX/HUT/LCK BS24 ....127 F1
Leeming Wy AVONM BS11......28 C5
Lees HI KCWD/HNM BS15 ....59 E1
Leeside PTSHD/EG BS20 ....39 H3
Lees La OLD/WMLY/WICK BS30...77 G1
Leewood Rd WSM BS23 ....120 D2
Leicester Sq MANG/FISH BS16...48 D5
Leicester St BMSTR BS3 ....73 E2
Leicester Wk
　BRSG/KWL/STAPK BS4.......75 E1
Leigh Cl CBATH/BATHN BA1 ...102 D2
Leigh La YATE/CS BS37 ....37 F4
Leigh Rd CFTN/FAIL BS8 ....55 F3
Leigh St BMSTR BS3 ....72 B2
Leighton Rd BMSTR BS3.........72 C3
　BRSG/KWL/STAPK BS4.......74 A4
　CBATH/BATHN BA1 ....101 F1
Leigh View Rd PTSHD/EG BS20...39 H1
Leignwood Dr NAIL BS48 ....66 C5
Leinster Av
　BRSG/KWL/STAPK BS4.......85 E1
Leisure Rd KCWD/HNM BS15 ...76 B1
Lena Av EVILLE/WHL BS5 ....57 E2
Lena St EVILLE/WHL BS5 ....56 D2
Leonder Gdns
　BMSTRD/HC/WWD BS13....84 C5
Leonard La CBRIS/FH BS1 ....4 E5
Leonard Rd EVILLE/WHL BS5 ...57 E4
Leonards Av EVILLE/WHL BS5 ...57 E2
Leopold Blds
　CBATH/BATHN BA1 * 102 D4
Leopold Rd RDLND/MONT BS6...56 A1
Lescren Wy AVONM BS11.......28 C4
Lester Dr MTN/WRL BS22 .....117 H5
Lewins Md CBRIS/FH BS1 ....4 E4
Lewin St CBRISNE BS2..........57 F4
Lewton La FRCTL/WBN BS36....23 E3
Leyland Wk
　BMSTRD/HC/WWD BS13....84 A5
The Leys CLVDN BS21 ....64 B4
Leyton Vls RDLND/MONT BS6 ...55 F1
Liberty Gdns CBRIS/FH BS1 * 4 C7
Lichfield Rd
　BRSG/KWL/STAPK BS4.......57 C5
Lilac Cl HNBRY/STHM BS10 .....31 C4
Lilac Wy MTN/WRL BS22 ......117 H3
Lillian St EVILLE/WHL BS5.......57 E5
Lilliput Av YATE/CS BS37........26 C2
Lilliput Ct YATE/CS BS37 ....26 C2
Lilstock Av HORF/LLZ BS7 ......46 B4
Lilton Wk
　BMSTRD/HC/WWD BS13....72 B5
Lilymead Av
　BRSG/KWL/STAPK BS4.......73 H3
Lime Breach Wd NAIL BS48 * ...67 G3
Lime Cl HNBRY/STHM BS10 ....31 F2
　MTN/WRL BS22 ....117 E5
　OMX/HUT/LCK BS24 ....127 E2
Lime Ct YATE/CS BS37 ....14 C3
Lime Gv BATHSE BA2 ....3 J5
Lime Grove Gdns BATHSE BA2...3 J5
Lime Kiln Cl BRSTK/PCHW BS34...34 D3
Lime Kiln Gdns ALMDB BS32 ...11 F4
Lime Kiln La CLVDN BS21 ....64 D5
Lime Kiln Rd CFTN/FAIL BS8 .....4 B5
Limekilns Cl KEYN BS31 ....88 C4
Limerick Rd RDLND/MONT BS6...55 G1
Lime Rd BMSTR BS3 ....72 C2
　KCWD/HNM BS15 ....75 H1
Limestone Link BATHSE BA2 ...104 B2
　CBATH/BATHN BA1 ....91 E5
Lime Tree Gv PTSHD/EG BS20...40 D4
Lime Trees Rd
　RDLND/MONT BS6 ....45 H2
Lincoln Cl KEYN BS31 ....87 H5
Lincoln St EVILLE/WHL BS5.....56 D4
Lincombe Av MANG/FISH BS16...48 C3
Lincombe Rd MANG/FISH BS16...48 C3
Linden Cl FRCTL/WBN BS36 .....23 E4
Linden Cl HNBRY/STHM BS10...58 B1
　MANG/FISH BS16............48 D5
Linden Dr ALMDB BS32.........21 E4
Linden Gdns
　CBATH/BATHN BA1 ....102 A4
Linden Rd CLVDN BS21 ....64 D1
　RDLND/MONT BS6 ....45 F4
The Lindens MTN/WRL BS22 ...117 F4
Lindrea St BMSTR BS3 ....72 C3
Lindsay Rd HORF/LLZ BS7 ......46 C2
Lindsey Cl PTSHD/EG BS20.....38 D4
Linemere Cl NAIL BS48 ....80 C5
Lines Wy HGRV/WHIT BS14.....97 F1
Lingfield Pk MANG/FISH BS16...35 F4

Link La BOAV BA15 ....105 G4
Link Rd BRSTK/PCHW BS34 ....32 B2
NAIL BS48 ....67 G4
PTSHD/EG BS20 ....39 G3
YATE/CS BS37 ....26 B1
Linkside CLVDN BS21 ....62 C4
Links Rd WSM BS23 ....124 B4
Linley Cl BATHSE BA2 ....107 F2
The Linleys
CBATH/BATHN BA1 ....101 H5
Linnell Cl HORF/LLZ BS7 ....46 D2
Linnet Cl BRSTK/PCHW BS34 ....20 A2
MTN/WRL BS22 ....122 B2
Lintern Crs
OLD/WMLY/WICK BS30 ....59 G5
Lintham Dr KGWD/HNM BS15 ....59 F5
Linton's Wk HGRV/WHIT BS14 ....85 H2
Lion Cl NAIL BS48 ....66 D4
Lisburn Rd
BRSG/KWL/STAPK BS4 ....73 F5
Lisle Rd MTN/WRL BS22 ....118 A4
Litfield Pl CFTN/FAIL BS8 * 54 D4
Litfield Rd CFTN/FAIL BS8 ....54 D3
Little Ann St CBRISNE BS2 ....5 K2
Little Birch Cft
HGRV/WHIT BS14 ....96 D1
Little Bishop St CBRISNE BS2 ....56 A3
Little Caroline Pl
CFTN/FAIL BS8 ....72 A1
Littledean YATE/CS BS37 ....26 A4
Little Dowles
OLD/WMLY/WICK BS30 ....76 D2
Little George St CBRISNE BS2 ....5 K1
WSM BS23 ....7 F4
Little Halt PTSHD/EG BS20 ....38 C4
Little Ham CLVDN BS21 ....64 C5
Little Hayes MANG/FISH BS16 ....48 B3
Little Headley Cl
BMSTRD/HC/WWD BS13 ....84 C2
Little King St CBRIS/FH BS1 ....5 F5
Little Md AVONM BS11 ....29 H4
Little Mead Cl
OMX/HUT/LCK BS24 ....126 B3
Little Meadow ALMDB BS32 ....21 H4
Little Meadow End NAIL BS48 ....79 F1
Little Orch WSM BS23 ....124 C5
Little Paradise BMSTR BS3 ....73 E2
Little Parr Cl
MANG/FISH BS16 ....47 E3
Little Paul St CBRISNE BS2 ....55 G3
Little Stanhope St
CBATH/BATHN BA1 * 2 D4
Little Stoke La
BRSTK/PCHW BS34 ....21 E3
Little Stoke Rd
HNLZ/SM/SNYPK/WT BS9 ....44 C4
Littleton La
BLAG/CWMG/WR BS40 ....94 B5
Littleton Rd BMSTR BS3 ....73 E4
Littleton St EVILLE/WHL BS5 ....57 E2
Little Withey Md
HNLZ/SM/SNYPK/WT BS9 ....44 D2
Littlewood Cl HGRV/WHIT BS14 ....97 E1
Littlewood La
YTN/CONG BS49 ....113 H1
Livingstone Rd BATHSE BA2 ....2 A6
Livingstone Ter BATHSE BA2 ....2 B7
Llewellyn Wy MTN/WRL BS22 ....118 A5
Lockemor Rd
BMSTRD/HC/WWD BS13 ....85 G5
Lockes Paddock
MTN/WRL BS22 ....118 B5
Lock Gdns
BMSTRD/HC/WWD BS13 ....83 H2
Locking Head Dro
OMX/HUT/LCK BS24 ....126 C1
Locking Moor Rd
MTN/WRL BS22 ....121 H3
Locking Rd MTN/WRL BS22 ....122 A3
WSM BS23 ....7 F4
Lockingwell Rd KEYN BS31 ....88 A4
Lockleaze Rd HORF/LLZ BS7 ....46 C2
Locksbrook Pl
CBATH/BATHN BA1 * 101 H5
Locksbrook Rd
CBATH/BATHN BA1 ....107 G1
MTN/WRL BS22 ....118 A3
Lockside PTSHD/EG BS20 ....40 A1
Lodge Cswy MANG/FISH BS16 ....47 H5
Lodge Cl YTN/CONG BS49 ....112 B3
Lodge Ct
HNLZ/SM/SNYPK/WT BS9 ....44 C4
Lodge Dr LGASH BS41 ....71 E4
OLD/WMLY/WICK BS30 ....77 F4
WSM BS23 ....121 F2
Lodge Gdns BATHSE BA2 ....110 B1
Lodge Hl KGWD/HNM BS15 ....58 C1
Lodge La NAIL BS48 ....67 H3
Lodge Pl CBRIS/FH BS1 ....4 D3
Lodge Rd KGWD/HNM BS15 ....58 C1
OLD/WMLY/WICK BS30 ....61 E3
YATE/CS BS37 ....13 E5
Lodgeside Av
KGWD/HNM BS15 ....58 C2
Lodgeside Gdns
KGWD/HNM BS15 ....58 C2
Lodge St CBRIS/FH BS1 ....4 D3
Lodge Wk MANG/FISH BS16 ....48 D2
Lodore Rd MANG/FISH BS16 ....47 H5
Lodway PTSHD/EG BS20 ....42 B4
Lodway Cl PTSHD/EG BS20 ....42 B3
Lodway Gdns PTSHD/EG BS20 ....42 C4
Lodway Rd
BRSG/KWL/STAPK BS4 ....74 B4
Logan Rd HORF/LLZ BS7 ....45 H5
Logus Ct
OLD/WMLY/WICK BS30 ....76 C2
Lombard St BMSTR BS3 ....73 E2
Lombardy Cl MTN/WRL BS22 ....122 B3
Lomond Rd HORF/LLZ BS7 ....32 B4
London Rd CBATH/BATHN BA1 ....3 G1
CBRISNE BS2 ....56 B2
OLD/WMLY/WICK BS30 ....60 A4
London Rd East
CBATH/BATHN BA1 ....104 B1
London Rd West
CBATH/BATHN BA1 ....103 F3
London Sq PTSHD/EG BS20 ....40 A1
London St KGWD/HNM BS15 ....58 D3
Long Acre CBATH/BATHN BA1 ....102 D4
Longacre CLVDN BS21 ....64 B5
Longacre Rd HGRV/WHIT BS14 ....96 D1
Long Acres Cl
HNLZ/SM/SNYPK/WT BS9 ....44 B1
Long Ashton Rd LGASH BS41 ....70 D5
Long Av CLVDN BS21 ....64 B3
Long Beach Rd
OLD/WMLY/WICK BS30 ....76 D4
Long Cl ALMDB BS32 ....21 G4
MANG/FISH BS16 ....48 C2
Long Cft YATE/CS BS37 ....13 H2
Long Cross AVONM BS11 ....29 E5
BLAG/CWMG/WR BS40 ....93 E5
Longden Rd MANG/FISH BS16 ....49 F2
Longdown Dr MTN/WRL BS22 ....118 A4
Long Eaton Dr
HGRV/WHIT BS14 ....86 A1
Longfellow Av BATHSE BA2 ....108 C3
Longfield Rd HORF/LLZ BS7 ....46 A5
Longford YATE/CS BS37 ....25 G2
Longford Av
HNBRY/STHM BS10 ....31 H5
Long Handstones
OLD/WMLY/WICK BS30 ....76 D2
Long Hay Cl BATHSE BA2 ....107 G2
Longleat Cl
HNLZ/SM/SNYPK/WT BS9 ....45 G3
Longleaze Gdns
OMX/HUT/LCK BS24 ....126 C3
Long Md YATE/CS BS37 ....14 A2
Longmead Av HORF/LLZ BS7 ....45 H3
Long Meadow
MANG/FISH BS16 ....47 F3
Longmeadow Rd KEYN BS31 ....87 H5
Longmead Rd
MANG/FISH BS16 ....35 H4
Longmoor Ct BMSTR BS3 ....72 B4
Longmoor Rd BMSTR BS3 ....72 B4
Longney Pl BRSTK/PCHW BS34 ....20 B1
Longreach Gv
HGRV/WHIT BS14 ....86 C2
Longridge Wy
OMX/HUT/LCK BS24 ....122 B4
Long Rd MANG/FISH BS16 ....49 G3
Long Rw CBRIS/FH BS1 * 5 G5
Longs Dr YATE/CS BS37 ....13 G4
Long-Thorn NAIL BS48 ....79 G3
Longthorne Pl BATHSE BA2 * 108 C5
Longton Grove Rd WSM BS23 ....6 E2
Long Valley Rd BATHSE BA2 ....107 E2
Longway Av HGRV/WHIT BS14 ....85 G5
Longwood
BRSG/KWL/STAPK BS4 ....75 F4
Longwood La CFTN/FAIL BS8 ....70 B2
Lonsdale Av WSM BS23 ....125 E2
Lorain Wk HNBRY/STHM BS10 ....30 D3
Lorton Cl HNBRY/STHM BS10 ....31 F4
Lorton Rd HNBRY/STHM BS10 ....31 F4
Lotts' Av NAIL BS48 ....80 A4
Loughman Cl
KGWD/HNM BS15 * 59 E3
Louisa St CBRISNE BS2 ....5 K4
Louise Av MANG/FISH BS16 ....49 G3
Love La YATE/CS BS37 ....26 C2
Lovelinch Gdns LGASH BS41 ....70 C5
Lovell Av
OLD/WMLY/WICK BS30 ....77 G2
Lovell's Hl KGWD/HNM BS15 ....75 G1
Loveridge Ct FRCTL/WBN BS36 ....23 H3
Loveringe Cl
HNBRY/STHM BS10 ....30 D1
Lowbourne HGRV/WHIT BS14 ....85 G3
Lower Ashley Rd
RDLND/MONT BS6 ....56 B2
Lower Borough Walls
CBATH/BATHN BA1 * 3 F5
Lower Bristol Rd BATHSE BA2 ....101 E5
Lower Burlington Rd
PTSHD/EG BS20 ....40 A1
Lower Camden Pl
CBATH/BATHN BA1 * 102 D4
Lower Castle St CBRIS/FH BS1 ....5 H2
Lower Chapel La
FRCTL/WBN BS36 ....24 A3
Lower Chapel Rd
KGWD/HNM BS15 ....75 H1
Lower Cheltenham Pl
RDLND/MONT BS6 ....56 B2
Lower Church La CBRIS/FH BS1 ....4 D3
Lower Church Rd WSM BS23 ....6 D2
Lower Clifton Hl CFTN/FAIL BS8 ....4 A4
Lower Cock Rd
KGWD/HNM BS15 ....59 F4
Lower College St CBRIS/FH BS1 ....4 C5
Lower Conham V
KGWD/HNM BS15 ....75 E1
Lower Court Rd ALMDB BS32 ....10 C2
Lower Down Rd
PTSHD/EG BS20 ....39 F3
Lower East Hayes
CBATH/BATHN BA1 * 103 E4
Lower Fallow Cl
HGRV/WHIT BS14 ....85 G5
Lower Gay St CBRISNE BS2 ....55 H3
Lower Grove Rd
MANG/FISH BS16 * 47 G4
Lower Guinea St CBRIS/FH BS1 ....5 F7
Lower Hanham Rd
KGWD/HNM BS15 ....58 C5
Lower Hedgemead Rd
CBATH/BATHN BA1 ....3 G1
Lower High St AVONM BS11 ....28 D5
Lower House Crs
BRSTK/PCHW BS34 ....32 D1
Lower Kingsdown Rd
COR/BOX SN13 ....105 G1
Lower Knole La
HNBRY/STHM BS10 ....31 E2
Lower Knowles Rd
CLVDN BS21 ....64 C3
Lower Lamb St CBRIS/FH BS1 ....4 C5
Lower Linden Rd CLVDN BS21 ....64 D2
Lower Maudlin St
CBRIS/FH BS1 ....5 F2
Lower Moor Rd YATE/CS BS37 ....14 A3
Lower Northend
CBATH/BATHN BA1 ....91 E4
Lower Norton La
MTN/WRL BS22 ....116 C4
Lower Oldfield Pk BATHSE BA2 ....2 C6
Lower Parade Ground Rd
OMX/HUT/LCK BS24 ....127 E1
Lower Park Rw CBRIS/FH BS1 ....4 E3
Lower Queen's Rd CLVDN BS21 ....64 D2
Lower Redland Rd
RDLND/MONT BS6 ....55 F1
Lower Sidney St BMSTR BS3 ....72 B2
Lower Station Approach Rd
CBRIS/FH BS1 ....5 J6
Lower Station Rd
MANG/FISH BS16 ....47 H4
Lower Stone Cl
FRCTL/WBN BS36 ....24 A2
Lowlis Cl HNBRY/STHM BS10 ....30 D2
Lowther Rd
HNBRY/STHM BS10 ....31 G3
Loxley Gdns BATHSE BA2 ....107 H3
Loxton Dr BATHSE BA2 ....107 G1
Loxton Rd WSM BS23 ....125 E3
Loxton Sq HGRV/WHIT BS14 ....85 H3
Lucas Cl BRSG/KWL/STAPK BS4 ....86 C1
Luccombe Hl
RDLND/MONT BS6 ....55 F1
Luckington Rd HORF/LLZ BS7 ....32 A5
Lucklands Rd
CBATH/BATHN BA1 ....101 H3
Luckley Av
BMSTRD/HC/WWD BS13 ....84 D4
Luckwell Rd BMSTR BS3 ....72 C3
Lucky La BMSTR BS3 ....73 E2
Ludlow Cl CBRISNE BS2 ....56 B2
KEYN BS31 ....88 A4
OLD/WMLY/WICK BS30 ....77 E4
Ludlow Ct
OLD/WMLY/WICK BS30 ....77 E4
Ludlow Rd HORF/LLZ BS7 ....46 C1
Ludwell Cl FRCTL/WBN BS36 ....22 D5
Lullington Rd
BRSG/KWL/STAPK BS4 ....74 A4
Lulsgate Rd
BMSTRD/HC/WWD BS13 ....84 B1
Lulworth Crs MANG/FISH BS16 ....35 F5
Lulworth Rd KEYN BS31 ....88 B5
Lunty Md NAIL BS48 ....79 H3
Lurgan Wk
BRSG/KWL/STAPK BS4 ....73 E5
Lutyens Cl MANG/FISH BS16 ....33 G5
Lux Furlong
HNLZ/SM/SNYPK/WT BS9 ....43 H1
Luxton St EVILLE/WHL BS5 ....56 D3
Lychgate Pk
OMX/HUT/LCK BS24 ....126 D2
Lydbrook Cl YATE/CS BS37 ....25 H2
Lyddington Rd HORF/LLZ BS7 ....32 A4
Lyddon Rd MTN/WRL BS22 ....118 A5
Lydford Wk BMSTR BS3 ....72 D4
Lydiard Cft KGWD/HNM BS15 ....75 H2
Lydney Rd HNBRY/STHM BS10 ....31 H5
MANG/FISH BS16 ....49 E4
Lydstep Ter BMSTR BS3 ....72 D2
Lyefield Rd MTN/WRL BS22 ....117 F4
The Lyes YTN/CONG BS49 ....114 D3
Lyme Gdns CBATH/BATHN BA1 ....101 F5
Lyme Rd CBATH/BATHN BA1 ....101 G5
Lymore Av BATHSE BA2 ....107 H2
Lymore Gdns BATHSE BA2 ....107 H2
Lymore Ter BATHSE BA2 ....107 H3
Lympsham Gn BATHSE BA2 ....110 B1
Lynbrook LGASH BS41 ....70 C5
Lynbrook La BATHSE BA2 ....108 C4
Lynch Cl MTN/WRL BS22 ....117 G5
Lynch Ct
OLD/WMLY/WICK BS30 * 76 C2
Lyncombe Hl BATHSE BA2 ....3 H7
Lyncombe V BATHSE BA2 ....108 D3
Lyncombe Vale Rd
BATHSE BA2 ....108 D4
Lyncombe Wk
MANG/FISH BS16 ....58 B1
Lyndale Av
HNLZ/SM/SNYPK/WT BS9 ....44 A3
Lyndale Rd EVILLE/WHL BS5 ....57 F3
YATE/CS BS37 ....25 H1
Lynde Cl
BMSTRD/HC/WWD BS13 ....84 C5
Lyndhurst Rd BATHSE BA2 ....107 H1
HNLZ/SM/SNYPK/WT BS9 ....44 D1
KEYN BS31 ....98 A1
WSM BS23 ....124 D2
Lyndhurst Ter
CBATH/BATHN BA1 ....102 D4
Lynfield Pk
CBATH/BATHN BA1 ....101 G2
Lynmouth Cl MTN/WRL BS22 ....122 D1
Lynmouth Rd CBRISNE BS2 ....56 C1
Lynn Rd MANG/FISH BS16 ....47 F3
Lynton Cl PTSHD/EG BS20 ....40 A4
Lynton Pl EVILLE/WHL BS5 ....57 E3
Lynton Rd BMSTR BS3 ....73 E5
Lynton Wy MANG/FISH BS16 ....34 B4
Lynx Crs OMX/HUT/LCK BS24 ....125 G4
Lyons Ct WSM BS23 ....7 G4
Lyons Court Rd
HGRV/WHIT BS14 ....86 C2
Lyppiatt Rd EVILLE/WHL BS5 ....57 F3
Lyppincourt Rd
HNBRY/STHM BS10 ....31 E2
Lysander Rd
HNBRY/STHM BS10 ....19 F4
Lysander Wk
BRSTK/PCHW BS34 ....21 G5
Lytchet Dr MANG/FISH BS16 ....35 F5
Lytes Cary Rd KEYN BS31 ....98 B2
Lytton Gdns BATHSE BA2 ....107 G3
Lytton Gv HORF/LLZ BS7 ....32 C5
KEYN BS31 ....88 D4
Lyveden Gdns
BMSTRD/HC/WWD BS13 ....84 C4
Lyvedon Wy LGASH BS41 ....71 E5

M

Mabberley Cl MANG/FISH BS16 ....50 A3
Macaulay Blds BATHSE BA2 ....109 F3
Macauley Rd HORF/LLZ BS7 ....32 C5
Macdonald Wk
KGWD/HNM BS15 ....58 D3
Macey's Rd
BMSTRD/HC/WWD BS13 ....96 A1
Macfarlane Cha WSM BS23 ....125 F1
Machin Cl HNBRY/STHM BS10 ....30 D2
Machin Gdns
HNBRY/STHM BS10 ....31 E2
Machin Rd HNBRY/STHM BS10 ....30 D2
The Macies
CBATH/BATHN BA1 ....101 G1
Mackie Av BRSTK/PCHW BS34 ....32 D3
Mackie Gv BRSTK/PCHW BS34 ....32 D3
Mackie Rd BRSTK/PCHW BS34 ....32 D3
Macleod Cl CLVDN BS21 ....64 A3
Macquarie Farm Cl
YTN/CONG BS49 ....112 A2
Macrae Ct KGWD/HNM BS15 * 59 E3
Macrae Rd PTSHD/EG BS20 ....43 E4
Madam La MTN/WRL BS22 ....122 C1
Madeira Rd CLVDN BS21 ....64 D2
WSM BS23 ....6 A1
Madeline Rd MANG/FISH BS16 ....57 H1
Madison Cl YATE/CS BS37 ....13 H5
Maesbury KGWD/HNM BS15 ....59 E5
Maesbury Rd KEYN BS31 ....98 B2
Maesknoll La PLTN/PENS BS39 ....96 D4
Maesknoll Rd
BRSG/KWL/STAPK BS4 ....73 H3
Magdalen Av BATHSE BA2 ....2 E7
Magdalene Pl CBRISNE BS2 ....56 B2
Magdalen Rd BATHSE BA2 ....2 E7
Magdalen Wy MTN/WRL BS22 ....117 H5
Magellan Cl MTN/WRL BS22 ....117 G4
Maggs Cl HNBRY/STHM BS10 ....31 G2
Maggs La EVILLE/WHL BS5 ....57 G1
HGRV/WHIT BS14 ....86 A5
Magnolia Av MTN/WRL BS22 ....122 D2
Magnolia Cl MTN/WRL BS22 ....122 A4
Magpie Bottom La
EVILLE/WHL BS5 ....58 B5
Magpie Cl MTN/WRL BS22 ....122 B3
Maidenhead Rd
BMSTRD/HC/WWD BS13 ....96 A1
Maiden Wy AVONM BS11 ....42 C1
Maidstone Gv
OMX/HUT/LCK BS24 ....125 F5
Maidstone St BMSTR BS3 ....73 G3
Main Rd MANG/FISH BS16 ....50 A4
NAIL BS48 ....81 E2
OMX/HUT/LCK BS24 ....126 A4
YTN/CONG BS49 ....113 H3
Main Vw FRCTL/WBN BS36 ....24 B3
Maisemore YATE/CS BS37 ....25 H4
Maisemore Av
BRSTK/PCHW BS34 ....20 D1
Makin Cl
OLD/WMLY/WICK BS30 ....77 F1
Malago Rd BMSTR BS3 ....72 D3
Malago Wk
BMSTRD/HC/WWD BS13 ....83 H5
Malden Md HGRV/WHIT BS14 ....85 H4
Maldowers La EVILLE/WHL BS5 ....58 A2
Mallard Cl ALMDB BS32 ....11 F5
EVILLE/WHL BS5 ....57 H2
YATE/CS BS37 ....26 C2
Mallow Cl CLVDN BS21 ....65 E2
THNB/SVB BS35 ....9 E2
The Mall CBATH/BATHN BA1 * 3 G6
CFTN/FAIL BS8 ....54 D4
Malmains Dr MANG/FISH BS16 ....34 B4
Malmesbury Cl
OLD/WMLY/WICK BS30 ....76 C1
RDLND/MONT BS6 ....45 G4
The Maltings MTN/WRL BS22 ....122 C1
RDLND/MONT BS6 * 56 B1
Maitlands MTN/WRL BS22 ....122 A3
Malvern Blds
CBATH/BATHN BA1 ....102 D2
Malvern Ct EVILLE/WHL BS5 ....57 H4
Malvern Dr
OLD/WMLY/WICK BS30 ....77 F1
THNB/SVB BS35 ....9 E4
Malvern Rd
BRSG/KWL/STAPK BS4 ....74 C3
EVILLE/WHL BS5 ....57 H4
WSM BS23 ....124 D1
Malvern Ter
CBATH/BATHN BA1 ....102 D3
Malvern Vls
CBATH/BATHN BA1 ....102 D3
Mancroft Av AVONM BS11 ....43 F1
Mangotsfield Rd
MANG/FISH BS16 ....49 F4
Manilla Crs WSM BS23 ....6 B1
Manilla Rd CFTN/FAIL BS8 ....55 E4
Manmoor La CLVDN BS21 ....65 G4
Manor Cl FRCTL/WBN BS36 ....24 A4
PTSHD/EG BS20 ....42 A4
PTSHD/EG BS20 ....39 E3
The Manor Cl CFTN/FAIL BS8 ....53 G3
Manor Ct NAIL BS48 ....79 H4
Manor Court Dr HORF/LLZ BS7 ....46 A1
Manor Dr CBATH/BATHN BA1 ....104 C2
Manor Farm Crs ALMDB BS32 ....21 F2
OMX/HUT/LCK BS24 ....125 G4
Manor Gdns MTN/WRL BS22 ....116 C4
OMX/HUT/LCK BS24 ....126 D2
Manor Gv BRSTK/PCHW BS34 ....10 D5
MANG/FISH BS16 ....49 G4
Manor La CFTN/FAIL BS8 ....53 F3
FRCTL/WBN BS36 ....23 F3
Manor Pk CBATH/BATHN BA1 ....101 G4
RDLND/MONT BS6 ....45 F5
Manor Pl BRSTK/PCHW BS34 ....34 A1
Manor Rd
BMSTRD/HC/WWD BS13 ....84 A3
CBATH/BATHN BA1 ....101 H3
CFTN/FAIL BS8 ....53 F5
HORF/LLZ BS7 ....46 A4
KEYN BS31 ....98 B1
MANG/FISH BS16 ....49 G4
MANG/FISH BS16 ....47 H3
WSM BS23 ....7 H1
Manor Va WSM BS23 ....7 J1
Manor Vls
CBATH/BATHN BA1 ....101 H3
Manor Wk THNB/SVB BS35 ....8 C1
Manor Wy CFTN/FAIL BS8 ....69 H2
YATE/CS BS37 ....15 E5
Mansel Cl KEYN BS31 ....98 D1
Mansfield Av WSM BS23 ....121 G3
Mansfield Cl WSM BS23 ....121 G3
Mansfield St BMSTR BS3 ....72 C4
Manston Cl HGRV/WHIT BS14 ....86 B2
Manvers St CBATH/BATHN BA1 ....3 G5
Manworthy Rd
BRSG/KWL/STAPK BS4 ....74 C3
Manx Rd HORF/LLZ BS7 ....46 B1
Maple Av MANG/FISH BS16 ....48 C5
THNB/SVB BS35 ....8 D3
Maple Cl BRSTK/PCHW BS34 ....21 E3
HGRV/WHIT BS14 ....86 C4
OLD/WMLY/WICK BS30 ....77 E2
WSM BS23 ....7 K3
Maple Gdns BATHSE BA2 ....108 B3
Maple Gv BATHSE BA2 ....108 B3
Mapleleaze
BRSG/KWL/STAPK BS4 ....74 C3
Maplemeade HORF/LLZ BS7 ....45 G4
Mapleridge La YATE/CS BS37 ....15 H1
Maple Rd
BRSG/KWL/STAPK BS4 ....74 C1
HORF/LLZ BS7 ....45 H3
The Maples NAIL BS48 ....66 D5
Maplestone Rd
HGRV/WHIT BS14 ....96 D1
Maple Wk KEYN BS31 ....88 A5
MANG/FISH BS16 ....51 G3
Mapstone Cl MANG/FISH BS16 ....34 B2
Marbeck Rd
HNBRY/STHM BS10 ....31 F4
Marchfields Wy WSM BS23 ....7 H7
Marconi Cl WSM BS23 ....121 G4
Marconi Rd PTSHD/EG BS20 ....38 D4
Mardale Cl HNBRY/STHM BS10 ....31 G3
Marden Rd KEYN BS31 ....88 D5
Mardon Rd
BRSG/KWL/STAPK BS4 ....57 F5
Mardyke Ferry Rd
CBRIS/FH BS1 ....4 A6
Margarets Blds
CBATH/BATHN BA1 * 2 E2
Margate St BMSTR BS3 ....73 F3
Marguerite Rd
BMSTRD/HC/WWD BS13 ....84 A1
Marigold Wk BMSTR BS3 ....72 B4
Marina Gdns MANG/FISH BS16 ....47 G5
Marindrin Dr MTN/WRL BS22 ....118 A4
Marine Hl CLVDN BS21 ....64 C1
Marine Pde CLVDN BS21 ....64 C1
PTSHD/EG BS20 ....42 C3
WSM BS23 ....6 C7
Mariners Cl NAIL BS48 ....79 H3
Mariner's Cl MTN/WRL BS22 ....122 A2
Mariners Dr
HNLZ/SM/SNYPK/WT BS9 ....44 B4
NAIL BS48 ....79 H3
Mariner's Wy PTSHD/EG BS20 ....42 C3
Marion Rd KGWD/HNM BS15 ....75 G3
Marion Wk EVILLE/WHL BS5 ....58 A4
Marissal Cl HNBRY/STHM BS10 ....30 C2
Marissal Rd HNBRY/STHM BS10 ....30 C2
Mariston Wy
OLD/WMLY/WICK BS30 ....60 A5
Marjoram Pl ALMDB BS32 ....21 H3
Marjoram Wy PTSHD/EG BS20 ....40 B3
Market Av MTN/WRL BS22 ....118 B5
Market La WSM BS23 ....6 D2
Market Pl
BLAG/CWMG/WR BS40 ....93 G5
Market Sq MANG/FISH BS16 ....48 C5
Mark La CBRIS/FH BS1 ....4 D4
Marksbury Rd BMSTR BS3 ....72 D4
Marlborough Av
EVILLE/WHL BS5 * 47 G5
Marlborough Blds
CBATH/BATHN BA1 ....2 D2
Marlborough Dr
MANG/FISH BS16 ....34 B4
MTN/WRL BS22 ....118 A5
Marlborough Hl
RDLND/MONT BS6 ....4 E1
Marlborough Hill Pl
CBRISNE BS2 ....4 E1
Marlborough La
CBATH/BATHN BA1 ....2 C3
Marlborough St
CBATH/BATHN BA1 ....2 D1
CBRIS/FH BS1 ....4 E2
EVILLE/WHL BS5 ....47 G5
Marlepit Gv
BMSTRD/HC/WWD BS13 ....83 H3
Marle Pits NAIL BS48 ....79 H3
Marlfield Wk
BMSTRD/HC/WWD BS13 ....83 H2
Marling Rd EVILLE/WHL BS5 ....57 H3
Marlwood Dr
HNBRY/STHM BS10 ....31 E2
Marmaduke St BMSTR BS3 ....73 G3
Marmion Crs
HNBRY/STHM BS10 ....30 D2
Marne Cl HGRV/WHIT BS14 ....86 C4
Marsden Rd BATHSE BA2 ....107 G4
Marshall Wk
BRSG/KWL/STAPK BS4 * 85 E2
Marsham Wy
OLD/WMLY/WICK BS30 ....76 B1
Marsh Cl FRCTL/WBN BS36 ....35 E1
Marshfield Rd
MANG/FISH BS16 ....48 B4
Marshfield Wy
CBATH/BATHN BA1 ....102 D3
Marsh La BMSTR BS3 ....72 B4
EVILLE/WHL BS5 ....57 E4
PTSHD/EG BS20 ....41 G2
Marsh Rd BMSTR BS3 ....72 A3
YTN/CONG BS49 ....112 B4
Marsh St AVONM BS11 ....28 C5
CBRIS/FH BS1 ....4 E4
Marshwall La ALMDB BS32 ....10 B1
Marson Rd CLVDN BS21 ....64 D2
Marston Rd
BRSG/KWL/STAPK BS4 ....74 A4
Martcombe Rd
PTSHD/EG BS20 ....42 B5
Martha's Orch
BMSTRD/HC/WWD BS13 ....83 H2
Martin Cl BRSTK/PCHW BS34 ....20 A2
Martindale Ct MTN/WRL BS22 ....121 H3
Martindale Rd
MTN/WRL BS22 ....122 A3

Martingale Rd
 BRSG/KWL/STAPK BS4....74 C2
Martins Cl *KGWD/HNM BS15*...75 H1
Martins Gv *MTN/WRL BS22*...122 D1
Martin's Rd *KGWD/HNM BS15*...75 H1
The Martins *PTSHD/EG BS20*...40 C2
Martin St *BMSTR BS3*...72 C5
Martock Crs *BMSTR BS3*...72 D5
Martock Rd *BMSTR BS3*...72 D5
 KEYN BS31...98 B1
Marwood Rd
 BRSG/KWL/STAPK BS4....85 F1
Marybush La *CBRISNE BS2*....5 H5
Mary Carpenter Pl
 *CBRISNE BS2 **...56 B2
Marygold Leaze
 OLD/WMLY/WICK BS30...76 D2
Mary St *EVILLE/WHL BS5*...57 F3
Mascot Rd *BMSTR BS3*...73 E5
Maserield Wy *HORF/LLZ BS7*...46 C1
Maskelyne Av
 HNBRY/STHM BS10...45 H1
Masons Vw *FRCTL/WBN BS36*...23 E3
Materman Rd
 HGRV/WHIT BS14...86 D4
Matford Cl *FRCTL/WBN BS36*...23 E5
 HNBRY/STHM BS10...31 H1
Matthews Cl *HGRV/WHIT BS14*...86 C4
Matthew's Rd *EVILLE/WHL BS5*...57 E4
Maules La *MANG/FISH BS16*...33 H5
Maunsell Rd *AVONM BS11*...27 H1
 OMX/HUT/LCK BS24...122 B4
Maurice Rd *RDLND/MONT BS6*...56 C1
Mautravers Cl *ALMDB BS32*...21 F5
Maxse Rd
 BRSG/KWL/STAPK BS4....74 A3
Maybec Gdns *EVILLE/WHL BS5*...58 A5
Maybourne
 BRSG/KWL/STAPK BS4....75 F4
Maybrick Rd *BATHSE BA2*....2 A7
Maycliffe Pk
 RDLND/MONT BS6...56 B1
Mayfair Av *NAIL BS48*...67 F5
Mayfield Av
 MANG/FISH BS16...58 A1
 MTN/WRL BS22...122 D2
Mayfield Pk *MANG/FISH BS16*...58 A1
Mayfield Pk North
 MANG/FISH BS16...58 A1
Mayfield Pk South
 MANG/FISH BS16...58 A1
Mayfield Rd *BATHSE BA2*....2 A7
Mayflower Gdns *NAIL BS48*...67 H4
May La *CBATH/BATHN BA1*...101 G4
Maynard Cl
 BMSTRD/HC/WWD BS13...84 D4
 CLVDN BS21...65 F2
Maynard Rd
 BMSTRD/HC/WWD BS13...84 D4
 CLVDN BS21...65 F2
Maypole Sq *KGWD/HNM BS15 **...75 H1
Maytree Av
 BMSTRD/HC/WWD BS13...84 C2
Maytree Cl
 BMSTRD/HC/WWD BS13...84 C2
May Tree Cl *NAIL BS48 **...66 D4
Mayville Av *BRSTK/PCHW BS34*...32 A2
Maywood Crs *MANG/FISH BS16*...48 B4
Maywood Rd *MANG/FISH BS16*...48 C4
Maze St *EVILLE/WHL BS5*...56 D5
McCrae Rd
 OMX/HUT/LCK BS24...127 E1
McLaren Rd *AVONM BS11 **...28 B4
Mead Cl *AVONM BS11 **...43 C2
 BATHSE BA2...108 B4
Meadgate *MANG/FISH BS16*...35 H5
Meadlands *BATHSE BA2*...100 A5
Meadowbank *MTN/WRL BS22*...117 G5
Meadow Cl *MANG/FISH BS16*...49 F1
 NAIL BS48...80 A3
 NAIL BS48...67 F5
Meadow Cft...38 D3
 OLD/WMLY/WICK BS30...77 F5
Meadowcroft
 MANG/FISH BS16...35 G5
Meadow Crt
 OMX/HUT/LCK BS24...125 G4
Meadow Dr *BATHSE BA2*...110 B2
 OMX/HUT/LCK BS24...126 D2
Meadow Gdns
 CBATH/BATHN BA1...101 F5
Meadow Gv *AVONM BS11 **...42 D1
Meadowland *YTN/CONG BS49*...112 A2
Meadowland Rd
 HNBRY/STHM BS10...30 C1
Meadowlands
 MTN/WRL BS22...123 F1
Meadow La *BATHSE BA2*...103 G3
Meadow Md *FRCTL/WBN BS36*...23 H2
 YATE/CS BS37...26 C1
Meadow Pk *CBATH/BATHN BA1*...91 C5
Meadow Pl *MTN/WRL BS22*...117 G5
Meadow Rd *CLVDN BS21*...64 D3
 YATE/CS BS37...26 C1
Meadowside *THNB/SVB BS35*....9 E4
Meadowside Dr
 Midland Av...96 D1
The Meadows
 KGWD/HNM BS15...76 A2
Meadow St *AVONM BS11*...28 A4
 WS23....6 D4
Meadowsweet Av
 BRSTK/PCHW BS34...32 D2
Meadow V *EVILLE/WHL BS5*...58 A2
Meadow Vw
 FRCTL/WBN BS36...24 A3
Meadow Wy *ALMDB BS32*...21 G3
Mead Ri *BMSTR BS3*...72 C5
Mead Rd *BRSTK/PCHW BS34*...21 H4
 PTSHD/EG BS20...39 C5
 YATE/CS BS37...27 E2
The Meads *MANG/FISH BS16*...49 F1
Mead St *BMSTR BS3*...73 G2

The Mead *BRSTK/PCHW BS34*...32 D1
 LGASH BS41...94 C2
Mead V *MTN/WRL BS22*...122 R5
Meadway
 HNLZ/SM/SNYPK/WT BS9...44 A2
Mead Wy *THNB/SVB BS35*....8 C5
Meadway Av *NAIL BS48*...67 E4
Meardon Rd *HGRV/WHIT BS14*...86 D3
Meare Rd *BATHSE BA2*...108 B5
Mede Cl *CBRIS/FH BS1 **....5 G7
Medical Av *CFTN/FAIL BS8*....4 D3
Medina Cl *THNB/SVB BS35*....8 D5
Medway Cl *KEYN BS31*...98 A1
Medway Ct *THNB/SVB BS35*....9 E4
Medway Dr *FRCTL/WBN BS36*...23 H5
 KEYN BS31...98 B1
Meere Bank *AVONM BS11*...29 H4
Meetinghouse La
 YTN/CONG BS49...113 G2
Meg Thatchers Gn
 EVILLE/WHL BS5...58 B4
Melbourne Dr *YATE/CS BS37*...26 D1
Melbourne Rd *HORF/LLZ BS7*...45 H4
Melbourne Ter *CLVDN BS21*...64 D3
Melbury Rd
 BRSG/KWL/STAPK BS4....73 H4
Melcombe Rd *BATHSE BA2*....2 A7
Melita Rd *RDLND/MONT BS6*...46 A5
Mellent Av
 BMSTRD/HC/WWD BS13...95 H1
Mells Cl *KEYN BS31*...98 B2
Melrose Av *CFTN/FAIL BS8*...55 F3
 YATE/CS BS37...14 B5
Melrose Cl *YATE/CS BS37*...14 C5
Melrose Gv *BATHSE BA2*...107 C4
Melrose Pl *CFTN/FAIL BS8*...55 F3
Melrose Ter
 *CBATH/BATHN BA1 **...102 D2
Melton Crs *HORF/LLZ BS7*...46 C1
Melville Rd *RDLND/MONT BS6*...55 F2
Melvin Ter *BMSTR BS3*...72 D5
Melvin Sq
 BRSG/KWL/STAPK BS4....73 F5
Memorial Cl *KGWD/HNM BS15*...75 G2
Memorial Rd
 KGWD/HNM BS15...75 G2
Mendip Av *MTN/WRL BS22*...122 B1
 NAIL BS48...67 F5
Mendip Cl *KEYN BS31*...88 A4
Mendip Crs *MANG/FISH BS16*...49 C1
Mendip Gdns *BATHSE BA2*...110 B2
 YTN/CONG BS49...112 B4
Mendip Rd *BMSTR BS3*...73 E3
 OMX/HUT/LCK BS24...127 F2
 PTSHD/EG BS20...39 E3
 WSM BS23....7 J4
 YTN/CONG BS49...112 B5
Mendip Vw
 OLD/WMLY/WICK BS30...61 G4
Mendip View Av
 MANG/FISH BS16...48 A5
Mendip Vw Cv *HNBRY/STHM BS10*...31 F2
Merchants Quay *CBRIS/FH BS1*....4 E6
Merchants Rd *CBRIS/FH BS1*...72 B1
 CFTN/FAIL BS8...55 E4
Merchants Rw *CBRIS/FH BS1 **....4 C7
Merchant St *CBRIS/FH BS1*....5 G4
Mercia Dr *CBRISNE BS2*...56 C1
Mercier Cl *YATE/CS BS37*...14 B5
Merfield Rd
 BRSG/KWL/STAPK BS4....74 A1
Meridian Pl *CFTN/FAIL BS8*....4 A3
Meridian Rd *RDLND/MONT BS6*...55 G2
Meridian Ter *HORF/LLZ BS7*...45 H5
Meridian V *CFTN/FAIL BS8*....4 A3
Meriet Av
 BMSTRD/HC/WWD BS13...84 C5
Merioneth St *BMSTR BS3*...73 C4
Meriton St *CBRISNE BS2*...74 A1
Merlin Cl
 HNLZ/SM/SNYPK/WT BS9...30 D5
 MTN/WRL BS22...122 B5
Merlin Pk *PTSHD/EG BS20*...38 D4
Merlin Rdg *MANG/FISH BS16*...51 C4
Merlin Rd *BRSTK/PCHW BS34*...19 F3
Merlin Wy *YATE/CS BS37*...26 B3
Merrimans Rd *AVONM BS11*...28 C5
Merryweather Cl *ALMDB BS32*...21 E2
Merrywood Cl *BMSTR BS3*...72 D2
Merrywood Rd *BMSTR BS3*...72 D2
Merstham Rd *CBRISNE BS2*...56 C1
Merton Dr
 OMX/HUT/LCK BS24...122 D3
Merton Rd *HORF/LLZ BS7*...46 A3
Mervyn Rd *HORF/LLZ BS7*...46 A3
Metford Gv *RDLND/MONT BS6*...45 F5
Metford Pl *RDLND/MONT BS6*...45 F5
Metford Rd *RDLND/MONT BS6*...45 F5
Methwyn Cl *MTN/WRL BS22*...121 H4
The Mews *CBATH/BATHN BA1*...101 F4
Mezellion Pl
 *CBATH/BATHN BA1 **...102 D3
Middle Av *CBRIS/FH BS1 **....5 F5
Middle La *CBATH/BATHN BA1*...103 E5
Middlepiece La *KEYN BS31*...98 C5
Middleton Rd *KGWD/HNM BS15*...49 E5
Middleton Rd *AVONM BS11*...29 F5
Middlewood Cl *BATHSE BA2*...110 A1
Middle Yeo Gn *NAIL BS48 **...67 F4
Midford Hi *BATHSE BA2*...111 C4
Midford La *BATHSE BA2*...111 G4
Midford Rd *BATHSE BA2*...110 D2
Midhaven Ri *MTN/WRL BS22*...117 H4
Midland Bridge Rd
 CBATH/BATHN BA1....2 D5
Midland Rd *BATHSE BA2*....2 B4
 CBRISNE BS2....5 K3
 MANG/FISH BS16...48 D4
Midland St *CBRISNE BS2*....5 J5
Midland Ter *MANG/FISH BS16*...48 D4
Midland Wy *THNB/SVB BS35*....8 C4
Midsummer Blds
 CBATH/BATHN BA1...102 D3
Midway Rd *WSM BS23*....7 H2
Milbury Gdns *MTN/WRL BS22*...121 G1
Mildred Cl *EVILLE/WHL BS5*...57 E4
Mile End *CBATH/BATHN BA1 **...103 E5
Miles Cl *BATHSE BA2*....3 H6
Miles Rd *CFTN/FAIL BS8*...55 E2

Miles's Blds *CBATH/BATHN BA1*....3 F3
Miles St *BATHSE BA2*....3 H6
Milestone Ct *MTN/WRL BS22*...123 C1
Mile Wk *HGRV/WHIT BS14*...85 H2
Milford Av
 OLD/WMLY/WICK BS30...61 F4
Milk St *CBATH/BATHN BA1*....3 F4
Millard Cl *HNBRY/STHM BS10*...31 C5
Mill Av *CBRIS/FH BS1*....5 F5
Millbank Cl
 BRSG/KWL/STAPK BS4....74 D3
Millbrook Cl
 OLD/WMLY/WICK BS30...60 A5
Millbrook Pl *BATHSE BA2*....3 H7
Millbrook Rd *YATE/CS BS37*...13 F5
Mill Cl *FRCTL/WBN BS36*...24 A3
Mill Crs *YATE/CS BS37*...37 F1
Millcross *CLVDN BS21*...64 C4
Millennium Cl
 FRCTL/WBN BS36...24 B3
Miller Ct *WSM BS23*....7 G3
Millers Cl *PTSHD/EG BS20*...42 C4
Millers Dr
 OLD/WMLY/WICK BS30...77 F1
Millers Rd *MTN/WRL BS22*...117 H4
Miller Wk *BATHSE BA2*...103 H3
Millfield Dr
 THNB/SVB BS35....9 E5
Millfield Dr
 OLD/WMLY/WICK BS30...60 A5
Millground Rd
 BMSTRD/HC/WWD BS13...83 H5
Mill Hill *YTN/CONG BS49*...113 G2
Milliman Cl
 BMSTRD/HC/WWD BS13...84 D4
Mill La *BATHSE BA2*...107 G1
 BATHSE BA2...104 A2
 BATHSE BA2...108 B5
 FRCTL/WBN BS36...23 H1
 OLD/WMLY/WICK BS30...77 F1
 YATE/CS BS37...27 F3
 YTN/CONG BS49...114 D2
Mill Leg *YTN/CONG BS49*...115 E2
Mill Pond Cl *BATHSE BA2*...107 H2
Millpill Cl
 HNLZ/SM/SNYPK/WT BS9...44 B5
Mill Rd *FRCTL/WBN BS36*...34 D1
Millward Gv *MANG/FISH BS16*...48 C4
Milner Gn
 OLD/WMLY/WICK BS30...76 D1
Milner Rd *HORF/LLZ BS7*...46 B3
Milsom St *BMSTR BS3 **....3 F5
 EVILLE/WHL BS5...56 D4
Milton Av *BATHSE BA2*...108 C5
 WSM BS23....7 J3
Milton Brow *MTN/WRL BS22*...121 C1
Milton Cl *NAIL BS48*...67 G5
 YATE/CS BS37...14 D5
Milton Gn *MTN/WRL BS22*...121 H2
Milton Hi *MTN/WRL BS22*...121 C1
Milton Pk *EVILLE/WHL BS5*...57 E4
Milton Park Rd
 MTN/WRL BS22...121 G2
Milton Ri *MTN/WRL BS22*...121 G2
Milton Rd *HORF/LLZ BS7*...46 A2
 MTN/WRL BS22...121 H3
 WSM BS23....7 G3
 YATE/CS BS37...13 H5
Miltons Cl
 BMSTRD/HC/WWD BS13...85 E5
Milverton Gdns *CBRISNE BS2*...56 B1
Milward Rd *KEYN BS31*...88 B3
Mina Rd *CBRISNE BS2*...56 C1
Minehead Rd
 BRSG/KWL/STAPK BS4....73 C5
Miners Cl *LGASH BS41*...70 C4
Minerva Gdns *BATHSE BA2*...107 H3
Minor's La *HNBRY/STHM BS10*...17 G2
Minsmere Rd *KEYN BS31*...98 B1
Minto Rd *CBRISNE BS2*...56 C1
Mission Rd *YATE/CS BS37*...13 E3
Mitchell Cl *CBRIS/FH BS1*....5 G5
Mitchell La *CBRIS/FH BS1*....5 G5
Mitchell Wk
 OLD/WMLY/WICK BS30...60 B5
Mivart St *EVILLE/WHL BS5*...57 E2
Mizzymead Cl *NAIL BS48*...67 E5
Mizzymead Rd *NAIL BS48*...67 E5
Mizzymead Ri *NAIL BS48*...67 F4
Modecombe Gv
 HNBRY/STHM BS10...30 D2
Mogg St *CBRISNE BS2*....5 J2
Molesworth Cl
 BMSTRD/HC/WWD BS13...84 B5
Molesworth Dr
 BMSTRD/HC/WWD BS13...84 B5
Monarch's Wy
 BLAG/CWMG/WR BS40...94 A5
 BRSG/KWL/STAPK BS4....75 E2
 CFTN/FAIL BS8...53 C5
 EVILLE/WHL BS5...54 A5
 KEYN BS31...88 C2
 KGWD/HNM BS15...59 H5
 LGASH BS41...70 B4
 OLD/WMLY/WICK BS30...61 F5
 OLD/WMLY/WICK BS30...89 C1
 YATE/CS BS37...37 G5
Monks Av *KGWD/HNM BS15*...58 D1
Monksdale Rd *BATHSE BA2*...108 A3
Monks Hill *MTN/WRL BS22*...116 C5
Monk's Park Av *HORF/LLZ BS7*...32 A4
Monks Park Wy
 HORF/LLZ BS7...32 A4
Monkton Av
 OMX/HUT/LCK BS24...125 F4
Monkton Rd *KGWD/HNM BS15*...58 D5
Monmouth Cl *PTSHD/EG BS20*...38 D4
Monmouth Hi
 CBATH/BATHN BA1...101 F4
Monmouth Rd *HORF/LLZ BS7*...45 H4
 KEYN BS31...88 A3
 PTSHD/EG BS20...42 C3
Monmouth St *BMSTR BS3*...73 C3
 CBATH/BATHN BA1....2 E4

Monsdale Cl
 HNBRY/STHM BS10...31 E3
Monsdale Dr
 HNBRY/STHM BS10...31 E2
Montacute Circ
 OMX/HUT/LCK BS24...122 C3
Montague Cl
 BRSTK/PCHW BS34...21 E3
Montague Hi
 RDLND/MONT BS6...55 H3
Montague Hi South
 CBRISNE BS2....5 F1
Montague Rd *KEYN BS31*...99 E2
Montpelier *WSM BS23*....7 G3
Montgomery St *BMSTR BS3*...73 G2
Montpelier East *WSM BS23*....7 G3
Montreal Av *HORF/LLZ BS7*...32 B5
Montrose Av
 RDLND/MONT BS6...55 G2
Montrose Dr
 OLD/WMLY/WICK BS30...59 H5
Montrose Pk
 BRSG/KWL/STAPK BS4....74 C4
Moon St *CBRIS/FH BS1*....5 G1
Moor Croft Dr
 OLD/WMLY/WICK BS30...59 H5
Moor Croft Rd
 OMX/HUT/LCK BS24...126 B5
Moordell Av *YATE/CS BS37*...25 H1
Moorend Farm Av
 AVONM BS11...43 F1
Moorend Gdns *AVONM BS11*...43 F1
Moor End Spout *NAIL BS48*...67 E4
Moorfield Rd *NAIL BS48*...79 C2
Moorfields Cl *EVILLE/WHL BS5*...57 E4
Moorfields Rd *BATHSE BA2*...108 A4
Moor Ga *PTSHD/EG BS20*...40 B4
Moor Gv *AVONM BS11*...29 F5
Moorhill St *EVILLE/WHL BS5*...56 D2
Moorhouse La *AVONM BS11*...16 B4
 HNBRY/STHM BS10...16 D3
The Moorings *PTSHD/EG BS20*...42 C4
Moorland Rd *BATHSE BA2*...107 H3
 WSM BS23...124 C2
 YATE/CS BS37...25 H1
Moorlands Cl *NAIL BS48*...67 E4
Moorlands Rd
 MANG/FISH BS16...58 A1
Moor La *CLVDN BS21*...64 D3
 MTN/WRL BS22...122 C2
 NAIL BS48...79 C3
 OMX/HUT/LCK BS24...125 H1
Moorlay Crs
 BLAG/CWMG/WR BS40...93 G4
Moor Pk *CLVDN BS21*...65 E3
Moorpark Av *YATE/CS BS37*...25 G1
Moorside *YTN/CONG BS49*...112 B2
Moravian Ct *KGWD/HNM BS15*...58 D3
Moravian Rd *KGWD/HNM BS15*...58 D3
Morden Wk *HGRV/WHIT BS14*...17 E5
Moreton Cl *HGRV/WHIT BS14*....3 F2
Morford St *CBATH/BATHN BA1*....3 F2
Morgan Cl *KEYN BS31*...99 E2
 OMX/HUT/LCK BS24...123 E3
Morgan St *CBRISNE BS2*...56 B2
Morley Av *MANG/FISH BS16*...48 D5
Morley Cl *BRSTK/PCHW BS34*...20 D3
 MANG/FISH BS16...48 D5
Morley Sq *HORF/LLZ BS7*...46 A4
Morley St *CBRISNE BS2*...56 B2
 KGWD/HNM BS15...58 D2
Morley Ter *BATHSE BA2 **...107 H1
 KGWD/HNM BS15...58 D2
Mornington Rd *CFTN/FAIL BS8*...55 E1
Morpeth Rd
 BRSG/KWL/STAPK BS4....85 E1
Morris Cl *CBATH/BATHN BA1*...104 C4
Morris La *CBATH/BATHN BA1*...104 C4
Morris Rd *HORF/LLZ BS7*...46 C3
Morse Rd *EVILLE/WHL BS5*...57 E4
Morston Ct *MTN/WRL BS22*...121 H4
Mortimer Cl
 CBATH/BATHN BA1...101 G2
Mortimer Rd
 BRSTK/PCHW BS34...32 D4
 CFTN/FAIL BS8...55 E4
Morton St *EVILLE/WHL BS5*...56 D4
Morton Wy *THNB/SVB BS35*....9 E1
Moseley Gv *WSM BS23*...124 D4
Mountain Ash
 CBATH/BATHN BA1...102 A3
Mountain Wd
 CBATH/BATHN BA1...104 D4
Mountbatten Cl
 MTN/WRL BS22...117 F4
 YATE/CS BS37...13 H4
Mount Beacon
 CBATH/BATHN BA1...102 C3
Mount Beacon Rw
 *CBATH/BATHN BA1 **...102 C3
Mount Cl *FRCTL/WBN BS36*...23 E5
Mount Crs *FRCTL/WBN BS36*...23 E5
Mount Gdns *KGWD/HNM BS15*...58 D4
Mount Gv *BATHSE BA2*...107 G4
Mount Hill Rd
 KGWD/HNM BS15...58 C5
Mount Pleasant
 PTSHD/EG BS20...42 D4
Mount Pleasant Ter
 BMSTR BS3....73 E2
Mount Rd *BATHSE BA2*...107 G4
 CBATH/BATHN BA1...102 C4
Mount Vw *BATHSE BA2*...107 G3
Mow Barton
 BMSTRD/HC/WWD BS13...83 H3
 YATE/CS BS37...26 A2
Mowbray Rd *HGRV/WHIT BS14*...86 B2
Mowcroft Rd
 BMSTRD/HC/WWD BS13...84 D5
Moxham Dr
 BMSTRD/HC/WWD BS13...84 D5

Mud La *YTN/CONG BS49*...113 G1
Muirfield
 OLD/WMLY/WICK BS30...59 G5
Mulberry Av *PTSHD/EG BS20*...40 A3
Mulberry Cl *KGWD/HNM BS15*...59 E3
 MTN/WRL BS22...122 D2
 NAIL BS48...79 H3
 PTSHD/EG BS20...40 A3
Mulberry Dr *KGWD/HNM BS15*...59 F2
Mulberry Gdns
 *CBRISNE BS2 **...48 D5
Mulberry Wk
 HNLZ/SM/SNYPK/WT BS9...30 A5
Mulberry Rd *YTN/CONG BS49*...115 E3
Muller Av *HORF/LLZ BS7*...46 B4
Muller Rd *EVILLE/WHL BS5*...47 E5
 HORF/LLZ BS7...46 B2
Mulready Cl *HORF/LLZ BS7*...47 E2
Murdoch Sq *HORF/LLZ BS7*...32 B5
Murford Av
 BMSTRD/HC/WWD BS13...84 C4
Murford Wk
 BMSTRD/HC/WWD BS13...84 C5
Murray St *BMSTR BS3*...72 D2
Musgrove Cl *AVONM BS11*...43 H3
Myrtleberry Md...117 H3
Myrtle Dr *AVONM BS11*...43 E3
Myrtle Gdns *YTN/CONG BS49*...112 B5
Myrtle Hi *PTSHD/EG BS20*...42 C3
Myrtle Rd *CBRISNE BS2*....4 D1
Myrtle St *BMSTR BS3*...72 C2
Myrtle Tree Crs
 MTN/WRL BS22...116 B2

N

Nags Head Hi *EVILLE/WHL BS5*...58 A5
Nailsea Cl
 BMSTRD/HC/WWD BS13...84 B2
Nailsea Ct *NAIL BS48*...78 C4
Nailsea Moor La *NAIL BS48*...78 A2
Nailsea Pk *NAIL BS48*...67 G4
Nailsea Park Cl *NAIL BS48*...67 G4
Nailsea Wall *NAIL BS48*...65 H5
Nailsworth Av *YATE/CS BS37*...26 A1
Naishcombe Hi
 OLD/WMLY/WICK BS30...61 G4
Naish La *NAIL BS48*...93 E1
Napier Miles Rd *AVONM BS11*...29 G5
Napier Rd *AVONM BS11*...28 B4
 CBATH/BATHN BA1...101 F1
 RDLND/MONT BS6...55 F1
Napier Sq *AVONM BS11*...28 A4
Napier St *EVILLE/WHL BS5*...56 C5
Narroways Rd *CBRISNE BS2*...46 C5
Narrow La *AMNG/FISH BS16*...49 E4
Narrow Pln *CBRISNE BS2*....5 E5
Narrow Quay *CBRIS/FH BS1*....4 E5
Naseby Wk *EVILLE/WHL BS5*...57 H2
Nash Cl *KEYN BS31*...88 D4
Nash Dr *HORF/LLZ BS7*...47 E1
Naunton Wy *MTN/WRL BS22*...121 G1
Neads Dr
 OLD/WMLY/WICK BS30...77 F1
Neale Wy *AVONM BS11 **...28 C4
Neath Rd *EVILLE/WHL BS5*...57 F3
Nelson Ct *AVONM BS11 **...48 D4
Nelson Pde *BMSTR BS3*....73 E2
Nelson Pl East
 CBATH/BATHN BA1....3 G1
Nelson Pl West
 CBATH/BATHN BA1....2 D4
Nelson Rd *MANG/FISH BS16*...48 D3
Nelson St *BMSTR BS3*...72 B4
 CBRIS/FH BS1....5 F5
Nelson Ter *CBATH/BATHN BA1*....3 G1
Nelson Vls *CBATH/BATHN BA1*....2 C4
Neston Wk
 BRSG/KWL/STAPK BS4....85 G1
Netham Rd *EVILLE/WHL BS5*...57 F4
Netherton Wood La *NAIL BS48*...78 A4
Nettleton Cl *OLD/WMLY/WICK BS30*...64 B3
Nettlestone Cl
 HNBRY/STHM BS10...30 C1
Nevalan Dr *EVILLE/WHL BS5*...58 A5
Neva Rd *WSM BS23*....6 E6
Neville Rd *KGWD/HNM BS15*...59 F1
Nevil Rd *HORF/LLZ BS7*...46 A4
Newbolt Cl *WSM BS23*...125 F2
New Bond St *CBATH/BATHN BA1*....3 G4
Newbourne Rd
 MTN/WRL BS22...121 H4
Newbrick Rd
 BRSTK/PCHW BS34...22 A5
New Br *CBATH/BATHN BA1*...101 E4
Newbridge Cl
 BRSG/KWL/STAPK BS4....57 F5
Newbridge Gdns
 CBATH/BATHN BA1...101 E4
Newbridge Hi
 CBATH/BATHN BA1...101 F4
Newbridge Rd
 BRSG/KWL/STAPK BS4....57 F5
 CBATH/BATHN BA1...101 F5
New Bristol Rd
 KGWD/HNM BS15...122 C2
New Brunswick Av
 EVILLE/WHL BS5...58 B4
New Blds *MANG/FISH BS16*...47 H4
Newbury Rd *HORF/LLZ BS7*...46 C1
New Charlotte St *BMSTR BS3*...73 E2
New Charlton Wy
 HNBRY/STHM BS10...19 E4
New Cheltenham Rd
 KGWD/HNM BS15...58 D2
New Church Rd *WSM BS23*...124 C4
Newcombe Dr
 HNLZ/SM/SNYPK/WT BS9...44 A4
Newcombe Rd
 HNLZ/SM/SNYPK/WT BS9...44 D1
Newditch La
 BLAG/CWMG/WR BS40...92 D3
Newent Av *EVILLE/WHL BS5*...58 B4

New Fosseway Rd
HGRV/WHIT BS14 86 A3
Newfoundland Rd
CBRISNE BS2 56 B3
Newfoundland St CBRIS/FH BS1 5 J1
Newfoundland Wy
CBRISNE BS2 5 K1
PTSHD/EG BS20 40 A1
Newgate CBRIS/FH BS1 5 G3
Newhaven Pl PTSHD/EG BS20 38 C4
Newhaven Rd PTSHD/EG BS20 38 B5
New John St BMSTR BS3 * 72 D3
New Kings Ct HORF/LLZ BS7 45 G4
New Kingsley Rd CBRISNE BS2 * 5 J4
New King St CBATH/BATHN BA1 2 E4
Newland Dr
BMSTRD/HC/WWD BS13 84 B5
Newland Rd
BMSTRD/HC/WWD BS13 84 B5
WSM BS23 7 G7
Newlands Av FRCTL/WBN BS36 24 A3
Newlands Gn CLVDN BS21 64 D4
Newlands Hl PTSHD/EG BS20 39 G4
Newlands Rd KEYN BS31 88 A5
The Newlands
MANG/FISH BS16 48 B1
Newland Wk
BMSTRD/HC/WWD BS13 95 F1
New Leaze ALMDB BS32 11 E4
Newlyn Av
HNLZ/SM/SNYPK/WT BS9 44 B3
Newlyn Wk
BRSG/KWL/STAPK BS4 74 A5
Newlyn Wy YATE/CS BS37 14 B5
Newman Cl YATE/CS BS37 37 F1
New Mdw HGRV/WHIT BS14 85 H3
Newnham Cl HGRV/WHIT BS14 86 C2
Newnham Pl
BRSTK/PCHW BS34 20 B1
New Orchard St
CBATH/BATHN BA1 3 G5
Newport Cl CLVDN BS21 64 C3
PTSHD/EG BS20 38 D4
Newport Rd PTSHD/EG BS20 42 C3
Newport St BMSTR BS3 73 F3
Newquay Rd
BRSG/KWL/STAPK BS4 85 G1
New Queen St BMSTR BS3 73 F2
KGWD/HNM BS15 58 B2
New Rd BNWL BS29 127 H2
BRSTK/PCHW BS34 32 B2
CBATH/BATHN BA1 104 D2
CLVDN BS21 64 D3
PTSHD/EG BS20 42 C4
Newry Wk
BRSG/KWL/STAPK BS4 73 F5
Newsome Av PTSHD/EG BS20 42 C4
New Stadium Rd
EVILLE/WHL BS5 56 D1
New Station Rd
MANG/FISH BS16 48 A4
New Station Wy
MANG/FISH BS16 48 A4
New St CBATH/BATHN BA1 2 E4
CBRISNE BS2 5 J2
New Thomas St CBRISNE BS2 5 J3
Newton Cl KGWD/HNM BS15 59 G2
Newton Gn NAIL BS48 78 D1
Newton Rd BATHSE BA2 107 E1
OLD/WMLY/WICK BS30 76 D1
WSM BS23 124 D1
Newton's Rd MTN/WRL BS22 117 F4
Newton St EVILLE/WHL BS5 56 C3
New Wk KGWD/HNM BS15 75 G1
New Walls
BRSG/KWL/STAPK BS4 73 G2
Niblett Cl KGWD/HNM BS15 59 F5
Niblett's Hl EVILLE/WHL BS5 58 A5
Nibley La YATE/CS BS37 12 D4
Nibley Rd AVONM BS11 43 E3
Nicholas La EVILLE/WHL BS5 58 A5
Nicholas Rd EVILLE/WHL BS5 56 D2
Nicholas St BMSTR BS3 73 F2
Nicholettes
OLD/WMLY/WICK BS30 77 G1
Nicholls La FRCTL/WBN BS36 23 E3
Nichol's Rd PTSHD/EG BS20 38 D2
Nigel Pk AVONM BS11 43 E1
Nightingale Cl
BRSG/KWL/STAPK BS4 57 G5
FRCTL/WBN BS36 23 G4
MTN/WRL BS22 122 B2
THNB/SVB BS35 9 E2
Nightingale Gdns NAIL BS48 66 D4
Nightingale La
FRCTL/WBN BS36 23 F2
Nightingale Ri PTSHD/EG BS20 38 D5
Nile St CBATH/BATHN BA1 2 D4
Nine Tree Hl RDLND/MONT BS6 55 H2
Ninth Av HORF/LLZ BS7 32 D4
Nithsdale Rd WSM BS23 124 D2
Noble Av
OLD/WMLY/WICK BS30 77 F2
Nomis Pk YTN/CONG BS49 115 E4
Nore Gdns PTSHD/EG BS20 39 G2
Nore Park Dr PTSHD/EG BS20 38 D3
Nore Rd PTSHD/EG BS20 38 C4
Norfolk Av CBRISNE BS2 5 H1
RDLND/MONT BS6 56 A1
Norfolk Blds CBATH/BATHN BA1 2 D4
Norfolk Crs CBATH/BATHN BA1 2 D4
Norfolk Gv KEYN BS31 87 H5
Norfolk Pl BMSTR BS3 72 D3
Norfolk Rd PTSHD/EG BS20 40 A4
WSM BS23 125 E1
Norland Rd CFTN/FAIL BS8 54 D3
Norley Rd HORF/LLZ BS7 46 B1
Normanby Rd EVILLE/WHL BS5 56 D2
Norman Gv KGWD/HNM BS15 58 D1
Norman Rd CBRISNE BS2 56 C1
KEYN BS31 99 E1
OLD/WMLY/WICK BS30 59 H3
The Normans BATHSE BA2 104 A3
Normans Wy PTSHD/EG BS20 41 H1
Normanton Rd CFTN/FAIL BS8 55 E1
Norrisville Rd
RDLND/MONT BS6 56 A2
Northampton St
CBATH/BATHN BA1 2 E1
Northcote Rd CFTN/FAIL BS8 54 D2
EVILLE/WHL BS5 57 G3
MANG/FISH BS16 49 F2
Northcote St EVILLE/WHL BS5 56 D2
North Cft
OLD/WMLY/WICK BS30 77 G2
North Devon Rd
MANG/FISH BS16 48 A3
North Dro NAIL BS48 66 C4
North East Rd THNB/SVB BS35 8 D2
North End YTN/CONG BS49 112 A1
Northend Av KGWD/HNM BS15 58 D1
Northend Rd KGWD/HNM BS15 59 E1
Northern Wy CLVDN BS21 65 F2
Northfield YATE/CS BS37 25 H2
Northfield Av KGWD/HNM BS15 76 A1
Northfield Rd EVILLE/WHL BS5 58 B4
PTSHD/EG BS20 38 B5
Northfields
CBATH/BATHN BA1 102 C3
Northfields Cl
CBATH/BATHN BA1 102 C3
Northgate St CBATH/BATHN BA1 3 G4
North Green St CFTN/FAIL BS8 54 D5
North Gv PTSHD/EG BS20 42 C4
North Hills Cl
OMX/HUT/LCK BS24 125 G4
North La BATHSE BA2 109 G2
NAIL BS48 66 C5
Northleach Wk AVONM BS11 43 F3
North Leaze LGASH BS41 71 E4
Northleigh Av MTN/WRL BS22 121 H2
Northmead La YATE/CS BS37 12 B1
Northover Rd
HNLZ/SM/SNYPK/WT BS9 30 D4
North Parade Blds
CBATH/BATHN BA1 * 3 G5
North Parade Rd BATHSE BA2 3 H5
North Pk KGWD/HNM BS15 59 E2
North Rd BATHSE BA2 111 F1
BMSTR BS3 72 B2
BRSTK/PCHW BS34 33 G1
CFTN/FAIL BS8 54 B5
FRCTL/WBN BS36 23 F3
RDLND/MONT BS6 55 H1
THNB/SVB BS35 8 D2
YATE/CS BS37 13 F4
North Side Rd NAIL BS48 92 A4
North St BMSTR BS3 72 B2
CBRIS/FH BS1 5 G1
MANG/FISH BS16 48 D3
NAIL BS48 66 C5
OLD/WMLY/WICK BS30 77 F2
WSM BS23 6 D3
Northumberland Blds
CBATH/BATHN BA1 * 3 F4
Northumberland Pl
CBATH/BATHN BA1 3 G4
Northumberland Rd
RDLND/MONT BS6 55 G1
Northumbria Dr
HNLZ/SM/SNYPK/WT BS9 45 F3
North Vw MANG/FISH BS16 48 D4
RDLND/MONT BS6 45 E4
North View Cl BATHSE BA2 107 G2
Northville Rd HORF/LLZ BS7 32 C4
North Wy BATHSE BA2 107 F2
Northway BRSTK/PCHW BS34 32 D1
Northwick Rd HORF/LLZ BS7 32 B5
LGASH BS41 96 A5
Northwoods Wk
HNBRY/STHM BS10 31 H2
Norton Cl KGWD/HNM BS15 59 F4
Norton La HGRV/WHIT BS14 97 F3
MTN/WRL BS22 116 D4
PLTN/PENS BS39 96 B5
Norton Rd
BRSG/KWL/STAPK BS4 73 H4
Nortons Wood La CLVDN BS21 63 F5
Norwich Dr
BRSG/KWL/STAPK BS4 57 G5
Norwood Av BATHSE BA2 109 H3
Norwood Gv PTSHD/EG BS20 38 D3
Notgrove Cl MTN/WRL BS22 121 G1
Nottingham Rd HORF/LLZ BS7 46 A5
Nottingham St BMSTR BS3 73 F3
Nova Scotia Pl CBRIS/FH BS1 * 72 B1
Nova Wy AVONM BS11 28 B4
Novers Crs
BRSG/KWL/STAPK BS4 84 D1
Novers Hl BMSTR BS3 72 D5
BRSG/KWL/STAPK BS4 84 D1
Novers La
BRSG/KWL/STAPK BS4 84 D2
Novers Park Cl
BRSG/KWL/STAPK BS4 73 E5
Novers Park Dr
BRSG/KWL/STAPK BS4 84 D1
Novers Park Rd
BRSG/KWL/STAPK BS4 85 E1
Novers Rd
BRSG/KWL/STAPK BS4 84 D1
Nowhere La NAIL BS48 * 67 H5
Nugent Hl RDLND/MONT BS6 55 H2
Nunney Cl KEYN BS31 98 B2
Nursery Gdns
HNBRY/STHM BS10 31 E2
The Nursery BMSTR BS3 72 C3
Nutfield Gv BRSTK/PCHW BS34 32 D3
Nutgrove Av BMSTR BS3 73 F3
Nuthatch Dr MANG/FISH BS16 47 H2
Nuthatch Gdns
MANG/FISH BS16 48 A2
Nutwell Rd MTN/WRL BS22 122 B1
Nutwell Sq MTN/WRL BS22 122 B1
Nympsfield KGWD/HNM BS15 59 E1

O

Oak Av BATHSE BA2 107 H4
Oak Cl BRSTK/PCHW BS34 21 F3
YATE/CS BS37 13 H4
Oak Ct MTN/WRL BS22 118 B5
Oakdale Av MANG/FISH BS16 34 D5
Oakdale Cl MANG/FISH BS16 35 E5
Oakdale Ct MANG/FISH BS16 48 D1
Oakdale Gdns MTN/WRL BS22 122 C1
Oakdale Rd HGRV/WHIT BS14 85 H1
MANG/FISH BS16 35 E5
Oakdene Av EVILLE/WHL BS5 47 F5
Oak Dr PTSHD/EG BS20 39 F4
Oakenhill Rd
BRSG/KWL/STAPK BS4 74 D4
Oakenhill Wk
BRSG/KWL/STAPK BS4 74 D4
Oakfield Cl CBATH/BATHN BA1 2 A1
Oakfield Ct CFTN/FAIL BS8 * 55 F3
Oakfield Gv CFTN/FAIL BS8 4 A1
Oakfield Pl CFTN/FAIL BS8 4 A1
PTSHD/EG BS20 * 39 H5
Oakfield Rd CFTN/FAIL BS8 55 E3
KEYN BS31 98 A1
KGWD/HNM BS15 58 D4
Oakford Av WSM BS23 7 H3
Oakford La
CBATH/BATHN BA1 91 F1
Oak Gv PTSHD/EG BS20 42 C4
Oakhanger Dr AVONM BS11 29 H4
Oakhill Av
OLD/WMLY/WICK BS30 77 F4
Oakhill Cl NAIL BS48 68 A5
Oakhill La HNBRY/STHM BS10 30 A1
Oakhill Rd BATHSE BA2 108 C5
Oakhurst Rd
HNLZ/SM/SNYPK/WT BS9 44 D3
Oakland Rd EVILLE/WHL BS5 57 G3
RDLND/MONT BS6 55 F2
Oaklands Cl MANG/FISH BS16 49 H3
Oaklands Dr ALMDB BS32 10 C3
MANG/FISH BS16 34 A5
OLD/WMLY/WICK BS30 77 F4
Oaklands Rd MANG/FISH BS16 49 G3
Oak La EVILLE/WHL BS5 57 H1
Oakleaze Rd THNB/SVB BS35 8 D3
Oakleigh Av EVILLE/WHL BS5 57 F3
Oakleigh Cl NAIL BS48 80 A4
Oakleigh Gdns
OLD/WMLY/WICK BS30 77 F4
Oakley BATHSE BA2 109 H2
CLVDN BS21 64 B5
Oakley Rd HORF/LLZ BS7 46 B1
Oakmeade Pk
BRSG/KWL/STAPK BS4 74 A4
Oakridge Cl KGWD/HNM BS15 59 G4
Oak Rd HORF/LLZ BS7 46 A3
Oaksey Gv NAIL BS48 67 H4
The Oaks
BLAG/CWMG/WR BS40 93 G5
NAIL BS48 67 H4
Oak St BATHSE BA2 2 E6
Oaktree Av MANG/FISH BS16 51 G3
Oak Tree Cl KGWD/HNM BS15 75 H3
Oaktree Ct AVONM BS11 43 E1
Oaktree Crs ALMDB BS32 10 D5
Oaktree Gdns
BMSTRD/HC/WWD BS13 83 H4
Oaktree Pl MTN/WRL BS22 118 B5
Oakwood Av
HNLZ/SM/SNYPK/WT BS9 45 F2
Oakwood Gdns
FRCTL/WBN BS36 24 C3
Oakwood Rd
HNLZ/SM/SNYPK/WT BS9 45 F2
Oatfield NAIL BS48 92 A3
Oatlands Av HGRV/WHIT BS14 85 H3
Oberon Av EVILLE/WHL BS5 57 G1
Odins Rd BATHSE BA2 110 B1
Okebourne Cl
HNBRY/STHM BS10 31 F1
Okebourne Rd
HNBRY/STHM BS10 31 F2
Oldacre Rd HGRV/WHIT BS14 96 D2
Old Ashley Hl
RDLND/MONT BS6 56 B1
Old Aust Rd ALMDB BS32 11 E1
Old Banwell Rd
OMX/HUT/LCK BS24 127 E2
Old Barrow Hl AVONM BS11 42 D1
Old Bond St CBATH/BATHN BA1 3 F4
Old Bread St CBRISNE BS2 5 J4
Oldbridge Rd HGRV/WHIT BS14 97 F1
Old Bristol Rd MTN/WRL BS22 122 D1
Oldbury Cha
OLD/WMLY/WICK BS30 76 D4
Oldbury Court Dr
MANG/FISH BS16 48 A2
Oldbury Court Rd
MANG/FISH BS16 48 A3
Old Chapel La NAIL BS48 78 A2
Old Chelsea La CFTN/FAIL BS8 69 H3
Old Church Cl
OLD/WMLY/WICK BS30 * 60 B4
Old Church Rd CLVDN BS21 64 A3
NAIL BS48 79 E1
WSM BS23 124 C4
Old Farm La EVILLE/WHL BS5 58 B5
Old Ferry Rd BATHSE BA2 107 G1
Oldfield La BATHSE BA2 108 A3
Oldfield Pl CFTN/FAIL BS8 72 A1
Oldfield Rd BATHSE BA2 2 C7
CFTN/FAIL BS8 72 B1
Old Fosse Rd BATHSE BA2 110 A1
Old Frome Rd BATHSE BA2 110 C2
Old Gloucester Rd
FRCTL/WBN BS36 22 B3
MANG/FISH BS16 34 B5
Old Hl BLAG/CWMG/WR BS40 93 E5
Old Junction Rd WSM BS23 125 G1
Old King St CBATH/BATHN BA1 3 F3
Old King Street Ct
CBRIS/FH BS1 * 5 G2
Oldlands Av FRCTL/WBN BS36 24 A4
Old La CLVDN BS21 66 D2
MANG/FISH BS16 50 A2
Old Market St CBRISNE BS2 5 J3
Oldmead Wk
BMSTRD/HC/WWD BS13 83 H2
Old Midford Rd BATHSE BA2 111 E3
Old Mill Cl YATE/CS BS37 37 F1
Old Mill Rd PTSHD/EG BS20 39 H3
Old Mill Wy MTN/WRL BS22 122 C3
OMX/HUT/LCK BS24 122 C3
Oldmixon Crs
OMX/HUT/LCK BS24 125 F3
Old Mixon Rd
OMX/HUT/LCK BS24 125 H4
Oldmixon Rd
OMX/HUT/LCK BS24 125 F5
Old Newbridge Hl
CBATH/BATHN BA1 101 F4
Old Orch CBATH/BATHN BA1 3 G2
Old Orchard St
CBATH/BATHN BA1 3 G5
Old Pk CBRISNE BS2 4 D2
Old Park Hl CBRISNE BS2 4 D3
Old Park Rd AVONM BS11 42 D1
CLVDN BS21 62 B5
Old Pooles Yd
BRSG/KWL/STAPK BS4 74 D4
Old Post Office La WSM BS23 * 6 D2
Old Priory Rd PTSHD/EG BS20 42 B4
Old Quarry BATHSE BA2 108 A5
Old Quarry Ri AVONM BS11 43 E1
Old Quarry Rd AVONM BS11 42 D1
Old School Hl BATHSE BA2 110 D3
Old Sneed Av
HNLZ/SM/SNYPK/WT BS9 44 B4
Old Sneed Pk
HNLZ/SM/SNYPK/WT BS9 44 B4
Old Sneed Rd
HNLZ/SM/SNYPK/WT BS9 44 B4
Old St CLVDN BS21 65 E2
Old Vicarage Pl
CFTN/FAIL BS8 * 55 E2
Oldville Av CLVDN BS21 64 D3
Old Wells Rd BATHSE BA2 108 C4
Old Weston Rd NAIL BS48 81 G2
YTN/CONG BS49 114 A1
Olveston Rd HORF/LLZ BS7 46 A3
Olympus Cl BRSTK/PCHW BS34 21 F4
Olympus Rd
BRSTK/PCHW BS34 19 H3
Onega Ter CBATH/BATHN BA1 2 C3
Oolite Gv BATHSE BA2 110 B1
Oolite Rd BATHSE BA2 110 B1
Oram Ct OLD/WMLY/WICK BS30 76 C2
Orange Gv CBATH/BATHN BA1 3 G4
Orange St CBRISNE BS2 5 J1
Orchard Av CBRIS/FH BS1 * 4 D4
THNB/SVB BS35 8 D3
Orchard Bvd
OLD/WMLY/WICK BS30 77 E2
Orchard Cl
BLAG/CWMG/WR BS40 92 D4
FRCTL/WBN BS36 23 E4
HNLZ/SM/SNYPK/WT BS9 44 D3
KEYN BS31 87 H3
KGWD/HNM BS15 59 E3
MTN/WRL BS22 116 C5
NAIL BS48 81 F1
PTSHD/EG BS20 39 H3
YATE/CS BS37 14 B5
YTN/CONG BS49 114 D2
Orchard Ct YTN/CONG BS49 113 F2
Orchard Crs AVONM BS11 42 D1
Orchard Dr
BMSTRD/HC/WWD BS13 84 B3
Orchard Gdns
KGWD/HNM BS15 59 F3
Orchard Ga ALMDB BS32 11 E5
Orchard Gra THNB/SVB BS35 8 C2
Orchard La CBRIS/FH BS1 4 D4
Orchard Lea PTSHD/EG BS20 42 D4
Orchard Pl WSM BS23 6 E4
Orchard Rd CLVDN BS21 64 D4
EVILLE/WHL BS5 57 H3
FRCTL/WBN BS36 24 B3
HORF/LLZ BS7 46 A4
KGWD/HNM BS15 59 E3
LGASH BS41 70 C4
MANG/FISH BS16 51 F3
NAIL BS48 66 D5
OMX/HUT/LCK BS24 126 A4
Orchard Sq EVILLE/WHL BS5 57 F4
The Orchards
KGWD/HNM BS15 59 F3
PTSHD/EG BS20 * 42 C4
Orchard St CBRIS/FH BS1 4 D4
WSM BS23 6 E3
Orchard Ter BATHSE BA2 107 G1
The Orchard BATHSE BA2 100 A4
BRSTK/PCHW BS34 21 H5
OMX/HUT/LCK BS24 126 C1
PTSHD/EG BS20 42 C4
Orchard V KGWD/HNM BS15 59 F4
Orchid Dr BATHSE BA2 110 A1
Oriel Gdns CBATH/BATHN BA1 103 F2
Oriel Gv BATHSE BA2 107 G3
Orion Dr BRSTK/PCHW BS34 21 F4
Orland Wy
OLD/WMLY/WICK BS30 76 D3
Orlebar Gdns AVONM BS11 29 H3
Orme Dr CLVDN BS21 62 B5
Ormerod Rd
HNLZ/SM/SNYPK/WT BS9 44 C4
Ormonds Cl ALMDB BS32 11 G5
Ormsley Cl BRSTK/PCHW BS34 21 E2
Orpen Gdns HORF/LLZ BS7 46 D3
Orpen Pk ALMDB BS32 10 D4
Orpheus Av BRSTK/PCHW BS34 21 F4
Orwell Dr KEYN BS31 88 C5
Orwell St BMSTR BS3 73 F3
Osborne Av HORF/LLZ BS7 46 B5
WSM BS23 7 H4
Osborne Cl BRSTK/PCHW BS34 33 F1
Osborne Rd BMSTR BS3 72 D2
CBATH/BATHN BA1 107 G1
CFTN/FAIL BS8 55 E2
WSM BS23 7 H4
Osborne Ter BMSTR BS3 72 C4
Osborne Vls CBRISNE BS2 4 C1
Osmond Rd
OMX/HUT/LCK BS24 122 C4
Osprey Gdns MTN/WRL BS22 122 C2
Osprey Pk THNB/SVB BS35 9 E1
Osprey Rd EVILLE/WHL BS5 57 E4
Ostlings La
CBATH/BATHN BA1 104 C2
Ottawa Rd WSM BS23 125 E3
Otterford Cl HGRV/WHIT BS14 86 A4
Otter Rd CLVDN BS21 64 D4
Ottery Cl AVONM BS11 29 G4
Ottrells Md ALMDB BS32 11 E4
The Oval BATHSE BA2 107 H4
Overhill PTSHD/EG BS20 42 C5
Over La ALMDB BS32 10 A5
Overndale Rd
MANG/FISH BS16 48 C3
Overnhill Ct MANG/FISH BS16 48 C3
Overnhill Rd MANG/FISH BS16 48 C3
Overton Rd RDLND/MONT BS6 55 H1
Owen Dr CFTN/FAIL BS8 69 G2
Owen Gv
HNLZ/SM/SNYPK/WT BS9 45 F3
Owen St EVILLE/WHL BS5 57 E3
Owls Head Rd
KGWD/HNM BS15 59 E5
Oxbarton BRSTK/PCHW BS34 21 H5
Oxenham Ct EVILLE/WHL BS5 57 F3
Oxen Leaze ALMDB BS32 11 F5
Oxford Pl CFTN/FAIL BS8 54 D5
EVILLE/WHL BS5 56 D2
WSM BS23 * 6 D4
Oxford Rw CBATH/BATHN BA1 3 F2
Oxford Sq
OMX/HUT/LCK BS24 123 E5
Oxford St BMSTR BS3 73 G2
RDLND/MONT BS6 55 G3
WSM BS23 6 D5
Oxhouse Gdns
HNBRY/STHM BS10 30 C2
Oxhouse La CFTN/FAIL BS8 69 G1
Oxleaze
BMSTRD/HC/WWD BS13 85 E5
Oxleaze La LGASH BS41 94 D2
Ozleworth KGWD/HNM BS15 59 G3

P

Pack Horse La BATHSE BA2 110 D3
Paddock Cl ALMDB BS32 11 F5
MANG/FISH BS16 49 H2
Paddock Gdn HGRV/WHIT BS14 85 G5
Paddock Gdns
HGRV/WHIT BS14 85 G5
Paddock Park Homes
MTN/WRL BS22 * 123 E1
The Paddocks BATHSE BA2 111 F1
MANG/FISH BS16 35 G4
THNB/SVB BS35 9 E3
WSM BS23 124 C4
The Paddock CLVDN BS21 64 D4
PTSHD/EG BS20 39 H4
Paddock Woods
BATHSE BA2 109 G5
Padfield Cl BATHSE BA2 107 G2
Padleigh Hl BATHSE BA2 107 F5
Padstow Rd
BRSG/KWL/STAPK BS4 85 F1
Page Rd MANG/FISH BS16 48 D4
Pages Md AVONM BS11 28 C5
Painswick Av
BRSTK/PCHW BS34 20 D2
Painswick Dr YATE/CS BS37 26 A1
Palace Yard Ms
CBATH/BATHN BA1 2 E4
Palmdale Cl
OLD/WMLY/WICK BS30 76 D3
Palmer Rw WSM BS23 6 E3
Palmers Cl
OLD/WMLY/WICK BS30 59 G5
Palmers Leaze ALMDB BS32 22 A3
Palmerston Rd
RDLND/MONT BS6 45 F4
Palmerston St BMSTR BS3 72 C3
Palmer St WSM BS23 6 E3
Palmyra Rd BMSTR BS3 72 C4
Parade Ct EVILLE/WHL BS5 57 H2
The Parade AVONM BS11 43 E2
BMSTRD/HC/WWD BS13 * 84 B3
BRSTK/PCHW BS34 * 20 A3
HGRV/WHIT BS14 * 85 H1
YATE/CS BS37 26 C1
Paragon Blds
CBATH/BATHN BA1 3 G2
Paragon Rd WSM BS23 6 A1
The Paragon CBATH/BATHN BA1 3 G2
CFTN/FAIL BS8 54 D5
Parfitt's Hl EVILLE/WHL BS5 57 H5
Parish Brook Rd NAIL BS48 66 C5
Park Av ALMDB BS32 10 C5
BATHSE BA2 2 E7
BMSTR BS3 73 F3
EVILLE/WHL BS5 57 G3
FRCTL/WBN BS36 23 E4
YTN/CONG BS49 112 B2
Park Cl KEYN BS31 88 A4
KGWD/HNM BS15 59 E4
OLD/WMLY/WICK BS30 77 E1
Park Ct WSM BS23 124 D1
Park Crs EVILLE/WHL BS5 57 F3
MANG/FISH BS16 34 C4
OLD/WMLY/WICK BS30 77 E1
Park End BNWL BS29 127 H2
Parkers Av
OLD/WMLY/WICK BS30 61 G4
Parkers Barton
EVILLE/WHL BS5 56 D5
Parkers Cl HNBRY/STHM BS10 32 A1
Parker St BMSTR BS3 72 C3
Parkes Rd
OMX/HUT/LCK BS24 127 F1
Park Farm Ct
OLD/WMLY/WICK BS30 * 76 C2
Parkfield Av EVILLE/WHL BS5 57 F4
Parkfield Rd MANG/FISH BS16 51 E1
Park Gdns CBATH/BATHN BA1 2 A1
Park Gv
HNLZ/SM/SNYPK/WT BS9 45 G2
Park Hl AVONM BS11 43 E2
Parkhurst Av MANG/FISH BS16 48 B4
Parkhurst Rd WSM BS23 7 K4
Parklands KGWD/HNM BS15 59 E3
Parklands Av MTN/WRL BS22 117 G4
Parklands Rd BMSTR BS3 71 H2
Parkland Wy THNB/SVB BS35 8 C1
Park La CBATH/BATHN BA1 2 B2
FRCTL/WBN BS36 23 G5
Park Leaze BRSTK/PCHW BS34 20 A1
Park Pl CBATH/BATHN BA1 2 D1
CFTN/FAIL BS8 4 A2
EVILLE/WHL BS5 47 G5
WSM BS23 6 C2
Park Rd AVONM BS11 43 E2
BMSTR BS3 4 B7
CBATH/BATHN BA1 101 G5

144 Par - Que

CLVDN RS21 .... 64 D1
HORF/LLZ BS7 .... 32 C4
KEYN BS31 .... 88 B4
KGWD/HNM BS15 .... 58 C2
MANG/FISH BS16 .... 49 E3
MANG/FISH BS16 .... 47 F3
OLD/WMLY/WICK BS30 .... 77 E1
THNB/SVB BS35 .... 8 D2
YTN/CONG BS49 .... 115 E5
Park Rw *CBRIS/FH* BS1 * 4 C3
FRCTL/WBN BS36 .... 23 E4
Parkside Av *FRCTL/WBN* BS36 .... 23 E4
Parkside Gdns *EVILLE/WHL* BS5 .... 46 C3
Parkstone Av *HORF/LLZ* BS7 .... 46 C2
Park St *BRSG/KWL/STAPK* BS4 .... 73 H2
CBATH/BATHN BA1 .... 102 B4
CBRIS/FH BS1 .... 4 C3
EVILLE/WHL BS5 .... 57 H3
YATE/CS BS37 .... 12 B3
Park Street Av *CBRIS/FH* BS1 * 4 C3
Park Street Ms
CBATH/BATHN BA1 .... 2 D1
The Park *ALMDB* BS32 .... 11 E4
KEYN BS31 .... 88 B3
KGWD/HNM BS15 .... 59 E3
MANG/FISH BS16 .... 34 B4
OLD/WMLY/WICK BS30 .... 77 E5
YTN/CONG BS49 .... 112 B2
Park Vw *KGWD/HNM* BS15 .... 59 E4
THNB/SVB BS35 * 8 D2
Park View Av *THNB/SVB* BS35 .... 8 D2
Parkwall Crs
OLD/WMLY/WICK BS30 .... 76 C2
Parkwall Rd
OLD/WMLY/WICK BS30 .... 76 D2
Parkway *BRSTK/PCHW* BS34 .... 34 A1
Park Wy *MTN/WRL* BS22 .... 123 E2
Parnall Crs *HGRV/WHIT* BS14 .... 13 C5
Parnall Rd *MANG/FISH* BS16 .... 48 A1
Parnell Rd *CLVDN* BS21 .... 65 E2
MANG/FISH BS16 .... 47 G1
Parry Cl *BATHSE* BA2 .... 107 G3
Parry's Cl
HNLZ/SM/SNYPK/WT BS9 .... 44 C3
Parrys Gv
HNLZ/SM/SNYPK/WT BS9 .... 44 C3
Parry's La
HNLZ/SM/SNYPK/WT BS9 .... 44 C3
Parslow Barton
EVILLE/WHL BS5 .... 58 A4
Parsonage Ct *PTSHD/EG* BS20 .... 39 H4
Parsonage La
CBATH/BATHN BA1 .... 3 G4
Parsonage Rd *LGASH* BS41 .... 71 F4
Parsons Av *BRSTK/PCHW* BS34 .... 21 H5
Parsons Gn *CLVDN* BS21 .... 64 C5
MTN/WRL BS22 .... 117 H5
Parsons Paddock
HGRV/WHIT BS14 .... 85 H2
Parson St *BMSTR* BS3 .... 72 C5
Parsons Wk
OLD/WMLY/WICK BS30 .... 60 B4
Partis Wy *CBATH/BATHN* BA1 .... 101 F4
Partition St *CBRIS/FH* BS1 * 4 C5
Partridge Cl *MTN/WRL* BS22 .... 122 C2
YATE/CS BS37 .... 14 B3
Partridge Rd *MANG/FISH* BS16 .... 48 C2
Partridge Rd *MANG/FISH* BS16 .... 48 C2
Passage Leaze *AVONM* BS11 .... 42 D2
Passage Rd *HNBRY/STHM* BS10 .... 30 D1
HNBRY/STHM BS10 .... 19 E5
Passage Road Brentry Hl
HNBRY/STHM BS10 .... 31 E2
Passage St *CBRIS/FH* BS1 .... 5 H4
Pastures Av *MTN/WRL* BS22 .... 122 A1
The Pasture *ALMDB* BS32 .... 21 F1
Patch Ct *MANG/FISH* BS16 .... 34 C3
Patch Cft *CLVDN* BS21 .... 64 A4
Paulman Gdns *LGASH* BS41 .... 82 C1
Paul's Cswy *YTN/CONG* BS49 .... 114 D2
Paul St *CBRISNE* BS2 .... 5 F1
Paulton Rd *HORF/LLZ* BS7 .... 45 G4
Paultow Av *BMSTR* BS3 .... 73 F3
Paultow Rd *BMSTR* BS3 .... 73 F3
Pavey Cl
BMSTRD/HC/WWD BS13 .... 84 D5
Pavey Rd
BMSTRD/HC/WWD BS13 .... 84 D5
The Pavilions
BRSG/KWL/STAPK BS4 .... 74 B5
Pawlett Rd
BMSTRD/HC/WWD BS13 .... 95 H1
Pawlett Wk
BMSTRD/HC/WWD BS13 .... 95 H1
Paxton *MANG/FISH* BS16 .... 33 C5
Paybridge Rd
BMSTRD/HC/WWD BS13 .... 84 A5
Payne Dr *EVILLE/WHL* BS5 .... 56 D4
Payne Rd *OMX/HUT/LCK* BS24 .... 126 A4
Peache Rd *MANG/FISH* BS16 .... 49 E2
Peacocks La *KGWD/HNM* BS15 .... 58 C3
Pearces Hl *MANG/FISH* BS16 .... 48 B3
Pearl St *BMSTR* BS3 .... 72 C3
Pearsall Rd
OLD/WMLY/WICK BS30 .... 76 D4
Pearse Cl *MTN/WRL* BS22 .... 118 A3
Peart Cl
BMSTRD/HC/WWD BS13 .... 83 H4
Peart Dr
BMSTRD/HC/WWD BS13 .... 83 H5
Peartree Cl
BMSTRD/HC/WWD BS13 .... 84 C5
Peartree Fld *PTSHD/EG* BS20 .... 40 B3
Pear Tree Hey *YATE/CS* BS37 .... 14 A2
Peartree La *EVILLE/WHL* BS5 .... 58 B5
KGWD/HNM BS15 .... 58 B5
Pear Tree Rd *ALMDB* BS32 .... 11 E5
Pedder Rd *CLVDN* BS21 .... 64 D4
Peel St *EVILLE/WHL* BS5 .... 56 B4
Pegasus Rd *BRSTK/PCHW* BS34 .... 19 H5
Peg Hl *YATE/CS* BS37 .... 14 B3
Pelican Cl *MTN/WRL* BS22 .... 122 D3
Pemberton Ct
MANG/FISH BS16 .... 48 B3
Pembery Rd *BMSTR* BS3 .... 72 C3
Pembroke Av *AVONM* BS11 .... 43 E2

Pembroke Gv *CFTN/FAIL* BS8 .... 55 E4
Pembroke Pl *CFTN/FAIL* BS8 .... 72 B1
Pembroke Rd *AVONM* BS11 .... 41 F2
BMSTR BS3 .... 55 E2
CFTN/FAIL BS8 .... 55 E2
KGWD/HNM BS15 .... 59 E1
PTSHD/EG BS20 .... 38 B5
Pembroke St *CBRISNE* BS2 .... 5 H1
Pembroke V *CFTN/FAIL* BS8 .... 55 E3
Penard Wy *KGWD/HNM* BS15 .... 59 F4
Penarth Dr
OMX/HUT/LCK BS24 .... 125 F5
Pendennis Av *MANG/FISH* BS16 .... 48 D4
Pendennis Pk
BRSG/KWL/STAPK BS4 .... 74 C3
Pendennis Rd
MANG/FISH BS16 .... 48 D3
Pendlesham Gdns *WSM* BS23 .... 121 F2
Pendock Cl
OLD/WMLY/WICK BS30 .... 77 F5
Pendock Rd *FRCTL/WBN* BS36 .... 23 E5
MANG/FISH BS16 .... 48 B2
Penfield Rd *CBRISNE* BS2 .... 57 F4
Penlea Ct *AVONM* BS11 .... 42 D1
Pennant Pl *PTSHD/EG* BS20 .... 40 B1
Pennard Ct *HGRV/WHIT* BS14 .... 86 A4
Pennard Gn *BATHSE* BA2 .... 107 F1
Penn Dr *MANG/FISH* BS16 .... 34 C4
Penn Gdns *CBATH/BATHN* BA1 .... 101 F4
Penngrove
OLD/WMLY/WICK BS30 .... 76 D3
Penn Hill Rd
CBATH/BATHN BA1 .... 101 F3
Pennine Gdns *WSM* BS23 .... 7 J1
Pennine Rd
BMSTRD/HC/WWD BS13 .... 84 C2
Pennlea
BMSTRD/HC/WWD BS13 .... 84 C2
The Penns *CLVDN* BS21 .... 65 E3
Penn St *CBRIS/FH* BS1 .... 5 H2
Pennycress *MTN/WRL* BS22 .... 122 A4
Pennyquick *BATHSE* BA2 .... 106 B1
Pennyroyal Gv
MANG/FISH BS16 .... 47 G3
Pennywell Rd
EVILLE/WHL BS5 .... 56 C2
Pen Park Rd
HNBRY/STHM BS10 .... 31 G2
Penpole Av *AVONM* BS11 .... 43 E2
Penpole Cl *AVONM* BS11 .... 42 D1
Penpole La *AVONM* BS11 .... 43 E1
Penpole Pk *AVONM* BS11 .... 43 E1
Penpole Pl *AVONM* BS11 .... 43 E2
Penrice Cl *MTN/WRL* BS22 .... 121 H1
Penrith Gdns
HNBRY/STHM BS10 .... 31 H4
Penrose *HGRV/WHIT* BS14 .... 85 G3
Pensfield Pk
HNBRY/STHM BS10 .... 31 H1
Pensford Ct *HGRV/WHIT* BS14 .... 86 C4
Penthouse Hl
CBATH/BATHN BA1 .... 91 E5
Pentire Av
BMSTRD/HC/WWD BS13 .... 84 B2
Pentland Av *THNB/SVB* BS35 .... 9 F4
Pepys Cl *KEYN* BS31 .... 99 E2
Pera Rd *CBATH/BATHN* BA1 .... 102 D4
Percival Rd *CFTN/FAIL* BS8 .... 54 D4
Percy Pl *CBATH/BATHN* BA1 .... 103 E5
Peregrine Cl *MTN/WRL* BS22 .... 122 C2
Perfect Vw
CBATH/BATHN BA1 .... 102 D3
The Perrings *NAIL* BS48 .... 67 F5
Perrott Rd *KGWD/HNM* BS15 .... 59 G2
Perry Cl *FRCTL/WBN* BS36 .... 34 D1
Perrycroft Av
BMSTRD/HC/WWD BS13 .... 84 B3
Perrycroft Rd
BMSTRD/HC/WWD BS13 .... 84 B3
Perrymans Cl *MANG/FISH* BS16 .... 48 A2
Perrymead *BATHSE* BA2 .... 109 E4
Perrymead *MTN/WRL* BS22 .... 118 A3
Perry Rd *CBRIS/FH* BS1 .... 4 D3
Perrys Lea *ALMDB* BS32 .... 11 F5
Perry St *EVILLE/WHL* BS5 .... 56 C3
Pesley Cl
BMSTRD/HC/WWD BS13 .... 84 A5
Petercole Dr
BMSTRD/HC/WWD BS13 .... 84 B3
Peterson Sq
BMSTRD/HC/WWD BS13 .... 95 H1
Peter's Ter *EVILLE/WHL* BS5 .... 56 D4
Petersway Gdns
EVILLE/WHL BS5 .... 58 A5
Petherbridge Wy
HORF/LLZ BS7 .... 46 C3
Petherton Cl *KGWD/HNM* BS15 .... 59 E4
Petherton Gdns
HGRV/WHIT BS14 .... 86 A2
Petherton Rd
HGRV/WHIT BS14 .... 86 A1
Pettigrew Gdns
MANG/FISH BS16 .... 59 E4
Pettigrove Rd
KGWD/HNM BS15 .... 59 E5
Pevensey Wk
BRSG/KWL/STAPK BS4 .... 85 E2
Peverell Cl *HNBRY/STHM* BS10 .... 30 D2
Peverell Dr *HNBRY/STHM* BS10 .... 30 D2
Philadelphia Ct *CBRIS/FH* BS1 * 5 H2
Philippa Cl *HGRV/WHIT* BS14 .... 85 H2
Philip St *BMSTR* BS3 .... 73 E2
CBRISNE BS2 .... 74 A1
Phillips Rd *WSM* BS23 .... 7 K7
Phippen St *CBRIS/FH* BS1 .... 5 G6
Phipps Barton
KGWD/HNM BS15 .... 58 B3
Phipps St *BMSTR* BS3 .... 72 C2
Phoenix Gv *HORF/LLZ* BS7 .... 45 G3
Phoenix Wy *PTSHD/EG* BS20 .... 40 B2
Piccadilly Pl
CBATH/BATHN BA1 .... 103 E3
Pickwick Rd
CBATH/BATHN BA1 .... 102 D2
Picton La *RDLND/MONT* BS6 .... 56 A2
Picton Ms *RDLND/MONT* BS6 .... 56 A2

Picton St *RDLND/MONT* BS6 .... 56 A2
Pier Cl *PTSHD/EG* BS20 .... 40 A1
Pierrepont Pl
CBATH/BATHN BA1 .... 3 G5
Pierrepont St
CBATH/BATHN BA1 .... 3 G5
Pier Rd *PTSHD/EG* BS20 .... 39 H1
Pigeon House Dr
BMSTRD/HC/WWD BS13 .... 85 E5
Pigott Av
BMSTRD/HC/WWD BS13 .... 84 B5
Pilemarsh *EVILLE/WHL* BS5 .... 57 F4
Pilgrims Wy *AVONM* BS11 * 42 C1
MANG/FISH BS16 .... 34 D5
MTN/WRL BS22 .... 122 B1
Pilgrims Whf
BRSG/KWL/STAPK BS4 .... 57 G4
Pilkington Cl *MTN/WRL* BS22 ...
Pilkington Cl
BRSTK/PCHW BS34 .... 33 E3
Pillgrens Gdns
RDLND/MONT BS6 .... 55 F1
Pillingers Rd
KGWD/HNM BS15 .... 58 D3
Pill Rd *CFTN/FAIL* BS8 .... 53 F2
PTSHD/EG BS20 .... 42 D5
Pill Wy *CLVDN* BS21 .... 64 B3
Pimms La *MTN/WRL* BS22 .... 116 C5
Pimm's La *MTN/WRL* BS22 .... 121 G1
Pimpernel Md *ALMDB* BS32 .... 21 G5
Pine Cl *MTN/WRL* BS22 .... 122 A1
THNB/SVB BS35 .... 8 D3
Pinecroft *HGRV/WHIT* BS14 .... 85 G2
Pine Cv *HORF/LLZ* BS7 .... 32 B4
Pine Grove Pl *HORF/LLZ* BS7 .... 55 H1
Pine Hl *MTN/WRL* BS22 .... 122 A1
Pine Ridge Cl
HNLZ/SM/SNYPK/WT BS9 * 44 A4
Pine Rd *HNBRY/STHM* BS10 .... 31 F2
Pines Rd
OLD/WMLY/WICK BS30 .... 77 F5
The Pines *KGWD/HNM* BS15 .... 59 G1
Pinetree Rd
OMX/HUT/LCK BS24 .... 127 F2
Pinewood *KGWD/HNM* BS15 .... 59 F2
Pinewood Cl
HNLZ/SM/SNYPK/WT BS9 .... 45 F1
Pinhay Rd
BMSTRD/HC/WWD BS13 .... 84 C3
Pinkers Md *MANG/FISH* BS16 .... 50 A2
Pinkhams Twist *HGRV/WHIT* BS14 .... 85 G4
Pioneer Av *BATHSE* BA2 .... 110 D1
Pioneer Pk
BRSG/KWL/STAPK BS4 .... 74 B1
Pipe La *CBRIS/FH* BS1 * 4 D4
Piper Rd *YATE/CS* BS37 .... 14 A4
Pippin Ct
BMSTRD/HC/WWD BS13 .... 84 A2
The Pippins *PTSHD/EG* BS20 .... 40 B3
Pitch And Pay La
HNLZ/SM/SNYPK/WT BS9 .... 44 C5
Pitch And Pay Pk
HNLZ/SM/SNYPK/WT BS9 .... 44 C5
Pitchcombe *YATE/CS* BS37 .... 25 G3
Pitchcombe Gdns
HNLZ/SM/SNYPK/WT BS9 .... 44 A4
Pitch La *RDLND/MONT* BS6 .... 55 H2
Pithay Ct *CBRIS/FH* BS1 .... 5 F3
The Pithay *CBRIS/FH* BS1 .... 5 F3
Pitt La *NAIL* BS48 .... 79 H5
Pitlochry Cl *HORF/LLZ* BS7 .... 32 B4
Pitman Ct *CBATH/BATHN* BA1 .... 102 D2
Pitman Rd *WSM* BS23 .... 6 A3
Pitt Rd *HORF/LLZ* BS7 .... 46 A3
Pittville Cl *THNB/SVB* BS35 .... 8 D1
Pitville Pl *RDLND/MONT* BS6 * 55 F2
Pixash La *KEYN* BS31 .... 89 E4
Pizey Av *CLVDN* BS21 .... 64 B3
Pizey Cl *CLVDN* BS21 .... 64 B3
Players Cl *MANG/FISH* BS16 .... 34 B1
Playford Gdns *AVONM* BS11 .... 29 E5
Pleasant Rd *MANG/FISH* BS16 .... 48 D3
Ploughed Paddock *NAIL* BS48 .... 67 E5
Plover Cl *MTN/WRL* BS22 .... 122 C2
YATE/CS BS37 .... 13 G5
Plumers Cl *CLVDN* BS21 .... 65 E4
Plummer's Hl *EVILLE/WHL* BS5 .... 57 E3
Plumpton Ct *MANG/FISH* BS16 .... 35 F4
Plumtree Rd *MTN/WRL* BS22 .... 122 B3
Plunder St *YTN/CONG* BS49 .... 113 H4
Podgers Dr
CBATH/BATHN BA1 .... 101 G2
The Podium
CBATH/BATHN BA1 .... 3 G4
Poets' Cl *EVILLE/WHL* BS5 .... 57 E3
Polden Cl *NAIL* BS48 .... 67 F5
Polden Rd *PTSHD/EG* BS20 .... 39 E3
WSM BS23 .... 7 H2
Pollard Rd
OMX/HUT/LCK BS24 .... 122 C3
Polly Barnes Cl
KGWD/HNM BS15 .... 75 G1
Polly Barnes Hl
KGWD/HNM BS15 .... 75 G1
Polygon Rd *CFTN/FAIL* BS8 .... 54 D5
The Polygon *CFTN/FAIL* BS8 .... 54 D5
Pomfrett Gdns
HGRV/WHIT BS14 .... 86 D4
Pomphrey Hl *MANG/FISH* BS16 .... 49 H3
Ponsford Rd
BRSG/KWL/STAPK BS4 .... 74 A5
Ponting Cl *EVILLE/WHL* BS5 .... 58 A2
Poole Court Dr *YATE/CS* BS37 .... 14 B5
Poolemead Rd *BATHSE* BA2 .... 107 E2
Poole St *AVONM* BS11 .... 28 D5
Pooles Whf *CFTN/FAIL* BS8 .... 72 B1
Pooles Wharf Ct
CFTN/FAIL BS8 .... 72 B1
Pool Rd *MANG/FISH* BS16 .... 49 E5
Pope's Wk *BATHSE* BA2 .... 109 E3
Poplar Av
HNLZ/SM/SNYPK/WT BS9 .... 44 B2
Poplar Cl *BATHSE* BA2 .... 108 A3
Poplar Fld *MANG/FISH* BS16 .... 51 F3
Poplar Pl
OLD/WMLY/WICK BS30 * 60 B5
WSM BS23 .... 6 E3
Poplar Rd *BATHSE* BA2 .... 110 B2
BMSTRD/HC/WWD BS13 .... 84 A2

EVILLE/WHL BS5 .... 57 H2
KGWD/HNM BS15 .... 75 F1
The Poplars *MTN/WRL* BS22 .... 122 C2
PTSHD/EG BS20 .... 60 B5
Poplar Ter *KGWD/HNM* BS15 .... 59 F5
Poplar Wk
OMX/HUT/LCK BS24 .... 126 D1
Poplar Way East *AVONM* BS11 .... 17 E5
Poplar Way West *AVONM* BS11 .... 16 D4
Pople Wk *HORF/LLZ* BS7 .... 46 B1
Poppy Cl *MTN/WRL* BS22 .... 117 H3
Poppy Md *ALMDB* BS32 .... 21 G3
Porlock Cl *CLVDN* BS21 .... 65 E4
WSM BS23 .... 7 K4
Porlock Gdns *NAIL* BS48 .... 67 F5
Porlock Rd *BATHSE* BA2 .... 108 D5
BMSTR BS3 .... 73 G3
Portal Rd *OMX/HUT/LCK* BS24 .... 127 G2
Portbury Common
PTSHD/EG BS20 .... 40 A4
Portbury Gv *AVONM* BS11 .... 42 D2
The Portbury Hundred
PTSHD/EG BS20 .... 40 C5
Portbury Wk *AVONM* BS11 .... 42 D2
Portbury Wy *PTSHD/EG* BS20 .... 41 F3
Portishead Rd
MTN/WRL BS22 .... 118 B5
Portland Ct *MANG/FISH* BS16 .... 48 D5
Portland Dr *PTSHD/EG* BS20 .... 40 A4
Portland Pl *CBATH/BATHN* BA1 .... 2 E1
CBRISNE BS2 * 55 H3
MANG/FISH BS16 .... 48 D5
Portland Sq *CBRISNE* BS2 .... 5 H1
Portland St *CFTN/FAIL* BS8 .... 54 D4
MANG/FISH BS16 .... 48 D5
Portland Ter *CBATH/BATHN* BA1 .... 2 E1
Portmeirion Cl
HGRV/WHIT BS14 .... 85 H4
Port Side Cl *EVILLE/WHL* BS5 * 57 H5
Port Vw *PTSHD/EG* BS20 .... 42 C3
Portview Rd *AVONM* BS11 .... 28 B5
Portwall La *CBRIS/FH* BS1 * 5 H6
Portwall La East *CBRIS/FH* BS1 * 5 H6
Portway *AVONM* BS11 .... 42 D2
CFTN/FAIL BS8 .... 54 C2
HNLZ/SM/SNYPK/WT BS9 .... 44 C1
Portway La *YATE/CS* BS37 .... 15 E5
Post Office La *NAIL* BS48 .... 81 E2
Post Office Rd
OMX/HUT/LCK BS24 .... 127 E1
Potterswood Cl
KGWD/HNM BS15 .... 58 D4
Pottery Cl *WSM* BS23 .... 7 J7
Pound Dr *MANG/FISH* BS16 .... 47 H3
Pound La *MANG/FISH* BS16 .... 47 H4
Pound Md
BLAG/CWMG/WR BS40 .... 92 D4
The Pound *ALMDB* BS32 .... 10 C2
Pountney Dr *EVILLE/WHL* BS5 .... 57 E2
Powells Acres *CLVDN* BS21 .... 65 E2
Powis Cl *MTN/WRL* BS22 .... 121 H1
Powlett Ct *BATHSE* BA2 .... 3 J2
Powlett Rd *BATHSE* BA2 .... 3 J1
Pow's Rd *KGWD/HNM* BS15 .... 58 D4
Poyntz Ct
OLD/WMLY/WICK BS30 .... 76 C3
Poyntz Rd
BRSG/KWL/STAPK BS4 .... 85 G1
Preacher Cl *EVILLE/WHL* BS5 .... 58 A4
Preanes Gn *MTN/WRL* BS22 .... 122 C1
Preddy's La *EVILLE/WHL* BS5 .... 58 A1
Prescot Cl *MTN/WRL* BS22 .... 121 G2
Prescott *YATE/CS* BS37 .... 25 H2
Press Moor Dr
OLD/WMLY/WICK BS30 .... 76 C2
Prestbury *YATE/CS* BS37 .... 25 H2
Preston Wk
BRSG/KWL/STAPK BS4 .... 73 H5
Prestwick Cl
BRSG/KWL/STAPK BS4 .... 74 C5
Pretoria Rd
BRSTK/PCHW BS34 .... 20 B2
Prewett St *CBRIS/FH* BS1 .... 5 G6
Priddy Cl *BATHSE* BA2 .... 107 G2
Priddy Ct *HGRV/WHIT* BS14 .... 86 A4
Priddy Dr *HGRV/WHIT* BS14 .... 86 A4
Priests Wy *MTN/WRL* BS22 .... 122 A1
Primrose Cl *ALMDB* BS32 .... 11 F5
KGWD/HNM BS15 .... 58 B2
Primrose Dr *THNB/SVB* BS35 .... 9 F4
Primrose La
CBATH/BATHN BA1 .... 102 A3
Primrose La *KGWD/HNM* BS15 .... 58 B2
Princes Bldgs
CBATH/BATHN BA1 * 3 F5
CFTN/FAIL BS8 .... 54 D5
Princes Ct
OLD/WMLY/WICK BS30 .... 76 C2
Princes' La *CFTN/FAIL* BS8 .... 54 D5
Princes' Pl *HORF/LLZ* BS7 .... 46 A5
Prince's Rd *CLVDN* BS21 .... 64 D2
Prince's St *CBRISNE* BS2 .... 88 B4
Princess Gdns
MANG/FISH BS16 .... 47 F2
Princess Rw *CBRISNE* BS2 .... 55 F1
Princess Royal Gdns
EVILLE/WHL BS5 .... 57 E3
Princess St *BMSTR* BS3 .... 73 F2
CBRISNE BS2 .... 56 C5
Princes St *CBATH/BATHN* BA1 .... 3 F5
CBRISNE BS2 .... 56 C5
Prince's Victoria St
CBRIS/FH BS1 .... 54 D5
Prince St *CBRIS/FH* BS1 .... 4 E6
Prince Street Rbt *CBRIS/FH* BS1 .... 4 E6
Prior Park Blds *BATHSE* BA2 .... 3 J7
Prior Park Gdns *BATHSE* BA2 .... 3 J7
Prior Park Rd *BATHSE* BA2 .... 3 J7
Priors Lea *YATE/CS* BS37 .... 26 A1
Priory Av
HNLZ/SM/SNYPK/WT BS9 .... 45 F1
Priory Cl *BATHSE* BA2 .... 109 E4
Priory Court Rd
HNLZ/SM/SNYPK/WT BS9 .... 45 E1

Priory Dene
HNLZ/SM/SNYPK/WT BS9 .... 45 E1
Priory Gdns *AVONM* BS11 .... 42 D2
HORF/LLZ BS7 .... 32 B3
PTSHD/EG BS20 .... 42 B4
Priory Ms *WSM* BS23 .... 7 K4
Priory Rd *AVONM* BS11 .... 42 D2
BRSG/KWL/STAPK BS4 .... 74 A4
CFTN/FAIL BS8 .... 54 D3
KEYN BS31 .... 88 B2
PTSHD/EG BS20 .... 41 F5
WSM BS23 .... 7 K4
Priston Cl *MTN/WRL* BS22 .... 118 A3
Pritchard St *CBRISNE* BS2 .... 5 H1
Privet Dr
BMSTRD/HC/WWD BS13 .... 84 D4
Probyn Cl *MANG/FISH* BS16 .... 48 A1
Pro-Cathedral La *CFTN/FAIL* BS8 .... 4 B3
Proctor Cl
BRSG/KWL/STAPK BS4 .... 74 C5
The Promenade
HORF/LLZ BS7 * 55 H1
Prospect Av *KGWD/HNM* BS15 .... 58 B1
Prospect Cl *FRCTL/WBN* BS36 .... 35 E1
Prospect Crs *KGWD/HNM* BS15 .... 59 G3
Prospect Gdns
CBATH/BATHN BA1 .... 91 E4
Prospect La *FRCTL/WBN* BS36 .... 23 F2
Prospect Pl *BATHSE* BA2 * 2 E1
EVILLE/WHL BS5 .... 57 E3
MANG/FISH BS16 .... 6 E3
Prospect Rd *BATHSE* BA2 .... 109 F3
Prospect Ter *BMSTR* BS3 .... 72 D3
Providence La *LGASH* BS41 .... 70 C4
Providence Pl *CBRISNE* BS2 * 5 J4
Providence Vw *LGASH* BS41 .... 70 C5
Prowse Cl *THNB/SVB* BS35 .... 8 D3
Prudham St *EVILLE/WHL* BS5 .... 57 E2
Puffin Cl *MTN/WRL* BS22 .... 122 C3
Pullin Ct
OLD/WMLY/WICK BS30 .... 77 G1
Pulteney Av *BATHSE* BA2 .... 3 J4
Pulteney Br *BATHSE* BA2 .... 3 G4
Pulteney Gdns *BATHSE* BA2 .... 3 J5
Pulteney Ms *BATHSE* BA2 * 3 J5
Pulteney Rd *BATHSE* BA2 .... 3 J4
Pulteney Ter *BATHSE* BA2 .... 3 J5
Pump House La
BRSG/KWL/STAPK BS4 .... 75 E1
Pump La *CBATH/BATHN* BA1 .... 104 C3
CBRIS/FH BS1 .... 5 G7
Pump Sq *PTSHD/EG* BS20 .... 42 D3
Purcell Wk
BRSG/KWL/STAPK BS4 .... 85 E2
Purdown Rd *HORF/LLZ* BS7 .... 46 B3
Purdue Cl *MTN/WRL* BS22 .... 118 A5
Puriewent Dr
CBATH/BATHN BA1 .... 101 H3
Pursey Dr *ALMDB* BS32 .... 21 G4
Purton Cl *KGWD/HNM* BS15 .... 59 E5
Purton Rd *HORF/LLZ* BS7 .... 55 H1
Puttingthorpe Dr
MTN/WRL BS22 .... 121 H4
Puxley Cl *HGRV/WHIT* BS14 .... 86 D3
Puxton Rd
OMX/HUT/LCK BS24 .... 119 H5
Pye Cft *ALMDB* BS32 .... 11 G4
Pyecroft Av
HNLZ/SM/SNYPK/WT BS9 .... 45 F1
Pylle Hill Crs *BMSTR* BS3 .... 73 G1
Pyne Point *CLVDN* BS21 .... 64 C2
Pynne Cl *HGRV/WHIT* BS14 .... 86 D3
Pynne Rd *HGRV/WHIT* BS14 .... 87 E4
Pyracantha Wk
HGRV/WHIT BS14 .... 85 H3

Q

The Quadrangle *YATE/CS* BS37 .... 37 G1
Quadrant East
MANG/FISH BS16 .... 48 C5
The Quadrant *R* 45 F5
Quadrant West
MANG/FISH BS16 .... 48 C5
Quaker La *THNB/SVB* BS35 .... 8 C3
Quaker's Rd *MANG/FISH* BS16 .... 34 D5
Quaker's Rd *MANG/FISH* BS16 .... 34 D5
Quantock Cl
OLD/WMLY/WICK BS30 .... 77 F1
Quantock Rd *BMSTR* BS3 .... 73 E3
PTSHD/EG BS20 .... 39 F3
WSM BS23 .... 124 C2
Quantocks *BATHSE* BA2 .... 109 H5
The Quarries *ALMDB* BS32 .... 10 D2
Quarrington Rd *HORF/LLZ* BS7 .... 46 A3
Quarry Barton
MANG/FISH BS16 .... 34 C1
Quarry Cl *BATHSE* BA2 .... 110 D1
Quarry La *AVONM* BS11 .... 30 A4
FRCTL/WBN BS36 .... 35 E1
Quarrymans Ct *BATHSE* BA2 .... 111 F1
Quarry Rd *OMX/HUT/LCK* BS24 .... 125 E5
Quarry Rd *BATHSE* BA2 .... 109 H5
KGWD/HNM BS15 .... 58 D5
YATE/CS BS37 .... 26 C1
Quarry Rock Gdns
BATHSE BA2 .... 109 J3
Quarry Steps *CFTN/FAIL* BS8 .... 55 E1
Quarry Wy *MANG/FISH* BS16 .... 47 G3
MANG/FISH BS16 .... 35 G4
NAIL BS48 .... 67 E4
Quay Head *CBRIS/FH* BS1 * 4 E5
Quays Av *PTSHD/EG* BS20 .... 40 A3
Quay Side *CBRIS/FH* BS1 * 5 H4
Quayside La *EVILLE/WHL* BS5 .... 57 H5
Quay St *CBRIS/FH* BS1 .... 4 E4
Quedgeley *YATE/CS* BS37 .... 25 G2
Queen Charlotte St
CBRIS/FH BS1 .... 5 F4
Queen Charlton La
HGRV/WHIT BS14 .... 97 G1
Queen Quay *CBRIS/FH* BS1 * 4 E5
Queen's Av *CFTN/FAIL* BS8 .... 55 E3

PTSHD/EG BS20 ....39 G3
Queenscote PTSHD/EG BS20 ...40 B3
Queensdale Crs
 BRSG/KWL/STAPK BS4............74 A3
Queens Dr KGWD/HNM BS15....75 G2
Queen's Dr BATHSE BA2 ....108 D5
 HORF/LLZ BS7 ....45 G4
Queens Ga
 HNLZ/SM/SNYPK/WT BS9.......44 B3
Queenshill Rd
 BRSG/KWL/STAPK BS4............73 H5
Queensholm Av
 MANG/FISH BS16 ....35 E4
Queensholm Cl
 MANG/FISH BS16 ....35 E4
Queensholm Crs
 MANG/FISH BS16 ....34 D4
Queensholm Dr
 MANG/FISH BS16 ....35 E5
Queen's Pde
 CBATH/BATHN BA1 ....2 E3
 CBRIS/FH BS1 ....4 B5
Queen's Parade Pl
 CBATH/BATHN BA1 ....2 E3
Queens Pl BATHSE BA2 ....3 J6
Queen Sq CBRIS/FH BS1 ....4 E5
Queen Square Av
 CBRIS/FH BS1 * 4 F5
Queens Rd
 BRSG/KWL/STAPK BS4............73 H5
 KEYN BS31 ....88 A5
 NAIL BS48 ....79 F1
 PTSHD/EG BS20 ....38 C4
Queen's Rd
 BMSTRD/HC/WWD BS13.........84 A5
 CFTN/FAIL BS8...................55 E4
 CLVDN BS21 ....64 D2
 EVILLE/WHL BS5..................57 H4
 HORF/LLZ BS7 ....46 B4
 LGASH BS41 ....95 E1
 MANG/FISH BS16 ....51 F3
 NAIL BS48 ....66 D5
 OLD/WMLY/WICK BS30 ....76 D2
 WSM BS23 ....6 D1
Queens Sq CBATH/BATHN BA1 ...3 F4
Queen St AVONM BS11 ....28 D4
 CBATH/BATHN BA1 ....3 F4
 CBRISNE BS2.....................5 H3
 EVILLE/WHL BS5..................47 E5
 KGWD/HNM BS15 ....58 B4
Queen's Wk MTHN/SVB BS35...8 C4
Queensway BRSTK/PCHW BS34...21 G4
Queens Wy PTSHD/EG BS20......38 C4
Queen's Wy MTN/WRL BS22 ....117 F4
Queen Victoria Rd
 RDLND/MONT BS6 ....45 E4
Queen Victoria St CBRISNE BS2...56 C5
Queenwood Av
 CBATH/BATHN BA1 ....102 D5
Quickthorn Cl
 HGRV/WHIT BS14 ....85 H3
Quilet St CBATH/BATHN BA1 .....3 F4
Quilter Gv
 BRSG/KWL/STAPK BS4 * 85 E2

R

Raby Ms BATHSE BA2 ....3 J3
Raby Pl BATHSE BA2 ....3 J3
Rackfield Pl BATHSE BA2 ....107 G1
Rackham Cl HORF/LLZ BS7 ......46 D2
Rackhay CBRIS/FH BS1 * 5 F4
Radley Rd MANG/FISH BS16 .....48 B4
Radnor Rd
 HNLZ/SM/SNYPK/WT BS9.......45 F3
Raeburn Rd EVILLE/WHL BS5 ....58 B4
Ragland La
 CBATH/BATHN BA1 ....102 D5
Ragland St CBATH/BATHN BA1...102 D5
Raglan La
 BLAG/CWMG/WR BS40..........93 F5
 CBATH/BATHN BA1 ....102 D5
Raglan Pl HORF/LLZ BS7 ....45 H5
 THNB/SVB BS35 ....8 C4
Raglan Rd HORF/LLZ BS7 ....45 H5
Raglan St
 CBATH/BATHN BA1 ....102 D2
Raglan Ter
 CBATH/BATHN BA1 * 102 D2
Raglan Vis
 CBATH/BATHN BA1 ....102 D2
Railton Jones Cl
 BRSTK/PCHW BS34 ....33 G2
Railway Pl CBATH/BATHN BA1...3 H6
Railway Ter MANG/FISH BS16 ...48 A4
Railway Vw MANG/FISH BS16 *...34 D2
Raleigh Cl KEYN BS31 ....98 D2
Raleigh Ri PTSHD/EG BS20 ....39 F2
Raleigh Rd BMSTER BS3 ....72 B2
Ralph Allen Dr BATHSE BA2 ....109 E5
Ralph Rd HORF/LLZ BS7 ....46 B4
Ram Hi FRCTL/WBN BS36..........36 B1
Ramsay Cl MTN/WRL BS22 ......117 F4
Ramscombe La
 CBATH/BATHN BA1 ....91 E5
Ramsey Rd HORF/LLZ BS7 ....46 B1
Ranchways PTSHD/EG BS20 ......38 D4
Randall Cl KGWD/HNM BS15 ....59 F1
Randall Rd CFTN/FAIL BS8 ....55 E5
Randolph Av
 BMSTRD/HC/WWD BS13.........84 C4
 YATE/CS BS37 ....13 H3
Randolph Cl
 BMSTRD/HC/WWD BS13.........84 C4
Rangers Wk KGWD/HNM BS15...75 H2
Rannoch Rd
 BRSTK/PCHW BS34 ....32 B5
Ranscombe Av
 MTN/WRL BS22 ....122 A1
Ransford CLVDN BS21 ....64 B4
Ratcliffe Dr BRSTK/PCHW BS34...21 G4
Rathbone Cl FRCTL/WBN BS36...24 A5
Ravel Cl MTN/WRL BS22 ....122 D2
Ravendale Dr
 OLD/WMLY/WICK BS30 ....77 E3

Ravenglass Crs
 HNBRY/STHM BS10 ....31 G3
Ravenhead Dr
 HGRV/WHIT BS14 ....86 A1
Ravenhill Av BMSTER BS3 ....73 H3
Ravenhill Rd BMSTER BS3.........73 H3
Ravenswood Rd
 RDLND/MONT BS6 ....55 G2
Rawens Wd
 OLD/WMLY/WICK BS30 ....77 E3
Rawlins Av MTN/WRL BS22 ....117 H5
Rayens Cross Rd LGASH BS41 ...70 C5
Rayleigh Rd
 HNLZ/SM/SNYPK/WT BS9.......44 B1
Raymend Rd BMSTER BS3 ....73 F3
Raymend Wk BMSTER BS3 ....73 F4
Raymill BRSG/KWL/STAPK BS4 ...75 F4
Raymore Ri LGASH BS41 ....82 C1
Raynes Rd BMSTER BS3 ....72 B3
Reading Ct KGWD/HNM BS15 ...58 D3
Rector's Wy WSM BS23 ....7 G7
Rectory Cl FRCTL/WBN BS36.....67 H4
 YATE/CS BS37 ....14 A3
Rectory Dr YTN/CONG BS49 ....112 C4
Rectory Gdns
 HNBRY/STHM BS10 ....30 D3
Rectory La BRSTK/PCHW BS34...32 C2
Rectory Rd FRCTL/WBN BS36.....23 G2
 PTSHD/EG BS20 ....42 B5
Rectory Wy YTN/CONG BS49 ...112 C4
Redcar Ct MANG/FISH BS16 .....47 F5
Redcatch Rd BMSTER BS3 ....73 G4
Redcliff Backs CBRIS/FH BS1 .....5 G5
Redcliffe Cl PTSHD/EG BS20 .....38 C5
Redcliffe Pde East
 CBRIS/FH BS1 ....5 F6
Redcliffe Pde West
 CBRIS/FH BS1 ....5 F6
Redcliffe Wy CBRIS/FH BS1 ......5 F6
Redcliff Hl CBRIS/FH BS1 * 5 F6
Redcliff Mead La CBRIS/FH BS1...5 G7
Redcliff St CBRIS/FH BS1 ....5 G5
Redcross Ms CBRISNE BS2 * 5 J3
Redcross St CBRISNE BS2 ....5 J3
The Reddings
 KGWD/HNM BS15 ....59 F1
Redfield Hl
 OLD/WMLY/WICK BS30 ....77 G2
Redfield Rd BRSTK/PCHW BS34...94 D1
Redford Crs
 BMSTRD/HC/WWD BS13.........83 H5
Redford Wk
 BMSTRD/HC/WWD BS13.........95 E1
Redhill Cl MANG/FISH BS16 ......47 G5
Redhill Dr MANG/FISH BS16 .....47 G5
Red House La ALMDB BS22 ....10 B5
Redland Av PTSHD/EG BS20 .....39 H1
Redland Ct Rd RDLND/MONT BS6...55 G1
Redland Court Rd
 RDLND/MONT BS6 ....41 H2
Redland Green Rd
 RDLND/MONT BS6 ....55 G1
Redland Gv RDLND/MONT BS6 ...55 G1
Redland Hl RDLND/MONT BS6 ...55 E1
Redland Pk BATHSE BA2 ....107 E1
 RDLND/MONT BS6 ....55 F1
Redland Rd RDLND/MONT BS6...55 E1
Redland Ter RDLND/MONT BS6...55 F1
Redpoll Dr PTSHD/EG BS20 ......40 D2
Redshelf Wk
 HNBRY/STHM BS10 ....31 G2
Redwick Cl AVONM BS11 ....30 A3
Redwing Dr MTN/WRL BS22 ...122 D2
Redwing Gdns
 MANG/FISH BS16 ....47 G2
Redwood Cl NAIL BS48 ....67 H4
Redwood La NAIL BS48 ....76 D3
Redwood La NAIL BS48 ....81 H2
Reed Cl HNBRY/STHM BS10 .....45 H2
Reed Ct
 OLD/WMLY/WICK BS30 * 76 C5
Reedley Rd
 HNLZ/SM/SNYPK/WT BS9.......44 C3
Reedling Cl MANG/FISH BS16 *...47 G2
Reed Wy MTN/WRL BS22 ....118 B5
Regency Dr
 BRSG/KWL/STAPK BS4...........75 F4
Regent Rd BMSTER BS3 ....73 E2
Regents Cl THNB/SVB BS35 ....8 B1
Regents St CFTN/FAIL BS8 ....55 E5
Regent St KGWD/HNM BS15.....58 D3
 WSM BS23 ....6 D4
The Regina CBATH/BATHN BA1 *...3 F2
Remenham Dr
 HNLZ/SM/SNYPK/WT BS9.......45 E3
Remenham Pk
 HNLZ/SM/SNYPK/WT BS9.......45 F3
Rendcomb Cl MTN/WRL BS22 ...121 G1
Repton Rd
 BRSG/KWL/STAPK BS4...........74 B3
Retort Rd AVONM BS11 ....28 C2
Reubens Ct MTN/WRL BS22 ....117 G5
Reynolds Cl KEYN BS31 ....88 A4
Reynold's Wk HORF/LLZ BS7 ....46 C1
Rhode Cl KEYN BS31 ....98 B2
Rhodyate Hl YTN/CONG BS49...113 H4
Rhodyate La YTN/CONG BS49...113 G4
Rhyne Ter WSM BS24 ....124 C4
Rhyne Vw NAIL BS48 ....66 C5
Ribblesdale THNB/SVB BS35 ......8 D4
Richards Cl MTN/WRL BS22 .....118 A4
Richeson Cl
 HNBRY/STHM BS10 ....30 D3
Richeson Wk
 HNBRY/STHM BS10 ....30 D3
Richmond Av
 BRSTK/PCHW BS34 ....21 G5
 RDLND/MONT BS6 ....56 B1
Richmond Cl KEYN BS31 ....88 A5
 PTSHD/EG BS20 ....40 A3
Richmond Dl CFTN/FAIL BS8 * ...46 C1
Richmond Gn NAIL BS48 ....67 G5
Richmond Hts
 CBATH/BATHN BA1 ....102 C3
Richmond Hl
 CBATH/BATHN BA1 ....102 C3
 CFTN/FAIL BS8....................4 A2
Richmond Hill Av CFTN/FAIL BS8...4 A3

Richmond La
 CBATH/BATHN BA1 ....102 C3
 CFTN/FAIL BS8....................55 E4
Richmond Ms CFTN/FAIL BS8 ...55 E4
Richmond Park Rd
 CFTN/FAIL BS8....................55 E4
Richmond Pl
 CBATH/BATHN BA1 ....102 C3
Richmond Rd
 CBATH/BATHN BA1 ....102 C2
 EVILLE/WHL BS5..................57 G3
 MANG/FISH BS16 ....49 E5
 RDLND/MONT BS6 ....56 A1
Richmond St BMSTER BS3 ....73 G2
 WSM BS23 ....6 D4
Richmond Ter AVONM BS11 .....28 A4
 CFTN/FAIL BS8....................55 E4
Ricketts La MTN/WRL BS22 ....122 D1
Rickford Rd NAIL BS48 ....67 G5
The Ride KGWD/HNM BS15 ......59 G1
Ridge Cl PTSHD/EG BS20 ....39 E4
Ridge Green Cl BATHSE BA2 ....110 B2
Ridgehill
 HNLZ/SM/SNYPK/WT BS9.......45 G2
The Ridge AVONM BS11 ....43 E1
 FRCTL/WBN BS36.................24 A3
 YTN/CONG BS49 ....71 E4
Ridgeview LGASH BS41 ....71 E4
Ridgeway FRCTL/WBN BS36 .....24 A3
 NAIL BS48 ....66 D5
 YATE/CS BS37 ....14 C5
Ridgeway Av WSM BS23 ....7 F7
Ridgeway Ct
 HNLZ/SM/SNYPK/WT BS9.......30 D4
Ridgeway Gdns
 HGRV/WHIT BS14 ....86 B4
Ridgeway La
 HGRV/WHIT BS14 ....86 A5
Ridgeway Pde
 EVILLE/WHL BS5..................47 G5
Ridgeway Rd LGASH BS41 ....70 D5
 MANG/FISH BS16 ....47 G5
The Ridgeway
 HNBRY/STHM BS10 ....31 E4
 MTN/WRL BS22 ....121 G1
Riding Barn Hl
 OLD/WMLY/WICK BS30 ....60 D5
Ridingleaze AVONM BS11 ....29 G4
Ridings Cl YATE/CS BS37 ....27 E1
Ridings Rd FRCTL/WBN BS36.....24 A4
The Ridings
 BMSTRD/HC/WWD BS13.........83 H5
 FRCTL/WBN BS36.................24 A4
Ridley Av KGWD/HNM BS15 .....49 H5
Ringspit La PLTN/PENS BS39 .....97 H4
Ringswell Gdns
 CBATH/BATHN BA1 ....103 F3
Ringwood Crs
 HNBRY/STHM BS10 ....31 H4
Ringwood Gv WSM BS23 ....121 F2
Ringwood Rd BATHSE BA2 ......107 H1
Ripley Rd EVILLE/WHL BS5........58 A2
Ripon Ct MANG/FISH BS16 ......35 F4
Ripon Rd
 BRSG/KWL/STAPK BS4...........57 G5
Rippleside PTSHD/EG BS20 ......39 G3
Rippleside Rd CLVDN BS21 ....62 C5
The Ripple CLVDN BS21 ....67 E2
Risdale Rd BMSTER BS3 ....71 H5
Rivendell MTN/WRL BS22 ......117 H4
Riverland Dr
 BMSTRD/HC/WWD BS13.........84 A4
Riverleaze
 HNLZ/SM/SNYPK/WT BS9.......43 H3
 PTSHD/EG BS20 ....38 D2
River Md CLVDN BS21 ....64 D5
River Rd YATE/CS BS37 ....26 C1
Riverside Cl AVONM BS11 ....43 F3
 CLVDN BS21 ....64 B4
 MTN/WRL BS22 ....118 B5
Riverside Ct BATHSE BA2 ....2 E5
 BRSG/KWL/STAPK BS4 * 57 H5
Riverside Gdns
 CBATH/BATHN BA1 ....2 E5
Riverside Ms
 BRSG/KWL/STAPK BS4...........57 H5
Riverside Rd BATHSE BA2 ....2 E5
Riverside Steps
 BRSG/KWL/STAPK BS4 * 57 G4
Riverside Wy KGWD/HNM BS15...75 H3
Rivers Rd CBATH/BATHN BA1...102 D4
Rivers St CBATH/BATHN BA1 .....2 E3
Rivers Street Ms
 CBATH/BATHN BA1 * 2 F2
Rivers Street Pl
 CBATH/BATHN BA1 * 3 F2
River St CBRISNE BS2 ....5 J2
River Ter KEYN BS31 * 88 C4
River Vw MANG/FISH BS16 ......47 G3
River Wk MTN/WRL BS22 ....123 G1
Riverway NAIL BS48 ....67 G3
Riverwood Rd
 MANG/FISH BS16 ....34 C4
Riviera Crs MANG/FISH BS16 ....49 E4
Riviera Wy BRSTK/PCHW BS34...34 B1
Roath Rd PTSHD/EG BS20 ....39 H3
Robbins Cl ALMDB BS32 ....21 H4
Robbins Ct MANG/FISH BS16 ...49 H2
Robel Av FRCTL/WBN BS36 ......23 F2
Robert Ct MANG/FISH BS16 .....49 H1
Robertson Dr
 BRSG/KWL/STAPK BS4...........57 H5
Robertson Rd EVILLE/WHL BS5...57 E1
Robert St EVILLE/WHL BS5 ....56 D4
Robin Cl HNBRY/STHM BS10 ....31 F3
 HGRV/WHIT BS14 ....85 F4
Robin Dr OMX/HUT/LCK BS24...126 B4
Robinia Wk HGRV/WHIT BS14...85 G2
Robin La CLVDN BS21 ....62 B5
Robinson Cl NAIL BS48 ....79 H4
Robinson Dr EVILLE/WHL BS5 ...56 C5
Robinson Wy NAIL BS48 ....79 H4
Robin Wy YATE/CS BS37 ....26 B3
Rochester Cl
 OMX/HUT/LCK BS24 ....125 F5
Rochester Rd
 BRSG/KWL/STAPK BS4...........74 D1
Rochfort Pl BATHSE BA2 ....3 H1
Rock Av NAIL BS48 ....66 D4

Rock Hall La BATHSE BA2 ....111 F1
Rockingham Gdns
 AVONM BS11 ....29 G5
Rockingham Gv WSM BS23 .....121 F2
Rockland Gv MANG/FISH BS16...47 F2
Rockland Rd
 MANG/FISH BS16 ....48 C1
Rock La BATHSE BA2 ....111 F1
 BRSTK/PCHW BS34 ....21 H5
Rockleaze
 HNLZ/SM/SNYPK/WT BS9.......54 C1
Rockleaze Av
 HNLZ/SM/SNYPK/WT BS9.......44 C5
Rockleaze Rd
 HNLZ/SM/SNYPK/WT BS9.......54 C1
Rockliffe Av BATHSE BA2 ....3 K1
Rockliffe Rd BATHSE BA2 ....3 J1
Rock Rd KEYN BS31 ....88 D4
 YTN/CONG BS49 ....112 C4
Rockside Av MANG/FISH BS16...35 F5
Rockside Dr
 HNLZ/SM/SNYPK/WT BS9.......45 F2
Rockside Gdns
 FRCTL/WBN BS36.................24 A2
 MANG/FISH BS16 ....35 F5
Rocks La
 BLAG/CWMG/WR BS40..........93 E5
Rockstowes Wy
 HNBRY/STHM BS10 ....31 H2
Rock St THNB/SVB BS35 ....8 C4
The Rock
 BRSG/KWL/STAPK BS4...........74 D3
Rockwell Av AVONM BS11 ....29 H4
Rodborough YATE/CS BS37 ......25 G3
Rodbourne Rd
 HNBRY/STHM BS10 ....45 H1
Rodfords Md HGRV/WHIT BS14...85 H2
Rodford Wy YATE/CS BS37 ......25 G3
Rodmead Wk
 BMSTRD/HC/WWD BS13.........84 B5
Rodmoor Rd PTSHD/EG BS20...39 H2
Rodney Av KGWD/HNM BS15 ...58 B5
Rodney Crs BRSTK/PCHW BS34...32 C1
Rodney Rd KEYN BS31 ....99 F2
 KGWD/HNM BS15 ....58 A2
Rodney Wk KGWD/HNM BS15...58 B5
Rodway Hl MANG/FISH BS16 ....49 G4
Rodway Rd BRSTK/PCHW BS34...20 D3
 MANG/FISH BS16 ....49 G4
Rodway Vw KGWD/HNM BS15...49 F5
Roebuck Cl MTN/WRL BS22 ....117 H4
Roegate Dr
 BRSG/KWL/STAPK BS4...........58 D1
Rogers Cl
 OLD/WMLY/WICK BS30 ....77 E1
Rogers Ct YATE/CS BS37 ....27 F1
Rogers Wk
 OLD/WMLY/WICK BS30 ....60 B4
Rokeby Av RDLND/MONT BS6...55 G2
Roman Farm Ct AVONM BS11 *...30 A3
Roman Farm Rd
 BRSG/KWL/STAPK BS4...........85 F2
Roman Rd BATHSE BA2 ....110 A2
 BMSTRD/HC/WWD BS13.........84 B3
Roman Wk
 BRSG/KWL/STAPK BS4...........58 B1
 BRSTK/PCHW BS34 ....21 G5
Roman Wy
 HNLZ/SM/SNYPK/WT BS9.......44 A4
Romney Av HORF/LLZ BS7 ....46 D3
Ronald Rd MANG/FISH BS16 ....47 H2
Ronayne Wk MANG/FISH BS16...48 C2
Rookery Cl MTN/WRL BS22 ....117 F5
Rookery Rd
 BRSG/KWL/STAPK BS4...........73 H3
Rookery Wy HGRV/WHIT BS14...85 F4
Rooksbridge Wk
 BATHSE BA2 * 107 G2
Rope Wk NAIL BS48 ....79 H4
Rosa Acre HNBRY/STHM BS10...31 E2
Rosebay Md MANG/FISH BS16...47 G4
Roseberry Pk EVILLE/WHL BS5...57 F3
Roseberry Pl BATHSE BA2 * 107 H1
Roseberry Rd BATHSE BA2 ......107 H1
 EVILLE/WHL BS5..................57 F4
Rosebery Av CBRISNE BS2 ....56 C2
Rosebery Ter CFTN/FAIL BS8 .....4 A4
Rose Cl FRCTL/WBN BS36 ....24 B5
Rosedale Av WSM BS23 ....7 J5
Rosedale Rd MANG/FISH BS16...48 D5
Rose Gdns MTN/WRL BS22 .....118 A4
Rose Green Rd
 EVILLE/WHL BS5..................57 F1
Rose Hl CBATH/BATHN BA1 ....103 E2
Roseland Cl
 CBATH/BATHN BA1 ....103 F1
Rose La FRCTL/WBN BS36 ....24 B3
Roselarge Gdns
 HNBRY/STHM BS10 ....31 E3
Rosemary Cl ALMDB BS32 ....21 H3
Rosemary Crs
 PTSHD/EG BS20 ....40 B3
Rosemary La EVILLE/WHL BS5...57 E1
Rose Md HORF/LLZ BS7 ....46 D3
Rosemont La BATHSE BA2 ......108 D5
Rosemount Rd NAIL BS48 ....81 G1
Rose Oak Dr
 FRCTL/WBN BS36.................24 B3
Rose Oak Gdns
 FRCTL/WBN BS36.................24 B3
Rose Oak La FRCTL/WBN BS36...24 B3
Rose Rd EVILLE/WHL BS5 ....57 G4
Rosery Cl
 HNLZ/SM/SNYPK/WT BS9.......31 G5
The Rosery MANG/FISH BS16 ...48 D5
Roseville Av
 OLD/WMLY/WICK BS30 ....76 D4
Rose Wk MANG/FISH BS16 ......48 C5
Rosewarn Cl BATHSE BA2 ......107 F3
Rosewell Ct CBATH/BATHN BA1...2 E4
Rosling Rd HORF/LLZ BS7 ....46 B2
Roslyn Av MTN/WRL BS22 .....121 H2
Roslyn Rd RDLND/MONT BS6 ...55 F1
Rossall Av BRSTK/PCHW BS34...21 E4
Rossall Rd CLVDN BS21 ....62 E3
Ross Cl YATE/CS BS37 ....14 C5
Rossendale Cl MTN/WRL BS22...117 G5

Rossiter Gra
 BMSTRD/HC/WWD BS13.........84 A5
Rossiter's La EVILLE/WHL BS5...58 A5
Rosslyn Cl CBATH/BATHN BA1...101 G5
Rosslyn Rd
 CBATH/BATHN BA1 ....101 G5
Rosslyn Wy THNB/SVB BS35 .....8 D1
Roundhill Gv BATHSE BA2 ......107 G4
Roundhill Pk BATHSE BA2 ......107 F3
Roundmoor Cl KEYN BS31 ....99 E1
Roundmoor Gdns
 HNLZ/SM/SNYPK/WT BS9.......30 C4
Roundways FRCTL/WBN BS36...24 A4
Rousham Rd EVILLE/WHL BS5...46 C5
Rowacres BATHSE BA2 ....107 G4
 HGRV/WHIT BS14 ....85 G3
Rowan Cl MANG/FISH BS16 .....58 A1
 NAIL BS48 ....67 H4
Rowan Pl OMX/HUT/LCK BS24...123 G2
Rowan Wy KGWD/HNM BS15...75 G3
Rowberrow MANG/FISH BS16 ...85 C2
Rowberrow Wy NAIL BS48 ....67 F5
Rowbrow Rd MANG/FISH BS16...47 E4
Rowlands Cl
 CBATH/BATHN BA1 ....104 C2
Rowlandson Gdns
 HORF/LLZ BS7 ....46 D2
Rowley St BMSTER BS3 ....72 D3
Rownham Cl BMSTER BS3 ....71 H2
Rownham Md CFTN/FAIL BS8 ...54 B4
The Rows MTN/WRL BS22 ......122 B1
Royal Albert Rd
 RDLND/MONT BS6 ....45 E4
Royal Av CBATH/BATHN BA1 .....2 C3
Royal Cl HNBRY/STHM BS10 ....30 B2
Royal Crs CBATH/BATHN BA1 ...2 D2
 WSM BS23 ....6 C2
Royal Fort Rd CFTN/FAIL BS8 ....4 D2
Royal Pde WSM BS23 ....6 C3 *
Royal Pk CFTN/FAIL BS8 ....55 E4
Royal Portbury Dock Rd
 PTSHD/EG BS20 ....41 G2
Royal Rd MANG/FISH BS16 ......48 C1
Royal Sands WSM BS23 ....124 C2
Royal Victoria Pk
 HNBRY/STHM BS10 ....31 F3
Royal York Crs CFTN/FAIL BS8...54 D5
Royal York Ms
 CBATH/BATHN BA1 * 3 F5
Royal York Vls CFTN/FAIL BS8...54 D5
Rovate Hl EVILLE/WHL BS5 ......57 F1
Roycroft Rd
 BRSTK/PCHW BS34 ....32 C3
Roy King Gdns
 OLD/WMLY/WICK BS30 ....77 F1
Royston Wk
 HNBRY/STHM BS10 ....31 H3
Rozel Rd HORF/LLZ BS7 ....46 A2
Rubens Cl KEYN BS31 ....88 D4
Ruby St BMSTER BS3 ....72 C3
Ruddymead CLVDN BS21 ....64 D3
Rudford Cl
 BRSTK/PCHW BS34 ....20 D1
Rudge Cl KGWD/HNM BS15 ....59 F1
Rudgewood Cl
 BMSTRD/HC/WWD BS13.........84 B5
Rudgleigh Av PTSHD/EG BS20...42 C4
Rudgleigh Rd PTSHD/EG BS20...42 C4
Rudhall Gv
 HNBRY/STHM BS10 ....46 A1
Rudmore Pk
 CBATH/BATHN BA1 ....101 F5
Ruffet Rd FRCTL/WBN BS36 .....35 H1
Rugby Rd
 BRSG/KWL/STAPK BS4...........73 H3
Runnymead Av
 BRSG/KWL/STAPK BS4...........74 C5
Runnymede
 KGWD/HNM BS15 ....59 G2
Runswick Rd
 BRSG/KWL/STAPK BS4...........74 B5
Rupert St CBRIS/FH BS1 ....5 F3
 EVILLE/WHL BS5..................57 E4
Rush Cl ALMDB BS32 ....11 F5
Rush Hl BATHSE BA2 ....107 G5
Rushmoor CLVDN BS21 ....64 A4
Rushmoor Gv NAIL BS48 ....79 G4
Rushmoor La NAIL BS48 ....79 H4
Rushton Dr FRCTL/WBN BS36...35 G2
Rushy OLD/WMLY/WICK BS30...76 D2
Rushy Wy MANG/FISH BS16 .....35 G4
Russell Av KGWD/HNM BS15 ...58 D4
Russell Gv RDLND/MONT BS6...45 G3
Russell Rd CLVDN BS21 ....64 C2
 MANG/FISH BS16 ....58 B1
 OMX/HUT/LCK BS24 ....45 F4
Russell St CBATH/BATHN BA1 ...3 F2
Russell Town Av
 EVILLE/WHL BS5..................56 D3
The Russets PTSHD/EG BS20 ....40 B4
Russett Cl NAIL BS48 ....80 A5
Russett Gv NAIL BS48 ....78 D1
Russ St CBRISNE BS2 ....5 J4
Rutherford Cl
 OLD/WMLY/WICK BS30 ....76 D5
Ruthven Rd
 BRSG/KWL/STAPK BS4...........85 F1
Rutland Av
 OLD/WMLY/WICK BS30 ....76 D4
Rutland Cl MTN/WRL BS22 ....121 H3
Rutland Rd HORF/LLZ BS7 ....46 A5
Ryde Rd BRSG/KWL/STAPK BS4...74 B5
Ryde Rd WSM BS23 ....125 E2
Ryde Rd
 BRSG/KWL/STAPK BS4...........74 B5
Rye Cl BMSTRD/HC/WWD BS13...83 H3
Ryecroft Av MTN/WRL BS22 ...122 C2
Ryecroft Ri LGASH BS41 ....95 F3
Ryecroft Rd FRCTL/WBN BS36...24 A2
Ryedown La
 OLD/WMLY/WICK BS30 ....77 F5
Ryland Pl CBRISNE BS2 * 56 C1
Rylestone Gv
 HNLZ/SM/SNYPK/WT BS9.......44 D3

Rysdale Rd
HNLZ/SM/SNYPK/WT BS9 ... **44** D2

S

Sabin Cl *BATHSE* BA2 ... **107** G4
Sabrina Wy
HNLZ/SM/SNYPK/WT BS22 ... **118** A4
Sadbury Cl *MTN/WRL* BS22 ... **118** A4
Sadlier Cl *AVONM* BS11 ... **29** F5
Saffron Cl *EVILLE/WHL* BS5 * ... **57** E3
Saffron Ct *CBATH/BATHN* BA1 ... **102** D4
The Saffrons *MTN/WRL* BS22 ... **118** A4
Sage Cl *PTSHD/EG* BS20 ... **38** C4
Sages Md *ALMDB* BS32 ... **21** C2
St Agnes Av
BRSG/KWL/STAPK BS4 ... **73** C4
St Agnes Cl
BRSG/KWL/STAPK BS4 ... **73** C4
NAIL BS48 ... **67** H5
St Agnes Gdns
BRSG/KWL/STAPK BS4 * ... **73** C4
St Agnes Wk
BRSG/KWL/STAPK BS4 * ... **73** C4
St Aidan's Cl *EVILLE/WHL* BS5 ... **58** A5
St Aidan's Rd *EVILLE/WHL* BS5 ... **58** A5
St Alban's Rd
RDLND/MONT BS6 ... **45** H5
St Aldams Dr *MANG/FISH* BS16 ... **51** F3
St Aldwyn's Cl *HORF/LLZ* BS7 ... **32** B5
St Andrews
OLD/WMLY/WICK BS30 ... **59** H5
YATE/CS BS37 ... **26** B1
St Andrews Cl
MTN/WRL BS22 * ... **117** C5
NAIL BS48 ... **67** H5
St Andrew's Cl
YTN/CONG BS49 * ... **114** D2
St Andrew's Dr *CLVDN* BS21 ... **64** A3
St Andrews Rd *NAIL* BS48 ... **80** A4
St Andrew's Rd *AVONM* BS11 ... **28** B2
RDLND/MONT BS6 ... **56** A1
St Andrews Ter
CBATH/BATHN BA1 * ... **3** F3
St Anne's Av *KEYN* BS31 ... **88** B4
St Annes Cl *EVILLE/WHL* BS5 * ... **57** H5
St Anne's Cl
OLD/WMLY/WICK BS30 ... **77** G2
St Annes Dr
OLD/WMLY/WICK BS30 ... **77** F4
St Annes Dr
FRCTL/WBN BS36 ... **24** A5
OLD/WMLY/WICK BS30 ... **61** F4
St Anne's Park Rd
BRSG/KWL/STAPK BS4 ... **74** D1
St Anne's Rd
BRSG/KWL/STAPK BS4 ... **57** F5
St Anne's Ter
BRSG/KWL/STAPK BS4 ... **74** D1
St Anns Pl *CBATH/BATHN* BA1 ... **2** D4
St Anns Wy *BATHSE* BA2 ... **3** K4
St Aubyn's Av *WSM* BS23 ... **124** C4
St Aubyn's Av
BRSG/KWL/STAPK BS4 ... **75** E3
St Augustine's Cl
PTSHD/EG BS20 ... **38** C4
St Augustine's Pde
CBRIS/FH BS1 * ... **4** E4
St Augustine's Pl
CBRIS/FH BS1 * ... **4** E4
St Augustines Yd
CBRIS/FH BS1 * ... **4** D4
St Austell Cl *NAIL* BS48 ... **79** H1
St Austell Rd *MTN/WRL* BS22 ... **121** G3
St Barnabas Cl
OLD/WMLY/WICK BS30 ... **60** A4
St Bartholomew's Rd
HORF/LLZ BS7 ... **46** B5
St Bede's Rd *KGWD/HNM* BS15 ... **58** C1
St Bernard's Rd *AVONM* BS11 ... **43** E2
St Brelades Gv
BRSG/KWL/STAPK BS4 ... **74** D1
St Brendan's Wy *AVONM* BS11 ... **28** B4
St Briavels Dr *YATE/CS* BS37 ... **25** H2
St Bridges Cl *MTN/WRL* BS22 ... **116** B2
St Catherine's Cl *BATHSE* BA2 ... **109** F1
St Catherines Ct *BMSTR* BS3 * ... **73** C5
St Catherines Hospital
CBATH/BATHN BA1 * ... **3** G5
St Catherine's Md
PTSHD/EG BS20 ... **42** D5
St Catherines Pl *BMSTR* BS3 * ... **73** C5
St Christophers Cl
BATHSE BA2 ... **103** F5
St Clements Ct *KEYN* BS31 ... **88** B5
St Clements Rd *KEYN* BS31 ... **88** B4
St David Ms *CBRIS/FH* BS1 * ... **4** C5
St David's Av
OLD/WMLY/WICK BS30 ... **77** E1
St David's Cl *MTN/WRL* BS22 ... **121** G1
St David's Crs
BRSG/KWL/STAPK BS4 ... **74** D1
St David's Rd *THNB/SVB* BS35 ... **8** B3
St Dunstans Cl *KEYN* BS31 ... **88** B5
St Dunstan's Rd *BMSTR* BS3 ... **72** D4
St Edward's Rd *CFTN/FAIL* BS8 * ... **4** A5
St Edyth's Rd
HNLZ/SM/SNYPK/WT BS9 ... **43** H2
St Fagans Ct
OLD/WMLY/WICK BS30 ... **77** E4
St Francis Dr *FRCTL/WBN* BS36 ... **23** F3
OLD/WMLY/WICK BS30 ... **61** F4
St Francis Rd *BMSTR* BS3 ... **72** B2
KEYN BS31 ... **87** H5
St Gabriel's Rd *EVILLE/WHL* BS5 ... **56** D2
St Georges Av
EVILLE/WHL BS5 * ... **57** G3
St Georges Blds
CBATH/BATHN BA1 * ... **2** C3
St George's Hl *BATHSE* BA2 ... **103** G4
PTSHD/EG BS20 ... **42** A5
St Georges House
EVILLE/WHL BS5 * ... **57** G3
St Georges Pl
CBATH/BATHN BA1 * ... **2** D3
St George's Rd *CBRIS/FH* BS1 * ... **4** E4
KEYN BS31 ... **88** B5

PTSHD/EG BS20 ... **41** G1
St Gregory's Rd *HORF/LLZ* BS7 ... **32** B5
St Gregory's Wk
HORF/LLZ BS7 * ... **32** C5
St Helena Rd
RDLND/MONT BS6 ... **45** F4
St Helens Dr
OLD/WMLY/WICK BS30 ... **77** F4
St Helen's Wk *EVILLE/WHL* BS5 ... **58** A2
St Helier Av
BRSG/KWL/STAPK BS4 * ... **75** E3
St Hilary Cl
HNLZ/SM/SNYPK/WT BS9 ... **44** B3
St Ivel Wy
OLD/WMLY/WICK BS30 ... **60** A5
St Ives Cl *NAIL* BS48 * ... **67** H5
St Ives Rd *WSM* BS23 ... **125** F1
St James Cl *ALMDB* BS32 ... **11** E4
St James Pl *MANG/FISH* BS16 ... **49** C3
St James's Pde
CBATH/BATHN BA1 ... **3** F5
St James's Pl
CBATH/BATHN BA1 * ... **2** D1
St James's Sq
CBATH/BATHN BA1 ... **2** D1
St James's St
CBATH/BATHN BA1 * ... **2** E1
MANG/FISH BS16 ... **49** C3
St James St *WSM* BS23 ... **6** C4
St John's Av *CLVDN* BS21 ... **64** D2
St John's Cl *WSM* BS23 ... **6** C1
St Johns Ct *KEYN* BS31 ... **88** B3
St Johns Crs *BMSTR* BS3 ... **73** F4
St Johns Hospital
CBATH/BATHN BA1 * ... **3** F5
St John's La *BMSTR* BS3 ... **72** D3
St Johns Ms *CFTN/FAIL* BS8 * ... **55** F3
St John's Pl *CBATH/BATHN* BA1 ... **3** F4
St John's Rd *BATHSE* BA2 ... **3** G2
BMSTR BS3 ... **72** D3
CBATH/BATHN BA1 ... **101** H5
CFTN/FAIL BS8 ... **55** E2
CLVDN BS21 ... **64** D2
NAIL BS48 ... **80** A4
St John's St *BMSTR* BS3 ... **72** D3
St John's Ter *THNB/SVB* BS35 ... **8** C3
St Johns Wy *YATE/CS* BS37 ... **27** F1
St Joseph's Rd
HNBRY/STHM BS10 ... **31** F2
St Jude's Ter *MTN/WRL* BS22 ... **121** H2
St Keyna Rd *KEYN* BS31 ... **88** B4
St Kilda's Rd *BATHSE* BA2 ... **2** A7
St Ladoc Rd *KEYN* BS31 ... **88** A3
St Laud Cl
HNLZ/SM/SNYPK/WT BS9 ... **44** A3
St Lawrence Cl *AVONM* BS11 ... **29** E5
St Leonard's Rd
EVILLE/WHL BS5 ... **57** E1
HORF/LLZ BS7 ... **46** A2
St Lucia Cl *HORF/LLZ* BS7 ... **32** A5
St Lucia Crs *HORF/LLZ* BS7 ... **46** A1
St Lukes Cl *MANG/FISH* BS16 ... **49** H1
St Luke's Crs *BMSTR* BS3 ... **73** G2
St Luke's Gdns
BRSG/KWL/STAPK BS4 ... **74** D4
St Luke's Ms
BMSTR BS3 ... **73** G2
St Luke's Rd *BATHSE* BA2 ... **108** C4
BMSTR BS3 ... **73** F2
St Luke St *EVILLE/WHL* BS5 * ... **56** D4
St Margarets Cl *NAIL* BS48 ... **79** H4
St Margaret's Cl *KEYN* BS31 ... **88** A3
St Margaret's Dr
HNLZ/SM/SNYPK/WT BS9 ... **45** C3
St Margaret's La *NAIL* BS48 ... **79** H4
St Margaret's Ter *WSM* BS23 ... **6** C3
St Marks Cl *KEYN* BS31 ... **88** B3
St Marks Gdns *BATHSE* BA2 ... **3** G6
St Marks Rd *BATHSE* BA2 ... **3** G7
MTN/WRL BS22 ... **117** C5
St Mark's Rd *EVILLE/WHL* BS5 ... **56** D2
St Mark's Ter *EVILLE/WHL* BS5 * ... **56** D2
St Martins Cl
BRSG/KWL/STAPK BS4 * ... **74** A5
St Martins Ct
MTN/WRL BS22 * ... **117** F5
St Martin's Gdns
BRSG/KWL/STAPK BS4 ... **74** A4
St Martin's Rd
BRSG/KWL/STAPK BS4 ... **74** A4
St Martin's Wk
BRSG/KWL/STAPK BS4 * ... **74** A5
St Marys Blds *BATHSE* BA2 ... **2** E6
St Marys Cl *BATHSE* BA2 * ... **3** K3
OLD/WMLY/WICK BS30 ... **77** E1
St Mary's Cl *BATHSE* BA2 ... **3** K4
OMX/HUT/LCK BS24 ... **126** A4
St Mary's Ct
OMX/HUT/LCK BS24 ... **125** F5
St Mary's Gv *NAIL* BS48 ... **78** D1
St Mary's Pk *NAIL* BS48 ... **78** D1
St Mary's Rd *AVONM* BS11 ... **42** D1
CFTN/FAIL BS8 ... **54** B5
OMX/HUT/LCK BS24 ... **126** A4
PTSHD/EG BS20 ... **39** C4
St Mary St *THNB/SVB* BS35 ... **8** C2
St Mary's Wk *AVONM* BS11 ... **42** D2
St Mary's Wy *YATE/CS* BS37 ... **14** B5
St Matthew's Av
RDLND/MONT BS6 ... **55** H2
St Matthew's Cl *WSM* BS23 ... **6** D1
St Matthew's Pl *BATHSE* BA2 * ... **3** J6
St Matthew's Rd
RDLND/MONT BS6 ... **55** H2
St Matthias Pk *CBRISNE* BS2 ... **5** J2
St Michael's Av *CLVDN* BS21 ... **64** D4
MTN/WRL BS22 ... **117** H5
St Michaels Cl *HORF/LLZ* BS7 ... **45** H4
St Michael's Cl
FRCTL/WBN BS36 ... **23** E5
St Michaels Ct
KGWD/HNM BS15 ... **58** B3
St Michael's Hl *CFTN/FAIL* BS8 ... **55** C3
St Michaels Rd *BATHSE* BA2 ... **4** C1
St Michaels Rd *BATHSE* BA2 ... **107** F2
St Michael's Rd
CBATH/BATHN BA1 ... **2** A2
St Nicholas Market
CBRIS/FH BS1 * ... **5** F4

St Nicholas Pk
EVILLE/WHL BS5 * ... **56** D2
St Nicholas Rd
HGRV/WHIT BS14 ... **86** B5
WSM BS23 ... **124** C4
St Nicholas' Rd *CBRISNE* BS2 ... **56** B2
St Nicholas St *CBRIS/FH* BS1 ... **5** F4
St Oswald's Rd
RDLND/MONT BS6 ... **45** F5
St Patricks Ct *BATHSE* BA2 ... **3** K4
St Paul's Rd *BMSTR* BS3 ... **73** F3
CFTN/FAIL BS8 ... **4** A2
St Paul St *CBRISNE* BS2 ... **5** H1
St Peter's Av *WSM* BS23 ... **6** C1
St Peter's Crs
FRCTL/WBN BS36 ... **23** H3
St Peter's Rd
BMSTR/HD/HC/WWD BS13 ... **84** B2
St Peters Rd *PTSHD/EG* BS20 ... **39** H4
St Peters Ter *BATHSE* BA2 ... **2** B4
St Peter's Wk
EVILLE/WHL BS5 ... **45** F3
St Philips Cswy
BRSG/KWL/STAPK BS4 ... **74** B2
CBRISNE BS2 ... **56** D5
St Philips Rd *CBRISNE* BS2 ... **5** K3
St Phillips Rd *CBRISNE* BS2 ... **56** C5
St Pierre Dr
OLD/WMLY/WICK BS30 * ... **59** H5
St Ronan's Av
RDLND/MONT BS6 ... **55** C2
St Saviour's Rd
FRCTL/WBN BS36 ... **23** H4
St Saviour's Rd
CBATH/BATHN BA1 ... **103** F3
St Saviours Ter
CBATH/BATHN BA1 ... **103** F3
St Saviours Wy
CBATH/BATHN BA1 ... **103** F3
St Stephen's Av *CBRIS/FH* BS1 ... **4** E4
St Stephens Cl
HNBRY/STHM BS10 * ... **31** G3
MANG/FISH BS16 ... **49** E5
St Stephen's Ct
CBATH/BATHN BA1 ... **102** C4
St Stephens Cl
CBATH/BATHN BA1 ... **102** C4
St Stephens Pl
CBATH/BATHN BA1 ... **102** C4
St Stephen's Rd
CBATH/BATHN BA1 ... **102** C4
MANG/FISH BS16 ... **48** D5
St Stephen St *CBRIS/FH* BS1 ... **4** E3
St Thomas Pl *CBRIS/FH* BS1 * ... **5** C5
St Thomas St *CBRIS/FH* BS1 ... **5** C5
St Vincent's Hl
RDLND/MONT BS6 ... **55** E1
St Vincent's Rd *CFTN/FAIL* BS8 ... **55** C5
St Wy *BRSTK/PCHW* BS34 ... **34** A1
St Werburgh's Pk *CBRISNE* BS2 ... **56** C1
St Werburgh's Rd
CBRISNE BS2 ... **56** B1
St Whytes Rd
BRSG/KWL/STAPK BS4 ... **85** E1
St Winifreds Dr *BATHSE* BA2 ... **109** G5
St Wulfstans Av
HNBRY/STHM BS10 ... **31** E4
Salcombe Gdns *WSM* BS22 ... **122** D1
Salcombe Rd
BRSG/KWL/STAPK BS4 ... **85** H1
Salem Rd *FRCTL/WBN* BS36 ... **23** F3
Salisbury Av *MANG/FISH* BS16 * ... **48** D5
Salisbury Gdns
MANG/FISH BS16 ... **49** E3
Salisbury Rd
BRSG/KWL/STAPK BS4 ... **74** C1
CBATH/BATHN BA1 ... **103** E2
MANG/FISH BS16 ... **49** E2
MTN/WRL BS22 ... **121** H2
RDLND/MONT BS6 ... **56** D5
Salisbury St *EVILLE/WHL* BS5 ... **56** D5
Salisbury Ter *WSM* BS23 ... **6** D3
Sally Hl *PTSHD/EG* BS20 ... **40** A1
Sallysmead Cl
BMSTRD/HC/WWD BS13 ... **84** B3
Sallys Wy *FRCTL/WBN* BS36 ... **23** F3
Salmons Wy *MANG/FISH* BS16 ... **35** C5
Salthouse Rd *CLVDN* BS21 ... **64** B3
Salthrop Rd *HORF/LLZ* BS7 ... **46** A5
Saltings Cl *CLVDN* BS21 ... **64** B3
Saltmarsh Dr *AVONM* BS11 ... **29** C4
Saltwell Av *HGRV/WHIT* BS14 ... **86** B4
Sambourne La
PTSHD/EG BS20 ... **42** C3
Samian Wy *BRSTK/PCHW* BS34 ... **33** C5
Sampsons Rd
BMSTRD/HC/WWD BS13 ... **85** E5
Samuel St *EVILLE/WHL* BS5 ... **57** E3
Samuel White Rd
KGWD/HNM BS15 ... **75** H5
Samuel Wright Cl
OLD/WMLY/WICK BS30 ... **77** G1
Sandbach Rd
BRSG/KWL/STAPK BS4 ... **74** C2
Sandbed Rd *CBRISNE* BS2 ... **56** C1
Sandburrows Rd
BMSTRD/HC/WWD BS13 ... **83** H3
Sandburrows Wk
BMSTRD/HC/WWD BS13 ... **84** A3
Sandcroft *HGRV/WHIT* BS14 ... **85** G4
Sandcroft Av *WSM* BS23 ... **124** C4
Sanderling Pl *PTSHD/EG* BS20 ... **40** B2
Sand Farm La *MTN/WRL* BS22 ... **116** D2
Sandford Cl *CLVDN* BS21 ... **64** A3
Sandford Rd *CFTN/FAIL* BS8 ... **72** B1
WSM BS23 ... **122** B3
Sandgate Rd
BRSG/KWL/STAPK BS4 ... **74** D1
Sand Hl *BRSG/KWL/STAPK* BS4 ... **74** D1
Sandholme Cl *MANG/FISH* BS16 ... **35** E5
Sandholme Rd
MANG/FISH BS16 ... **49** C3
Sandhurst *YATE/CS* BS37 ... **25** H2
Sandhurst Cl
BRSTK/PCHW BS34 ... **20** D1

Sandhurst Rd
BRSG/KWL/STAPK BS4 ... **74** B3
Sandling Av *HORF/LLZ* BS7 ... **46** C1
Sandown Cl *MANG/FISH* BS16 ... **35** F4
Sandown Rd
BRSG/KWL/STAPK BS4 ... **74** C2
BRSTK/PCHW BS34 ... **33** E2
Sandpiper Dr *MTN/WRL* BS22 ... **122** C2
Sandringham Av
MANG/FISH BS16 ... **35** G5
Sandringham Pk
MANG/FISH BS16 ... **35** G5
Sandringham Rd
BRSG/KWL/STAPK BS4 ... **74** C3
BRSTK/PCHW BS34 ... **33** F1
WSM BS23 ... **125** E1
Sand Rd *MTN/WRL* BS22 ... **116** C3
Sandstone Ri *FRCTL/WBN* BS36 ... **34** C5
Sandwich Rd
BRSG/KWL/STAPK BS4 ... **74** C2
Sandy Cl *ALMDB* BS32 ... **21** C4
Sandy La *CFTN/FAIL* BS8 ... **52** A3
EVILLE/WHL BS5 ... **47** E5
Sandyleaze
HNLZ/SM/SNYPK/WT BS9 ... **44** C1
Sandy Ldg *YATE/CS* BS37 ... **26** A2
Sandy Park Rd
BRSG/KWL/STAPK BS4 ... **74** B2
Sarah St *CBATH/BATHN* BA1 * ... **3** J3
Sarah St *EVILLE/WHL* BS5 ... **56** D4
Sargent St *BMSTR* BS3 ... **73** F2
Sarum Cl *MANG/FISH* BS16 ... **50** A2
Sarum Crs *HNBRY/STHM* BS10 ... **31** G4
Sassoon Ct
OLD/WMLY/WICK BS30 ... **76** C1
Satchfield Cl
HNBRY/STHM BS10 ... **30** D3
Satchfield Crs
HNBRY/STHM BS10 ... **30** D3
Sates Wy
HNLZ/SM/SNYPK/WT BS9 ... **45** C2
Saunders Rd *MANG/FISH* BS16 ... **49** E4
Saunton Wk
BRSG/KWL/STAPK BS4 ... **85** F1
Savages Wood Rd
ALMDB BS32 ... **21** F2
Savernake Rd *MTN/WRL* BS22 ... **117** C5
Saville Crs *MTN/WRL* BS22 ... **121** H3
Saville Gate Cl
HNLZ/SM/SNYPK/WT BS9 ... **44** D4
Saville Ms *RDLND/MONT* BS6 * ... **55** E5
Saville Pl *CFTN/FAIL* BS8 ... **55** E5
Saville Rd
HNLZ/SM/SNYPK/WT BS9 ... **44** D4
MTN/WRL BS22 ... **121** H3
Saville Rw *CBATH/BATHN* BA1 ... **3** F2
Savoy Rd
BRSG/KWL/STAPK BS4 ... **74** C2
Saw Cl *CBATH/BATHN* BA1 ... **3** F4
Saw Mill La *THNB/SVB* BS35 ... **9** E4
Sawyers Cl *NAIL* BS48 ... **67** H4
Sawyers Ct *CLVDN* BS21 ... **65** E2
Saxby Cl *CLVDN* BS21 ... **64** B4
MTN/WRL BS22 ... **118** A4
Saxon Cl *MTN/WRL* BS22 ... **121** H3
Saxon Rd *CBRISNE* BS2 ... **56** C1
MTN/WRL BS22 ... **121** H3
Saxon Wy *ALMDB* BS32 ... **21** E1
Say Wk
OLD/WMLY/WICK BS30 ... **60** B4
Scafell Cl *WSM* BS23 ... **7** K1
Scandrett Cl
HNBRY/STHM BS10 ... **30** C2
Scantleberry Cl
MANG/FISH BS16 ... **34** D5
The Scaurs *MTN/WRL* BS22 ... **122** C1
School Cl *BRSTK/PCHW* BS34 ... **21** E2
EVILLE/WHL BS5 ... **57** F1
HGRV/WHIT BS14 ... **85** G5
School Ct *BRSTK/PCHW* BS34 ... **34** A1
School La *CBATH/BATHN* BA1 ... **118** A1
NAIL BS48 ... **82** A4
School Rd
BRSG/KWL/STAPK BS4 ... **73** H5
FRCTL/WBN BS36 ... **23** F2
KGWD/HNM BS15 ... **58** C3
OLD/WMLY/WICK BS30 ... **76** D2
School Vw *NAIL* BS48 ... **68** A5
School Wk *EVILLE/WHL* BS5 * ... **57** F2
Scaurs *MTN/WRL* BS22 ... **14** A5
The Scop *ALMDB* BS32 ... **10** D1
Scotch Horn Cl *NAIL* BS48 ... **67** G4
Scotch Horn Wy *NAIL* BS48 ... **67** G4
Scot Elm Dr
OMX/HUT/LCK BS24 ... **123** F2
Scotland La *HGRV/WHIT* BS14 ... **87** H3
Scots Pine Av *NAIL* BS48 ... **67** G4
Scott Ct *OLD/WMLY/WICK* BS30 ... **76** C1
Scott Lawrence Cl
MANG/FISH BS16 ... **48** A1
Scott Rd *WSM* BS23 ... **125** F2
Scott Wk
OLD/WMLY/WICK BS30 ... **60** B4
Scott Wy *YATE/CS* BS37 ... **26** B2
Seabrook Rd *MTN/WRL* BS22 ... **122** A2
Seagry Cl *HNBRY/STHM* BS10 ... **32** A4
Sea Mills La
HNLZ/SM/SNYPK/WT BS9 ... **44** A4
Searle Court Av
BRSG/KWL/STAPK BS4 ... **74** D1
Searle Crs *WSM* BS23 ... **7** K7
Seaton Rd *EVILLE/WHL* BS5 ... **57** E2
Seavale Rd *CLVDN* BS21 ... **64** C1
Seaview Rd *PTSHD/EG* BS20 ... **38** C1
Seawalls Rd
HNLZ/SM/SNYPK/WT BS9 ... **54** B1
Second Av *BATHSE* BA2 ... **108** A5
Second Wy *AVONM* BS11 ... **28** D4
Seddon Rd *CBRISNE* BS2 ... **56** C1
Sedgefield Gdns
MANG/FISH BS16 ... **35** F4
Sedgemoor Cl *NAIL* BS48 ... **79** F1
Sedgemoor Rd *BATHSE* BA2 ... **110** D1
WSM BS23 ... **124** C3
Sedgemoor Ter *BATHSE* BA2 * ... **108** D5
Sefton Park Rd *BRSTK/PCHW* BS7 ... **46** B5
Sefton Sq
OMX/HUT/LCK BS24 ... **123** D3
Selborne Rd *HORF/LLZ* BS7 ... **46** B3

Selbourne Cl *BATHSE* BA1 ... **101** F4
Selbourne Rd *WSM* BS23 ... **124** D2
Selbrooke Crs
MANG/FISH BS16 ... **48** C2
Selby Rd *EVILLE/WHL* BS5 ... **57** H2
Selden Rd *HGRV/WHIT* BS14 ... **86** D4
Sekirk Rd *KGWD/HNM* BS15 ... **58** C1
Selley Wk
BMSTRD/HC/WWD BS13 ... **84** B4
Selwood Cl *MTN/WRL* BS22 ... **121** H4
Selworthy *KGWD/HNM* BS15 ... **59** E4
Selworthy Cl *KEYN* BS31 ... **88** A4
Selworthy Rd
BRSG/KWL/STAPK BS4 ... **74** A4
WSM BS23 ... **125** E2
Selworthy Ter *BATHSE* BA2 * ... **108** D5
Seneca Pl *EVILLE/WHL* BS5 ... **57** F4
Seneca St *EVILLE/WHL* BS5 ... **57** F4
Serbert Cl *PTSHD/EG* BS20 ... **40** A3
Serbert Rd *PTSHD/EG* BS20 ... **40** A3
Serbert Wy *PTSHD/EG* BS20 ... **40** A3
Serlo Ct *MTN/WRL* BS22 ... **117** G4
Seven Acres La *CBATH/BATHN* BA1 ... **91** E4
The Seven Acres
OMX/HUT/LCK BS24 ... **122** C4
Seven Dials *CBATH/BATHN* BA1 * ... **3** F4
Seventh Av *HORF/LLZ* BS7 ... **32** D4
Seven View Rd *THNB/SVB* BS35 ... **8** C2
Severn Av *WSM* BS23 ... **124** D1
Severn Dr *THNB/SVB* BS35 ... **8** C2
Severnmeade *PTSHD/EG* BS20 ... **38** C4
Severn Rd *AVONM* BS11 ... **42** D2
HNBRY/STHM BS10 ... **17** C3
PTSHD/EG BS20 ... **42** C3
PTSHD/EG BS20 ... **39** C3
THNB/SVB BS35 ... **8** C3
Severn Wy *BRSTK/PCHW* BS34 ... **20** B1
KEYN BS31 ... **88** C5
Sevier St *CBRISNE* BS2 ... **56** C1
Seville Ct *PTSHD/EG* BS20 ... **40** A1
Seville Rd *PTSHD/EG* BS20 ... **40** A1
Seymour Av *HORF/LLZ* BS7 ... **46** A1
Seymour Cl *CLVDN* BS21 ... **65** E2
MTN/WRL BS22 ... **117** G4
Seymour Rd
CBATH/BATHN BA1 ... **102** D4
EVILLE/WHL BS5 ... **56** C2
KGWD/HNM BS15 ... **58** C2
Seyton Wk *BRSTK/PCHW* BS34 ... **21** G5
Shackel Hendy Ms
MANG/FISH BS16 ... **49** H3
Shackleton Av *YATE/CS* BS37 ... **26** B1
Shadow Wk
OMX/HUT/LCK BS24 ... **127** F3
Shadwell Rd *HORF/LLZ* BS7 ... **45** H5
Shaftesbury Av
CBATH/BATHN BA1 ... **101** H5
RDLND/MONT BS6 ... **56** A2
Shaftesbury Cl *NAIL* BS48 ... **79** E1
Shaftesbury Rd *BATHSE* BA2 ... **2** B7
WSM BS23 ... **121** G3
Shaft Rd *BATHSE* BA2 ... **111** H2
Shakespeare Av *BATHSE* BA2 ... **108** C5
HORF/LLZ BS7 ... **32** C5
Shaldon Rd *HORF/LLZ* BS7 ... **46** C4
The Shallows *KEYN* BS31 ... **99** G1
Sham Castle La *BATHSE* BA2 ... **3** K5
Shanklin Dr *BRSTK/PCHW* BS34 ... **32** D2
Shannon Ct *CBRIS/FH* BS1 * ... **5** F4
THNB/SVB BS35 ... **9** E4
Shapcott Cl
BRSG/KWL/STAPK BS4 ... **74** A5
Shaplands
HNLZ/SM/SNYPK/WT BS9 ... **44** D4
Sharland Gv
BMSTRD/HC/WWD BS13 ... **95** H1
Shaw Gdns *HGRV/WHIT* BS14 ... **85** H1
Shaws Wy *BATHSE* BA2 ... **107** G2
Shearmore Cl *HORF/LLZ* BS7 ... **46** C1
Sheene La *BMSTR* BS3 ... **72** D3
Sheene Rd *BMSTR* BS3 ... **72** D3
Sheene Wy *BMSTR* BS3 ... **72** D3
Sheeps Cft
BMSTRD/HC/WWD BS13 ... **84** B5
Sheepway *PTSHD/EG* BS20 ... **40** C4
Sheepwood Cl
HNBRY/STHM BS10 ... **31** E4
Sheepwood Rd
HNBRY/STHM BS10 ... **31** E3
Sheldare Barton
EVILLE/WHL BS5 ... **58** B4
Sheldon Cl *CLVDN* BS21 ... **65** F3
Sheldrake Dr *MANG/FISH* BS16 ... **47** H2
Sheliard Rd
BRSTK/PCHW BS34 ... **32** C2
Sheliards Rd
OLD/WMLY/WICK BS30 ... **76** C3
Shelley Av *CLVDN* BS21 ... **64** D3
Shelley Cl *EVILLE/WHL* BS5 ... **57** H3
Shelley Rd *BATHSE* BA2 ... **108** C5
WSM BS23 ... **125** F2
Shelley Wy *HORF/LLZ* BS7 ... **32** C5
Shellmoor Av
BRSTK/PCHW BS34 ... **20** D1
Shellmoor Cl *BRSTK/PCHW* BS34 ... **21** E1
Shepherds Cl *MANG/FISH* BS16 ... **35** G4
Shepherds Wk *ALMDB* BS32 ... **21** F1
Sheppard Rd *MANG/FISH* BS16 ... **48** C2
Sheppy's Mi *YTN/CONG* BS49 ... **114** D1
Shepton Wk *BMSTR* BS3 ... **72** D4
Sherbourne Av *ALMDB* BS32 ... **21** G3
Sherbourne Cl
KGWD/HNM BS15 ... **59** F1
Sherbourne St
EVILLE/WHL BS5 ... **57** G3
Sheridan Rd *BATHSE* BA2 ... **107** G2
HORF/LLZ BS7 ... **32** C4
Sheridan Wy
OLD/WMLY/WICK BS30 ... **76** D4
Sherperds Wy *MTN/WRL* BS22 ... **123** F1
Sherrin Wy
BMSTRD/HC/WWD BS13 ... **94** D1
Sherston Cl *MANG/FISH* BS16 ... **48** B3
NAIL BS48 ... **67** H5
Sherston Rd *HORF/LLZ* BS7 ... **32** A5

Sherwell Rd
BRSG/KWL/STAPK BS4 ....74 D3
Sherwood Cl *KEYN* BS31.........88 B4
Sherwood Crs
MTN/WRL BS22 ....117 G5
Sherwood Rd *KEYN* BS31.........88 B4
KGWD/HNM BS15 ....58 A2
Shetland Rd
HNBRY/STHM BS10 ....31 H4
Shetland Wy *NAIL* BS48 ....67 H5
Shickle Gv *BATHSE* BA2 ....110 A1
Shields Av *HORF/LLZ* BS7 ....32 C5
Shiels Dr *ALMDB* BS32 ....21 F3
Shilton Cl *KGWD/HNM* BS15 ....59 F4
Shimsey Cl *MANG/FISH* BS16 ....48 C2
Shiners Elms *YTN/CONG* BS49 ....112 A3
Shipham Cl *HGRV/WHIT* BS14 ....86 A4
NAIL BS48 ....79 C1
Ship La *CBRIS/FH* BS1 ....5 G7
Shipley Mow *MANG/FISH* BS16 ..49 H2
Shipley Rd
HNLZ/SM/SNYPK/WT BS9 ....31 E5
Shipman Ct *MANG/FISH* BS16 ....49 E4
Shire Gdns *AVONM* BS11 ....28 D5
Shirehampton Rd
AVONM BS11 ....43 F1
HNLZ/SM/SNYPK/WT BS9 ....44 A2
Shires Yd *CBATH/BATHN* BA1 .....3 F5
Shire Wy *YATE/CS* BS37 ....25 C4
Shockerwick La
CBATH/BATHN BA1 ....91 G5
Shophouse Rd *BATHSE* BA2 .....107 C2
Shorthill Rd *YATE/CS* BS37 ....37 G1
Shortlands Rd *AVONM* BS11 .....28 C4
Short La *LGASH* BS41 ....70 C4
Short St *CBRISNE* BS2 ....73 H1
Short Wy *CFTN/FAIL* BS8 ....69 G3
THNB/SVB BS35 ....8 C5
Shortwood Hl
MANG/FISH BS16 ....50 B3
Shortwood Rd
BMSTRD/HC/WWD BS13 ......96 B1
MANG/FISH BS16 ....51 E4
Shortwood Vw
KGWD/HNM BS15 ....59 F3
Shortwood Wk
BMSTRD/HC/WWD BS13 ......96 B1
Showering Cl *HGRV/WHIT* BS14 ..86 C4
Showering Rd
HGRV/WHIT BS14 ....86 C4
Shrewsbury Bow
OMX/HUT/LCK BS24 ....122 D3
Shrubbery Av *WSM* BS23 ....120 B2
Shrubbery Cots
RDLND/MONT BS6 ....55 F1
Shrubbery Rd
MANG/FISH BS16 ....48 D3
WSM BS23 ....6 B1
Shrubbery Ter *WSM* BS23 ....6 B1
WSM BS23 ....6 B1
Shrubbery Wk West
WSM BS23 * 6 C1
Shuter Rd
BMSTRD/HC/WWD BS13 ......83 H4
Sibland *THNB/SVB* BS35 ....9 E4
Sibland Cl *THNB/SVB* BS35 ....9 E4
Sibland Rd *THNB/SVB* BS35 ....9 E4
Sibland Wy *THNB/SVB* BS35 ....9 E4
Sidcot *BRSG/KWL/STAPK* BS4 .....75 F4
Sidcot La *HNLZ/SM/SNYPK/WT* BS9 ..86 D5
Sidelands Rd *MANG/FISH* BS16 ...48 C2
The Sidings *BRSTK/PCHW* BS34 ..33 E3
Sidmouth Gdns *BMSTR* BS3 ....73 E4
Sidmouth Rd *BMSTR* BS3 ....73 E4
Signal Rd *MANG/FISH* BS16 ....49 H4
Silbury Ri *KEYN* BS31 ....98 B2
Silbury Rd *BMSTR* BS3 ....71 H4
Silcox Rd
BMSTRD/HC/WWD BS13 ......84 D5
Silklands Gv
HNLZ/SM/SNYPK/WT BS9 * ...44 A2
Silverberry Rd
MTN/WRL BS22 ....122 D2
Silver Birch Cl
BRSTK/PCHW BS34 ....21 F3
Silvercourt Nail *NAIL* BS48 * 66 D4
Silverhill Rd
HNBRY/STHM BS10 ....30 C2
Silverlow Rd *NAIL* BS48 ....67 E4
Silver Mt *YTN/CONG* BS49 ....114 D4
Silverstone Wy
YTN/CONG BS49 ....114 D3
Silver St *CBRIS/FH* BS1 ....5 F2
NAIL BS48 ....67 E4
YTN/CONG BS49 ....114 D4
Silverthorne La *CBRISNE* BS2 ....56 C5
Silverton Ct
BRSG/KWL/STAPK BS4 * 73 G5
Simmonds Vw
BRSTK/PCHW BS34 ....21 H5
Simons Cl *MTN/WRL* BS22 ....122 D1
Singapore Rd *WSM* BS23 ....124 D3
Sion Hl *CBATH/BATHN* BA1 ......102 A3
CFTN/FAIL BS8 ....54 D4
Sion La *CBATH/BATHN* BA1 ......102 B3
Sion Pl *BATHSE* BA2 ....3 K4
CFTN/FAIL BS8 ....54 D4
Sion Rd
CBATH/BATHN BA1 ....102 B3
The Sion *NAIL* BS48 ....67 F4
Sir John's La *EVILLE/WHL* BS5 ....46 D4
Sir Johns Wd *NAIL* BS48 * 67 E3
Siskin Cl *PTSHD/EG* BS20 ....40 B2
Siston Cl *KGWD/HNM* BS15 ....59 H2
Siston Common
OLD/WMLY/WICK BS30 ....59 H2
Siston La
OLD/WMLY/WICK BS30 ....60 C2
Siston Pk *KGWD/HNM* BS15 ....59 G1
Sixth Av *HORF/LLZ* BS7 ....32 D5
Sixty Acres Cl *CFTN/FAIL* BS8 ....69 G3
Skippon Ct *KGWD/HNM* BS15 ....76 B1
Skylark Av *CLVDN* BS21 ....63 F1
Sladebrook Av *BATHSE* BA2 ....107 H4
Sladebrook Rd *BATHSE* BA2 ....107 H5
Slade La *NAIL* BS48 ....81 G5
Slade Rd *PTSHD/EG* BS20 ....39 H3

Slades Ct *NAIL* BS48 ....79 H3
Sleep La *HGRV/WHIT* BS14 ....97 G1
Slimbridge Cl *YATE/CS* BS37 ....26 D3
Sloan St *EVILLE/WHL* BS5 ....57 F3
Sloe Cl *MTN/WRL* BS22 ....122 A4
Slymbridge Av
HNBRY/STHM BS10 ....31 E1
Small La *MANG/FISH* BS16 ....47 G3
Small St *CBRIS/FH* BS1 ....4 E3
CBRISNE BS2 ....73 H1
Smallway *YTN/CONG* BS49 ....114 D1
Smarts Gn *YATE/CS* BS37 ....27 E2
Smeaton Rd *CBRIS/FH* BS1 ....72 A1
Smithcourt Dr
BRSTK/PCHW BS34 ....21 E4
Smithmead
BMSTRD/HC/WWD BS13 .....84 A1
Smoke La *AVONM* BS11 ....16 C4
Smythe Cft *HGRV/WHIT* BS14 ....96 D1
Smyth Rd *BMSTR* BS3 ....72 A3
Smyths Cl *AVONM* BS11 ....28 B4
Sneyd Park Ms
HNLZ/SM/SNYPK/WT BS9 * ...44 B5
Snowberry Cl *ALMDB* BS32 ......21 G2
MTN/WRL BS22 ....122 D2
Snowberry Wk
EVILLE/WHL BS5 ....57 G3
Snowdon Cl *MANG/FISH* BS16 ...47 H4
Snowdon Rd *MANG/FISH* BS16 ..47 H3
Snowdon V *WSM* BS23 ....7 J1
Snowdrop Cl *MTN/WRL* BS22 ...117 H5
Snow Hl *CBATH/BATHN* BA1 ......3 K1
Solent Wy *THNB/SVB* BS35 ....9 E5
Solsbury La *CBATH/BATHN* BA1 ..90 D5
Solsbury Wy
CBATH/BATHN BA1 ....102 D2
Somerby Cl *ALMDB* BS32 ....21 F3
Somerdale Av *BATHSE* BA2 ....108 A5
BRSG/KWL/STAPK BS4 ....73 H5
MTN/WRL BS22 ....121 H3
Somerdale Cl *MTN/WRL* BS22 ..121 H5
Somerdale Rd *KEYN* BS31 ....88 C2
Somerdale Rd North
KEYN BS31 ....88 C2
Somerdale Vw *BATHSE* BA2 ....107 H5
Somermead *BMSTR* BS3 ....72 D5
Somerset Av
OMX/HUT/LCK BS24 ....122 C4
YATE/CS BS37 ....14 B4
Somerset Crs
BRSTK/PCHW BS34 ....21 H5
Somerset La
CBATH/BATHN BA1 ....102 B3
Somerset Pl
CBATH/BATHN BA1 ....102 B3
Somerset Rd
BRSG/KWL/STAPK BS4 ....73 H3
CLVDN BS21 ....65 E2
PTSHD/EG BS20 ....38 D3
Somerset Sq *CBRIS/FH* BS1 ......5 G7
Somerset St *CBATH/BATHN* BA1 ..3 F6
CBRIS/FH BS1 ....5 G7
Somerset Ter *BMSTR* BS3 ....73 F5
Somerton Cl *KGWD/HNM* BS15 ..59 E4
Somerton Rd *CLVDN* BS21 ....65 E4
HORF/LLZ BS7 ....46 A2
Somerville Cl *KEYN* BS31 ....99 F2
Somerville Rd *HORF/LLZ* BS7 ....46 A2
Somerville Rd South
RDLND/MONT BS6 ....56 B1
Soper Gdns
BRSG/KWL/STAPK BS4 ....84 D1
Sophia Gdns *MTN/WRL* BS22 ...118 A4
Sorrel Cl *THNB/SVB* BS35 ....9 E2
Soundwell Rd
KGWD/HNM BS15 ....58 C2
Southampton Gdns
HORF/LLZ BS7 * 46 B3
Southampton Ms
HORF/LLZ BS7 * 46 B3
South Av *BATHSE* BA2 ....2 A6
PTSHD/EG BS20 ....39 H2
YATE/CS BS37 ....25 F1
Southbourne Gdns
CBATH/BATHN BA1 ....103 E3
Southcot Pl *BATHSE* BA2 ....3 H7
South Crs *WSM* BS23 ....6 C2
South Cft
HNLZ/SM/SNYPK/WT BS9 ....45 C1
South Dene
HNLZ/SM/SNYPK/WT BS9 ....44 C2
Southdown Rd *MTN/WRL* BS22 ..117 G4
Southdown Av *BATHSE* BA2 ....107 G4
Southdown Rd *BATHSE* BA2 ....107 G3
HNLZ/SM/SNYPK/WT BS9 ....30 D5
Southend Rd *WSM* BS23 ....124 D2
Southernhay *CFTN/FAIL* BS8.....4 A5
MANG/FISH BS16 ....48 C4
Southernhay Av *CFTN/FAIL* BS8 ...4 A5
Southernhay Crs *CFTN/FAIL* BS8 ..4 A5
Southern Wy *CLVDN* BS21 ....64 B3
Southey Av *KGWD/HNM* BS15 ....58 D2
Southey Rd *CLVDN* BS21 ....64 D5
Southey St *CBRISNE* BS2 ....56 B2
Southfield Av
KGWD/HNM BS15 ....59 E2
Southfield Cl *WSM* BS23 ....120 D3
Southfield Ct
HNLZ/SM/SNYPK/WT BS9 ....45 E1
Southfield Rd
HNLZ/SM/SNYPK/WT BS9 ....45 E1
NAIL BS48 ....67 H3
RDLND/MONT BS6 ....55 H2
Southgate *CBATH/BATHN* BA1 ....3 G5
South Green St *CFTN/FAIL* BS8 ..54 D5
South Gv *PTSHD/EG* BS20 ....42 C4
RDLND/MONT BS6 ....45 G3
South Hayes *EVILLE/WHL* BS5 ....46 D4
Southlands
CBATH/BATHN BA1 ....101 F4
Southlands Wy
YTN/CONG BS49 ....114 D1
South Lawn
OMX/HUT/LCK BS24 ....126 C2
South Lawn Cl
OMX/HUT/LCK BS24 ....126 C2
South Lea Rd
CBATH/BATHN BA1 ....101 F4

Southleigh Rd *CFTN/FAIL* BS8 .....4 A1
South Liberty La *BMSTR* BS3 .....72 B5
Southmead Rd
HNBRY/STHM BS10 ....31 G5
HNLZ/SM/SNYPK/WT BS9 ....45 F1
MTN/WRL BS22 ....121 G4
Southmead Wy
HNBRY/STHM BS10 ....31 H5
Southover Cl
HNLZ/SM/SNYPK/WT BS9 ....31 E5
South Pde *BATHSE* BA2 ....3 H5
WSM BS23 ....6 D3
South Rd *ALMDB* BS32 ....11 F1
BMSTR BS3 ....72 D3
KGWD/HNM BS15 ....58 D3
PTSHD/EG BS20 ....39 H2
RDLND/MONT BS6 ....55 G1
WSM BS23 ....120 B2
Southsea Rd
BRSTK/PCHW BS34 ....20 C3
Southside *WSM* BS23 ....6 E2
South Side *YTN/CONG* BS49 ....115 E1
Southside Cl
HNLZ/SM/SNYPK/WT BS9 ....43 H1
Southside Crs *MTN/WRL* BS22 ..116 B4
Southstoke La *BATHSE* BA2 ....110 D3
Southstoke Rd *BATHSE* BA2 ....110 D1
South St *BMSTR* BS3 ....72 C3
South Ter *RDLND/MONT* BS6 .....55 H1
South Vw *FRCTL/WBN* BS36 ....23 H5
MANG/FISH BS16 ....49 E3
PTSHD/EG BS20 ....39 H1
Southview Cl
OMX/HUT/LCK BS24 ....126 B4
South View Crs
FRCTL/WBN BS36 ....24 B4
South View Rd
FRCTL/WBN BS36 ....24 B4
South View Ter
YTN/CONG BS49 ....112 B2
Southville Pl *BMSTR* BS3 ....73 E2
Southville Rd *BMSTR* BS3 ....72 D2
WSM BS23 ....124 D3
Southville Ter *BATHSE* BA2 ....108 D3
Southway Dr
OLD/WMLY/WICK BS30 ....77 C1
Southwell St *CBRISNE* BS2 ....4 D1
Southwood Av
HNLZ/SM/SNYPK/WT BS9 ....30 A5
Southwood Dr
HNLZ/SM/SNYPK/WT BS9 ....29 H5
Southwood Dr East
HNLZ/SM/SNYPK/WT BS9 ....30 A5
Spa La *CBATH/BATHN* BA1 ....103 F2
Spalding Cl *HORF/LLZ* BS7 ....46 C5
Spar Rd *AVONM* BS11 ....28 C1
YATE/CS BS37 ....13 H5
Spartley Dr
BMSTRD/HC/WWD BS13 .....84 A3
Spartley Wk
BMSTRD/HC/WWD BS13 .....84 A3
Speedwell Av *EVILLE/WHL* BS5 ..57 E2
Speedwell Cl *THNB/SVB* BS35 ....9 E2
Speedwell Rd *EVILLE/WHL* BS5 ..57 F2
Spencer Dr *MTN/WRL* BS22 ....118 A4
Spencers Belle Vue
CBATH/BATHN BA1 ....2 E1
Spey Cl *THNB/SVB* BS35 ....9 E2
Spindleberry Gv *NAIL* BS48 ....67 H4
Spinners End *MTN/WRL* BS22 ...118 A4
Spinney Rd
OMX/HUT/LCK BS24 ....127 G2
The Spinney *ALMDB* BS32 ....21 G3
FRCTL/WBN BS36 ....23 H1
OMX/HUT/LCK BS24 ....127 G2
PTSHD/EG BS20 ....39 G5
Spires Vw *MANG/FISH* BS16 * 47 G3
Springfield *THNB/SVB* BS35 ....9 E4
Springfield Av *AVONM* BS11 ....42 D3
HORF/LLZ BS7 ....46 B3
MANG/FISH BS16 ....49 E3
WSM BS23 ....122 A2
Springfield Cl *BATHSE* BA2 ......107 G2
MANG/FISH BS16 ....49 G1
Springfield Gv
RDLND/MONT BS6 ....45 F3
Springfield Pl
CBATH/BATHN BA1 ....102 C3
Springfield Rd
MANG/FISH BS16 ....49 G1
PTSHD/EG BS20 ....39 F2
RDLND/MONT BS6 ....55 H1
Springfields
BRSTK/PCHW BS34 ....32 C3
Spring Gdns
BRSG/KWL/STAPK BS4 ....73 H5
Spring Gardens Rd
CBATH/BATHN BA1 ....3 G3
Spring Hl *KGWD/HNM* BS15 ....59 E1
MTN/WRL BS22 ....121 H1
RDLND/MONT BS6 ....55 H3
Spring La *CBATH/BATHN* BA1 ..103 E2
LGASH BS41 ....33 F5
Springleaze
MANG/FISH BS16 ....49 G1
RDLND/MONT BS6 ....55 G3
Springly Ct *KGWD/HNM* BS15 * ..59 G3
Spring Ri *PTSHD/EG* BS20 ....39 G4
Spring St *BMSTR* BS3 ....73 F2
Spring Street Pl *BMSTR* BS3 .....73 F2
Spring Ter *MTN/WRL* BS22 ......121 H1
Spring V *CBATH/BATHN* BA1 .....90 D5
Spring Valley *MTN/WRL* BS22 ...121 H1
Springville Cl
OLD/WMLY/WICK BS30 ....76 D3
Springwood Dr
HNBRY/STHM BS10 ....30 B2
Spring Wood Gdns
OMX/HUT/LCK BS24 ....127 G2
Spruce Wy
BRSTK/PCHW BS34 ....20 A3
MTN/WRL BS22 ....122 B3
The Square *BATHSE* BA2 ....2 E6
BRSG/KWL/STAPK BS4 ....73 H5
CBRIS/FH BS1 ....5 J5
MANG/FISH BS16 * 49 E4

Stavordale Gv
HGRV/WHIT BS14 ....86 A3
Staynes Crs *KGWD/HNM* BS15 ...59 E3
Steanbridge Rd *ALMDB* BS32 ....21 F4
Steel Cl *OLD/WMLY/WICK* BS30 ..76 C3
Steel Mills *KEYN* BS31 ....88 C5
Stella Gv *BMSTR* BS3 ....72 B4
Stephens Dr
OLD/WMLY/WICK BS30 ....76 C1
Stephen St *EVILLE/WHL* BS5 .....57 E1
Stepney Rd *EVILLE/WHL* BS5 .....57 E2
Stepney Wk *EVILLE/WHL* BS5 ....57 E2
The Stepping Stones
BRSG/KWL/STAPK BS4 * 75 C5
Sterncourt Rd
MANG/FISH BS16 ....48 A1
Stevens Crs *BMSTR* BS3 ....73 G2
Stevens Wk *ALMDB* BS32 ....21 F2
Steway La *CBATH/BATHN* BA1 ...91 H1
Stibbs Ct
OLD/WMLY/WICK BS30 ....76 C2
Stibbs Hl *EVILLE/WHL* BS5 ....58 A1
Stickland *CLVDN* BS21 ....64 C4
Stile Acres *AVONM* BS11 ....28 C4
Stillhouse La *BMSTR* BS3 ....73 E2
Stillingfleet Rd
BMSTRD/HC/WWD BS13 .....84 D4
Stillman Cl
BMSTRD/HC/WWD BS13 .....83 H5
Stinchcombe *YATE/CS* BS37 ....26 A1
Stirchel Cl *YATE/CS* BS37 ....13 H3
Stirling Rd
BRSG/KWL/STAPK BS4 ....74 B2
Stirling Wy *KEYN* BS31 ....88 B5
Stirtingale Av *BATHSE* BA2 ......107 H4
Stirtingale Rd *BATHSE* BA2 ......107 H4
Stock La *YTN/CONG* BS49 ....115 F5
Stockton Cl *HGRV/WHIT* BS14 ....85 C5
OLD/WMLY/WICK BS30 ....77 E3
Stock Wy North *NAIL* BS48 ....67 F4
Stock Wy South *NAIL* BS48 ....67 F4
Stockwell Av *MANG/FISH* BS16 ..50 B2
Stockwell Cl *MANG/FISH* BS16 ...49 F1
Stockwell Dr *MANG/FISH* BS16 ..49 G2
Stockwood Crs
BRSG/KWL/STAPK BS4 ....74 B4
Stockwood Hl *KEYN* BS31 ....87 H2
Stockwood La
HGRV/WHIT BS14 ....86 D4
Stockwood Ms
BRSG/KWL/STAPK BS4 ....75 E1
Stockwood Rd
BRSG/KWL/STAPK BS4 ....75 E5
HGRV/WHIT BS14 ....87 H1
Stodelegh Cl *MTN/WRL* BS22 ...118 A5
Stoke Bridge Av
BRSTK/PCHW BS34 ....21 F4
Stokefield Cl *THNB/SVB* BS35 .....8 C5
Stoke Gv
HNLZ/SM/SNYPK/WT BS9 ....44 C2
Stoke Hamlet
HNLZ/SM/SNYPK/WT BS9 ....44 D2
Stoke Hl
HNLZ/SM/SNYPK/WT BS9 ....44 C4
Stoke La *BRSTK/PCHW* BS34 ....21 E2
HNLZ/SM/SNYPK/WT BS9 ....44 C4
MANG/FISH BS16 ....33 G5
Stokeleigh Wk
HNLZ/SM/SNYPK/WT BS9 ....44 A3
Stokemead *BRSTK/PCHW* BS34 ..21 E2
Stoke Mdw *ALMDB* BS32 ....21 F1
Stoke Paddock Rd
HNLZ/SM/SNYPK/WT BS9 ....44 B2
Stoke Park Rd
HNLZ/SM/SNYPK/WT BS9 ....44 C4
Stoke Park Rd South
HNLZ/SM/SNYPK/WT BS9 ....44 C5
Stoke Rd
HNLZ/SM/SNYPK/WT BS9 ....44 C4
PTSHD/EG BS20 ....39 H3
Stokes Ct
OLD/WMLY/WICK BS30 ....76 D2
Stokes Cft *CBRIS/FH* BS1 ....56 A3
Stoke View Rd
MANG/FISH BS16 ....47 H5
Stoneberry Rd
HGRV/WHIT BS14 ....96 D1
Stonebridge *CLVDN* BS21 ....64 D4
Stonebridge Pk
EVILLE/WHL BS5 ....57 F1
Stonebridge Rd *WSM* BS23 ....125 E2
Stonechat Gdns
MANG/FISH BS16 ....47 G2
Stonechat Gn *PTSHD/EG* BS20 ..39 G4
Stone Cl *FRCTL/WBN* BS36 ....35 E1
Stonehenge La *FRCTL/WBN* BS36 ..23 F2
Stonehill *KGWD/HNM* BS15 ....76 B2
Stonehouse Cl *BATHSE* BA2 ....111 F1
Stonehouse La *BATHSE* BA2 ....109 E5
Stone La *FRCTL/WBN* BS36 ....35 E1
Stoneleigh Crs
BRSG/KWL/STAPK BS4 ....73 H4
Stoneleigh Dr
OLD/WMLY/WICK BS30 ....76 C1
Stoneleigh Rd
BRSG/KWL/STAPK BS4 ....73 H4
Stoneleigh Wk
BRSG/KWL/STAPK BS4 ....73 H4
Stonewell Cv *YTN/CONG* BS49 ..114 D3
Stonewell Dr *YTN/CONG* BS49 ..114 D3
Stonewell Park Rd
YTN/CONG BS49 ....114 D3
Stoneyfield Cl *PTSHD/EG* BS20 ..42 B4
Stoneyfields *PTSHD/EG* BS20 ....42 B4
Stoney Steep *NAIL* BS48 ....67 H1
PTSHD/EG BS20 ....39 G2
Stores Rd *AVONM* BS11 ....28 C1
Stormont Cl *WSM* BS23 ....125 E3
Stothard Rd
OMX/HUT/LCK BS24 ....122 B4
Stothard Rd *HORF/LLZ* BS7 ....46 D1
Stottbury Rd *HORF/LLZ* BS7 ....46 B3
Stoulton Gv
HNBRY/STHM BS10 ....31 E2
Stourden Cl *MANG/FISH* BS16 ...48 A1
Stourton Dr
OLD/WMLY/WICK BS30 ....76 C1
Stover Rd *YATE/CS* BS37 ....13 F5
Stowey Pk *YTN/CONG* BS49 ....112 D4

Stowey Rd YTN/CONG BS49 ...... 112 B2
Stowick Crs AVONM BS11 .... 30 A4
Stradbrook Av
  EVILLE/WHL BS5........................ 58 B4
Stradling Av MANG/FISH BS23 .. 125 E1
Stradling Rd AVONM BS11 .... 30 A3
Stradling Ter WSM BS23 *.......... 125 E1
Straight St CBRISNE BS2 .... 5 J4
Stratford Cl HGRV/WHIT BS14...... 96 C1
Strathearn Dr
  HNBRY/STHM BS10 .... 31 F3
Strathmore Rd HORF/LLZ BS7 .... 46 A2
Stratton Pl
Stratton Rd KEYN BS31 .... 99 F1
Strawberry Cl NAIL BS48.............. 67 E5
Strawberry Hl CLVDN BS21 .... 65 E1
Strawberry La LGASH BS41 .... 94 D1
Strawbridge Rd
  EVILLE/WHL BS5........................ 56 D4
Stream Cl HNBRY/STHM BS10...... 31 H3
Streamcross YTN/CONG BS49 .... 113 E1
Streamleaze THNB/SVB BS35........ 8 C3
Streamside CLVDN BS21 .... 64 D5
Stream Side MANG/FISH BS16...... 49 F2
Streamside Rd YATE/CS BS37 ...... 26 C1
The Stream MANG/FISH BS16...... 34 B3
Stretford Av EVILLE/WHL BS5 ...... 57 F3
Stretford Rd HORF/LLZ BS7 .... 57 F3
Strode Rd CLVDN BS21 .... 64 B4
Strode Wy CLVDN BS21 .... 64 B4
Stroud Rd AVONM BS11 .... 43 E3
  BRSTK/PCHW BS34.................... 20 A2
Stroud Wy
  OMX/HUT/LCK BS24 .... 122 B4
Stuart Pl BATHSE BA2 .... 2 A5
Stuart Rd WSM BS23 .... 125 F1
Stuart St EVILLE/WHL BS5 .... 57 E4
Sturden La MANG/FISH BS16 ...... 34 C2
Sturdon Rd BMSTR BS3................ 72 B3
Sturmer Cl YATE/CS BS37 .... 14 A3
Sturmey Wy PTSHD/EG BS20 ...... 42 D5
Sturminster Cl
  HGRV/WHIT BS14 .... 86 C3
Sturminster Rd
  HGRV/WHIT BS14 .... 86 B4
Sulis Manor Rd BATHSE BA2 ...... 110 B2
Sullivan Cl
  BRSG/KWL/STAPK BS4.............. 85 E3
Sumerlin Dr CLVDN BS21 .... 65 F2
Summerfield
  MTN/WRL BS22 .... 118 A5
Summerfield Rd
  CBATH/BATHN BA1 .... 102 D3
Summerfield Ter
  CBATH/BATHN BA1 *................ 102 D3
Summer Ground Dr
  BMSTRD/HC/WWD BS13 .... 84 B4
Summerhayes
  OLD/WMLY/WICK BS30 .... 77 G1
Summer Hl
  EVILLE/WHL BS5........................ 73 H2
Summerhill Rd
  CBATH/BATHN BA1 .... 102 A3
  EVILLE/WHL BS5........................ 57 H3
Summerhill Ter
  EVILLE/WHL BS5........................ 57 H4
Summerhouse CLVDN BS21 .... 67 E2
Summer House Wy
  OLD/WMLY/WICK BS30 .... 59 H4
Summerlands NAIL BS48.............. 80 A4
Summerlands Rd WSM BS23........ 7 J5
Summer La North
  BNWL BS29 .... 127 H2
  MTN/WRL BS22 .... 123 E2
Summer La North
Summerlays Ct BATHSE BA2 .... 3 J5
Summerleaze KEYN BS31 .... 88 D2
  MANG/FISH BS16 .... 48 C5
Summers Md YATE/CS BS37 .... 14 A2
Summers Rd CBRISNE BS2 .... 56 C2
Summer St BMSTR BS3 .... 72 D2
Summit Cl KGWD/HNM BS15........ 59 E3
Sundays Hl ALMDB BS32 .... 10 C3
Sunderland Pl CFTN/FAIL BS8 .... 4 A2
Sunderland St BATHSE BA2 .... 3 H3
Sundridge Pk YATE/CS BS37 .... 26 A2
Sunningdale CFTN/FAIL BS8 .... 55 F3
  YATE/CS BS37 .... 26 A2
Sunningdale Dr NAIL BS48............ 67 H5
Sunningdale Rd
  MTN/WRL BS22 .... 117 G5
Sunnybank BATHSE BA2 .... 109 E3
Sunny Bank KGWD/HNM BS15...... 58 D2
Sunny Bank Wy
  OMX/HUT/LCK BS24 .... 123 E2
Sunny Hl
  HNLZ/SM/SNYPK/WT BS9 .... 43 H1
Sunnyhill Dr AVONM BS11 .... 43 E4
Sunnymead KEYN BS31 .... 98 A1
Sunnymede Rd NAIL BS48............ 67 E4
Sunnyside FRCTL/WBN BS36........ 23 H3
  HNLZ/SM/SNYPK/WT BS9 .... 44 C1
Sunnyside Crs CLVDN BS21.......... 64 D2
Sunnyside La MANG/FISH BS16.... 34 B3
  YATE/CS BS37 .... 25 G1
Sunnyside Rd CLVDN BS21.......... 64 D2
Sunnyside Rd North WSM BS23...... 7 F7
Sunnyvale CLVDN BS21................ 64 A4
Sunnyvale Dr
  OLD/WMLY/WICK BS30 .... 77 E3
Sunny Wk KGWD/HNM BS15........ 58 B2
Sunridge MANG/FISH BS16.......... 48 D2
Sunrise Gv
  BRSG/KWL/STAPK BS4.............. 74 C2
Surrey Rd HORF/LLZ BS7 .... 46 A5
Surrey St CBRISNE BS2 .... 5 H1
Suspension Br CFTN/FAIL BS8 ...... 54 C4
Sussex Pl BATHSE BA2 * 3 J5
Sussex St CBRISNE BS2................ 56 C5
Sutherland Av
  MANG/FISH BS16 .... 49 E1
  YATE/CS BS37 .... 13 H3

Sutherland Dr
  OMX/HUT/LCK BS24 .... 126 A4
Sutherland Pl CFTN/FAIL BS8 .... 55 E1
Sutton Av
  BRSG/KWL/STAPK BS4.............. 74 C2
Sutton Cl MTN/WRL BS22 .... 122 B3
Sutton St BATHSE BA2.................... 3 J3
Swainswick MTN/WRL BS14 .... 85 G3
Swainswick Gdns
  CBATH/BATHN BA1 .... 103 F2
Swainswick La
  CBATH/BATHN BA1 .... 103 G1
Swaish Dr
  OLD/WMLY/WICK BS30 .... 76 C2
Swallow Dr BRSTK/PCHW BS34 .... 20 A2
Swallow Gdns MTN/WRL BS22 .. 122 A3
Swallow Pk THNB/SVB BS35.......... 8 D1
Swallows Ct
  BRSTK/PCHW BS34.................... 33 G1
The Swallows
  MANG/FISH BS22 .... 122 A4
Swallow St CBATH/BATHN BA1 ...... 3 G5
Swan Cl MTN/WRL BS22 .... 122 B3
Swane Rd HGRV/WHIT BS14 .... 87 E3
Swan Fld YATE/CS BS37 .... 14 B5
Swan La FRCTL/WBN BS36............ 22 C2
Swanmoor Crs
  HNBRY/STHM BS10 .... 31 F1
Sweetgrass Rd
  OMX/HUT/LCK BS24 .... 122 C3
Sweets Cl KGWD/HNM BS15........ 59 E1
Sweets Rd KGWD/HNM BS15...... 58 D1
Swift Cl MTN/WRL BS22 .... 122 C3
Swiss Rd BMSTR BS3 .... 72 A4
  WSM BS23.................................... 7 G4
Sycamore Cl EVILLE/WHL BS5 ...... 57 C2
  KGWD/HNM BS15 .... 75 G3
  NAIL BS48 .... 67 F4
  OMX/HUT/LCK BS24 .... 126 B1
  WSM BS23.................................... 7 J3
Sycamore Dr
  BRSTK/PCHW BS34.................... 20 A3
  THNB/SVB BS35........................ 8 D3
Sydenham Blds BATHSE BA2 .... 2 C6
Sydenham Hl
  RDLND/MONT BS6 .... 55 H2
Sydenham La
  RDLND/MONT BS6 .... 55 H2
Sydenham Rd BATHSE BA2 .... 2 D5
  BRSG/KWL/STAPK BS4.............. 73 H5
  RDLND/MONT BS6 .... 55 H2
Sydenham Wy
  KGWD/HNM BS15 .... 75 H3
Sydney Blds BATHSE BA2 .... 3 K5
Sydney Ms BATHSE BA2.................. 3 J3
Sydney Pl BATHSE BA2 .... 3 J3
Sydney Rd BATHSE BA2 .... 3 K5
Sydney Rw CBRIS/FH BS1 .... 4 A7
Sydney Whf BATHSE BA2.................. 3 K5
Sylvan Wy
  HNLZ/SM/SNYPK/WT BS9 .... 43 H2
Sylvia Av BMSTR BS3 .... 73 C3
Symes Pk CBATH/BATHN BA1 .... 101 F2
Symington Rd
  MANG/FISH BS16 .... 48 B3
Syston Wy KGWD/HNM BS15 ...... 58 D2

T

Tabernacle Rd
  KGWD/HNM BS15 .... 58 C5
Tackley Rd EVILLE/WHL BS5 .... 46 D5
Tadwick La CBATH/BATHN BA1 .... 90 A4
Tailors Ct CBRIS/FH BS1 .... 5 F3
Talbot Av KGWD/HNM BS15.......... 58 D4
Talbot Rd
  BRSG/KWL/STAPK BS4.............. 74 A4
Talgarth Rd HORF/LLZ BS7 .... 46 A4
Tallis Gv BRSG/KWL/STAPK BS4.. 85 E5
Tamar Cl THNB/SVB BS35 .... 9 E5
Tamar Dr KEYN BS31 .... 88 D5
Tamar Rd CBRISNE BS2 .... 57 E5
  MTN/WRL BS22 .... 122 B1
Tamworth Rd KEYN BS31 .... 88 B5
Tankard's Cl CFTN/FAIL BS8 .... 4 C2
Tanner Cl
  OLD/WMLY/WICK BS30 .... 76 C1
Tanners Ct THNB/SVB BS35 .... 8 C4
Tanners Wk BATHSE BA2 .... 107 E2
Tanorth Cl HGRV/WHIT BS14 ...... 96 C1
Tanorth Rd HGRV/WHIT BS14 ...... 96 C1
Tansy La PTSHD/EG BS20 .... 40 B3
The Tanyard
  OLD/WMLY/WICK BS30 .... 77 E4
Tapsters
  OLD/WMLY/WICK BS30 *.......... 76 D2
Tara Cl FRCTL/WBN BS36.............. 23 F1
Tarnock Av HGRV/WHIT BS14 ...... 85 H2
Tarragon Pl ALMDB BS32 .... 21 H5
Taunton Rd MTN/WRL BS22 ...... 118 A4
Taunton Wk HORF/LLZ BS7 .... 46 C1
Taverner Wk NAIL BS48 * 67 G3
Taverna Cl WSM BS23.................. 106 C2
Taverner Cl
  BRSG/KWL/STAPK BS4.............. 85 E2
Tavistock Rd
  BRSG/KWL/STAPK BS4.............. 73 G5
  MTN/WRL BS22 .... 122 D1
Tavistock Wk
  BRSG/KWL/STAPK BS4.............. 73 G5
Tawny Wy MTN/WRL BS22 .... 122 C3
Taylor Cl KGWD/HNM BS15.......... 59 F3
Taylor Ct MTN/WRL BS22 .... 118 A4
Taylor Gdns
  BMSTRD/HC/WWD BS13 .... 84 A5
Tayman Cl HNBRY/STHM BS10...... 46 A5
Tayman Rdg
  OLD/WMLY/WICK BS30 .... 89 G1
Taynton Cl
  OLD/WMLY/WICK BS30 * 77 E4
Teal Cl ALMDB BS32 .... 11 F5
  MTN/WRL BS22 .... 122 C4
Teal Wy PTSHD/EG BS20.............. 40 D2
Teasel Md ALMDB BS32 .... 21 G3
Teasel Wk MTN/WRL BS22 .... 122 C4
Teddington Cl BATHSE BA2 .... 107 H5
Teesdale Cl MTN/WRL BS22 ...... 122 A3

Teewell Av MANG/FISH BS16 ...... 49 E4
Teewell Cl MANG/FISH BS16 * 49 E4
Teewell Hl MANG/FISH BS16 ...... 49 E4
Teignmouth Rd
  BRSG/KWL/STAPK BS4.............. 73 G5
  CLVDN BS21................................ 65 E2
Telephone Av CBRIS/FH BS1........ 4 E4
Telford Wk EVILLE/WHL BS5........ 58 A2
Templar Rd YATE/CS BS37 .... 14 B2
Temple Back CBRIS/FH BS1.......... 5 H4
Temple Back East CBRIS/FH BS1 .. 5 J5
Temple Ga CBRIS/FH BS1 .... 5 H6
Templeland Rd
  BMSTRD/HC/WWD BS13............ 84 A4
Temple Rose St CBRIS/FH BS1 ...... 5 H5
Temple St BMSTR BS3 .... 72 C4
  CBRIS/FH BS1 .... 5 G4
  KEYN BS31 .... 88 B4
Temple Wy CBRIS/FH BS1 .... 5 H5
Temple Wy U/P CBRISNE BS2 .... 5 J3
Tenby Rd KEYN BS31 .... 88 A4
Tenby St EVILLE/WHL BS5 .... 56 D4
Tennessee Gv
  RDLND/MONT BS6 .... 45 G3
Tenniscourt Rd
  KGWD/HNM BS15 .... 59 G2
Tennis Rd
  BRSG/KWL/STAPK BS4.............. 73 G5
Tennyson Av CLVDN BS21............ 64 B3
Tennyson Cl KEYN BS31 .... 88 C3
Tennyson Rd CBATH/BATHN BA1 .. 2 A2
  HORF/LLZ BS7 .... 46 A3
  WSM BS23................................ 125 E3
Tenth Av HORF/LLZ BS7 .... 32 D4
Tereslake Gn
  HNBRY/STHM BS10 .... 31 H1
Terrace Wk CBATH/BATHN BA1 .... 3 G5
Terrell Gdns EVILLE/WHL BS5 ...... 57 F4
Terrell St CBRISNE BS2 .... 4 E2
Tetbury Cl BRSTK/PCHW BS34 .... 21 E2
Tetbury Gdns NAIL BS48.............. 67 H5
Tetbury Rd KGWD/HNM BS15...... 58 B3
Teviot Rd KEYN BS31 .... 88 D5
Tewkesbury Rd CBRISNE BS2 ...... 56 C1
Tewther Rd
  BMSTRD/HC/WWD BS13 .... 95 H1
Teyfant Rd
  BMSTRD/HC/WWD BS13 .... 96 B1
Teyfant Wk
  BMSTRD/HC/WWD BS13 .... 96 B1
Thackeray HORF/LLZ BS7 .... 32 C5
Thackeray Av CLVDN BS21 .... 64 D1
Thackeray Rd HORF/LLZ BS7 ...... 32 C5
Thanet Rd BMSTR BS3 .... 72 C4
Thatcher Cl BRSTK/PCHW BS34 .. 39 H4
Thatchers Cl EVILLE/WHL BS5...... 58 B4
Theme-And-Back-Again La
  CFTN/FAIL BS8 *.......................... 4 C3
Theresa Av HORF/LLZ BS7 .... 46 A4
Theynes Cft LGASH BS41 .... 71 E5
Thicket Av MANG/FISH BS16 ...... 49 E4
Thicket Rd MANG/FISH BS16 ...... 48 C4
Thicket Wk THNB/SVB BS35 .... 8 D3
Thiery Rd
  BRSG/KWL/STAPK BS4.............. 74 B4
Thingwall Pk MANG/FISH BS16.... 47 G5
Third Av BATHSE BA2 .... 107 J2
  HORF/LLZ BS7 .... 32 C4
Third Wy AVONM BS11 .... 28 C3
Thirlmere Ct
  OLD/WMLY/WICK BS30 .... 60 B5
Thirlmere Rd
  BRSTK/PCHW BS34.................... 20 C2
  WSM BS23................................ 125 F2
Thistle St BMSTR BS3 .... 72 C5
Thomas Av MANG/FISH BS16 ...... 35 H5
Thomas La CBRIS/FH BS1.............. 5 G3
Thomas Pring Wk
  EVILLE/WHL BS5........................ 58 A2
Thomas St CBATH/BATHN BA1 .. 102 A3
  CBRISNE BS2 .... 56 A3
Thomas St North
  RDLND/MONT BS6 .... 55 H2
Thomas Wy MANG/FISH BS16 .... 47 C1
Thompson Rd
  HGRV/WHIT BS14 .... 86 D3
Thornbank Pl BATHSE BA2 .... 56 D3
Thornbury Dr WSM BS23 .... 124 B4
Thornbury Rd WSM BS23 .... 124 B4
Thorn Cl MTN/WRL BS22 .... 123 E1
  YATE/CS BS37 .... 14 C4
Thorndale CFTN/FAIL BS8 .... 55 E3
Thorndale Ms CFTN/FAIL BS8 ...... 55 E3
Thornhayes
  FRCTL/WBN BS36........................ 23 C2
The Thornhills
  MANG/FISH BS16 .... 48 C1
Thornleigh Rd HORF/LLZ BS7...... 46 A3
Thornmead Gv
  HNBRY/STHM BS10 .... 31 E3
Thorns Farm YATE/CS BS37 * 26 A1
Thornycroft Cl HORF/LLZ BS7 ...... 46 D1
Three Oaks Cl MANG/FISH BS16.. 48 C4
Three Peaks Wk LGASH BS41 ...... 95 H5
Three Queens La CBRIS/FH BS1 .. 5 G5
Three Wells Rd
  BMSTRD/HC/WWD BS13............ 84 A5
Thrissell St EVILLE/WHL BS5 .... 56 C3
Throgmorton Rd
  BRSG/KWL/STAPK BS4.............. 85 G2
Thrush Cl MTN/WRL BS22............ 122 B5
Thurlestone HGRV/WHIT BS14 .... 85 G4
Thurlow Rd EVILLE/WHL BS5........ 57 F1
Thurstons Barton
  EVILLE/WHL BS5........................ 57 G2
Thyme Cl HORF/LLZ BS20 .... 40 B3
Tibberton KGWD/HNM BS15 .... 59 H3
Tibbott Rd HGRV/WHIT BS14 ...... 86 D4
Tibbott Wk HGRV/WHIT BS14 ...... 86 D4
Tichborne Rd EVILLE/WHL BS5 .... 57 E4
  WSM BS23 .... 6 E2
Tickenham Rd CLVDN BS21 .... 65 H1
Tide Gv AVONM BS11 .... 29 G5
Tidenham Wy
  BRSTK/PCHW BS34.................... 20 B1
Tilley Cl KEYN BS31 .... 98 D2
Tilling Rd HNBRY/STHM BS10...... 46 A1

Tilling Wk HNBRY/STHM BS10...... 46 A1
Tilting Rd THNB/SVB BS35 .... 8 C2
Timber Dene MANG/FISH BS16.... 47 F4
Timbercombe Wk
  HGRV/WHIT BS14 .... 06 A1
Timsbury Rd BMSTR BS3 .... 72 C4
Tindell Ct
  OLD/WMLY/WICK BS30 .... 76 C2
Tintern Av EVILLE/WHL BS5 .... 57 F3
Tintern Ct
  OLD/WMLY/WICK BS30 .... 59 F5
Tippetts Rd KGWD/HNM BS15...... 58 D5
Tirley Wy MTN/WRL BS22 .... 121 C1
Titan Barrow
  CBATH/BATHN BA1 .... 104 D2
Tiverton Gdns
  MTN/WRL BS22 .... 122 D1
Tiverton Rd CLVDN BS21 .... 65 E4
Tiverton Wk MANG/FISH BS16 .... 58 A1
Tivoli La WSM BS23 .... 6 E2
Tockington La ALMDB BS32 .... 10 C1
Toll Bridge Rd
  CBATH/BATHN BA1 .... 103 H1
Tone Rd CLVDN BS21 .... 64 D3
Tormarton Crs
  HNBRY/STHM BS10 .... 30 D1
Tormarton Rd
  MTN/WRL BS22 .... 122 D1
Toronto Rd HORF/LLZ BS7 .... 32 C5
Torpoint Rd BMSTR BS3................ 73 E4
Torrance Cl
  OLD/WMLY/WICK BS30 .... 60 B5
Torridge Rd KEYN BS31 .... 88 D5
Torrington Av
  BRSG/KWL/STAPK BS4.............. 85 C1
Torrington Crs
  MTN/WRL BS22 .... 117 H5
Tortworth Rd HORF/LLZ BS7 ...... 46 A3
Totnes Cl MTN/WRL BS22 .... 122 D1
Totshill Dr
  BMSTRD/HC/WWD BS13 .... 85 F5
Totshill Gv
  BMSTRD/HC/WWD BS13............ 85 F5
Tottenham Pl CFTN/FAIL BS8 .... 4 A3
Totterdown La
  OMX/HUT/LCK BS24 .... 125 F5
Totterdown Rd WSM BS23 .... 125 E3
Touchstone Av
  BRSTK/PCHW BS34.................... 21 G5
Tovey Cl MTN/WRL BS22 .... 117 H4
Tower Hl CBRISNE BS2 .... 5 H4
  OMX/HUT/LCK BS24 .... 127 G2
Tower House La NAIL BS48 .... 67 C2
Tower La CBRIS/FH BS1 .... 5 F3
  OLD/WMLY/WICK BS30 .... 59 G5
Towerleaze
  HNLZ/SM/SNYPK/WT BS9 .... 44 B5
Tower Rd KGWD/HNM BS15 .... 59 H4
  PTSHD/EG BS20 .... 39 E4
Tower Rd North
  OLD/WMLY/WICK BS30 .... 59 H5
Tower Rd South
  OLD/WMLY/WICK BS30 .... 59 H5
Tower St WSM BS23 .... 120 C2
Townsend ALMDB BS32 .... 10 B3
Townsend Cl HGRV/WHIT BS14 .. 87 E4
Townsend La ALMDB BS32............ 10 B3
Townsend Rd
  HGRV/WHIT BS14 .... 87 E4
Townshend Rd
  MTN/WRL BS22 .... 117 H3
Tozers Hl
  BRSG/KWL/STAPK BS4.............. 74 B4
Tracy Cl HGRV/WHIT BS14 .... 85 G2
Trafalgar Rd
  CBATH/BATHN BA1 .... 101 G3
Trafalgar Ter BMSTR BS3 .... 72 B5
Tralee Wk
  BRSG/KWL/STAPK BS4.............. 73 E5
Tramway Rd
  BRSG/KWL/STAPK BS4.............. 74 B3
Tranmere Av
  HNBRY/STHM BS10 .... 31 E1
Tranmere Gv
  HNBRY/STHM BS10 .... 31 E1
Tratman Wk
  HNBRY/STHM BS10 .... 30 D2
Travers Cl
  BRSG/KWL/STAPK BS4.............. 85 E3
Travers Wk BRSTK/PCHW BS34.... 21 G5
Trawden Cl WSM BS23 .... 121 F2
Tredegar Rd MANG/FISH BS16 .... 48 B5
Treefield Pl CBRISNE BS2 .... 56 C5
Treefield Rd CLVDN BS21 .... 64 D3
Tree Leaze YATE/CS BS37 .... 14 B5
Tregarth Rd BMSTR BS3 .... 72 A5
Trelawn Cl MTN/WRL BS22 .... 123 C1
Trelawney Av EVILLE/WHL BS5 .... 57 F3
Trelawney Pk
  RDLND/MONT BS6 .... 55 G2
Trelawney Rd
  BRSG/KWL/STAPK BS4.............. 74 C3

Trevethin Cl
  KGWD/HNM BS15 .... 58 C4
Trevisa Gv HNBRY/STHM BS10 .... 31 G1
Trewartha Cl WSM BS23 .... 7 C2
Trewartha Pk WSM BS23................ 7 G2
Trewint Gdns
  BRSG/KWL/STAPK BS4.............. 85 C1
Triangle East BATHSE BA2 .... 2 A6
Triangle North BATHSE BA2 .... 2 A6
Triangle South CFTN/FAIL BS8 ...... 4 A3
Triangle Vls BATHSE BA2................ 2 A6
Triangle West BATHSE BA2 .... 2 A6
  CFTN/FAIL BS8............................ 4 B3
Trident Cl MANG/FISH BS16 .... 35 G4
Trim Br CBATH/BATHN BA1 .... 3 F4
Trim St CBATH/BATHN BA1............ 3 F4
Trinder Rd PTSHD/EG BS20.......... 42 B4
Trinity Cl BATHSE BA2.................... 2 E5
Trinity Ct KGWD/HNM BS15 .... 59 E3
Trinity La YATE/CS BS37 .... 5 J3
Trinity Ms CBRISNE BS2 .... 5 J3
Trinity Rd BATHSE BA2 .... 109 E5
  CBRISNE BS2 .... 56 C4
  NAIL BS48 .... 120 B2
  WSM BS23................................ 120 B2
Trinity St CBATH/BATHN BA1 .... 3 F5
  CBRIS/FH BS1 .... 4 D5
  CBRISNE BS2 .... 56 C4
Trinity Wk CBRISNE BS2 .... 5 K2
Trin Mills CBRIS/FH BS1 .... 5 F6
Tripps Cnr YTN/CONG BS49 ...... 112 D4
Tripps Rw LGASH BS41................ 70 D5
Troon YATE/CS BS37 .... 26 A2
Troon Dr
  OLD/WMLY/WICK BS30 .... 59 H5
Troopers' Hill Rd
  BRSG/KWL/STAPK BS4.............. 57 H5
Trossachs Dr BATHSE BA2 .... 103 G4
Trowbridge Rd
  HNBRY/STHM BS10 .... 31 G4
Trowbridge Wk
  HNBRY/STHM BS10 .... 31 G4
Trubshaw Cl HORF/LLZ BS7 .... 46 B2
Trumpet La EVILLE/WHL BS5........ 58 B4
Truro Rd BMSTR BS3 .... 72 C3
  NAIL BS48 .... 79 H1
Trym Cross Rd
  HNLZ/SM/SNYPK/WT BS9 .... 44 A3
Trym Leaze
  HNLZ/SM/SNYPK/WT BS9 .... 44 A3
Trym Rd
  HNLZ/SM/SNYPK/WT BS9 .... 45 E1
Trym Side
  HNLZ/SM/SNYPK/WT BS9 .... 44 A3
Trymwood Cl
  HNLZ/SM/SNYPK/WT BS9 .... 30 D3
Trymwood Pde
  HNLZ/SM/SNYPK/WT BS9 * 44 B2
Tuckett La MANG/FISH BS16........ 48 C1
Tucking Mill Cots BATHSE BA2 .. 111 H3
Tuckmill CLVDN BS21 .... 64 B4
Tudor Cl OLD/WMLY/WICK BS30.. 58 B2
Tudor Rd CBRISNE BS2.................. 56 B2
  KGWD/HNM BS15 .... 75 H1
  MTN/WRL BS22 .... 117 H4
Tuffley Rd HNBRY/STHM BS10 .... 31 G5
Tufton Av AVONM BS11 .... 31 G5
Tugela Rd
  BMSTRD/HC/WWD BS13 .... 84 A2
Tunbridge Wy
  MANG/FISH BS16 .... 35 G5
Tunstall Cl
  HNLZ/SM/SNYPK/WT BS9 .... 44 C4
Turley Rd EVILLE/WHL BS5............ 57 F2
Turnberry
  OLD/WMLY/WICK BS30 .... 59 H5
  YATE/CS BS37 .... 26 A2
Turnberry Wk
  BRSG/KWL/STAPK BS4 * 74 C5
Turnbridge Cl
  HNBRY/STHM BS10 .... 31 H1
Turnbridge Rd
  HNBRY/STHM BS10 .... 31 G1
Turnbury Av NAIL BS48 .... 67 H5
Turnbury Cl MTN/WRL BS22 ...... 117 G5
Turner Cl KEYN BS31 .... 88 D4
Turner Dr YATE/CS BS37 .... 117 G5
Turner Gdns HORF/LLZ BS7 .... 46 D1
Turners Ct
  OLD/WMLY/WICK BS30 .... 76 C2
Turner Wk
  OLD/WMLY/WICK BS30 .... 60 B4
Turner Wy CLVDN BS21 .... 64 B4
Turnpike Cl YATE/CS BS37 .... 14 C5
Turtlegate Av
  BMSTRD/HC/WWD BS13 .... 83 H5
Turtlegate Wk
  BMSTRD/HC/WWD BS13............ 83 H5
Tutton Wy CLVDN BS21 .... 64 D5
Tweed Cl THNB/SVB BS35 .... 8 D4
Tweed Rd CLVDN BS21 .... 64 D3
Tweeny La
  OLD/WMLY/WICK BS30 .... 60 B5
Twenty Acres Rd
  HNBRY/STHM BS10 .... 31 F3
Twerton Farm Cl BATHSE BA2 .. 107 G1
Twickenham Rd
  RDLND/MONT BS6 .... 45 G3
Two Acres Rd
  HGRV/WHIT BS14 .... 85 H2
Two Mile Ct KGWD/HNM BS15 * .. 58 C3
Twomile Hill Rd
  KGWD/HNM BS15 .... 58 B3
Two Rivers Wy
  BLAG/CWMG/WR BS40............ 115 G3
  KEYN BS31 .... 98 A1
  YTN/CONG BS49 .... 115 E2
The Twynings
  KGWD/HNM BS15 .... 59 E1
Tybalt Wy BRSTK/PCHW BS34 .... 21 G5
Tydeman Rd PTSHD/EG BS20 ...... 40 B5
Tyler Cl KGWD/HNM BS15............ 59 G3
Tyler Gn MTN/WRL BS22 .... 118 A3
Tyler's La MANG/FISH BS16 .... 48 D3
Tylers Wy YATE/CS BS37.............. 14 C5
Tyler's Farm MANG/FISH BS16 .... 48 D3
Tyndale Av MANG/FISH BS16...... 48 A4
  YATE/CS BS37 .... 13 H4

Tyndale Rd *KGWD/HNM* BS15 .... 59 E1
Tyndale Vw *THNB/SVB* BS35 .... 8 C4
Tyndall Av *CFTN/FAIL* BS8 .... 4 C2
Tyndall Rd *EVILLE/WHL* BS5 .... 56 D3
Tyndalls Park Ms *CFTN/FAIL* BS8 .... 4 C1
Tyndall's Park Rd *CFTN/FAIL* BS8 ... 4 B1
Tyndalls Wy
   HNBRY/STHM BS10 .... 32 A5
Tyne Gv *PTSHD/EG* BS20 .... 40 B2
Tyne Rd *HORF/LLZ* BS7 .... 45 H5
Tyne St *CBRISNE* BS2 .... 56 C1
Tyning Cl *HGRV/WHIT* BS14 .... 85 H2
   YATE/CS BS37 .... 14 A5
Tyning End *BATHSE* BA2 .... 3 K7
Tyning La *CBATH/BATHN* BA1 ..... 103 E3
Tyning Rd *BATHSE* BA2 .... 109 F5
   BATHSE BA2 .... 104 A3
   BMSTR BS3 .... 73 G3
   KEYN BS31 .... 99 F2
Tynings Ms *WSM* BS23 .... 124 D2
The Tynings *CLVDN* BS21 .... 64 A4
Tyning Ter *CBATH/BATHN* BA1 .... 102 D3
The Tyning *BATHSE* BA2 .... 3 K7
Tynte Av
   BMSTRD/HC/WWD BS13 .... 96 A1
Tyntesfield Rd
   BMSTRD/HC/WWD BS13 .... 84 B2
Tyrone Wk
   BRSG/KWL/STAPK BS4 .... 85 F1
Tyrrel Wy *PCHW* BS34 .... 21 G4

U

Ullswater Cl
   OLD/WMLY/WICK BS30 .... 60 B5
   WSM BS23 .... 125 F2
   YATE/CS BS37 .... 14 A4
Ullswater Dr
   CBATH/BATHN BA1 .... 102 D2
Ullswater Rd
   HNBRY/STHM BS10 .... 31 F4
Uncombe Cl *NAIL* BS48 .... 67 F3
Underbanks *PTSHD/EG* BS20 .... 42 D4
Underhill Dr *WSM* BS23 .... 124 C4
Underwood Av
   MTN/WRL BS22 .... 121 G2
Underwood Rd
   PTSHD/EG BS20 .... 39 G5
Unicorn Business Pk
   BRSG/KWL/STAPK BS4 .... 74 C1
Union Gallery *CBRIS/FH* BS1 * 5 G2
Union Pas *CBATH/BATHN* BA1 .... 3 G4
Union Pl *WSM* BS23 * 6 D4
Union Rd *CBRISNE* BS2 .... 5 K4
Union St *CBATH/BATHN* BA1 .... 3 F3
   NAIL BS48 .... 66 D5
   CBRIS/FH BS1 .... 5 F4
   CBRISNE BS2 .... 5 H4
Unity Av *KEYN* BS31 .... 88 D4
Unity St *CBRIS/FH* BS1 .... 4 D4
   CBRISNE BS2 .... 5 J3
   KGWD/HNM BS15 .... 58 C3
University Cl
   HNLZ/SM/SNYPK/WT BS9 .... 44 D4
University Hall
   HNLZ/SM/SNYPK/WT BS9 .... 44 D4
University Rd *CFTN/FAIL* BS8 .... 4 B3
University Wk *CFTN/FAIL* BS8 .... 4 B3
Uphill Dr *CBATH/BATHN* BA1 ...... 103 E2
Uphill Rd *HORF/LLZ* BS7 .... 46 B3
Uphill Rd North *WSM* BS23 .... 124 C5
Uphill Rd South *WSM* BS23 .... 124 C5
Uphill Wy *WSM* BS23 .... 124 C5
Upjohn Crs
   BMSTRD/HC/WWD BS13 .... 96 A1
Uplands Dr *KEYN* BS31 .... 99 G2
Uplands Rd *KEYN* BS31 .... 99 F2
   MANG/FISH BS16 .... 48 C5
The Uplands *NAIL* BS48 .... 78 D2
Upper Bath Rd *THNB/SVB* BS35 ..... 8 C4
Upper Belgrave Rd
   CFTN/FAIL BS8 .... 55 E1
Upper Belmont Rd
   HORF/LLZ BS7 .... 46 A5
Upper Bloomfield Rd
   BATHSE BA2 .... 110 B1
Upper Borough Walls
   CBATH/BATHN BA1 .... 3 F4
Upper Bristol Rd *WSM* BS23 .... 7 K1
Upper Byron Pl *CFTN/FAIL* BS8 .... 4 B5
Upper Camden Pl
   CBATH/BATHN BA1 * 102 D4
Upper Chapel La
   FRCTL/WBN BS36 .... 24 A3
Upper Cheltenham Pl
   RDLND/MONT BS6 .... 56 A2
Upper Church La *CBRISNE* BS2 ..... 4 D3
Upper Church Rd *WSM* BS23 .... 6 C1
Upper Church St
   CBATH/BATHN BA1 .... 2 E2
Upper Conham V
   KGWD/HNM BS15 .... 75 F1
Upper Cranbrook Rd
   RDLND/MONT BS6 .... 45 F4
Upper East Hayes
   CBATH/BATHN BA1 .... 103 E3
Upper Hedgemead Rd
   CBATH/BATHN BA1 .... 3 F1
Upper Lambridge St
   CBATH/BATHN BA1 .... 103 F2
Upper Lansdown Ms
   CBATH/BATHN BA1 .... 102 C3
Upper Maudlin St *CBRIS/FH* BS1 .... 4 E2
Upper Oldfield Pk *BATHSE* BA2 ...... 2 C6
Upper Perry HI *BMSTR* BS3 .... 72 D2
Upper Sandhurst Rd
   BRSG/KWL/STAPK BS4 .... 74 C2
Upper Station Rd
   MANG/FISH BS16 .... 48 C4
Upper Stone Cl
   FRCTL/WBN BS36 .... 24 A3
Upper Sydney St *BMSTR* BS3 .... 72 C2
Upper Ter *AVONM* BS11 * 29 H3
Upper Town La
   BLAG/CWMG/WR BS40 .... 92 D4
Upper Wells St *CBRIS/FH* BS1 * 4 D3

Upton La *LGASH* BS41 .... 95 E3
Upton Rd *BMSTR* BS3 .... 72 C2
Urchinwood La
   YTN/CONG BS49 .... 115 F2
Urfords Dr *MANG/FISH* BS16 .... 48 C2

V

Valda Rd *MTN/WRL* BS22 .... 121 H1
Vale Crs *MTN/WRL* BS22 .... 123 F1
Vale End *NAIL* BS48 .... 67 E5
Vale La *BMSTR* BS3 .... 84 D1
Vale Mill Wy
   OMX/HUT/LCK BS24 .... 122 C3
Valentine Cl *HGRV/WHIT* BS14 ..... 86 A4
Valerian Cl *AVONM* BS11 .... 43 F2
Vale St *BRSG/KWL/STAPK* BS4 ...... 73 H5
The Vale *MANG/FISH* BS16 .... 50 D1
Valetta Cl *WSM* BS23 .... 125 E3
Vale View Pl
   CBATH/BATHN BA1 .... 103 E5
Vale View Ter
   CBATH/BATHN BA1 .... 104 A1
Valley View Rd
   CBATH/BATHN BA1 .... 103 F1
Valley Way Rd *NAIL* BS48 .... 67 F3
The Valls *ALMDB* BS32 .... 11 H2
Valma Rocks *EVILLE/WHL* BS5 ...... 57 H5
Vanbrugh La *MANG/FISH* BS16 .... 47 G1
Van Diemen's La
   CBATH/BATHN BA1 .... 102 B2
Vandyck Av *KEYN* BS31 .... 88 C3
Vane St *BATHSE* BA2 .... 3 J3
Varsity Wy
   OMX/HUT/LCK BS24 .... 123 E5
Vassall Ct *MANG/FISH* BS16 .... 48 B3
Vassall Rd *MANG/FISH* BS16 .... 48 B5
Vaughan Cl *HNBRY/STHM* BS10 ... 30 D2
Vauxhall Ter *BMSTR* BS3 * 72 B2
Vayre Cl *YATE/CS* BS37 .... 27 E1
Vee La *BLAG/CWMG/WR* BS40 ..... 93 E4
Vellore La *BATHSE* BA2 .... 3 K3
Ventnor Rd *BRSTK/PCHW* BS34 ..... 32 D2
   EVILLE/WHL BS5 .... 57 F1
Venus St *YTN/CONG* BS49 .... 115 E4
Vera Rd *MANG/FISH* BS16 .... 47 G5
Verbena Wy *MTN/WRL* BS22 ...... 122 D2
Vereland Rd
   OMX/HUT/LCK BS24 .... 126 B4
Verlands *YTN/CONG* BS49 .... 115 E1
Vernham Gv *BATHSE* BA2 .... 110 A1
Vernhamwood Cl
   BATHSE BA2 .... 110 A1
Vernon La *KEYN* BS31 .... 99 E1
Vernon Pk *BATHSE* BA2 .... 107 H1
Vernon St
   BRSG/KWL/STAPK BS4 .... 73 G2
Vernon Ter *BATHSE* BA2 * 107 H1
Vernslade *CBATH/BATHN* BA1 .... 101 G5
Verrier Rd *EVILLE/WHL* BS5 .... 57 E4
Verwood Dr
   OLD/WMLY/WICK BS30 .... 77 F5
Vian End *MTN/WRL* BS22 .... 117 G4
Vicarage Cl *MTN/WRL* BS22 .... 117 G5
Vicarage Ct *KGWD/HNM* BS15 ..... 75 C1
Vicarage La *NAIL* BS48 .... 81 H3
Vicarage Rd *BMSTR* BS3 .... 73 C2
   BMSTRD/HC/WWD BS13 .... 84 A5
   CFTN/FAIL BS8 .... 55 F3
   EVILLE/WHL BS5 .... 57 E1
   FRCTL/WBN BS36 .... 24 A5
   KGWD/HNM BS15 .... 75 C1
Victor Rd *BMSTR* BS3 * 73 H3
Victoria Av *EVILLE/WHL* BS5 .... 57 E4
Victoria Bridge Rd *BATHSE* BA2 .... 2 C4
Victoria Blds *BATHSE* BA2 .... 2 B4
Victoria Cl *BATHSE* BA2 .... 107 H2
   PTSHD/EG BS20 .... 39 H5
   THNB/SVB BS35 .... 8 C1
Victoria Gdns
   CBATH/BATHN BA1 .... 104 A1
   RDLND/MONT BS6 .... 55 H2
Victoria Gv *BMSTR* BS3 .... 73 F2
Victoria Ms *BMSTR* BS3 * 72 D3
Victoria Pde *EVILLE/WHL* BS5 .... 57 E3
Victoria Pk *KGWD/HNM* BS15 ...... 58 D3
   WSM BS23 .... 6 C1
Victoria Pl *BMSTR* BS3 .... 72 D3
   CBATH/BATHN BA1 .... 103 F5
   WSM BS23 .... 6 C1
Victoria Qd *WSM* BS23 .... 6 D2
Victoria Rd *AVONM* BS11 .... 28 B5
   CBRISNE BS2 .... 73 H1
   CLVDN BS21 .... 64 C2
   KEYN BS31 .... 99 E1
   KGWD/HNM BS15 .... 58 D3
   OLD/WMLY/WICK BS30 .... 77 G1
Victoria Sq *CFTN/FAIL* BS8 .... 55 E4
   PTSHD/EG BS20 .... 39 H5
   WSM BS23 .... 6 C4
Victoria St *CBRIS/FH* BS1 * 5 C4
   MANG/FISH BS16 .... 48 D4
Victoria Ter *BATHSE* BA2 .... 3 J6
   CBRISNE BS2 .... 74 A1
   CFTN/FAIL BS8 .... 55 E4
Victoria Vw *RDLND/MONT* BS6 ..... 55 H2
Victor Rd *BMSTR* BS3 .... 72 D3
Victor St *CBRISNE* BS2 .... 73 G2
   EVILLE/WHL BS5 .... 56 D5
Vigor Rd
   BMSTRD/HC/WWD BS13 .... 84 B3
Village Cl *YATE/CS* BS37 .... 25 H1
The Village *MANG/FISH* BS16 * 50 A1
Villiers Rd *EVILLE/WHL* BS5 .... 56 D2
The Villings *BMSTR* BS3 * 71 H5

Vilner La *THNB/SVB* BS35 .... 8 C5
Vimpany Cl *HNBRY/STHM* BS10 ... 30 D2
Vimpennys La *THNB/SVB* BS35 ..... 18 B1
Vincent Cl *AVONM* BS11 .... 30 A3
Vine Gdns *MTN/WRL* BS22 .... 122 D1
Vineyards *CBATH/BATHN* BA1 .... 3 F2
Vining Wk *EVILLE/WHL* BS5 .... 56 D5
Vinny Av *MANG/FISH* BS16 .... 49 G1
Vintery Leys
   HNLZ/SM/SNYPK/WT BS9 .... 45 F1
Virginia Cl *YATE/CS* BS37 .... 26 C1
Vivian St *BMSTR* BS3 .... 73 E3
Vowell Cl
   BMSTRD/HC/WWD BS13 .... 84 C5
Vowles Cl *NAIL* BS48 .... 67 H5
Voyager Cl *BRSTK/PCHW* BS34 ..... 34 A1
Vynes Cl *NAIL* BS48 .... 67 H5
Vynes Wy *NAIL* BS48 .... 68 A5
Vyvyan Rd *CFTN/FAIL* BS8............. 55 E4
Vyvyan Ter *CFTN/FAIL* BS8 .... 55 E4

W

Wade Rd *YATE/CS* BS37 .... 13 E4
Wades Rd *BRSTK/PCHW* BS34 ...... 32 D2
Wade St *CBRISNE* BS2 .... 5 J1
Wadham Dr *MANG/FISH* BS16 ..... 34 B4
Wadham Gv *MANG/FISH* BS16 .... 49 H5
Wadham St *WSM* BS23 .... 6 D2
Wagtail Gdns *MTN/WRL* BS22 .... 122 B3
Wainbrook Dr *EVILLE/WHL* BS5 .... 57 F1
Wains Cl *CLVDN* BS21 .... 64 C3
Wainwright Cl
   MTN/WRL BS22 .... 118 A4
Wakedean Gdns
   YTN/CONG BS49 .... 112 A2
Wakeford Rd *MANG/FISH* BS16 .... 35 C5
Wakeford Wy
   OLD/WMLY/WICK BS30 .... 60 B4
Walcot Blds
   CBATH/BATHN BA1 * 102 D4
Walcot Ga *CBATH/BATHN* BA1 ...... 3 G1
Walcot Pde
   CBATH/BATHN BA1 * 102 D4
Walcot St *CBATH/BATHN* BA1 .... 3 G3
Walcot Ter
   CBATH/BATHN BA1 * 102 D4
Waldegrave Rd
   BATHSE BA2 .... 102 B3
Walden Rd *KEYN* BS31 .... 88 D5
Walford Av *MTN/WRL* BS22 .... 118 A4
Walker Cl *EVILLE/WHL* BS5 .... 56 D4
Walker St *CBRISNE* BS2 .... 49 G1
Walkers Dr
   OMX/HUT/LCK BS24 .... 122 C4
Walker St *CBRISNE* BS2 .... 4 D1
Walker Wy *THNB/SVB* BS35 .... 8 C5
Wallace Rd
   CBATH/BATHN BA1 .... 103 E3
Wallingford Rd
   BRSG/KWL/STAPK BS4 .... 85 G2
Walliscote Av
   HNLZ/SM/SNYPK/WT BS9 .... 45 G2
Walliscote Rd
   HNLZ/SM/SNYPK/WT BS9 .... 45 G2
   WSM BS23 .... 6 E4
Walliscote Rd South
   WSM BS23 .... 124 C2
Walliscourt Rd
   BRSTK/PCHW BS34 .... 33 E5
Walliscourt Rd South
   HORF/LLZ BS7 .... 32 D4
Walmesley Ter
   CBATH/BATHN BA1 * 102 D3
Walnut Av *YATE/CS* BS37 .... 14 C5
Walnut Cl *FRCTL/WBN* BS36 .... 24 A4
   KEYN BS31 .... 87 H5
   NAIL BS48 .... 79 F1
   OMX/HUT/LCK BS24 .... 125 F4
   PTSHD/EG BS20 .... 42 A5
   THNB/SVB BS35 .... 8 C5
Walnut Crs *KGWD/HNM* BS15 ...... 59 F3
Walnut Dr *BATHSE* BA2 .... 108 B3
Walnut La *KGWD/HNM* BS15 .... 59 G3
Walnut Tree Cl *ALMDB* BS32 .... 10 C2
Walnut Wk
   BMSTRD/HC/WWD BS13 .... 84 B3
Walsh Av *HGRV/WHIT* BS14 .... 85 H2
Walsh Cl *OMX/HUT/LCK* BS24 ... 125 G4
Walshe Av *YATE/CS* BS37 .... 27 E1
Walsingham Rd
   RDLND/MONT BS6 .... 56 A1
Walter St *BMSTR* BS3 .... 72 B2
Waltham End
   OMX/HUT/LCK BS24 .... 122 D3
Walton Av
   BRSG/KWL/STAPK BS4 .... 74 C1
Walton Cl *KEYN* BS31 .... 88 A5
   OLD/WMLY/WICK BS30 .... 77 F5
Walton Crs
   BLAG/CWMG/WR BS40 .... 93 C4
Walton Dro *CLVDN* BS21 .... 63 F3
Walton Heath *YATE/CS* BS37 .... 26 B1
Walton Ri
   HNLZ/SM/SNYPK/WT BS9 .... 31 E5
Walton Rd *AVONM* BS11 .... 42 D4
   CLVDN BS21 .... 65 F1
Walton St *EVILLE/WHL* BS5 .... 56 D2
Walwyn Cl *BATHSE* BA2 .... 107 F1
Wansbeck Rd *KEYN* BS31 .... 88 D5
Wansbrough Rd
   MTN/WRL BS22 .... 118 A4
Wanscow Wk
   HNLZ/SM/SNYPK/WT BS9 .... 45 F2
Wansdyke Rd *BATHSE* BA2 .... 110 A1
Wapping Rd *CBRIS/FH* BS1 .... 4 E6
Warden Rd *BMSTR* BS3 .... 72 D2
Wardour Rd
   BMSTRD/HC/WWD BS13 .... 84 B5
Wareham Cl *NAIL* BS48 .... 67 E5
Warleigh Dr
   CBATH/BATHN BA1 .... 104 B1
Warleigh La
   CBATH/BATHN BA1 .... 104 C4
Warleys La
   OMX/HUT/LCK BS24 .... 123 F2
Warman Cl *HGRV/WHIT* BS14 ...... 87 E3

Warman Rd *HGRV/WHIT* BS14 ..... 87 E3
Warmington Rd
   HGRV/WHIT BS14 .... 86 B1
Warminster Rd *BATHSE* BA2 .... 103 F4
   CBRISNE BS2 .... 56 C2
Warner Cl *KGWD/HNM* BS15 .... 59 F5
   YTN/CONG BS49 .... 113 G4
Warne Rd *WSM* BS23 .... 7 K5
The Warns
   OLD/WMLY/WICK BS30 .... 76 D2
Warren Cl *ALMDB* BS32 .... 11 F4
   OMX/HUT/LCK BS24 .... 123 F4
Warren Gdns *HGRV/WHIT* BS14 ... 87 E4
Warren La *LGASH* BS41 .... 82 B1
Warren Rd *BRSTK/PCHW* BS34 ..... 32 D2
Warren Wy *YATE/CS* BS37 .... 14 A4
Warrilow Cl *MTN/WRL* BS22 ...... 118 A3
Warrington Rd
   BRSG/KWL/STAPK BS4 .... 74 C4
Warry Cl *NAIL* BS48 .... 68 D4
Warwick Av *EVILLE/WHL* BS5 ...... 57 E1
Warwick Cl *MTN/WRL* BS22 .... 121 H3
   OLD/WMLY/WICK BS30 .... 77 E4
Warwick Pl *THNB/SVB* BS35 .... 8 B3
Warwick Rd
   CBATH/BATHN BA1 .... 101 G5
   KEYN BS31 .... 88 A5
   RDLND/MONT BS6 .... 55 F2
Washingpool La *AVONM* BS11 .... 18 A1
Washing Pound La
   CBRISNE BS2 .... 66 C2
   HGRV/WHIT BS14 .... 86 A5
Washington Av
   EVILLE/WHL BS5 .... 57 G2
Washpool La *BATHSE* BA2 .... 107 E5
Watch Elm Cl *ALMDB* BS32 .... 21 G4
Watch House Pl
   PTSHD/EG BS20 .... 40 A2
Watchhouse Rd
   PTSHD/EG BS20 .... 42 D4
Watchill Av
   BMSTRD/HC/WWD BS13 .... 84 A3
Watchill Cl
   BMSTRD/HC/WWD BS13 .... 84 A3
Watcombe Cl *MTN/WRL* BS22 .... 122 B2
Wateridge Rd
   BMSTRD/HC/WWD BS13 .... 84 A3
Watercress Rd *NAIL* BS48 .... 68 A4
Watercress Rd *HORF/LLZ* BS7 ...... 46 B5
Waterdaie Cl
   HNLZ/SM/SNYPK/WT BS9 .... 45 G1
Waterdale Gdns
   HNLZ/SM/SNYPK/WT BS9 .... 45 G1
Waterford Cl *THNB/SVB* BS35 .... 9 E4
Waterford Rd
   HNLZ/SM/SNYPK/WT BS9 .... 45 F2
Water La *BMSTR* BS3 .... 73 G5
   CBRIS/FH BS1 .... 5 H4
   PTSHD/EG BS20 .... 42 C4
Waterloo Blds *BATHSE* BA2 .... 107 C1
Waterloo Pl *CBRISNE* BS2 .... 5 K3
Waterloo Rd *CBRISNE* BS2 .... 5 K3
Waterloo St *CBRISNE* BS2 .... 5 K2
   CFTN/FAIL BS8 .... 54 D4
   WSM BS23 .... 6 F4
Watermore Cl
   FRCTL/WBN BS36 .... 24 A3
Waterside Dr *ALMDB* BS32 .... 10 D4
Waterside Pk
   PTSHD/EG BS20 .... 38 B4
Water's La
   HNLZ/SM/SNYPK/WT BS9 .... 45 E2
Waters Rd *KGWD/HNM* BS15 .... 58 C3
Watery La *BATHSE* BA2 .... 107 H4
   NAIL BS48 .... 66 C4
Wathen Rd *RDLND/MONT* BS6 ..... 46 B5
Watkins Yd
   HNLZ/SM/SNYPK/WT BS9 .... 31 E5
Watley's End Rd
   FRCTL/WBN BS36 .... 23 E5
Watling Wy *AVONM* BS11 .... 42 D4
Watson Av
   BRSG/KWL/STAPK BS4 .... 74 C2
Watson's Rd
   OLD/WMLY/WICK BS30 .... 76 C3
Watters Cl *FRCTL/WBN* BS36 .... 24 B4
Wavell Cl *YATE/CS* BS37 .... 13 H5
Waveney Rd *KEYN* BS31 .... 98 B1
Waverley Rd *AVONM* BS11 .... 43 F2
   NAIL BS48 .... 79 H2
   RDLND/MONT BS6 .... 55 F2
   WSM BS23 .... 125 E2
Waverley St *EVILLE/WHL* BS5 .... 56 C2
Wayfield Gdns
   CBATH/BATHN BA1 .... 91 E5
Wayford Cl *KEYN* BS31 .... 98 B1
Wayland Rd *MTN/WRL* BS22 ...... 117 F5
Wayleaze *FRCTL/WBN* BS36 .... 24 B3
Wayside *MTN/WRL* BS22 .... 122 A1
Wayside Cl *FRCTL/WBN* BS36 ...... 23 H3
Wayside Dr *CLVDN* BS21 .... 62 C5
The Weal *CBATH/BATHN* BA1 ..... 101 G2
Weatherley Dr *PTSHD/EG* BS20 .... 38 D5
Weatherly Av *BATHSE* BA2 .... 108 A5
Webbs Heath
   OLD/WMLY/WICK BS30 .... 60 B4
Webb St *EVILLE/WHL* BS5 .... 56 C3
Webbs Wood Rd *ALMDB* BS32 ..... 11 H4
Wedgewood Rd
   MANG/FISH BS16 .... 34 D4
Wedgwood Cl
   HGRV/WHIT BS14 .... 86 A4
Wedgwood Rd *BATHSE* BA2 .... 107 E2
Wedlock Wy *BMSTR* BS3 .... 72 A3
Wedmore Cl *BATHSE* BA2 .... 107 H4
   KGWD/HNM BS15 .... 59 F5
Wedmore Pk *BATHSE* BA2 .... 107 F4
Wedmore Rd *CLVDN* BS21 .... 64 D3
   KEYN BS31 .... 89 G5
   NAIL BS48 .... 68 A5
Wedmore V *BMSTR* BS3 .... 73 H4
Weedon Cl *CBRISNE* BS2 .... 56 C4
Weetwood Rd
   YTN/CONG BS49 .... 115 E1
Weight Rd *EVILLE/WHL* BS5 .... 57 E4
The Weind *MTN/WRL* BS22 .... 122 A1
Weir La *CFTN/FAIL* BS8 .... 70 B1

Weir Rd *YTN/CONG* BS49 .... 115 E3
Welland Rd *KEYN* BS31 .... 88 C5
Wellard Cl *MTN/WRL* BS22 * 118 A4
Well Cl *LGASH* BS41 .... 71 E5
Well Cl *OMX/HUT/LCK* BS24 ...... 125 G4
Wellgarth Rd
   BRSG/KWL/STAPK BS4 .... 73 H4
Wellgarth Wk
   BRSG/KWL/STAPK BS4 .... 73 H5
Well House Cl
   HNLZ/SM/SNYPK/WT BS9 .... 54 C1
Wellington Av
   RDLND/MONT BS6 .... 56 A2
Wellington Blds
   CBATH/BATHN BA1 .... 101 G2
Wellington Dr
   HNLZ/SM/SNYPK/WT BS9 .... 45 H2
   YATE/CS BS37 .... 13 F5
Wellington HI *HORF/LLZ* BS7 .... 46 A2
Wellington HI West
   HNLZ/SM/SNYPK/WT BS9 .... 45 H1
Wellington La
   RDLND/MONT BS6 .... 56 A2
Wellington Ms *AVONM* BS11 .... 42 D3
Wellington Pde *CFTN/FAIL* BS8 ..... 55 E2
Wellington Pl *WSM* BS23 * 6 D4
   KGWD/HNM BS15 .... 59 E2
   YATE/CS BS37 .... 12 D4
Wellington Rd *CFTN/FAIL* BS8 ...... 54 D5
   CLVDN BS21 .... 62 A5
Wellington Wk
   HNBRY/STHM BS10 .... 45 G1
Well La *BNWL* BS29 .... 127 H5
Well Pk *YTN/CONG* BS49 .... 115 E2
Wells Cl *HGRV/WHIT* BS14 .... 86 B4
Wells Rd *BATHSE* BA2 .... 2 E7
   BRSG/KWL/STAPK BS4 .... 73 C2
   HGRV/WHIT BS14 .... 86 A1
   LGASH BS41 .... 94 D5
Wells St *BMSTR* BS3 .... 72 C2
Wellstead Av *YATE/CS* BS37 .... 25 H1
Wellsway *BATHSE* BA2 .... 110 B2
Wellsway Pk *BATHSE* BA2 .... 110 B2
Wellsway *KEYN* BS31 .... 99 E1
Welsford Av *MANG/FISH* BS16 ..... 47 F4
Welsford Rd *MANG/FISH* BS16 .... 47 E4
Welsh Back *CBRIS/FH* BS1 .... 5 F6
Welton Wk *KGWD/HNM* BS15 ..... 58 C1
Wemberham Crs
   YTN/CONG BS49 .... 112 A2
Wemberham La
   YTN/CONG BS49 .... 112 A3
Wenmore Cl *MANG/FISH* BS16 .... 34 D4
Wentforth Dr
   KGWD/HNM BS15 .... 58 C1
Wentwood Dr
   OMX/HUT/LCK BS24 .... 125 F5
Wentworth
   OLD/WMLY/WICK BS30 .... 59 G5
   YATE/CS BS37 .... 26 A1
Wentworth Cl *MTN/WRL* BS22 ... 117 G5
Wentworth Rd *HORF/LLZ* BS7 ...... 45 H5
Wescott Gv *AVONM* BS11 * 30 A3
Wesley Av *KGWD/HNM* BS15 ...... 76 A1
Wesley Cl *EVILLE/WHL* BS5 .... 57 H2
   MANG/FISH BS16 * 48 D5
Wesley Dr *MTN/WRL* BS22 .... 117 H5
Wesley HI *KGWD/HNM* BS15 .... 58 D2
Wesley La
   OLD/WMLY/WICK BS30 .... 77 E1
Wesley Pl *CFTN/FAIL* BS8 .... 55 E1
Wesley Rd *HORF/LLZ* BS7 .... 46 A4
Wesley St *BMSTR* BS3 .... 72 D3
Wessex Av *HORF/LLZ* BS7 .... 46 B3
Wessex Ct *HORF/LLZ* BS7 * 46 B1
Wessex Rd
   OMX/HUT/LCK BS24 .... 125 G4
Westacre Cl
   HNBRY/STHM BS10 .... 31 E3
West Ar *CBRIS/FH* BS1 * 5 F4
West Av *BATHSE* BA2 .... 107 H2
Westaway Cl *YTN/CONG* BS49 .... 112 C4
Westaway Pk
   YTN/CONG BS49 .... 112 D4
Westbourne Av *CLVDN* BS21 .... 64 B3
   KEYN BS31 .... 88 B4
Westbourne Cl
   MANG/FISH BS16 .... 49 F1
Westbourne Crs *CLVDN* BS21 ...... 64 B3
Westbourne Pl *CFTN/FAIL* BS8 .... 4 A1
Westbourne Rd
   EVILLE/WHL BS5 .... 56 D5
   MANG/FISH BS16 .... 35 F5
West Broadway
   HNLZ/SM/SNYPK/WT BS9 .... 45 G2
Westbrooke Ct *CBRIS/FH* BS1 * 72 B1
Westbrook Rd
   CBATH/BATHN BA1 .... 101 F2
   BRSG/KWL/STAPK BS4 .... 86 C1
   MTN/WRL BS22 .... 122 A2
Westbury Court Rd
   HNLZ/SM/SNYPK/WT BS9 .... 44 D1
Westbury Crs *WSM* BS23 .... 125 E4
Westbury HI
   HNLZ/SM/SNYPK/WT BS9 .... 45 E1
Westbury La
   HNLZ/SM/SNYPK/WT BS9 .... 43 H1
Westbury Ms
   HNLZ/SM/SNYPK/WT BS9 .... 45 E1
Westbury Pk
   RDLND/MONT BS6 .... 45 E4
Westbury Rd
   RDLND/MONT BS6 .... 45 E4
West Cl *BATHSE* BA2 .... 107 F2
West Coombe
   HNLZ/SM/SNYPK/WT BS9 .... 44 B2
West Courtney
   OLD/WMLY/WICK BS30 .... 77 G2
West Cft *CLVDN* BS21 .... 64 B3
   HNLZ/SM/SNYPK/WT BS9 .... 45 G1

West Dene
HNLZ/SM/SNYPK/WT BS9 44 C2
West Dundry La LGASH BS41 94 D2
West End BMSTR BS3 72 D2
CBRISNE BS2 4 E1
West End La NAIL BS48 78 A2
Westering Cl MANG/FISH BS16 49 G3
Westerleigh Cl
MANG/FISH BS16 49 F1
Westerleigh Rd BATHSE BA2 111 F1
CLVDN BS21 64 B3
MANG/FISH BS16 51 F2
MANG/FISH BS16 49 E2
MANG/FISH BS16 37 G5
YATE/CS BS37 37 E2
Western Av FRCTL/WBN BS36 23 G2
Western Ct BRSTK/PCHW BS34 34 A1
Western Dr
BRSG/KWL/STAPK BS4 85 F2
Western Rd HORF/LLZ BS7 46 A2
Westfield CLVDN BS21 64 D5
Westfield Cl BATHSE BA2 108 B4
KEYN BS31 87 H4
KGWD/HNM BS15 76 A1
NAIL BS48 79 H3
WSM BS23 124 C4
Westfield Dr NAIL BS48 79 H3
Westfield La
BRSTK/PCHW BS34 33 G2
Westfield Pk
CBATH/BATHN BA1 101 F5
RDLND/MONT BS6 55 F2
Westfield Pl CFTN/FAIL BS8 54 D4
Westfield Rd
HNLZ/SM/SNYPK/WT BS9 31 E5
NAIL BS48 79 H3
Westfield Wy ALMDB BS32 11 F5
Westgate CBRIS/FH BS1 * 4 B6
Westgate Blds
CBATH/BATHN BA1 3 F4
Westgate St CBATH/BATHN BA1 3 F4
West Gv RDLND/MONT BS6 56 B2
Westhall Rd CBATH/BATHN BA1 2 A2
West Hl PTSHD/EG BS20 39 G3
West Hill Ct PTSHD/EG BS20 39 G2
West Hill Gdns PTSHD/EG BS20 39 G3
Westland Av
OLD/WMLY/WICK BS30 77 F2
West La BLAG/CWMG/WR BS40 92 C4
West Lea Rd
CBATH/BATHN BA1 101 F4
West Leaze Pl ALMDB BS32 21 G4
Westleigh Cl
HNBRY/STHM BS10 31 H4
YATE/CS BS37 25 G1
Westleigh Pk HGRV/WHIT BS14 85 H1
Westleigh Rd
HNBRY/STHM BS10 31 G4
West Links Cl MTN/WRL BS22 116 C5
West Ml CFTN/FAIL BS8 54 D4
Westmarch Wy
MTN/WRL BS22 117 H4
Westmead Gdns
CBATH/BATHN BA1 101 F2
Westmead Rd EVILLE/WHL BS5 58 B4
Westminster Cl
HNLZ/SM/SNYPK/WT BS9 * 45 E1
Westminster Rd
EVILLE/WHL BS5 57 F3
Westmoreland Dr BATHSE BA2 2 D5
Westmoreland Rd BATHSE BA2 2 D6
RDLND/MONT BS6 45 E5
Westmoreland Station Rd
BATHSE BA2 2 C6
Westmoreland St BATHSE BA2 2 D6
Weston Av EVILLE/WHL BS5 57 F4
Weston Cl
HNLZ/SM/SNYPK/WT BS9 44 A1
Weston Crs HORF/LLZ BS7 46 A2
Weston Farm La
CBATH/BATHN BA1 101 G2
Weston La CBATH/BATHN BA1 101 H3
Weston Ldg WSM BS23 * 6 D2
Weston Pk CBATH/BATHN BA1 101 H3
Weston Pk East
CBATH/BATHN BA1 102 A4
Weston Pk West
CBATH/BATHN BA1 101 H3
Weston Rd CBATH/BATHN BA1 2 A1
CFTN/FAIL BS8 69 H3
LGASH BS41 70 C5
NAIL BS48 82 A1
YTN/CONG BS49 114 A1
Westons Brake
MANG/FISH BS16 35 G4
Westons Hill Dr
MANG/FISH BS16 35 G5
Westons Wy
KGWD/HNM BS15 59 F4
Weston Wy
OMX/HUT/LCK BS24 126 B4
Weston Wood Rd
PTSHD/EG BS20 39 G5
Westover Cl
HNLZ/SM/SNYPK/WT BS9 30 D4
Westover Dr
HNLZ/SM/SNYPK/WT BS9 31 E5
Westover Gdns
HNLZ/SM/SNYPK/WT BS9 30 D5
Westover Ri
HNLZ/SM/SNYPK/WT BS9 31 E4
Westover Rd
HNLZ/SM/SNYPK/WT BS9 31 E5
West Pde
HNLZ/SM/SNYPK/WT BS9 44 A1
West Pk CFTN/FAIL BS8 55 F3
West Park Rd MANG/FISH BS16 49 E3
West Priory Cl
HNLZ/SM/SNYPK/WT BS9 45 E1
West Rdg FRCTL/WBN BS36 23 H3
West Rd YTN/CONG BS49 112 B4
West Rocke Av
HNLZ/SM/SNYPK/WT BS9 44 B1
West Shrubbery
RDLND/MONT BS6 55 F1
West St BMSTR BS3 72 C4
CBRISNE BS2 5 K3
KGWD/HNM BS15 58 D3
OLD/WMLY/WICK BS30 77 F2
WSM BS23 6 D3
West Town Dr
BRSG/KWL/STAPK BS4 86 C1
West Town Gv
BRSG/KWL/STAPK BS4 86 C1
West Town La
BRSG/KWL/STAPK BS4 74 C5
HGRV/WHIT BS14 86 A1
West Town Pk
BRSG/KWL/STAPK BS4 74 C5
West Town Rd AVONM BS11 42 C1
NAIL BS48 79 H4
West View Rd BMSTR BS3 72 C3
CBATH/BATHN BA1 104 B1
KEYN BS31 88 B4
Westward Dr PTSHD/EG BS20 42 C4
Westward Gdns LGASH BS41 71 E4
Westward Rd
BMSTRD/HC/WWD BS13 84 A2
West Wy CLVDN BS21 64 C2
HNBRY/STHM BS10 32 A1
Westway NAIL BS48 67 E4
West Wick
OMX/HUT/LCK BS24 123 F3
Westwood Cl MTN/WRL BS22 122 C1
Westwood Crs
BRSG/KWL/STAPK BS4 74 C1
Westwood Rd
BRSG/KWL/STAPK BS4 86 C1
Westwoods
CBATH/BATHN BA1 104 C1
Wetherby Ct MANG/FISH BS16 35 F4
Wetherell Pl CFTN/FAIL BS8 4 A3
Wetlands La PTSHD/EG BS20 39 G5
Wexford Rd
BRSG/KWL/STAPK BS4 85 E1
Weymouth Rd BMSTR BS3 73 E4
Weymouth St
CBATH/BATHN BA1 103 E4
Wharfedale THNB/SVB BS35 9 E4
Wharf La PTSHD/EG BS20 40 D3
Wharf Rd MANG/FISH BS16 47 H4
Wharnecliffe Cl
HGRV/WHIT BS14 86 A4
Wharnecliffe Gdns
HGRV/WHIT BS14 86 A4
Whatley Rd CFTN/FAIL BS8 55 E2
Wheatfield Dr ALMDB BS32 21 F1
MTN/WRL BS22 117 H3
Wheathill Cl KEYN BS31 87 H4
Wheelers Patch
MANG/FISH BS16 49 H3
Whinchat Gdns
MANG/FISH BS16 47 H2
Whippington Ct
CBRIS/FH BS1 * 5 G2
Whistle Rd KGWD/HNM BS15 59 H1
Whitby Rd
BRSG/KWL/STAPK BS4 74 B1
Whitchurch La
BMSTRD/HC/WWD BS13 84 B4
LGASH BS41 95 G3
Whitecross Av
HGRV/WHIT BS14 86 B3
Whitecross Rd WSM BS23 124 D1
Whitefield Av EVILLE/WHL BS5 58 A2
KGWD/HNM BS15 76 A1
Whitefield Cl
CBATH/BATHN BA1 91 G5
Whitefield Rd EVILLE/WHL BS5 58 A1
Whitefields YATE/CS BS37 27 E1
Whitehall Av EVILLE/WHL BS5 57 G2
Whitehall Gdns
EVILLE/WHL BS5 57 F2
Whitehall Rd EVILLE/WHL BS5 57 E3
Whitehouse La BMSTR BS3 73 E2
Whitehouse Pl BMSTR BS3 73 F2
White House Rd
YTN/CONG BS49 113 F3
Whitehouse St BMSTR BS3 73 F2
Whiteladies Ga
CFTN/FAIL BS8 * 55 F2
Whiteladies Rd CFTN/FAIL BS8 4 B1
Whiteleaze HNBRY/STHM BS10 31 G5
White Lodge Pk
PTSHD/EG BS20 39 H2
White Lodge Rd
MANG/FISH BS16 49 F4
Whiteoak Wy NAIL BS48 79 E1
Whitesfield Rd NAIL BS48 67 E5
Whites Hl EVILLE/WHL BS5 58 A5
Whiteshill MANG/FISH BS16 34 D2
White St EVILLE/WHL BS5 5 K1
Whitethorn V
HNBRY/STHM BS10 31 G2
White Tree Rd
HNLZ/SM/SNYPK/WT BS9 45 F4
Whitewall La THNB/SVB BS35 9 G2
Whiteway Cl
BRSG/KWL/STAPK BS4 57 G5
EVILLE/WHL BS5 58 A3
Whiteway Ct EVILLE/WHL BS5 58 A3
Whiteway Ms EVILLE/WHL BS5 58 A3
Whiteway Rd BATHSE BA2 107 E2
EVILLE/WHL BS5 58 A2
Whitewells Rd
CBATH/BATHN BA1 102 D2
Whitewood Rd
EVILLE/WHL BS5 57 H2
Whitfield Cl MANG/FISH BS16 48 D5
Whitfield Rd THNB/SVB BS35 8 D2
Whiting Rd
BMSTRD/HC/WWD BS13 84 B5
Whitland Av
BMSTRD/HC/WWD BS13 84 C4
Whitland Rd
BMSTRD/HC/WWD BS13 84 C4
Whitley Cl YATE/CS BS37 13 G4
Whitley Md BRSTK/PCHW BS34 33 G2
Whitmead Gdns
BMSTRD/HC/WWD BS13 84 D5
Whitmore Av
BRSG/KWL/STAPK BS4 75 F3
Whitson St CBRIS/FH BS1 5 F1
Whitting Rd WSM BS23 124 D2
Whittington Dr
MTN/WRL BS22 122 A1
Whittington Rd
MANG/FISH BS16 48 C2
Whittock Rd HGRV/WHIT BS14 86 C4
Whittock Sq HGRV/WHIT BS14 86 C2
Whittucks Cl KGWD/HNM BS15 76 A2
Whittucks Rd
KGWD/HNM BS15 75 H2
Whitwell Rd HGRV/WHIT BS14 86 A1
Whytes Cl
HNLZ/SM/SNYPK/WT BS9 31 E5
Wick Crs BRSG/KWL/STAPK BS4 74 C3
The Wickets HORF/LLZ BS7 32 B4
KGWD/HNM BS15 58 D1
Wickfield CLVDN BS21 64 C4
Wickham Cl YATE/CS BS37 27 F2
Wickham Ct MANG/FISH BS16 47 F3
Wickham Gln MANG/FISH BS16 47 F3
Wickham Hl MANG/FISH BS16 47 F3
Wickham Vw MANG/FISH BS16 47 F4
Wick House Cl KEYN BS31 99 E1
Wicklow Rd
BRSG/KWL/STAPK BS4 85 F1
Wick Rd BRSG/KWL/STAPK BS4 74 C2
MTN/WRL BS22 117 H1
OMX/HUT/LCK BS24 119 E3
Wicks Rd MTN/WRL BS22 118 A1
Wickwar Rd YATE/CS BS37 14 C4
Wick Wick Cl FRCTL/WBN BS36 35 G4
Widcombe HGRV/WHIT BS14 85 H4
Widcombe Cl EVILLE/WHL BS5 58 A4
Widcombe Crs BATHSE BA2 3 J7
Widcombe Hl BATHSE BA2 3 J7
Widcombe Pde BATHSE BA2 * 3 H7
Widcombe Ri BATHSE BA2 3 J7
Widcombe Ter BATHSE BA2 3 K7
Widmore Gv
BMSTRD/HC/WWD BS13 * 84 C4
Wight Rw PTSHD/EG BS20 40 B2
Wigmore Gdns
MTN/WRL BS22 121 H1
Wigton Crs HNBRY/STHM BS10 31 G3
Wilbye Gv
BRSG/KWL/STAPK BS4 85 E2
Wilcox Cl KGWD/HNM BS15 58 C4
Wildcountry La NAIL BS48 82 B4
Wildcroft Rd
HNLZ/SM/SNYPK/WT BS9 45 F3
Willada Cl BMSTR BS3 72 C4
William Mason Cl
EVILLE/WHL BS5 56 D4
Williams Cl
OLD/WMLY/WICK BS30 76 C4
Williamson Rd HORF/LLZ BS7 46 B5
William St BATHSE BA2 3 H3
BMSTR BS3 73 F2
CBRISNE BS2 56 B2
MANG/FISH BS16 48 B5
Willianstowe BATHSE BA2 111 G1
Willinton Rd
BRSG/KWL/STAPK BS4 85 G2
Willis Rd KGWD/HNM BS15 59 F1
Williton Crs WSM BS23 125 E4
Willment Wy AVONM BS11 28 D4
Willmott Cl HGRV/WHIT BS14 96 C1
Willoughby Cl
BMSTRD/HC/WWD BS13 84 B2
Willoughby Rd HORF/LLZ BS7 46 A3
Willow Bed Cl MANG/FISH BS16 48 B2
Willow Cl BATHSE BA2 110 B2
BRSTK/PCHW BS34 20 A3
CLVDN BS21 65 E2
LGASH BS41 70 C5
MTN/WRL BS22 123 G1
OLD/WMLY/WICK BS30 60 B5
PTSHD/EG BS20 39 G4
WSM BS23 124 D4
Willowdown MTN/WRL BS22 117 F4
Willow Dr OMX/HUT/LCK BS24 126 B4
The Willowfalls
CBATH/BATHN BA1 103 H1
Willow Gdns MTN/WRL BS22 123 G1
Willow Gn BATHSE BA2 108 B3
Willow Gv MANG/FISH BS16 58 C1
Willow Rd KGWD/HNM BS15 75 H2
The Willows ALMDB BS32 21 F2
NAIL BS48 67 G3
YATE/CS BS37 13 H5
Willow Wk HNBRY/STHM BS10 31 F2
KEYN BS31 88 A5
Willow Wy FRCTL/WBN BS36 24 A4
Willsbridge Hl
OLD/WMLY/WICK BS30 76 D4
Wills Dr EVILLE/WHL BS5 56 C3
Wills Wy
BMSTRD/HC/WWD BS13 85 E3
Willway St BMSTR BS3 73 F2
CBRISNE BS2 5 K3
Wilmot Ct
OLD/WMLY/WICK BS30 59 G5
Wilmots Wy PTSHD/EG BS20 42 D4
Wilshire Av KGWD/HNM BS15 76 A1
Wilson Pl CBRISNE BS2 56 B3
Wilson St CBRISNE BS2 5 H1
Wilton Cl HNBRY/STHM BS10 31 G5
Wilton Gdns WSM BS23 6 E6
Wiltshire Av YATE/CS BS37 14 C4
Wiltshire Pl MANG/FISH BS16 49 E5
Wiltshire Wy
CBATH/BATHN BA1 102 D2
Wimbledon Rd
RDLND/MONT BS6 45 G3
Wimborne Rd BMSTR BS3 72 D5
Winash Cl HGRV/WHIT BS14 86 C1
Wincanton Cl MANG/FISH BS16 35 F4
NAIL BS48 68 A5
Winchcombe Cl NAIL BS48 79 H1
Winchcombe Rd
FRCTL/WBN BS36 23 H2
Winchester Av
BRSG/KWL/STAPK BS4 74 C3
Winchester Rd BATHSE BA2 2 B6
BRSG/KWL/STAPK BS4 74 C3
Wincroft
OLD/WMLY/WICK BS30 77 F2
Windcliff Crs AVONM BS11 29 E5
Windermere
HNBRY/STHM BS10 * 31 H3
Windermere Av WSM BS23 125 E2
Windermere Rd
BRSTK/PCHW BS34 20 C2
Windermere Wy
OLD/WMLY/WICK BS30 60 B5
Windmill Cl BMSTR BS3 73 F2
Windmill Hl BMSTR BS3 73 E3
OMX/HUT/LCK BS24 126 D4
Windmill La
HNBRY/STHM BS10 30 B2
Windmill Rd CLVDN BS21 65 E5
Windrush Cl BATHSE BA2 107 E3
Windrush Ct THNB/SVB BS35 8 D4
Windrush Rd KEYN BS31 88 D5
Windscreens Av CBRISNE BS2 5 K3
Windsor Av EVILLE/WHL BS5 58 B5
KEYN BS31 88 B5
Windsor Bridge Rd
CBATH/BATHN BA1 2 A3
Windsor Cl BRSTK/PCHW BS34 33 G1
CLVDN BS21 64 C3
Windsor Ct MANG/FISH BS16 49 E1
Windsor Crs
HNBRY/STHM BS10 30 A1
Windsor Dr NAIL BS48 67 F4
YATE/CS BS37 13 H4
Windsor Gv EVILLE/WHL BS5 56 D3
Windsor Pl
CBATH/BATHN BA1 * 101 H5
CFTN/FAIL BS8 54 D5
MANG/FISH BS16 49 G3
Windsor Rd MTN/WRL BS22 121 H1
OLD/WMLY/WICK BS30 76 C4
RDLND/MONT BS6 56 A1
Windsor Ter BMSTR BS3 73 G2
CFTN/FAIL BS8 54 D5
Windsor Vls
CBATH/BATHN BA1 101 H5
Windwhistle Cir WSM BS23 125 E2
Windwhistle La WSM BS23 124 D3
Windwhistle Rd WSM BS23 124 C3
Wineberry Cl EVILLE/WHL BS5 57 F2
Wine St CBRIS/FH BS1 5 F3
Winfield Rd
OLD/WMLY/WICK BS30 60 A4
Winford Cl PTSHD/EG BS20 40 A4
Winford Gv
BMSTRD/HC/WWD BS13 84 B1
Winford La
BLAG/CWMG/WR BS40 94 A4
Wingard Cl WSM BS23 124 C4
Wingard Ct WSM BS23 124 D1
Wingfield Rd BMSTR BS3 73 F4
Winifred's La
CBATH/BATHN BA1 102 B3
Winkworth Pl CBRISNE BS2 56 B2
Winsbury Wy ALMDB BS32 21 E2
Winscombe Cl KEYN BS31 88 A3
Winscombe Rd WSM BS23 7 H5
Winsford St EVILLE/WHL BS5 * 56 C3
Winsham Cl HGRV/WHIT BS14 86 A4
Winsley Rd RDLND/MONT BS6 55 H2
Winterbourne Hl
FRCTL/WBN BS36 22 D5
Winterbourne Rd
BRSTK/PCHW BS34 21 H4
Winterstoke Cl BMSTR BS3 72 C4
Winterstoke Rd BMSTR BS3 72 A3
OMX/HUT/LCK BS24 125 G4
WSM BS23 7 J7
Winton St
BRSG/KWL/STAPK BS4 73 G2
Wistaria Av YATE/CS BS37 26 C1
Wisteria Av
OMX/HUT/LCK BS24 126 A4
Witchell Rd EVILLE/WHL BS5 57 E4
Witch Hazel Rd
BMSTRD/HC/WWD BS13 96 B1
Witcombe YATE/CS BS37 25 G3
Witcombe Cl KGWD/HNM BS15 59 E2
Witham Rd KEYN BS31 98 B1
Witherlies Rd
MANG/FISH BS16 47 H2
Withey Cl West H
NLZ/SM/SNYPK/WT BS9 44 C3
The Witheys HGRV/WHIT BS14 86 B5
Withington Cl
OLD/WMLY/WICK BS30 77 F4
Withleigh Rd
BRSG/KWL/STAPK BS4 74 A4
Withy Cl NAIL BS48 67 G3
Withy Cl East
HNLZ/SM/SNYPK/WT BS9 44 D3
Withymead YTN/CONG BS49 113 F2
Withypool Gdns
HGRV/WHIT BS14 86 A4
The Withys PTSHD/EG BS20 42 D4
Withywood Gdns
BMSTRD/HC/WWD BS13 * 84 A5
Withywood Rd
BMSTRD/HC/WWD BS13 84 A5
Witney Cl KEYN BS31 99 E1
Witney Md FRCTL/WBN BS36 23 H2
Woburn Cl
OLD/WMLY/WICK BS30 76 C1
Woburn Rd EVILLE/WHL BS5 46 D5
Wolferton Rd HORF/LLZ BS7 56 B1
Wolfridge Gdns
HNBRY/STHM BS10 31 E1
Wolseley Rd HORF/LLZ BS7 45 H5
Wolvers Hill Rd
OMX/HUT/LCK BS24 123 F3
Woodacre PTSHD/EG BS20 40 A1
Woodbine Rd EVILLE/WHL BS5 57 E3
Woodborough St
EVILLE/WHL BS5 56 D2
Woodbridge Rd
BRSG/KWL/STAPK BS4 73 H4
Woodchester
KGWD/HNM BS15 49 E5
YATE/CS BS37 26 A4
Woodchester Rd
HNBRY/STHM BS10 45 G1
Woodcliff Rd MTN/WRL BS22 121 H2
Woodcote KGWD/HNM BS15 58 D5
Woodcote Rd MANG/FISH BS16 58 B1
Woodcote Wk
MANG/FISH BS16 58 B1
Woodcroft Av EVILLE/WHL BS5 57 F3
Woodcroft Cl
BRSG/KWL/STAPK BS4 74 D2
Woodcroft Rd
BRSG/KWL/STAPK BS4 74 D2
Woodend KGWD/HNM BS15 58 D5
Woodend Rd FRCTL/WBN BS36 23 H3
Wood End Wk
HNLZ/SM/SNYPK/WT BS9 44 A2
Woodfield Rd
RDLND/MONT BS6 55 F2
Woodford Cl NAIL BS48 67 H5
Woodgrove Rd
HNBRY/STHM BS10 30 B3
Woodhall Cl MANG/FISH BS16 49 F2
Wood Hl YTN/CONG BS49 112 D5
Woodhill Av PTSHD/EG BS20 39 H2
Wood Hill Pk PTSHD/EG BS20 39 H1
Woodhill Rd PTSHD/EG BS20 39 H2
Woodhill Views NAIL BS48 67 G3
Woodhouse Gv HORF/LLZ BS7 46 A2
Woodhouse Rd BATHSE BA2 107 F1
Woodhurst Rd WSM BS23 7 J3
Woodington Ct
OLD/WMLY/WICK BS30 76 C2
Woodington Rd CLVDN BS21 64 C4
The Wood Kilns
YTN/CONG BS49 112 A2
Woodland Av
KGWD/HNM BS15 58 D1
Woodland Cl CFTN/FAIL BS8 69 G2
KGWD/HNM BS15 58 C1
Woodland Ct
MANG/FISH BS16 * 48 C2
Woodland Gld CLVDN BS21 62 C5
Woodland Gv BATHSE BA2 109 H2
HNLZ/SM/SNYPK/WT BS9 44 B2
Woodland Pl BATHSE BA2 109 G2
Woodland Rd CFTN/FAIL BS8 4 C2
NAIL BS48 67 F3
WSM BS23 124 C2
Woodlands ALMDB BS32 11 F4
CLVDN BS21 64 C1
MANG/FISH BS16 49 E2
Woodlands La ALMDB BS32 10 D5
Woodlands Pk
ALMDB BS32 10 D4
CBATH/BATHN BA1 103 F2
Woodlands Ri
MANG/FISH BS16 48 D2
Woodland Ter
KGWD/HNM BS15 58 D4
RDLND/MONT BS6 55 F1
Woodland Wy CFTN/FAIL BS8 69 G2
KGWD/HNM BS15 58 C1
Wood La WSM BS23 7 H1
Woodleaze
HNLZ/SM/SNYPK/WT BS9 43 H2
Woodleigh THNB/SVB BS35 8 D3
Woodleigh Gdns
HGRV/WHIT BS14 86 B3
Woodmancote YATE/CS BS37 25 H2
Woodmancote Rd
RDLND/MONT BS6 56 A2
Woodmans Cl YATE/CS BS37 26 D2
Woodmans Rd YATE/CS BS37 26 D2
Woodmans V YATE/CS BS37 27 E2
Woodmarsh Cl
HGRV/WHIT BS14 85 H5
Woodmead Gdns
BMSTRD/HC/WWD BS13 84 D5
Woodmill YTN/CONG BS49 112 A2
Woodpecker Crs
MANG/FISH BS16 51 G4
Woodpecker Dr
MTN/WRL BS22 122 B3
Wood Rd KGWD/HNM BS15 58 D3
Woodside
HNLZ/SM/SNYPK/WT BS9 * 44 B5
Woodside Av
OMX/HUT/LCK BS24 125 G4
Woodside Gdns
PTSHD/EG BS20 38 C3
Woodside Gv
HNBRY/STHM BS10 30 B2
Woodside Rd
BRSG/KWL/STAPK BS4 57 G5
CLVDN BS21 62 C5
FRCTL/WBN BS36 24 B3
KGWD/HNM BS15 58 C3
Woodspring Av
MTN/WRL BS22 116 B5
Woodspring Crs
MTN/WRL BS22 116 B5
Woodstock Av
RDLND/MONT BS6 55 G2
Woodstock Cl
KGWD/HNM BS15 59 F3
Woodstock Rd
KGWD/HNM BS15 59 F3
MTN/WRL BS22 121 G3
RDLND/MONT BS6 55 F1
Wood St BATHSE BA2 2 E6
CBATH/BATHN BA1 3 F4
EVILLE/WHL BS5 56 D1
Woodview CLVDN BS21 65 F2
Woodview Cl AVONM BS11 43 E1
Woodview Dr
YTN/CONG BS49 113 G3
Woodview Ter NAIL BS48 67 G4
WSM BS23 7 H6
Woodward Av YATE/CS BS37 25 F1
Woodward Dr
OLD/WMLY/WICK BS30 76 C2
Woodwell Rd AVONM BS11 43 E2
Woodyleaze Dr
KGWD/HNM BS15 58 C5
Wookey Cl NAIL BS48 79 G1
Woolcot St RDLND/MONT BS6 55 F1
Wooler Rd WSM BS23 7 F3
Woollard La HGRV/WHIT BS14 97 G2
Woolley Rd HGRV/WHIT BS14 86 D4
Woolvers Hill Rd BNWL BS29 127 H1
Woolvers Wy
OMX/HUT/LCK BS24 123 E5
Wootton Crs
BRSG/KWL/STAPK BS4 57 G5
Wootton Pk HGRV/WHIT BS14 74 A5
Wootton Rd
BRSG/KWL/STAPK BS4 57 G5
Worcester Blds
CBATH/BATHN BA1 103 E2
Worcester Cl MANG/FISH BS16 58 B1
Worcester Crs CFTN/FAIL BS8 54 D3
Worcester Gdns NAIL BS48 78 C1
Worcester Pk
CBATH/BATHN BA1 103 E3
Worcester Pl
CBATH/BATHN BA1 * 103 E2

Worcester Rd CFTN/FAIL BS8 ....55 E3
   KGWD/HNM BS15 ....58 D2
Worcester Ter
   CBATH/BATHN BA1 ....103 E5
   CFTN/FAIL BS8 ....55 E3
Worcester Vls
   CBATH/BATHN BA1 ....103 E2
Wordsworth Rd CLVDN BS21 ....64 C3
   HORF/LLZ BS7 ....46 C1
   WSM BS23 ....125 F5
Workshop Rd AVONM BS11 ......28 C1
World's End La KEYN BS31 ....89 F4
Worlebury Cl MTN/WRL BS22 ..116 C5
Worlebury Hill Rd
   MTN/WRL BS22 ....121 F1
   WSM BS23 ....121 E1
Worlebury Park Rd
   MTN/WRL BS22 ....116 B5
Worle Ct MTN/WRL BS22 ....117 C5
Worle Moor Rd
   OMX/HUT/LCK BS24 ....122 B4
Worrall Ms CFTN/FAIL BS8 ....55 F1
Worrall Rd CFTN/FAIL BS8 ....55 E1
Worrel's La MANG/FISH BS16 ...34 D2
Worsley St EVILLE/WHL BS5 .....57 F4
Worthing Rd
   BRSTK/PCHW BS34 ....20 B2
Worthy Cl KGWD/HNM BS15 ....59 F5
Worthy La WSM BS23 ....6 E3
Worthy Pl WSM BS23 ....6 D5
Worthy Rd AVONM BS11 ....16 D5
The Worthys ALMDB BS32 ....22 A4
Wotton Rd YATE/CS BS37 ....12 C3
Wrangle Farm Gn CLVDN BS21 ..65 E3

The Wrangle
   OMX/HUT/LCK BS24 ....122 C4
Wraxall Gv
   BMSTRD/HC/WWD BS13 ....84 A1
Wraxall Hl NAIL BS48 ....68 B1
Wraxall Rd KGWD/HNM BS15 ...59 C5
Wrenbert Rd
   MANG/FISH BS16 ....48 D3
Wren Cl MANG/FISH BS16 ....47 C1
   MTN/WRL BS22 ....122 A3
Wren Dr MANG/FISH BS16 ....47 H2
Wright Wy MANG/FISH BS16 ....33 C5
Wrington Cl
   BRSTK/PCHW BS34 ....21 E3
Wrington Crs
   BMSTRD/HC/WWD BS13 ....84 B2
Wrington La
   YTN/CONG BS49 ....115 E1
Wrington Md
   YTN/CONG BS49 ....115 E1
Wrington Rd YTN/CONG BS49 ..115 F2
Wroughton Dr
   BMSTRD/HC/WWD BS13 ....85 E5
Wroughton Gdns
   BMSTRD/HC/WWD BS13 ....85 E5
Wroxham Dr
   BRSTK/PCHW BS34 ....21 E2
Wyatt Av
   BMSTRD/HC/WWD BS13 ....84 A4
Wyatt Cl
   BMSTRD/HC/WWD BS13 ....84 A4
Wyatt's Cl NAIL BS48 ....67 E4
Wyatts Vw
   BRSG/KWL/STAPK BS4 ......57 G4

Wychwood
   KGWD/HNM BS15 ....58 D5
Wyck Beck Rd
   HNBRY/STHM BS10 ....31 E1
Wycliffe Rd
   HNLZ/SM/SNYPK/WT BS9 ...45 F1
Wycliffe Rw
   BMSTR BS5 ....73 G2
Wycombe Gv
   BRSG/KWL/STAPK BS4 ......74 C4
Wye Ct THNB/SVB BS35 ....8 D4
Wye Croft Cl
   HNBRY/STHM BS10 ....31 H2
Wyedale Av
   HNLZ/SM/SNYPK/WT BS9 ...43 H1
Wykis Ct
   BMSTRD/HC/WWD BS13 .....76 B1
Wyllie Ct MTN/WRL BS22 ....117 H3
Wymbush Crs
   BMSTRD/HC/WWD BS13 ....84 D4
Wymbush Gdns
   BMSTRD/HC/WWD BS13 ....84 D4
Wyndham Crs
   BRSG/KWL/STAPK BS4 ......75 E3
   PTSHD/EG BS20 ....42 B4
Wyndham Wy
   PTSHD/EG BS20 ....39 H2
The Wynstones
   MANG/FISH BS15 ....58 C4
Wynter Cl MTN/WRL BS22 .....117 H5
Wytherlies Dr
   MANG/FISH BS16 ....47 H2
Wyvern Cl
   WSM BS23 ....7 H5

Wyvern Ms WSM BS23 * 7 J5

Y

Yanieigh Cl
   BMSTRD/HC/WWD BS13 .....83 F3
Yanleigh Est LGASH BS41 ....83 E1
Yanley La LGASH BS41 ....83 E1
Yarbury Wy
   OMX/HUT/LCK BS24 ....123 E2
The Yard CBRISNE BS2 ....46 C5
Yate Rd YATE/CS BS37 ....12 E3
Yeates Ct CLVDN BS21 ....65 E2
Yeo Cl WSM BS23 ....125 F1
Yeolands Dr CLVDN BS21 ....64 B4
Yeo La LGASH BS41 ....70 C5
Yeomans Ct
   HNLZ/SM/SNYPK/WT BS9 ...44 B3
Yeomanside Cl
   HGRV/WHIT BS14 ....86 B4
Yeomead NAIL BS48 ....67 G3
Yeomeads LGASH BS41 ....70 C5
Yeo Moor CLVDN BS21 ....65 E3
Yeo Valley Wy NAIL BS48 ....68 A4
Yeoward Rd CLVDN BS21 ....65 E4
Yeo Vw CLVDN BS21 ....64 B3
Yewcroft Cl HGRV/WHIT BS14 ..86 B5
Yew Tree Cl NAIL BS48 * 66 D5
Yew Tree Dr KGWD/HNM BS15 ..46 D5
   OMX/HUT/LCK BS24 ....123 E5
Yew Tree Gdns NAIL BS48 ....66 D5

   PTSHD/EG BS20 * 42 C4
Yew Tree Pk YTN/CONG BS49 ..114 D3
Yomede Pk
   CBATH/BATHN BA1 ....101 F5
York Av HORF/LLZ BS7 ....46 B4
York Ct BRSTK/PCHW BS34 ......33 F1
   MANG/FISH BS16 ....35 F4
   MTN/WRL BS22 ....117 H4
York Gdns CFTN/FAIL BS8 ....54 D5
   FRCTL/WBN BS36 ....23 F2
York Pl CBATH/BATHN BA1 * ...103 E4
   CFTN/FAIL BS8 ....4 A5
York Rd BMSTR BS5 ....73 F2
   EVILLE/WHL BS5 ....57 E2
   MANG/FISH BS16 ....49 E4
   RDLND/MONT BS6 ....56 A2
York St CBATH/BATHN BA1 ....3 G1
   CBRISNE BS2 ....5 G1
   CFTN/FAIL BS8 ....55 E1
   EVILLE/WHL BS5 ....57 E4
   WSM BS23 ....6 D4
Youngs Ct MANG/FISH BS16 ....35 H5
Youngwood La NAIL BS48 ....78 D3

Z

Zetland Rd RDLND/MONT BS6 ...55 H1
Zig Zag CLVDN BS21 ....64 D1
Zinc Rd AVONM BS11 ....28 C2

Index - featured places

Abbey Wood Business Park
   BRSTK/PCHW BS34 ....32 D3
Abbotswood Primary School
   YATE/CS BS37 ....25 H3
Acton Court
   YATE/CS BS37 ....12 B2
Air Balloon Hill J & I School
   EVILLE/WHL BS5 ....58 A4
Alien School House
   OLD/WMLY/WICK BS30 ......76 D1
All Saints East Clevedon CE
   Primary School
   CLVDN BS21 ....65 F1
All Saints Exhibition Centre
   CBRIS/FH BS1 ....5 F3
Almonsbury Business Centre
   ALMDB BS32 ....11 F4
Almondsbury Cemetery
   ALMDB BS32 ....10 C1
Almondsbury CE Primary
   School
   ALMDB BS32 ....10 C2
Almondsbury Town FC
   ALMDB BS32 ....10 C3
Amelia Nutt Clinic
   BMSTRD/HC/WWD BS13 ....84 A5
AMF Bowling
   WSM BS23 ....6 D5
Anchor Business Centre
   CFTN/FAIL BS8 ....55 F2
Anchor Head Hotel
   WSM BS23 ....6 A1
Andalusia Academy Bristol
   CBRISNE BS2 ....56 B3
Arelans RFC
   BRSTK/PCHW BS34 ....20 D3
Arnolfini
   CBRIS/FH BS1 ....4 E6
Arnos Manor Hotel
   BRSG/KWL/STAPK BS4 ......74 B3
Arnos Vale Cemetery
   BRSG/KWL/STAPK BS4 ......74 A3
The Arosfa Hotel
   WSM BS23 ....6 D2
Arts Centre Cinema
   CBRISNE BS2 ....55 H3
Ashbrook House School
   WSM BS23 ....6 D6
Ashcombe Primary School
   WSM BS23 ....7 K4
Ashley Down J & I School
   HORF/LLZ BS7 ....46 A3
Ashley Trading Estate
   RDLND/MONT BS6 ....56 B1
Ashmead Industrial Estate
   KEYN BS31 ....89 E4
Ashton Court Estate
   LGASH BS41 ....71 F2
Ashton Gate Primary School
   BMSTR BS3 ....72 B2
Ashton Gate Trading Estate
   BMSTR BS3 ....71 H3
Ashton Park School
   BMSTR BS3 ....71 H3
Ashton Vale Primary School
   BMSTR BS3 ....72 A4
Atlantic Business Park
   WSM BS23 ....6 A1
Avonbank Industrial Centre
   AVONM BS11 ....42 B1
Avonbridge Trading Estate
   AVONM BS11 ....28 C5
Avon Business Park
   MANG/FISH BS16 ....47 H5
Avondale Business Centre
   MANG/FISH BS16 ....58 C1
Avon Friends of the Earth
   Depot
   CBRIS/FH BS1 ....98 C3
Avon Gorge Industrial Estate
   AVONM BS11 ....42 C1
Avon Gorge Nature Reserve
   CFTN/FAIL BS8 ....54 B4

Avonmouth CE Primary
   School
   AVONM BS11 ....28 C5
Avonmouth Medical Centre
   AVONM BS11 ....28 B5
Avon Primary School
   AVONM BS11 ....28 B5
Avon Riverside Estate
   AVONM BS11 ....42 B1
Avonside Industrial Park
   CBRISNE BS2 ....57 E5
Avon Trading Estate
   CBRISNE BS2 ....73 H1
Avon Valley Country Park
   KEYN BS31 ....89 G3
Avon Valley Railway
   OLD/WMLY/WICK BS30 ......89 F1
Avon View Cemetery
   EVILLE/WHL BS5 ....57 G4
Aztec Hotel
   ALMDB BS32 ....10 D5
B6 Sixth Form Centre
   KEYN BS31 ....88 A3
Backwell CE Junior School
   NAIL BS48 ....80 B4
Backwell Leisure Centre
   NAIL BS48 ....80 A3
Backwell Medical Centre
   NAIL BS48 ....80 A3
Backwell RFC
   NAIL BS48 ....79 H3
Backwell School
   NAIL BS48 ....80 A3
Badminton Road Trading
   Estate
   YATE/CS BS37 ....25 H3
Badminton School
   HNLZ/SM/SNYPK/WT BS9 ...45 E3
Badocks Wood Primary
   School
   HNBRY/STHM BS10 ....31 F5
Bailbrook House Hotel
   CBATH/BATHN BA1 ....103 G2
Baileys Court Primary School
   ALMDB BS32 ....21 H4
Balaclava Industrial Estate
   MANG/FISH BS16 ....47 H5
Bank Leaze Primary School
   AVONM BS11 ....29 H2
Bannerman Road
   Primary School
   EVILLE/WHL BS5 ....56 D2
Barley Close Primary School
   MANG/FISH BS16 ....49 G2
Barrack Trading Centre
   BMSTR BS3 ....72 D5
Barrow Hospital
   NAIL BS48 ....82 D3
Barrs Court Primary School
   OLD/WMLY/WICK BS30 ......76 C1
Barton Hill Infant School
   CBRISNE BS2 ....56 D5
Barton Hill Primary School
   EVILLE/WHL BS5 ....56 D5
Barton Hill Trading Estate
   EVILLE/WHL BS5 ....56 D5
Bath Abbey
   CBATH/BATHN BA1 ....3 G4
Bathampton Primary School
   BATHSE BA2 ....104 A2
Bath Boating Station
   BATHSE BA2 ....103 E4
Bath CC
   BATHSE BA2 ....3 J5
The Bath Clinic
   BATHSE BA2 ....109 H5
Bath College of Higher
   Education
   CBATH/BATHN BA1 ....102 B3
Batheaston CE Primary
   School
   CBATH/BATHN BA1 ....104 A1
Batheaston Medical Centre
   CBATH/BATHN BA1 ....91 E5

Bathford Primary School
   CBATH/BATHN BA1 ....104 D2
Bath Golf Club
   BATHSE BA2 ....109 C1
Bath Media College
   CBATH/BATHN BA1 ....3 F5
Bath Natural Health Clinic
   CBATH/BATHN BA1 ....1 D4
Bath Postal Museum
   CBATH/BATHN BA1 ....3 F3
The Bath Priory Hotel
   CBATH/BATHN BA1 ....101 H4
Bath Rugby
   (Recreation Ground)
   BATHSE BA2 ....3 H4
Bath Spa University
   (Newton Park Campus)
   BATHSE BA2 ....106 A2
Bath Sports & Leisure Centre
   BATHSE BA2 ....3 H4
Bathwick Cemetery
   BATHSE BA2 ....109 F2
Bathwick St Mary
   CE Primary School
   BATHSE BA2 ....103 F4
Baytree School
   MTN/WRL BS22 ....121 H5
Beachlands Hotel
   BATHSE BA2 ....124 C2
Beacon Rise Primary School
   KGWD/HNM BS15 ....58 D5
Beazer Garden Maze
   BATHSE BA2 ....3 H4
Becket Primary School
   MTN/WRL BS22 ....122 D1
Becks Business Park
   BMSTR BS3 ....7 K5
Bedminster Down School
   BMSTRD/HC/WWD BS13 ....84 A2
Beechen Cliff School
   BATHSE BA2 ....108 D3
Beeches Trading Estate
   YATE/CS BS37 ....13 E5
Beehive Trading Estate
   EVILLE/WHL BS5 ....57 G4
Begbrook Primary School
   MANG/FISH BS16 ....47 H2
Belgrave School
   CFTN/FAIL BS8 ....54 D1
Berkeley Square Hotel
   CFTN/FAIL BS8 ....4 B3
Best Western Abbey Hotel
   CBATH/BATHN BA1 ....3 G5
Best Western
   Victoria Square Hotel
   CFTN/FAIL BS8 ....55 E4
Best Western Walton Park
   Hotel
   CLVDN BS21 ....62 B4
Birdwell Primary School
   LGASH BS41 ....82 D1
Bishop Road
   Primary School
   HORF/LLZ BS7 ....45 H4
Bishopston House Clinic
   HORF/LLZ BS7 ....46 A4
Bishopsworth CE Junior School
   BMSTRD/HC/WWD BS13 ....84 A3
Bishopsworth Swimming Pool
   BMSTRD/HC/WWD BS13 ....84 B3
Bitton Station
   OLD/WMLY/WICK BS30 ......77 E5
Blackberry Hill Hospital
   MANG/FISH BS16 ....48 C2
Blackhorse Primary School
   MANG/FISH BS16 ....35 G5
Blaise Hamlet (NT)
   HNBRY/STHM BS10 ....30 B3
Blaise Primary School
   HNBRY/STHM BS10 ....30 D3
Bonville Business Centre
   BRSG/KWL/STAPK BS4 ......75 E4
Bonville Trading Estate
   BRSG/KWL/STAPK BS4 ......75 F4
Book Museum
   CBATH/BATHN BA1 ....3 H6

Bournville Junior School &
   Community Infant School
   WSM BS23 ....125 E1
Bowling Hill Business Park
   YATE/CS BS37 ....26 C1
The Bowl Inn Hotel
   ALMDB BS32 ....10 C2
Bowsland Green Primary
   School
   ALMDB BS32 ....11 F5
Bradley Stoke Community
   School ALMDB BS32 ....21 G2
Bradley Stoke Leisure Centre
   ALMDB BS32 ....21 G1
Brassmill Lane Trading Estate
   CBATH/BATHN BA1 ....101 F5
Brentry Hospital
   HNBRY/STHM BS10 ....31 F3
Brentry Primary School
   HNBRY/STHM BS10 ....31 F2
Briarwood Special School
   MANG/FISH BS16 ....48 B5
Bridge Farm Primary School
   WSM BS23 ....7 H6
Bridge Road Business Park
   WSM BS23 ....7 H6
Brimsham Green School
   YATE/CS BS37 ....13 H3
Brislington
   Enterprise College
   BRSG/KWL/STAPK BS4 ......87 C1
Brislington Retail Park
   BRSG/KWL/STAPK BS4 ......74 D5
Brislington Trading Estate
   BRSG/KWL/STAPK BS4 ......74 D4
Bristol & Clifton Golf Club
   CFTN/FAIL BS8 ....70 B1
Bristol Baptist College
   CFTN/FAIL BS8 ....54 D3
Bristol Business Park
   MANG/FISH BS16 ....33 C4
Bristol Cathedral
   CBRIS/FH BS1 ....4 D5
Bristol Cathedral School
   CFTN/FAIL BS8 ....4 C5
Bristol City FC (Ashton Gate)
   BMSTR BS3 ....72 A3
Bristol
   Civil Service Sports Club
   HORF/LLZ BS7 ....46 B2
Bristol County Sports Club
   CFTN/FAIL BS8 ....55 E6
Bristol Dental Hospital
   CBRIS/FH BS1 ....4 E2
Bristol Eye Hospital
   CBRIS/FH BS1 ....5 F2
Bristol Gateway School
   CBRISNE BS2 ....56 C1
Bristol General Hospital
   CBRIS/FH BS1 ....5 F7
Bristol Golf Club
   HNBRY/STHM BS10 ....19 F3
Bristol Grammar Lower School
   CFTN/FAIL BS8 ....4 D2
Bristol Grammar School
   CFTN/FAIL BS8 ....4 C2
Bristol Harlequins RFC
   BRSG/KWL/STAPK BS4 ......75 F4
Bristol Homeopathic Hospital
   CFTN/FAIL BS8 ....55 G3
Bristol Ice Rink
   CBRIS/FH BS1 ....4 D3
Bristol International Airport
   NAIL BS48 ....92 B5
Bristol Marriott Hotel
   CBRIS/FH BS1 ....5 H3
Bristol Marriott Royal Hotel
   CBRIS/FH BS1 ....4 D5
Bristol North Baths
   HORF/LLZ BS7 ....45 H5
Bristol & North Somerset
   Sports Club
   CFTN/FAIL BS8 ....70 A3
Bristol Old Vic (New Vic
   Theatre & Theatre Royal)
   CBRIS/FH BS1 ....4 E4

Bristol Rovers FC & Bristol RFC
   (Memorial Stadium)
   HORF/LLZ BS7 ....46 B2
Bristol Rovers FC
   BRSG/KWL/STAPK BS4 ......75 E5
Bristol Royal Hospital for
   Children
   CBRISNE BS2 ....4 D2
Bristol Royal Infirmary
   CBRISNE BS2 ....4 E1
Bristol's Blaise Castle House
   Museum
   HNBRY/STHM BS10 ....30 C3
Bristol's City Museum & Art
   Gallery
   CFTN/FAIL BS8 ....4 C3
Bristol's Georgian House
   CFTN/FAIL BS8 ....4 C4
Bristol South Swimming Pool
   BMSTR BS3 ....72 D2
Bristol's Red Lodge
   CBRIS/FH BS1 ....4 D3
Bristol Vale Trading Estate
   BMSTR BS3 ....72 C5
Bristol Zoo Gardens
   CFTN/FAIL BS8 ....54 D2
British Empire &
   Commonwealth Museum
   CBRIS/FH BS1 ....5 H6
Broadlands School
   KEYN BS31 ....88 A3
Broadmead Lane Industrial
   Estate
   KEYN BS31 ....88 D2
Broadoak Maths & Computing
   College
   WSM BS23 ....124 C5
Broadwalk Shopping Centre
   BRSG/KWL/STAPK BS4 ......74 A4
Broadway Infant School
   YATE/CS BS37 ....14 C5
Brockeridge Infant School
   FRCTL/WBN BS36 ....24 A3
Brock Street Clinic
   CBATH/BATHN BA1 ....2 E2
Brockway Medical Centre
   NAIL BS48 ....67 G4
Bromley Heath J & I School
   MANG/FISH BS16 ....35 E5
Brooklea Clinic
   BRSG/KWL/STAPK BS4 ......74 D1
Broomhill J & I School
   BRSG/KWL/STAPK BS4 ......75 E3
Browns Folly Nature Reserve
   CBATH/BATHN BA1 ....104 D3
Brunel's SS Great Britain
   CBRIS/FH BS1 ....4 B6
The Building of Bath Museum
   CBATH/BATHN BA1 ....3 F2
Burnbush Primary School
   HGRV/WHIT BS14 ....86 C4
Burnett Business Park
   KEYN BS31 ....98 D3
Bush Industrial Estate
   EVILLE/WHL BS5 ....57 F3
The Business Park
   BMSTRD/HC/WWD BS13 ....96 B1
Butcombe Pre-Preparatory
   School
   CFTN/FAIL BS8 ....54 D3
BW Estates
   OMX/HUT/LCK BS24 ....125 F3
Cabot Circus
   CBRIS/FH BS1 ....5 H2
Cabot Primary School
   CBRISNE BS2 ....56 B3
Cabot Tower
   CFTN/FAIL BS8 ....4 B4
Cadbury Camp
   PTSHD/EG BS20 ....66 B1
Cadbury Heath Health Centre
   OLD/WMLY/WICK BS30 ......76 D1
Cadbury Heath Primary School
   OLD/WMLY/WICK BS30 ......59 H5
Cadbury House Hotel
   YTN/CONG BS49 ....112 D3

Cailicroft Primary School
  BRSTK/PCHW BS34 .... 20 A2
Canford Cemetery
  HNLZ/SM/SNYPK/WT BS9 .. 44 C1
Canford Crematorium
  HNLZ/SM/SNYPK/WT BS9 .. 44 D1
Canons House
  CFTN/FAIL BS1 .... 4 D6
Canon's Marsh Amphitheatre
  CBRIS/FH BS1 .... 4 D6
Carla Trading Estate
  BMSTR BS3 .... 72 A3
Carlyle Business Centre
  CBRISNE BS2 .... 56 C5
Carmel Christian Centre &
  School
Carrick Business Park
  BRSG/KWL/STAPK BS4 ...... 74 D5
Castle Batch Primary School
  MTN/WRL BS22 .... 117 H3
Castlemead Shopping Centre
  MTN/WRL BS22 .... 117 H3
Central Health Clinic
  CBRISNE BS2 .... 5 H4
Central Trading Estate
  BRSG/KWL/STAPK BS4 ...... 74 A2
Chandag J & I School
  KEYN BS31 .... 88 D5
Chandos Trading Estate
  CBRISNE BS2 .... 73 H1
Charborough Road Primary
  School
  BRSTK/PCHW BS34 .... 32 B3
Charlotte Keel Health Clinic
  EVILLE/WHL BS5 .... 56 C2
Chatterton House
  CBRIS/FH BS1 .... 5 G6
Cheddar Grove Primary School
  BMSTRD/HC/WWD BS13 .... 84 B1
Cherry Garden Primary School
  OLD/WMLY/WICK BS30 ..... 77 E4
Chesterfield Hospital
  CFTN/FAIL BS8 .... 55 E5
Chester Park & I School
  MANG/FISH BS16 .... 48 A5
Chipping Edge Estate
  YATE/CS BS37 .... 26 D1
Chipping Sodbury Cemetery
  YATE/CS BS37 .... 26 D1
Chipping Sodbury Golf Club
  YATE/CS BS37 .... 15 E4
Chipping Sodbury School
  YATE/CS BS37 .... 26 D2
Chittening Industrial Estate
  AVONM BS11 .... 16 D3
Christchurch CE Junior School
  MANG/FISH BS16 .... 48 D3
Christchurch CE Primary
  School
  KGWD/HNM BS15 .... 75 G2
Christ Church CE VC Infant
  School
  MANG/FISH BS16 .... 48 D3
Christ Church Primary School
  CFTN/FAIL BS8 .... 7 F3
Christ the King RC Primary
  School
  THNB/SVB BS35 .... 8 D3
Church Farm Business Park
  BATHSE BA2 .... 99 H5
Churchill Business Park
  WSM BS23 .... 7 J5
Cinema de Lux
  CBRIS/FH BS1 .... 5 H2
Cineworld
  HNBRY/WHIT BS14 .... 85 F3
The City Academy Bristol
  EVILLE/WHL BS5 .... 57 E3
City Business Park
  CBRIS/FH BS1 .... 5 H2
City of Bath College
  CBATH/BATHN BA1 .... 3 F5
City of Bristol College
  (Bedminster Centre)
  BMSTR BS3 .... 73 E4
City of Bristol College
  (Brunel Centre)
  HORF/LLZ BS7 .... 46 B4
City of Bristol College
  (College Green Centre)
  CBRIS/FH BS1 .... 4 B5
City of Bristol College
  (Downend Centre)
  MANG/FISH BS16 .... 35 G5
City of Bristol College
  (Folly Lane Centre)
  CBRISNE BS2 .... 56 C5
City of Bristol College
  (Hartcliffe Centre)
  BMSTRD/HC/WWD BS13 .... 85 E5
City of Bristol College
  (Kingswood Centre)
  KGWD/HNM BS15 .... 59 E3
City of Bristol College
  (Lawrence Weston Centre)
  AVONM BS11 .... 29 H3
City of Bristol College
  (Parkway Transport
  Technology Centre)
  BRSTK/PCHW BS34 .... 33 F2
City of Bristol College
  (Soundwell Centre)
  MANG/FISH BS16 .... 59 E1
City & Port of Bristol Social &
  Sports Club
  AVONM BS11 .... 43 E3
Civil Service Sports Club
  BATHSE BA2 .... 109 H5
Claremont Special School
  RDLND/MONT BS6 .... 45 G3
Claverham CC
  YTN/CONG BS49 .... 112 D4
Clevedon Army Training Corps
  Squadron
  CLVDN BS21 .... 64 C1
Clevedon Cemetery
  CLVDN BS21 .... 64 A3
Clevedon Community School
  CLVDN BS21 .... 62 D5

Clevedon Court (NT)
  CLVDN BS21 .... 65 G1
Clevedon Craft Centre
  CLVDN BS21 .... 65 G1
Clevedon Fruit Market
  CLVDN BS21 .... 64 D2
Clevedon Golf Club
  CLVDN BS21 .... 62 D3
Clevedon Health Centre
  CLVDN BS21 .... 65 E2
Clevedon Hospital
  CLVDN BS21 .... 65 E2
Clevedon Pier
  CLVDN BS21 .... 62 A5
Cleve House School
  BRSG/KWL/STAPK BS4 ...... 74 A3
Clifton Cathedral Church
  CFTN/FAIL BS8 .... 55 E3
Clifton Clinic
  CFTN/FAIL BS8 .... 55 E4
Clifton College Preparatory
  School
  CFTN/FAIL BS8 .... 54 D2
Clifton College Sports Club
  CFTN/FAIL BS8 .... 53 H4
Clifton Down Shopping Centre
  CFTN/FAIL BS8 .... 55 F2
Clifton High School & Lower
  School
  CFTN/FAIL BS8 .... 54 D4
Clifton Hotel
  CFTN/FAIL BS8 .... 4 A2
Clifton RFC
  HNBRY/STHM BS10 .... 18 D5
Clifton Tutors
  CFTN/FAIL BS8 .... 55 E4
Coates Industrial Estate
  NAIL BS48 .... 67 G3
College House
  MANG/FISH BS16 .... 48 A3
Colston Hall
  CBRIS/FH BS1 .... 4 E3
Colstons Collegiate School
  MANG/FISH BS16 .... 47 E4
Colstons Girls School
  RDLND/MONT BS6 .... 56 A2
Colstons Primary School
  RDLND/MONT BS6 .... 55 G2
Combe Dean CE Primary
  School
  BATHSE BA2 .... 111 F1
Combe Down RFC
  BATHSE BA2 .... 109 E5
Commodore Hotel
  MTN/WRL BS22 .... 116 A5
The Compton Clinic
  RDLND/MONT BS6 .... 45 E4
Coniston Primary School
  BRSTK/PCHW BS34 .... 20 B1
Connaught Primary School
  BRSG/KWL/STAPK BS4 ...... 85 F1
Conygre Medical Centre
  BRSTK/PCHW BS34 .... 32 C2
Corbett House Clinic
  EVILLE/WHL BS5 .... 56 D4
Corpus Christi RC Primary
  School
  WSM BS23 .... 6 D7
Cossham Memorial Hospital
  KGWD/HNM BS15 .... 58 C1
Cotham Park RFC
  CFTN/FAIL BS8 .... 53 G5
Cotham School
  RDLND/MONT BS6 .... 55 G2
Country View Holiday Park
  MTN/WRL BS22 .... 116 C2
Court De Wyck Primary School
  YTN/CONG BS49 .... 113 F2
Courtney Primary School
  KGWD/HNM BS15 .... 59 F4
Cranleigh Court Infant School
  YATE/CS BS37 .... 13 H4
Create Centre
  CBRIS/FH BS1 .... 72 A1
Cribbs Causeway Regional
  Shopping Centre
  BRSTK/PCHW BS34 .... 19 H4
Cribbs Causeway Retail Park
  BRSTK/PCHW BS34 .... 19 G4
Cricket Pavilion
  BATHSE BA2 .... 3 H4
Crockerne CE Primary School
  PTSHD/EG BS20 .... 42 C5
Crofts End Industrial Estate
  EVILLE/WHL BS5 .... 57 G2
The Cross Bath
  CBATH/BATHN BA1 .... 3 F5
Crossways J & I School
  THNB/SVB BS35 .... 9 E3
Crown Industrial Estate
  OLD/WMLY/WICK BS30 ..... 59 H5
Culverhay School
  BATHSE BA2 .... 107 G5
Culverhay Sports Centre
  BATHSE BA2 .... 107 G5
Culverhill School
  YATE/CS BS37 .... 25 H3
Curzon Cinema
  CLVDN BS21 .... 64 C2
Custom House
  CBRIS/FH BS1 .... 5 F5
Daunceys Hotel
  WSM BS23 .... 120 A2
Days Inn
  PTSHD/EG BS20 .... 41 H4
Deers Wood Primary School
  KGWD/HNM BS15 .... 59 G1
Devon Road Trading Estate
  EVILLE/WHL BS5 .... 57 E2
Dixon Business Centre
  BRSG/KWL/STAPK BS4 ...... 75 E4
Docks Industrial Estate
  AVONM BS11 .... 17 E2
Dolphin Square Shopping
  Centre
  WSM BS23 .... 6 D5
Douglas Road Industrial Park
  KGWD/HNM BS15 .... 58 D3
Downend CC
  MANG/FISH BS16 .... 48 D2

Downend School
  MANG/FISH BS16 .... 49 F1
Downs Fitness & Health Centre
  RDLND/MONT BS6 .... 55 E1
Drove Road Hospital
  WSM BS23 .... 125 E1
Duckmoor Road Industrial
  Estate
  BMSTR BS3 .... 72 B2
Dukes Hotel
  BATHSE BA2 .... 3 H3
Dundry CE Primary School
  LGASH BS41 .... 94 C2
Eagles Wood Business Park
  ALMDB BS32 .... 11 E4
Eastgate Retail Park
  EVILLE/WHL BS5 .... 56 D1
Easton Business Centre
  EVILLE/WHL BS5 .... 56 D1
Easton CE Primary School
  EVILLE/WHL BS5 .... 56 C3
Easton Leisure Centre
  EVILLE/WHL BS5 .... 56 C3
Eastpark Trading Estate
  EVILLE/WHL BS5 .... 57 F2
Eastville Health Centre
  EVILLE/WHL BS5 .... 56 D1
Eldonwall Trading Estate
  BMSTR BS3 .... 72 D1
Elmfield Special School
  HNBRY/STHM BS10 .... 31 F5
Elmlea Junior School
  HNLZ/SM/SNYPK/WT BS9 .. 44 D3
Elm Park Primary School
  FRCTL/WBN BS36 .... 23 E4
Entry Hill Golf Course
  BATHSE BA2 .... 108 C5
Explore-At-Bristol
  CBRIS/FH BS1 .... 4 D5
Express by Holiday Inn
  BATHSE BA2 .... 2 C5
  BRSTK/PCHW BS34 .... 33 E2
  CBRIS/FH BS1 .... 5 H6
The Eye Clinic
  CBRIS/FH BS1 .... 5 G2
Fairfield High School
  RDLND/MONT BS6 .... 56 B1
Fairfield Park Health Centre
  RDLND/MONT BS6 .... 103 E3
Fairfield PNEU School
  BATHSE BA2 .... 80 B3
Fair Furlong Primary School
  BMSTRD/HC/WWD BS13 .... 84 B5
Fairway Industrial Centre
  BRSTK/PCHW BS34 .... 32 B2
Falconride Primary School
  HNBRY/STHM BS10 .... 59 E2
Fashion Museum
  CBATH/BATHN BA1 .... 3 F2
Ferry Steps Industrial Estate
  CBRISNE BS2 .... 73 H2
Filton Airfield
  HNBRY/STHM BS10 .... 19 H5
Filton Avenue
  J & I School
  HORF/LLZ BS7 .... 46 C1
Filton Cemetery
  MANG/FISH BS16 .... 33 G5
Filton Clinic
  HORF/LLZ BS7 .... 32 C3
Filton College
  BRSTK/PCHW BS34 .... 32 C1
Filton Golf Club
  BRSTK/PCHW BS34 .... 32 A1
Filton High School
  BRSTK/PCHW BS34 .... 33 F2
Filton Hill Primary School
  BRSTK/PCHW BS34 .... 32 D1
Filton Recreation Centre
  BRSTK/PCHW BS34 .... 32 C3
Filwood Broadway School
  BRSG/KWL/STAPK BS4 ...... 85 F1
Fishponds Health Centre
  MANG/FISH BS16 .... 48 B4
Fishponds Trading Estate
  EVILLE/WHL BS5 .... 57 H1
Five C Business Centre
  CLVDN BS21 .... 64 B4
Flax Bourton CE Primary
  School
  NAIL BS48 .... 81 E1
Florence Brown Community
  School
  BRSG/KWL/STAPK BS4 ...... 85 E1
Folk House
  CBRIS/FH BS1 .... 4 D3
Fonthill Primary School
  HNBRY/STHM BS10 .... 32 A3
Foster Almshouses
  CBRIS/FH BS1 .... 4 E3
Four Acres Primary School
  BMSTRD/HC/WWD BS13 .... 83 H5
Frampton Cotterell
  CE Primary School
  FRCTL/WBN BS36 .... 23 C2
Frenchay CE Primary School
  MANG/FISH BS16 .... 48 B1
Frenchay Hospital
  MANG/FISH BS16 .... 34 B5
Frenchay Village Museum
  MANG/FISH BS16 .... 34 A5
Frome Bank Junior School
  YATE/CS BS37 .... 13 H4
Fromeside Clinic
  MANG/FISH BS16 .... 47 H3
Gay Elms Primary School
  BMSTRD/HC/WWD BS13 .... 84 A5
Gillingstool Primary School
  THNB/SVB BS35 .... 8 C4
The Glebe Infant School
  YTN/CONG BS49 .... 114 C2
Glencoe Business Park
  WSM BS23 .... 7 K5
Glenfrome Primary School
  EVILLE/WHL BS5 .... 46 D4
Gloucestershire CCC
  (County Ground)
  HORF/LLZ BS7 .... 46 A4

Glynne Wickham Studio
  Theatre
  CFTN/FAIL BS8 .... 4 D3
Golden Valley Primary School
  NAIL BS48 .... 67 G4
Gordano RFC
  PTSHD/EG BS20 .... 41 E5
Gordano School
  PTSHD/EG BS20 .... 39 H5
Gracefield Preparatory School
  MANG/FISH BS16 .... 48 B3
Granby House Clinic
  BMSTR BS3 .... 72 D3
Grand Pier
  WSM BS23 .... 6 C4
The Grange Hotel
  FRCTL/WBN BS36 .... 22 B1
The Grange School & Sports
  College
  OLD/WMLY/WICK BS30 ..... 59 H4
Great Western Business Park
  YATE/CS BS37 .... 13 F4
Greenbank Cemetery
  EVILLE/WHL BS5 .... 57 F1
Greenfield Primary School
  BRSG/KWL/STAPK BS4 ...... 84 D2
Green Park Station Market
  CBATH/BATHN BA1 .... 2 D4
Greystoke Business Centre
  PTSHD/EG BS20 .... 39 H4
Grove Industrial Estate
  BRSTK/PCHW BS34 .... 20 D3
Grove Junior School
  NAIL BS48 .... 79 E1
Grove Road Day Hospital
  NAIL BS48 .... 55 E1
Grove Sports Centre
  NAIL BS48 .... 79 E1
Hambrook Primary School
  MANG/FISH BS16 .... 34 D2
Hambrook Sports Club
  MANG/FISH BS16 .... 34 D2
Hampset CE
  BATHSE BA2 .... 108 A5
Hanham Abbots Junior School
  KGWD/HNM BS15 .... 75 H2
Hanham Business Park
  KGWD/HNM BS15 .... 75 G1
Hanham High School
  KGWD/HNM BS15 .... 75 H2
Hanham More Infant School
  NAIL BS48 .... 79 E1
Hannah More Primary School
  CBRISNE BS2 .... 5 K4
Harbour Road Trading Estate
  PTSHD/EG BS20 .... 40 A2
Harcclive Primary School
  BMSTRD/HC/WWD BS13 .... 84 D5
Haringtons Hotel
  CBATH/BATHN BA1 .... 3 F4
Hartcliffe Engineering
  Community College
  BMSTRD/HC/WWD BS13 .... 85 F5
Hartcliffe Health Centre
  BMSTRD/HC/WWD BS13 .... 84 D5
Harveys Wine Museum
  CBRIS/FH BS1 .... 4 D4
Haslemere Industrial Estate
  AVONM BS11 .... 28 C2
Hawkfield Business Park
  HGRV/WHIT BS14 .... 85 E4
Hawkins Clinic
  CBATH/BATHN BA1 .... 3 F4
Haycombe Cemetery
  BATHSE BA2 .... 107 E3
Haycombe Crematorium
  BATHSE BA2 .... 107 E3
Hayesfield School Technology
  College
  BATHSE BA2 .... 2 C5
Hayward Road Industrial
  Estate
  MANG/FISH BS16 .... 48 D5
Headley Park Primary School
  BMSTRD/HC/WWD BS13 .... 84 C3
Heath House Priory Hospital
  HORF/LLZ BS7 .... 46 D4
The Helicopter Museum
  OMX/HUT/LCK BS24 .... 126 D1
Henbury Court Primary School
  HNBRY/STHM BS10 .... 30 C2
Henbury Golf Club
  HNBRY/STHM BS10 .... 30 C3
Henbury Lodge Hotel
  HNBRY/STHM BS10 .... 30 C3
Henbury Old Boys AFC
  HNBRY/STHM BS10 .... 30 D5
Henbury School
  HNBRY/STHM BS10 .... 30 C2
Henbury Swimming Pool
  HNBRY/STHM BS10 .... 30 D2
Henfield Business Park
  FRCTL/WBN BS36 .... 36 B3
Hengrove Community Arts
  College
  HGRV/WHIT BS14 .... 86 A2
Hengrove Leisure Park
  HGRV/WHIT BS14 .... 85 J3
Henleaze J & I School
  RDLND/MONT BS6 .... 45 G3
Heritage Centre
  WSM BS23 .... 6 D3
Herons Moor Community
  Primary School
  OMX/HUT/LCK BS24 .... 122 D5
The Herschel Museum of
  Astronomy
  CBATH/BATHN BA1 .... 2 E4
Heywood Health Centre
  PTSHD/EG BS20 .... 42 C4
Highcroft Junior School
  FRCTL/WBN BS36 .... 24 A2
High Down Infant School
  PTSHD/EG BS20 .... 39 E4
Highridge Infant School
  BMSTRD/HC/WWD BS13 .... 84 A3
Hillcrest Primary School
  BRSG/KWL/STAPK BS4 ...... 73 H5
Hillfield Primary School
  MANG/FISH BS16 .... 48 C5

Hillside First School
  MTN/WRL BS22 .... 122 B1
Hippodrome Theatre
  CBRIS/FH BS1 .... 4 E4
Hither Green Industrial Estate
  CLVDN BS21 .... 65 F2
HM Prison
  HORF/LLZ BS7 .... 45 H3
Holburne Museum of Art
  BATHSE BA2 .... 3 J2
Holloway Dental Health Centre
  HGRV/WHIT BS14 .... 86 D4
Hollywood Bowl
  CBRISNE BS2 .... 74 B1
Holy Cross Primary School
  BMSTR BS3 .... 72 D2
Holy Family RC Primary School
  BRSTK/PCHW BS34 .... 20 D2
Holymead Infant School
  BRSG/KWL/STAPK BS4 ...... 74 C4
Holymead Junior School
  BRSG/KWL/STAPK BS4 ...... 74 C3
Homefield Industrial Estate
  OMX/HUT/LCK BS24 .... 126 D1
Horfield Health Centre
  HORF/LLZ BS7 .... 46 C2
Horfield Primary School
  HNBRY/STHM BS10 .... 45 H1
Horfield Sports Centre
  HORF/LLZ BS7 .... 46 B1
Hornets RFC
  MTN/WRL BS22 .... 121 H4
HorseWorld
  HGRV/WHIT BS14 .... 97 G1
Hot Bath Gallery & College
  of Art
  CBATH/BATHN BA1 .... 3 F5
Hotel du Vin & Bistro
  CBRIS/FH BS1 .... 4 E3
Hotspots Indoor Sports
  Centre
  BRSG/KWL/STAPK BS4 ...... 75 E4
Hotwells Primary School
  CFTN/FAIL BS8 .... 54 D5
Hutton Moor Leisure Centre
  WSM BS23 .... 7 J5
Hutton Primary School
  OMX/HUT/LCK BS24 .... 126 B4
Hydro School
  AVONM BS11 .... 28 B2
IKEA Bristol EVILLE/WHL BS5 .. 46 D5
Illminster Avenue Primary
  School
  BRSG/KWL/STAPK BS4 ...... 85 H1
Iron Acton CE Primary School
  YATE/CS BS37 .... 12 C3
The Jane Austen Centre
  CBATH/BATHN BA1 .... 3 F3
John Cabot Academy
  KGWD/HNM BS15 .... 58 C4
The John Milton Health Clinic
  HNBRY/STHM BS10 .... 31 E2
Jorrocks Estate
  YATE/CS BS37 .... 37 G1
Jubilee Public Baths
  BRSG/KWL/STAPK BS4 ...... 74 A4
Jurys Bristol Hotel
  CBRIS/FH BS1 .... 4 E5
The Kendleshire Golf Club
  FRCTL/WBN BS36 .... 36 A1
Kenn Business Park
  CLVDN BS21 .... 65 E5
Kewstoke Primary School
  MTN/WRL BS22 .... 116 C5
Keynsham Cemetery
  KEYN BS31 .... 88 A2
Keynsham Hospital
  KEYN BS31 .... 88 C5
Keynsham Leisure Centre
  KEYN BS31 .... 88 C4
Keynsham RFC
  KEYN BS31 .... 88 A2
Keynsham Town FC
  KEYN BS31 .... 88 A2
King Edmund Community
  School
  YATE/CS BS37 .... 25 H1
King Edward Pre Preparatory
  School
  CBATH/BATHN BA1 .... 101 H4
King Edwards Junior School
  BATHSE BA2 .... 103 F5
King Edwards School
  BATHSE BA2 .... 103 F5
Kings Business Park
  CBRISNE BS2 .... 57 E5
Kings Chase Shopping Centre
  KGWD/HNM BS15 .... 58 D3
Kings Court Primary School
  YATE/CS BS37 .... 26 A2
Kingsdown Sports Centre
  RDLND/MONT BS6 .... 55 G2
Kingsfield School
  KGWD/HNM BS15 .... 59 G3
Kingshill CE Primary School
  NAIL BS48 .... 67 E3
Kingsland Trading Estate
  CBRISNE BS2 .... 73 H2
Kingsweston Special School
  AVONM BS11 .... 29 G5
Kingswood Health Centre
  KGWD/HNM BS15 .... 59 E3
Kingswood Leisure Centre
  MANG/FISH BS16 .... 48 D5
Kingswood Preparatory School
  CBATH/BATHN BA1 .... 102 B3
Kingswood School
  CBATH/BATHN BA1 .... 102 B2
Kingswood Trading Estate
  WSM BS23 .... 7 G2
Knowle Golf Club
  BRSG/KWL/STAPK BS4 ...... 86 C1
Knowle Park & I School
  BRSG/KWL/STAPK BS4 ...... 73 H5
Lambretta Scooter Museum
  WSM BS23 .... 7 F5
Lancaster House School
  WSM BS23 .... 7 G2
Lansdown Cemetery
  CBATH/BATHN BA1 .... 102 A1

Lansdown CC
CBATH/BATHN BA1 .... 101 G4
Larkhall FC
CBATH/BATHN BA1 .... 103 E1
Laura Place Fountain
BATHSE BA2 .... 3 H3
Lawnwood Road Industrial
Estate
EVILLE/WHL BS5 .... 56 D3
Lawrence Hill Health Centre
CBRISNE BS2 .... 56 C4
Lawrence Hill
Industrial Estate
EVILLE/WHL BS5 .... 57 E3
Lawrence Hill Industrial Park
EVILLE/WHL BS5 .... 56 D3
Leigh Court Business Centre
CFTN/FAIL BS8 .... 53 C1
Liberty Industrial Park
BMSTR BS3 .... 73 A5
Lime Grove Special School
BATHSE BA2 .... 3 J5
The Link Centre
BATHSE BA2 .... 110 C2
Little Mead Primary School
HNBRY/STHM BS10 .... 31 F4
Little Stoke Primary School
BRSTK/PCHW BS34 .... 21 F4
Little Theatre
CBATH/BATHN BA1 .... 3 F4
Locking Farm Industrial
Estate
OMX/HUT/LCK BS24 .... 126 D1
Locking Primary School
OMX/HUT/LCK BS24 .... 127 E2
Locking Road Business Park
WSM BS23 .... 7 J5
Locklease Primary School
HORF/LLZ BS7 .... 46 D2
Locksbrook Cemetery
CBATH/BATHN BA1 .... 101 H5
Locksbrook Road Trading
Estate
CBATH/BATHN BA1 .... 107 H1
Lodge Causeway Trading
Estate
MANG/FISH BS16 .... 47 H5
Long Ashton Business Park
LGASH BS41 .... 71 E5
Long Ashton Golf Club
LGASH BS41 .... 70 B3
Longbrook Trading Estate
BMSTR BS3 .... 71 H3
Longton Industrial Estate
BMSTR BS3 .... 7 J6
Longwell Green CP School
OLD/WMLY/WICK BS30 .... 76 C3
Lonsdale Business Centre
KGWD/HNM BS15 .... 58 C1
Luckwell Primary School
BMSTR BS3 .... 72 B3
Macdonald Bath Spa Hotel
BATHSE BA2 .... 103 F5
Maes Knoll Fort
HGRV/WHIT BS14 .... 96 D3
Malago Vale Trading Estate
BMSTR BS3 .... 73 E3
The Mall *CBRIS/FH* BS1 .... 5 G2
The Maltings
Industrial Estate
CBATH/BATHN BA1 .... 101 F5
Mangotsfield Cemetery
MANG/FISH BS16 .... 49 F1
Mangotsfield CE Primary
School
MANG/FISH BS16 .... 49 H2
Mangotsfield School
MANG/FISH BS16 .... 49 H4
Mangotsfield United FC
MANG/FISH BS16 .... 49 H3
Manor Brook Primary School
THNB/SVB BS35 .... 8 C1
The Manor CE Primary School
FRCTL/WBN BS36 .... 24 A4
Manor Farm Associated FC
HNLZ/SM/SNYPK/WT BS9 ...... 43 H3
Maritime Heritage Centre
CBRIS/FH BS1 .... 4 B6
Market Industrial Estate
YTN/CONG BS49 .... 112 B2
Mary Elton Primary School
CLVDN BS21 .... 64 B4
Max Park Primary School
EVILLE/WHL BS5 .... 57 E1
Mayshill Cemetery
FRCTL/WBN BS36 .... 24 D1
Meadowbrook Primary School
ALMDB BS32 .... 21 G2
Meadow School
OLD/WMLY/WICK BS30 .... 89 G1
Mead Vale Primary School
MTN/WRL BS22 .... 122 B2
Mendip Green First School
MTN/WRL BS22 .... 122 B2
Mendip Leisure Centre
PTSHD/EG BS20 .... 39 H4
Menzies Waterside Hotel
BATHSE BA2 .... 3 H6
Mercure Brigstow Hotel
CBRIS/FH BS1 .... 5 F4
Mercure Francis Hotel
CBATH/BATHN BA1 .... 3 F4
Mercure Holland House Hotel
CBRIS/FH BS1 .... 5 F7
Midland Way Business Park
THNB/SVB BS35 .... 8 C4
Millennium Exhibition Centre
CBRIS/FH BS1 .... 4 D6
Millennium Square
CBRIS/FH BS1 .... 4 C6
Millpond Primary School
EVILLE/WHL BS5 .... 56 C2
Milson Street Clinic
CBATH/BATHN BA1 .... 3 F3
Milton Infant School
MTN/WRL BS22 .... 121 H2
Milton Junior School
MTN/WRL BS22 .... 121 H2
Milton Road Cemetery
WSM BS23 .... 7 H2

Minto Road Industrial Centre
CBRISNE BS2 .... 56 B1
Mizzymean
Recreation Centre
NAIL BS48 .... 67 F5
Model Yacht Centre
WSM BS23 .... 6 C3
Monks Park School
HORF/LLZ BS7 .... 32 B4
Monkton Combe Junior
School
BATHSE BA2 .... 111 H1
Monkton Combe Pre
Preparatory School
BATHSE BA2 .... 111 G1
Monkton Farleigh & South
Wraxall CE Primary School
BOAV BA15 .... 105 F5
Montpelier Health Centre
RDLND/MONT BS6 .... 56 A2
Moorlands J & I School
BATHSE BA2 .... 108 A4
The Mount
CBATH/BATHN BA1 .... 91 H4
Museum of Bath at Work
CBATH/BATHN BA1 .... 3 F1
Museum of East Asian Art
CBATH/BATHN BA1 .... 2 E2
Nailsea Health Centre
NAIL BS48 .... 67 F4
Nailsea School
NAIL BS48 .... 67 G5
Netham Industrial Estate
EVILLE/WHL BS5 .... 57 F4
Netham Industrial Park
EVILLE/WHL BS5 .... 57 F4
New Birchfield Hotel
WSM BS23 .... 6 B1
Newbridge Industrial Estate
BRSG/KWL/STAPK BS4 .... 75 E5
Newbridge Junior School
CBATH/BATHN BA1 .... 101 G5
Newbridge Primary School
CBATH/BATHN BA1 .... 101 G5
Newbridge Trading Estate
BRSG/KWL/STAPK BS4 .... 57 F5
New Fosseway Special School
HGRV/WHIT BS14 .... 86 A2
New Oak Primary School
HGRV/WHIT BS14 .... 86 A2
New Ocean Hotel
WSM BS23 .... 6 A1
New Siblands Special School
THNB/SVB BS35 .... 9 E3
Newton Mill Caravan &
Camping Park
BATHSE BA2 .... 107 E1
No 1 Royal Crescent
BATHSE BA2 .... 2 E2
Norland College
CBATH/BATHN BA1 .... 103 E4
Northavon Business Centre
YATE/CS BS37 .... 13 G4
North Bristol RFC
ALMDB BS32 .... 10 C4
Northleaze Primary School
LGASH BS41 .... 71 E4
Northridge Business Centre
YATE/CS BS37 .... 13 G5
North Road Primary School
YATE/CS BS37 .... 13 F3
North Somerset Museum
WSM BS23 .... 7 E3
North Worle Shopping Centre
MTN/WRL BS22 .... 118 A5
Novers Hill Trading Estate
BMSTR BS3 .... 72 D5
Novotel
CBRIS/FH BS1 .... 5 H5
Oakfield Business Park
KGWD/HNM BS15 .... 58 D4
The Oaklands Business Park
YATE/CS BS37 .... 13 E4
Oatley Trading Estate
KGWD/HNM BS15 .... 58 D2
Odd Down FC
BATHSE BA2 .... 110 A2
Odeon Cinema
CBATH/BATHN BA1 .... 2 E5
CBRIS/FH BS1 .... 5 F3
WSM BS23 .... 6 E4
Old Bristolians Sports Club
CFTN/FAIL BS8 .... 70 C2
Oldbury Court Primary School
MANG/FISH BS16 .... 48 C1
Old Culverhaysians RFC
BATHSE BA2 .... 110 A1
Oldfield Old Boys RFC
BATHSE BA2 .... 2 D6
Oldfield Park Infant School
BATHSE BA2 .... 2 B5
Oldfield Park Junior School
BATHSE BA2 .... 107 H3
Oldfield School
CBATH/BATHN BA1 .... 101 E3
Old Knightstone Theatre
WSM BS23 .... 6 A2
Oldmixon Primary School
OMX/HUT/LCK BS24 .... 125 F4
Open University
CBRIS/FH BS1 .... 5 G6
Optimax Laser Eye Clinic
CBRIS/FH BS1 .... 4 E4
Oral Health Centre
CBATH/BATHN BA1 .... 3 F3
The Orchard Medical Centre
KGWD/HNM BS15 .... 58 D3
Orchard View
(Ham Green Hospital)
PTSHD/EG BS20 .... 43 E4
Our Lady of Lourdes RC
Primary School
KGWD/HNM BS15 .... 59 E4
Our Lady of the Rosary RC
Primary School
AVONM BS11 .... 29 G4
Outline Fitness Club
WSM BS23 .... 7 F6
Paragon School
BATHSE BA2 .... 108 D4

Parish Wharf Leisure Centre
PTSHD/EG BS20 .... 40 A2
The Park School
KGWD/HNM BS15 .... 59 E3
Parkwall Primary School
OLD/WMLY/WICK BS30 .... 76 D1
Parkway Trading Estate
CBRISNE BS2 .... 56 B1
Parnall Road Industrial Estate
MANG/FISH BS16 .... 48 A5
Parson Street Primary School
BMSTR BS3 .... 72 D4
Patchway Community College
ALMDB BS32 .... 20 C1
Patchway Health Clinic
BRSTK/PCHW BS34 .... 20 C2
Patchway Trading Estate
BRSTK/PCHW BS34 .... 19 H2
Pembroke Road Surgery
CFTN/FAIL BS8 .... 55 E2
Perry Court Junior School
HGRV/WHIT BS14 .... 85 H3
Phoenix Business Park
BMSTR BS3 .... 72 B4
Picturedrome Cinema
RDLND/MONT BS6 .... 45 E4
The Picture House
CBRIS/FH BS1 .... 5 G1
Picture This
CBRIS/FH BS1 .... 4 A7
Pines Way Industrial Estate
BATHSE BA2 .... 2 D5
Pizey Avenue
Industrial Estate
CLVDN BS21 .... 64 B3
Playhouse Theatre
WSM BS23 .... 6 D2
The Podium
Shopping Centre & Library
CBATH/BATHN BA1 .... 3 G3
Portbury Sawmills Industrial
Estate
PTSHD/EG BS20 .... 41 H1
Portishead Business Park
PTSHD/EG BS20 .... 39 H2
Portishead Cemetery
PTSHD/EG BS20 .... 39 G5
Portishead Health Centre
PTSHD/EG BS20 .... 39 H3
Portishead Lifeboat Station
PTSHD/EG BS20 .... 38 D2
Portishead Primary School
PTSHD/EG BS20 .... 40 A2
Portview Trading Estate
AVONM BS11 .... 28 B5
Portway Community School
AVONM BS11 .... 43 E1
Portway Trading Estate
AVONM BS11 .... 42 C1
Pratt's Hotel
BATHSE BA2 .... 3 H5
Premier Inn
BRSTK/PCHW BS34 .... 32 C2
PTSHD/EG BS20 .... 40 A3
Prior Park College
BATHSE BA2 .... 109 F5
Prior Park Landscape
Garden (NT)
BATHSE BA2 .... 109 F4
Priory Community School
MTN/WRL BS22 .... 118 A5
Priory Farm Trading Estate
PTSHD/EG BS20 .... 41 F5
Pucklechurch CE Primary
School
MANG/FISH BS16 .... 51 G2
Pucklechurch Trading Estate
MANG/FISH BS16 .... 51 F4
QEH Theatre
CFTN/FAIL BS8 .... 4 A3
Quakers Friars
CBRIS/FH BS1 .... 5 H2
Queen Elizabeth Hospital
CFTN/FAIL BS8 .... 4 B4
Queen Elizabeths Hospital
School
CFTN/FAIL BS8 .... 4 A3
The Queensberry Hotel
CBATH/BATHN BA1 .... 2 E2
Radnor Business Centre
HORF/LLZ BS7 .... 46 A3
Ralph Allen School
BATHSE BA2 .... 109 H5
Ramada Plaza Bristol
CBRIS/FH BS1 .... 5 H6
Ravenswood Special School
NAIL BS48 .... 67 G3
Raysfield J & I School
YATE/CS BS37 .... 26 B2
Redfield Edge Primary School
OLD/WMLY/WICK BS30 .... 77 G2
Redfield Leisure Centre
EVILLE/WHL BS5 .... 57 E4
Redgrave Theatre
BATHSE BA2 .... 54 D5
Redland Green School
RDLND/MONT BS6 .... 45 G5
Redland High Junior School
RDLND/MONT BS6 .... 55 G1
Redland High School for Girls
RDLND/MONT BS6 .... 55 G1
The Red Maids Junior School
HNLZ/SM/SNYPK/WT BS9 ..... 45 E2
The Red Maids School
HNLZ/SM/SNYPK/WT BS9 ..... 45 E2
Redwood Hotel
CFTN/FAIL BS8 .... 70 C2
Ridge Junior School
YATE/CS BS37 .... 14 B5
Ridgeway Industrial Centre
EVILLE/WHL BS5 .... 57 G1
Ridgeway Park Cemetery
EVILLE/WHL BS5 .... 57 F5
The Ridings High School
FRCTL/WBN BS36 .... 22 D4
Riverbank Medical Centre
MTN/WRL BS22 .... 118 A5
Riverside Business Park
BATHSE BA2 .... 2 E5
EVILLE/WHL BS5 .... 57 F5

Riverside Leisure Centre
CBRISNE BS2 .... 56 B3
Robin Cousins Sports Centre
AVONM BS11 .... 28 C5
Rodford Primary School
YATE/CS BS37 .... 25 G3
Rodney Hotel
CFTN/FAIL BS8 .... 54 D4
Roman Baths & Pump Room
CBATH/BATHN BA1 .... 3 G5
The Royal Crescent Hotel
CBATH/BATHN BA1 .... 2 D2
Royal High School Bath
GDST Senior School
CBATH/BATHN BA1 .... 102 C2
The Royal High School
(Junior Department)
CBATH/BATHN BA1 .... 102 C4
The Royal Hotel
WSM BS23 .... 6 C3
Royal National Hospital for
Rheumatic Diseases
CBATH/BATHN BA1 .... 3 F4
Royal Navy &
Royal Marines Careers
Information Office
CBRIS/FH BS1 .... 4 E3
Royal United Hospital
CBATH/BATHN BA1 .... 101 G4
Royal Victoria Park Bandstand
CBATH/BATHN BA1 .... 2 D3
Royal Victoria Park Pavilion
CBATH/BATHN BA1 .... 2 E3
RSPCA & Dogs Home
CBRISNE BS2 .... 73 H2
Russell Town Industrial Park
EVILLE/WHL BS5 .... 57 E4
St Andrews CE Primary
School
CBATH/BATHN BA1 .... 2 E1
St Andrews Junior School
YTN/CONG BS49 .... 114 C2
St Annes CE Primary School
OLD/WMLY/WICK BS30 .... 77 F3
St Annes J & I School
BRSG/KWL/STAPK BS4 .... 74 C1
St Annes Park
Primary School
BRSG/KWL/STAPK BS4 .... 74 D1
St Augustine of Canterbury
RC Primary School
MANG/FISH BS16 .... 49 F1
St Barnabas CE Primary
School
RDLND/MONT BS6 .... 56 B2
St Bedes Catholic College
AVONM BS11 .... 29 G3
St Bernadettes Catholic
Secondary School
HGRV/WHIT BS14 .... 86 A3
St Bernadettes RC Primary
School
HGRV/WHIT BS14 .... 86 A3
St Bernards RC Primary School
AVONM BS11 .... 43 E2
St Bonaventures RC Primary
School
RDLND/MONT BS6 .... 45 G4
St Brendans Trading Estate
AVONM BS11 .... 28 B3
St Catherines Industrial Estate
BMSTR BS3 .... 73 E2
St Chads Patchway CE Primary
School
BRSTK/PCHW BS34 .... 21 E1
St Christophers School
RDLND/MONT BS6 .... 45 E5
St Francis Catholic Primary
School
NAIL BS48 .... 67 G5
St Gabriel's Business Park
EVILLE/WHL BS5 .... 56 D3
St George Health Centre
CFTN/FAIL BS8 .... 58 A3
St Georges CE Primary School
CFTN/FAIL BS8 .... 4 B5
St Georges Industrial Estate
AVONM BS11 .... 28 B2
St Georges VA Primary School
MTN/WRL BS22 .... 118 B5
St Gregorys Catholic College
BATHSE BA2 .... 110 B2
St James Cemetery
CBRIS/FH BS1 .... 2 C5
St Johns CE Primary School
CFTN/FAIL BS8 .... 55 E1
St Johns Church & Old City Gate
CBRIS/FH BS1 .... 5 F3
St Johns Lane Health Centre
BMSTR BS3 .... 73 F4
St Johns Mead CE Primary
School
YATE/CS BS37 .... 26 D2
St Johns Primary School
KEYN BS31 .... 88 B4
St Johns RC Primary School
BATHSE BA2 .... 3 J4
St John the Evangelist CE
Primary School
CLVDN BS21 .... 64 C4
St Josephs Catholic Primary
School
PTSHD/EG BS20 .... 39 H5
St Joseph's RC Primary School
MANG/FISH BS16 .... 48 B5
St Katharine's Primary School
BLAG/CWMG/WR BS40 .... 92 B5
St Katherines School
PTSHD/EG BS20 .... 39 J3
St Keyna Primary School
KEYN BS31 .... 88 C3
St Marks CE School
CBATH/BATHN BA1 .... 103 E2
St Mark's Community Centre
BATHSE BA2 .... 3 G7
St Marks VA Primary School
MTN/WRL BS22 .... 117 G4
St Martins CE Junior School
MTN/WRL BS22 .... 122 A2

St Martins Garden
Primary School
BATHSE BA2 .... 110 C1
St Martins Hospital
BATHSE BA2 .... 110 C1
St Mary Redcliffe Cemetery
BRSG/KWL/STAPK BS4 .... 74 A2
St Mary Redcliffe CE VC Primary
School
BMSTR BS3 .... 73 F2
St Mary's Catholic Primary
School
ALMDB BS32 .... 22 A3
St Marys CE VA Primary School
PTSHD/EG BS20 .... 41 G5
St Marys Hospital
CFTN/FAIL BS8 .... 4 B3
St Marys RC Primary School
CBATH/BATHN BA1 .... 101 G3
St Mary's Redcliffe Church
CBRIS/FH BS1 .... 5 G6
St Marys RFC
FRCTL/WBN BS36 .... 11 H5
St Matthias & Dr Bells CE
Primary School
MANG/FISH BS16 .... 48 A4
St Michael on the Mount
Primary School
CFTN/FAIL BS8 .... 4 D5
St Michaels CE Junior School
BATHSE BA2 .... 107 E1
St Michael's Cemetery
CBATH/BATHN BA1 .... 101 H5
St Michaels CE Primary
School
BRSTK/PCHW BS34 .... 21 G5
St Michaels CE VC Primary
School
FRCTL/WBN BS36 .... 22 D4
St Michaels Hill Clinic
CBRISNE BS2 .... 4 E2
St Michaels Hospital
CBRISNE BS2 .... 4 D1
St Nicholas Chantry Primary
School
CLVDN BS21 .... 65 E1
St Nicholas Market
CBRIS/FH BS1 .... 5 F4
St Nicholas of Tolentine RC
Primary School
EVILLE/WHL BS5 .... 5 K1
St Patricks RC Primary School
EVILLE/WHL BS5 .... 57 F4
St Pauls Catholic Primary
School
YATE/CS BS37 .... 26 A2
St Peter & Paul RC Primary
School
RDLND/MONT BS6 .... 55 G5
St Peters CE Primary School
PTSHD/EG BS20 .... 39 H3
St Philips CE Primary School
BATHSE BA2 .... 108 A5
St Pius X RC Primary School
BMSTRD/HC/WWD BS13 .... 84 B4
St Saviours Infant School
CBATH/BATHN BA1 .... 103 E2
St Saviours Junior School
CBATH/BATHN BA1 .... 103 E2
St Stephens Business Centre
OLD/WMLY/WICK BS30 .... 77 F1
St Stephens CE Primary School
CBATH/BATHN BA1 .... 102 C3
St Stephens J & I School
KGWD/HNM BS15 .... 58 D1
St Teresas Catholic Primary
School
HORF/LLZ BS7 .... 32 A4
St Teresas Private Hospital
BATHSE BA2 .... 100 A4
St Ursulas High School
HNLZ/SM/SNYPK/WT BS9 ..... 45 E2
St Vincents Trading Estate
CBRISNE BS2 .... 57 E5
St Werburgh's Primary School
CBRISNE BS2 .... 56 C1
Sally Lunn's Refreshment
House & Museum
CBATH/BATHN BA1 .... 3 G5
Saltford CE Primary School
KEYN BS31 .... 99 E2
Saltford Golf Club
KEYN BS31 .... 99 F3
Sampson House Business Park
KGWD/HNM BS15 .... 18 B3
Samuel Whites Infant School
KGWD/HNM BS15 .... 75 H1
Saracens RFC
HNBRY/STHM BS10 .... 18 D5
Satellite Business Park
EVILLE/WHL BS5 .... 57 F4
Saville Court Business Centre
CFTN/FAIL BS8 .... 55 E4
Sawclose Health Clinic
CBATH/BATHN BA1 .... 3 F4
School of Christ the King
BRSG/KWL/STAPK BS4 .... 85 F2
Scotch Horn Community &
Sports Centre
NAIL BS48 .... 67 G4
Sea Mills Infant School
HNLZ/SM/SNYPK/WT BS9 ..... 44 A1
Sea Mills Junior School
HNLZ/SM/SNYPK/WT BS9 ..... 43 H3
SeaQuarium
WSM BS23 .... 6 C6
Sefton Park J & I School
HORF/LLZ BS7 .... 46 B5
Severnside Trading Estate
AVONM BS11 .... 28 C4
Sham Castle
BATHSE BA2 .... 109 G1
Sheene Court Industrial Estate
BMSTR BS3 .... 72 D3
The Sheiling School
THNB/SVB BS35 .... 8 B3
The Shield Retail Centre
BRSTK/PCHW BS34 .... 32 C2
Shield Road Primary School
HORF/LLZ BS7 .... 32 C4

Shirehampton Cemetery
AVONM BS11 ......42 D2
Shirehampton CC
AVONM BS11 ......43 F1
Shirehampton Health Centre
AVONM BS11 ......43 E2
Shirehampton Park Golf Club
AVONM BS11 ......43 F2
Shirehampton Primary School
AVONM BS11 ......42 D2
Shirehampton Swimming Pool
AVONM BS11 ......43 E2
Shortwood Lodge Golf Club
MANG/FISH BS16 ......50 A5
Showcase Cinema
CBRISNE BS2 ......74 B1
Silverhill School
FRCTL/WBN BS36 ......23 E3
Simplex Trading Estate
MANG/FISH BS16 ......77 G2
The Sir Bernard Lovell School
OLD/WMLY/WICK BS30 ......77 F2
Soaphouse Industrial Estate
EVILLE/WHL BS5 ......57 G3
Solsbury Hill Hill Fort
CBATH/BATHN BA1 ......90 C5
South Bristol Business Park
BRSG/KWL/STAPK BS4 ......85 E2
South Bristol Cemetery
BMSTRD/HC/WWD BS13 ......83 H1
South Bristol Crematorium
BMSTRD/HC/WWD BS13 ......84 A1
South Bristol Retail Park
BMSTR BS3 ......72 B5
Southdown J & I School
BATHSE BA2 ......107 G4
Southfield Road Trading Estate
NAIL BS48 ......67 G3
Southgate
CBATH/BATHN BA1 ......3 G6
Southmead Health Centre
HNBRY/STHM BS10 ......31 G3
Southmead Hospital
HNBRY/STHM BS10 ......45 H1
South Street Primary School
BMSTR BS3 ......72 C3
South View Business Centre
MANG/FISH BS16 ......49 E3
South View Business Park
MANG/FISH BS16 ......49 E3
Southville Primary School
BMSTR BS3 ......72 D2
Sovereign Shopping Centre
WSM BS23 ......6 D4
Speedwell Industrial Estate
CLVDN BS21 ......64 C3
Speedwell Swimming Baths
EVILLE/WHL BS5 ......57 H2
Speedwell Technology College
EVILLE/WHL BS5 ......58 A2
Spike Island Centre of Contemporary Art & Design
CBRIS/FH BS1 ......4 A7
Springfield School
RDLND/MONT BS6 ......56 A1
Springwater Park Trading Estate
EVILLE/WHL BS5 ......57 G4
Stafford Business Centre
WSM BS23 ......7 G4
Stanbridge Primary School
MANG/FISH BS16 ......49 F2
Staple Hill Primary School
MANG/FISH BS16 ......48 D4
Sterling College International
CBATH/BATHN BA1 ......3 G2

Stock Exchange
CBRIS/FH BS1 ......4 E4
Stockwood Green Primary School
HGRV/WHIT BS14 ......86 D5
Stockwood Open Space Nature Reserve
HGRV/WHIT BS14 ......87 E3
Stockwood Vale Golf Club
KEYN BS31 ......87 F3
Stoke Bishop CE Primary School
HNLZ/SM/SNYPK/WT BS9 ......44 B3
Stoke Gifford Medical Centre
BRSTK/PCHW BS34 ......33 G1
Stoke Lodge Primary School
BRSTK/PCHW BS34 ......21 E2
Stokes Medical Centre
BRSTK/PCHW BS34 ......21 E3
Stoke View Business Park
MANG/FISH BS16 ......47 H4
Stone Hill Business Centre
KGWD/HNM BS15 ......76 B2
Storybox Theatre
YTN/CONG BS49 ......113 G3
Stover Trading Estate
YATE/CS BS57 ......25 F1
Summerhill J & I School
EVILLE/WHL BS5 ......57 G3
Sun Life Sports Club
HNBRY/STHM BS10 ......30 D1
Sunnyside Farm Trading Estate
PTSHD/EG BS20 ......52 C1
Swainswick Primary School
CBATH/BATHN BA1 ......90 A4
Temple Quay
CBRIS/FH BS1 ......5 J5
Temple Trading Estate
CBRISNE BS2 ......74 A1
Teyfant Community School
BMSTRD/HC/WWD BS13 ......85 F5
Theatre Royal
CBATH/BATHN BA1 ......2 E4
Thermae Bath Spa
CBATH/BATHN BA1 ......3 F5
Thistle Hotel
CBRIS/FH BS1 ......5 F3
Thornbury Castle Hotel
THNB/SVB BS35 ......8 B2
Thornbury Cemetery
THNB/SVB BS35 ......8 B3
Thornbury Golf Lodge Hotel & Golf Centre
THNB/SVB BS35 ......8 A5
Thornbury Health Centre
THNB/SVB BS35 ......8 D3
Thornbury Hospital
THNB/SVB BS35 ......8 D3
Thornbury Leisure Centre
THNB/SVB BS35 ......8 C5
Three Ways School
BATHSE BA2 ......3 J4
BATHSE BA2 ......110 C2
CBATH/BATHN BA1 ......102 A3
Tickenham Primary School
CLVDN BS21 ......66 A2
Time Machine Museum
YATE/CS BS37 ......6 E3
Toll House Clinic
YATE/CS BS37 ......27 E1
Torwood House School
RDLND/MONT BS6 ......45 E5
Totterdown Bridge Industrial Estate CBRISNE BS2 ......73 H2
Travelodge
CBATH/BATHN BA1 ......3 G3
HNBRY/STHM BS10 ......19 E4

Trinity Theological College
HNLZ/SM/SNYPK/WT BS9 ......44 C4
TT Trading Estate
YATE/CS BS37 ......27 E1
Tudor Lodge Health Centre
WSM BS23 ......124 D2
Twerton Cemetery
BATHSE BA2 ......107 H1
Twerton Infant School
BATHSE BA2 ......107 E2
Two Mile Hill J & I School
KGWD/HNM BS15 ......58 B3
Twyford House CC
AVONM BS11 ......43 F1
The Tynings Primary School
MANG/FISH BS16 ......49 F4
Tyntesfield House (NT)
NAIL BS48 ......68 D2
Unicorn Business Park
CBRISNE BS2 ......74 B1
University of Bath
BATHSE BA2 ......109 H2
University of Bristol
CFTN/FAIL BS8 ......4 C1
University of Bristol Childrens Hospital
CFTN/FAIL BS8 ......4 C2
University of the West of England
BMSTR BS3 ......71 H2
CBRIS/FH BS1 ......5 F4
University of the West of England (Frenchay Campus)
MANG/FISH BS16 ......33 G5
University of the West of England (Glenside Campus)
MANG/FISH BS16 ......47 G3
University of the West of England (St Matthias Campus)
MANG/FISH BS16 ......48 A3
Uphill Primary School
WSM BS23 ......124 C4
Upper Horfield Primary School
HORF/LLZ BS7 ......32 B5
Victoria Art Gallery
BATHSE BA2 ......3 G4
Victoria Monument
CBATH/BATHN BA1 ......2 C2
Victoria Park Business Centre
CBATH/BATHN BA1 ......2 A3
Victoria Park Community Infant School
BMSTR BS3 ......73 F3
Vines Industrial Estate
NAIL BS48 ......67 H3
Vue Cinema
HNBRY/STHM BS10 ......19 G4
Wadehurst Industrial Park
CBRISNE BS2 ......56 C4
Walliscote Primary School
WSM BS23 ......6 E5
Wallis Estate
CBRISNE BS2 ......46 B5
Wansdyke Business Centre
BATHSE BA2 ......108 A3
Wansbrook Primary School
HGRV/WHIT BS14 ......85 G5
Warmley CE School
OLD/WMLY/WICK BS30 ......60 A5
Warmley Park School
OLD/WMLY/WICK BS30 ......59 H4
Watershed Cinema
CBRIS/FH BS1 ......4 E5
Watershed Media Centre
CBRIS/FH BS1 ......4 E5

Waycroft Primary School
HGRV/WHIT BS14 ......86 D4
Wellesley Primary School
YATE/CS BS37 ......25 H4
Wellsway School
KEYN BS31 ......88 D4
Wentworth House Hotel
BATHSE BA2 ......108 B3
Westbourne Hotel
CFTN/FAIL BS8 ......4 A1
Westbury on Trym CE Primary School
HNLZ/SM/SNYPK/WT BS9 ......31 E5
Westbury Park Primary School RDLND/MONT BS6 ......45 E4
Westcliff College of Further Education WSM BS23 ......120 A2
West Country Water Park
FRCTL/WBN BS36 ......11 H5
Westerleigh Crematorium
YATE/CS BS37 ......37 G4
Westhaven Special School
MANG/FISH BS16 ......124 B4
Westland Business Centre
OMX/HUT/LCK BS24 ......125 C3
West Leigh Infant School
NAIL BS48 ......79 G3
Weston All Saints Primary School
CBATH/BATHN BA1 ......101 F2
Weston Business Park
BNWL BS29 ......127 G3
OMX/HUT/LCK BS24 ......126 B1
Weston College
WSM BS23 ......6 C2
WSM BS23 ......125 E4
Weston Express Business Park
MTN/WRL BS22 ......121 H5
Weston Park Primary School
AVONM BS11 ......29 F5
Weston Retail Park
WSM BS23 ......7 J7
Weston St Johns Associated FC
WSM BS23 ......125 E3
Weston-super-Mare AFC (Woodspring Stadium)
OMX/HUT/LCK BS24 ......125 F2
Weston-super-Mare Borough Employees Sports Club
WSM BS23 ......7 G5
Weston-super-Mare Cemetery
MTN/WRL BS22 ......117 F4
Weston-super-Mare Crematorium
MTN/WRL BS22 ......117 F4
Weston-super-Mare CC
WSM BS23 ......124 D3
Weston-super-Mare General Hospital
WSM BS23 ......124 D4
Weston-super-Mare Golf Club
WSM BS23 ......124 B2
Weston-super-Mare RFC
WSM BS23 ......7 F6
Westpoint Trading Estate
KGWD/HNM BS15 ......58 D4
West Town Lane Primary School
BRSG/KWL/STAPK BS4 ......74 B5
Wheatfield Primary School
ALMDB BS32 ......21 F1
Whitchurch Health Centre
HGRV/WHIT BS14 ......85 H4
Whitchurch Primary School
HGRV/WHIT BS14 ......86 B5

Whitchurch Sports Centre
HGRV/WHIT BS14 ......85 G4
Whitefield Fishponds Community School
MANG/FISH BS16 ......47 H4
Whitehall Primary School
EVILLE/WHL BS5 ......57 F2
Whitehall Trading Estate
EVILLE/WHL BS5 ......57 E3
Wick CE Primary School
OLD/WMLY/WICK BS30 ......61 F5
Widcombe CE Junior School
BATHSE BA2 ......3 J6
Widcombe Infant School
BATHSE BA2 ......3 H6
William Budd Health Centre
BMSTR BS3 ......85 E1
Willsbridge Mill Museum & Nature Reserve
OLD/WMLY/WICK BS30 ......77 G4
Wilverley Trading Estate
BRSG/KWL/STAPK BS4 ......74 D5
Wincombe Trading Estate
CBRISNE BS2 ......73 H2
Windmill Farm Business Centre
BMSTR BS3 ......73 E2
Windmill Hill City Farm
BMSTR BS3 ......73 E2
Window Arts Centre
CBATH/BATHN BA1 ......3 F5
Windwhistle Primary School
WSM BS23 ......125 E3
Winford CE Primary School
BLAG/CWMG/WR BS40 ......93 G5
Winter Gardens & Pavilion
WSM BS23 ......6 C3
Withywood Community School
BMSTRD/HC/WWD BS13 ......84 B4
Woodlands Golf & Country Club
ALMDB BS32 ......11 H4
Wood Road Industrial Centre
KGWD/HNM BS15 ......58 D3
Woodspring Golf & Country Club
LGASH BS41 ......83 F3
Woodstock Special School
HNBRY/STHM BS10 ......30 C3
Worlebury Golf Club
MTN/WRL BS22 ......116 C5
Worlebury St Pauls CE VA First School
MTN/WRL BS22 ......121 G1
Worle Health Centre
MTN/WRL BS22 ......122 B1
Wraxall CE Primary School
NAIL BS48 ......68 A2
Wyvern Community School
WSM BS23 ......125 E1
Wyvern Sports Centre
WSM BS23 ......125 E1
Yate Leisure Centre
YATE/CS BS37 ......14 A5
Yate Outdoor Sports Complex
YATE/CS BS37 ......13 H2
Yate Town FC
YATE/CS BS37 ......13 F4
Yatton J & I School
YTN/CONG BS49 ......112 C3
Yeo Moor J & I School
CLVDN BS21 ......65 E3

Acknowledgements

Schools address data provided by Education Direct.

Petrol station information supplied by Johnsons.

Garden centre information provided by:

Garden Centre Association  Britains best garden centres

Wyevale Garden Centres

The statement on the front cover of this atlas is sourced, selected and quoted from a reader comment and feedback form received in 2004

SPEED READING

Speed camera locations

Speed camera locations provided in association with RoadPilot Ltd

RoadPilot is the developer of one of the largest and most accurate databases of speed camera locations in the UK and Europe. It has provided the speed camera information in this atlas. RoadPilot is the UK's pioneer and market leader in GPS (Global Positioning System) road safety technologies.

microGo (pictured right) is RoadPilot's latest in-car speed camera location system. It improves road safety by alerting you to the location of accident black spots,

fixed and mobile camera sites. RoadPilot's microGo does not jam police lasers and is therefore completely legal.

RoadPilot's database of fixed camera locations has been compiled with the full co-operation of regional police forces and the Safety Camera Partnerships.

For more information on RoadPilot's GPS road safety products, please visit **www.roadpilot.com** or telephone 0870 240 1701

RoadPilot

ALARM MODE

GPS Antenna
microGo is directional, so it only alerts you to cameras on your side of the road

Visual Countdown
To camera location

Your Speed
The speed you are travelling when approaching camera

Camera Types Located
Gatso, Specs, Truvelo, TSS/DS5, Traffipax, mobile camera sites, accident black spots, congestion charges, tolls

Voice Warnings
Only if you are exceeding the speed limit at the camera

Plug and Go
Easy to move from vehicle to vehicle

64 Colour Options
To match vehicle's illumination

Speed Limit at Camera
Screen turns red as visual alert

Single Button Operation
For easy access to speed display, camera warning, rescue me location, trip computer, congestion charge, max speed alarm, date and time

AA Street by Street QUESTIONNAIRE

Dear Atlas User
Your comments, opinions and recommendations are very important to us.
So please help us to improve our street atlases by taking a few minutes
to complete this simple questionnaire.

You do not need a stamp (unless posted outside the UK). If you do not want to remove
this page from your street atlas, then photocopy it or write your answers on a plain sheet
of paper.

Send to: Marketing Assistant, AA Publishing, 14th Floor Fanum House,
Freepost SCE 4598, Basingstoke RG21 4GY

ABOUT THE ATLAS...

Please state which city / town / county you bought:
_____

Where did you buy the atlas? (City, Town, County)
_____

For what purpose? (please tick all applicable)

To use in your local area ☐   To use on business or at work ☐

Visiting a strange place ☐   In the car ☐   On foot ☐

Other (please state)
_____

Have you ever used any street atlases other than AA Street by Street?

Yes ☐   No ☐

If so, which ones?
_____

Is there any aspect of our street atlases that could be improved?
(Please continue on a separate sheet if necessary)
_____
_____
_____
_____

ML060y

continued overleaf

Please list the features you found most useful:

_____
_____
_____

Please list the features you found least useful:

_____
_____
_____

LOCAL KNOWLEDGE...

Local knowledge is invaluable. Whilst every attempt has been made to make the information contained in this atlas as accurate as possible, should you notice any inaccuracies, please detail them below (if necessary, use a blank piece of paper) or e-mail us at *streetbystreet@theAA.com*

_____
_____
_____

ABOUT YOU...

Name (Mr/Mrs/Ms) _____

Address _____

_____ Postcode _____

Daytime tel no _____

E-mail address _____

Which age group are you in?

Under 25 ☐   25-34 ☐   35-44 ☐   45-54 ☐   55-64 ☐   65+ ☐

Are you an AA member?   YES ☐   NO ☐

Do you have Internet access?   YES ☐   NO ☐

Thank you for taking the time to complete this questionnaire. Please send it to us as soon as possible, and remember, you do not need a stamp (unless posted outside the UK).

We may use information we hold about you to telephone or email you about other products and services offered by the AA, we do NOT disclose this information to third parties.

Please tick here if you do not wish to hear about products and services from the AA. ☐